INSIGHT GUIDE

GREEK ISLANDS

 **APA** PUBLICATIONS **L**

Part of the Langenscheidt Publishing Group

ABOUT THIS BOOK

Editorial

Project Editor
Jeffery Pike
Managing Editor
Emily Hatchwell
Editorial Director
Brian Bell

Distribution

UK & Ireland
GeoCenter International Ltd
The Viables Centre
Harrow Way
Basingstoke
Hants RG22 4BJ
Fax: (44) 1256-817988

United States
Langenscheidt Publishers, Inc.
46–35 54th Road
Maspeth, NY 11378
Fax: (718) 784-0640

Worldwide
**APA Publications GmbH & Co.
Verlag KG (Singapore branch)**
38 Joo Koon Road
Singapore 628990
Tel: (65) 865-1600
Fax: (65) 861-6438

Printing

Insight Print Services (Pte) Ltd
38 Joo Koon Road
Singapore 628990
Tel: (65) 865-1600
Fax: (65) 861-6438

© 1999 APA Publications GmbH & Co.
Verlag KG (Singapore branch)
All Rights Reserved
First Edition 1990
Third Edition 1999

CONTACTING THE EDITORS
Although every effort is made to
provide accurate information in
this publication, we live in a
fast-changing world and would
appreciate it if readers would
call our attention to any errors or
outdated information that may
occur by writing to us at:
**Insight Guides, P.O. Box 7910,
London SE1 8ZB, England.
Fax: (44 171) 620-1074.**
e-mail:
insight@apaguide.demon.co.uk

Ing 12/98

This is far more than just a
guidebook. Like all the Insight
Guides, it combines informative,
entertaining and well-written text
with an exciting photojournalistic
approach, to give a thorough and
sympathetic insight into the Greek
Islands and their culture. For this
new edition, all the maps have
been redrawn, many new
photographs have been selected,
and all the text has been updated.

How to use the book

To understand Greece today, you
need to know something of its
turbulent past. The **History** and
Features section, with a yellow
colour bar, covers the country's
history from ancient times to the
struggle for independence and the
formation of the modern state. The
culture and everyday life of the
islands are explored in lively
essays by experts.

The central **Places** section, with
a blue bar, provides a detailed run-
down of just about every island
that it's possible to visit. The main
places of interest are coordinated
by number with full-colour maps.

The **Travel Tips** listings section, with an orange bar, provides all the information you need on travel, accommodation, eating and drinking, sports and language. You can locate information quickly by referring to the index on the back cover flap – and the flaps are designed to double as bookmarks.

The contributors

This new edition was edited by **Jeffery Pike**, a London-based freelance journalist and photographer for whom the Greek islands have an enduring appeal. He has drawn on the last edition of *Insight Guide: Greek Islands*, which was edited by

Martha Ellen Zenfell, one of Apa's senior editors.

John Chapple, who has lived in Greece since 1969, has revised our chapters on Athens, the Saronic Gulf, the Ionian islands and the Sporades, as well as updating the essays on Greek life.

Marc Dubin, a well-travelled American who has a house on Sámos, has updated the chapters on the Dodecanese and the Northeast Aegean islands, as well as writing on Greek music and attempts to cope with tourism.

Lance Chilton has published numerous guide books on Greece and Cyprus. He updated the Crete chapter, as well as supplying new material on island wildlife, wild flowers and the Palace of Knossós.

Stephanie Ferguson, an English journalist very familiar with Greece, has brought her story of an island family up to date, and contributed new pages on religious festivals and food and drink in the islands.

Jeffrey Carson, who has lived on Páros since 1970, has revised the chapter on the Cyclades.

This edition builds on previous editions of the guide, whose contributors also included **Rowlinson Carter** (history and Island Elections). **Mark Mazower** (history), **Marcus Brooke** (Ancient Delos, Lindos and Crete), **Rhoda Nottridge** (Corfu), **David Glenn** (Sailing), **Kerin Hope** (Athens), **Carol Reed, John Carr** (Cruising), **Anthony Wood** (Working the Land), **Jane Cocking, Nile Stanton, Anita Peltonen** (Cyclades and Northeast Aegean) and **Diana Fare Louis** and **Nikos Stavroualakis**, both of whom have helped update the guide for previous editions.

Map Legend

▬ ▪ ▬	International Boundary
▭ ▭ ▭	Province
⊖	Border Crossing
▬ ▪ ▬	National Park/Reserve
▭ ▭ ▭	Ferry Route
Ⓜ	Metro
✈ ✈	Airport International / Regional
🚌	Bus Station
℗	Parking
❶	Tourist Information
✉	Post Office
† ✝	Church / Ruins
✝	Monastery
☾	Mosque
✡	Synagogue
⌂ 🏚	Castle / Ruins
∴	Archaeological Site
∩	Cave
1	Statue / Monument
★	Place of Interest

The main places of interest in the Places section are coordinated by number with a full-colour map (e.g. ❶), and a symbol at the top of every right-hand page tells you where to find the map.

INSIGHT GUIDE
Greek Islands

CONTENTS

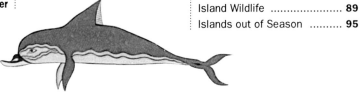

Pátmos, the Dodecanese

Travel Tips

Insight on ...

Information panels

♦ **Full Travel Tips index is on page 305**

Places

ISLAND MENTALITY

Greece has about 2,000 islands altogether. Despite their superficial similarities, each has a distinct identity and often an idiosyncratic history

It is one of those words that psychiatrists might use to trigger an automatic response from a patient stretched on the couch. Say "island" and childhood recollections of Robinson Crusoe may spring to mind. Often, islands are associated with the escape from a complex universe into a private, more manageable world that offers individuals control over their own destiny. Crusoe becomes comfortable in his reconstructed womb, and it's a surprise, when rescue is at hand, that he doesn't tell his saviours to push off.

"Greek island" would probably add some specific touches to the imagery: a cluster of blisteringly white buildings against a shimmering sea, donkeys slowly carrying their burdens against a backdrop of olive groves, small circles of weather-beaten fishermen bent over their nets, and jolly tavernas full of *retsina, moussaká*, shattered plates and an endless supply of *Never on Sunday* and *Zorba the Greek*. Accurate as far as it goes, perhaps, but any worthwhile generalisation about the Greek islands – anything, that is, more adventurous than the staringly obvious – would almost certainly be wrong.

Inter-island relations

Although the islands are classified as members of one group or another, each has a strong sense of separate identity and invariably an idiosyncratic history to back it up. Often, the feeling between neighbouring islands is mutual suspicion bordering on loathing, although this is something visitors would seldom be aware of unless they made a point of going down to the local *ouzerié* and chatting to the old boys entrenched there. Conditioned by long winter nights when nothing much happens, the old boys have developed the knack of waffling on

about any subject under the sun, and a new face in the audience is welcome.

As an example of inter-island relations, Skiáthos and Skópelos in the Sporades have never been able to see eye to eye on the matter of ice. The origins of the dispute are buried in history, but it may spring from days when mak-

ing ice depended on clanking contraptions which were partly home-made and therefore the focus of parochial pride. Neither side in the respective *ouzerié* will volunteer what is wrong with the other island's ice. Uncharacteristically, questions are turned aside, but hopeless shaking of grey heads hints at a truth so awful that they cannot bring themselves to utter it.

The telephone directories on Skiáthos and Skópelos reveal some of the same surnames. Could the families be related? The inquiry hits a nerve as painful as the ice business.

Only in one area, if the old boys are to be believed, are the two islands in full agreement, and that concerns Skýros, the largest island in

PRECEDING PAGES: a fishing boat in Mýkonos; a little blue-domed church in the Cyclades; an Orthodox priest on his way to work; sausages for sale.
LEFT: birds, cats and villager. RIGHT: a family group at Ambelákia, Salamína.

the chain. Skiáthos and Skópelos are within full view of one another, a distasteful but undeniable fact, whereas Skýros lies below the horizon. According to the miraculously united old boys, that means that Skýros may not exist.

Such theories are expounded with twinkling eyes and guffaws. Even if they should not be taken too literally, they are great fun, and the opportunity to move between neighbouring islands in order to compare notes should not be missed. It is sometimes said that if, against the odds, two islands struck the curious visitor as being practically identical, those islands would necessarily be at opposite ends of the Aegean.

with the skills which developed into the Minoan civilisation.

Intruders

To look at the history of Corfu, for instance, merely from the 11th century is to pick up that particular story a long way down the line. Nevertheless, the record from that date reveals an amazing cavalcade of intruders to the island (*see panel below*). All of them must have left a mark, even if the traces today would require more diligent research than most visitors would care to conduct while staying there on holiday. Dedicated scholars could probably assemble a

Apart from the natural tendency for small island communities to be staunchly independent, there is a historical basis for their individualism. From the time of the Phoenicians, the islands have been tossed around like loose pebbles in the cultural tides that have surged backwards and forwards through the eastern Mediterranean, and none has emerged from that experience quite like any other.

Momentous events were taking place on Crete and some of the Cyclades as early as 3000BC. The golden age of Athens under Pericles lay as far in the future then as, for us, it now lies in the past – more than two millennia either way. Settlers from Mesopotamia landed

---

FOREIGN OCCUPIERS

The history of Corfu is a typical saga of occupation by foreign powers, each of whom left some mark. From the 11th century, the island was ruled successively by Greeks (the Byzantine Empire), Normans, Sicilians, Venetians, Greeks ("the despotate of Epirus"), more Sicilians, Neapolitans and then the Venetians again – this time for 400 years. Then the procession of foreign rulers resumed: France, Russia and the Ottoman Empire, Britain, and then Greece. Italy occupied Corfu briefly in the 1920s and again during World War II. After Italy collapsed in 1943, Germany became the last foreign occupier, until the German surrender in 1944.

jigsaw, with pieces extant in Corfu, that would reflect each and every one of these waves.

The evidence does not necessarily consist of archeological ruins or excavated objects. Corfu extrapolated from one small chapter of its convoluted history an abiding passion for cricket. It is still played on the square in the middle of the town, albeit with local variations which would raise the eyebrows of traditionalists in England.

Other islands got almost as much unwanted outside attention as Corfu. Piracy was a perennial problem, hence the number of citadels (*kástra*) on high ground to which the island population retreated when danger threatened.

isn't mapped. A good tip for amateur archeologists would be to ask themselves where, taking into account security, prevailing winds, terrain, water supply etc, they themselves would have chosen to build something – and then start looking for evidence of past peoples.

The topographical differences among the islands are worth considering. If some of the islands look like mountain peaks, it is because much of the area now covered by the Aegean was once a solid land bridge between Greece and Asia Minor, which eventually fractured and "sank". These islands are the tips of what used to be ranges encroaching from either side.

Determined pirates

The defences did not always keep determined pirates like Khair-ed-din Barbarossa out, but they did mean that the pirates had to make an effort instead of lazily helping themselves to everything of value when they happened to be cruising by.

Crete and Rhodes have by far the richest and most thoroughly documented sites for historically-minded visitors, but on any island there is bound to be something to pick over, even if it

LEFT AND ABOVE: the Church and music are two of the common themes throughout Greece, providing a social bond within scattered communities.

The largest mountain ranges in mainland Greece caused famous military bottlenecks at places like Thermopylae where, in Xerxes' time, there was only the narrowest of passages between the mountains and the sea. Since then the sea has receded, so what used to be a death trap, where Spartan defenders calmly bathed and combed their hair (according to Herodotus) while waiting for the Persian onslaught, is now a coastal plain 5 km (3 miles) wide.

The contours of submerged mountains and valleys extending from the area around Thermopylae caused the seabed around the islands to drop precipitously to 1,800 metres (6,000 ft). On the Turkish side, the sea is generally much shallower, and it is the shallows which can cause the Aegean, quiet and bather-friendly one moment, to be transformed into a lethal cauldron within the space of an hour or two.

Anyone hiring a boat on holiday should never leave port without consulting the islanders. For thousands of years, lives have depended on accurate weather predictions, and local knowledge handed down is often more reliable than official forecasts carried on the radio or in newspapers.

If the purpose of a visit to the islands is nothing more than to settle on a stretch of agreeable beach and live cheaply, visitors should be lucky

on both counts. Greece has about 2,000 islands altogether and these, plus the islets, add up to technically the longest coastline of any country in Europe. Basic commodities, including restaurant meals, are price-controlled. They may rise with inflation, but against major foreign currencies the Greek drachma usually goes down, so the net result for foreigners is constant good value for money.

Advanced androgyny

The one exception may be Mýkonos, which in recent years seems to have cornered a market in advanced androgyny. The islanders used to ask themselves why there were so many churches on Mýkonos (hundreds of them); they now tend to say (stoically, while pocketing the money) that the gay birds of paradise who descend on them in summer are undoubtedly in urgent need of every one of them.

Mýkonos would not have been allowed to develop its exotic reputation under the puritanical military junta, when even topless sunbathing was discouraged. Since the overthrow of the glum colonels, what bathers choose to wear or discard has been a matter of personal choice, and there is usually at least one beach on an island where nudity is tolerated, even if it is not official.

The best way to enjoy the islands is to arrive with a certain attitude of mind. By all means, begin by uncritically enjoying the cluster of blisteringly white buildings against a shimmering sea, donkeys with a backdrop of olive groves, and so on – the vista, indeed, seared into the senses by island holiday brochures.

When the novelty wears off, or perhaps earlier, examine each island as if it were an onion, and start stripping off the skins. If not a longstanding dispute about ice, some other unexpected aspect is certain to be revealed.

How to strip the onion is a large part of what this book is about. It hopes to show by example. The book will never be written that says everything about 2,000 islands. The learned Helidorius once tried to set out all he had learned about the monuments of Athens, as they existed in the second century BC. Fifteen volumes later… ❏

ILLEGAL SUBSTANCES

The apparently tolerant attitude towards tourist behaviour in Greece does not extend to the use of drugs, and the more popular islands are subject to close undercover surveillance. Some humdrum medicines sold without prescription elsewhere may be illegal in Greece, and as the legal system seems to rest on the principle that the slightest suspicion warrants a spell in prison before the proceedings proper begin, it is wise to err on the side of extreme caution and leave nothing to chance. There are random drug searches at customs, and the minimum sentence for possessing even a small quantity of cannabis is seven years.

LEFT: fishing in local waters supplies tourists and villagers alike. **RIGHT:** preparing the evening meal of *hórta* – wild greens.

Decisive Dates

3200BC: Beginnings of Bronze Age cultures in Crete and the Cyclades.
2600–1450BC: Minoan civilisation in Crete.
c1500BC: Huge volcanic eruption on Santorini produces tidal waves that cause devastation. Major sites in central and southern Crete destroyed by fire.
c1450BC: Mycenaeans (originally from the northern Peloponnese) occupy Crete and Rhodes; establish a trading empire; adapt Minoan script into Linear B – the first written Greek.
1184BC: Traditional date for the fall of Troy.

11TH CENTURY BC: Dorians from the north invade the islands, destroying Mycenaean civilisation and bringing Iron-Age technology and new "geometric" pottery.
1150–750BC: The "Dark Ages". Cultural and economic development stagnates, the art of writing is forgotten. Refugee Mycenaeans (known as Ionians) settle on Aegean islands, in Asia Minor and in Attica.
900–750BC: The growth of city states. Athens becomes the foremost Ionian city.
776BC: Probable date of the first Olympic Games.
c770BC: Contact with Etruscans, Phoenicians and Egyptians spurs a revival of Greek cultural life. Greeks adopt the Phoenician alphabet.
750–700BC: The Homeric epics *The Odyssey* and *The Iliad* are written down for the first time.

c715BC: Archilochus, the first lyric poet, born on Paros
c650BC: Poetess Sappho born on Lesbos (Lésvos).
c570BC: Pythagoras born on Sámos.
546BC: The Persian empire expands to control Ionian Greek cities on west coast of Anatolia (now Turkey).
520–500BC: Persians, under Darius the Great, systematically conquer many Aegean islands. Revolts are ruthlessly put down.
499–479BC: Persian invasions of Greek mainland repulsed by united Greek front, led by Spartan army and Athenian navy. Ionian states freed from Persian rule.

The Classical Age

477BC: Athens establishes Delian League, comprising many islands and cities in Asia Minor; the treasury and nominal headquarters is on Delos.
471–465BC: Islands that attempt to secede from the League are brutally quashed by Athens.
460BC: Hippocrates, the "father of medicine", born on Kos.
454BC: The League's treasury is removed from Delos to Athens. Effectively, the island states are now part of an Athenian Empire.
431–404BC: Peloponnesian War between Athens (and her allies) and Sparta (and other Peloponnesian states) leaves Athens defeated and weakened.
338BC: Greeks defeated by Philip II of Macedon.
336–323BC: Philip succeeded by his son Alexander, who extends his empire as far as India and Egypt.
323BC: On Alexander's death, the empire is divided between his generals. Greek islands are controlled by Ptolemy and his successors.
c300BC: Thíra on Santoríni becomes capital of the Ptolemaic Aegean.
227BC: Earthquake destroys Colossus of Rhodes.

Romans and Byzantines

146BC: Romans annex Macedonia and Greece.
AD58: St Paul on Rhodes.
AD95: St John writes the Apocalypse on Pátmos.
3RD CENTURY: Christianity spreads; Goths threaten Greece's northen frontier.
323: Constantine becomes sole ruler of the Roman Empire; establishes his capital at Constantinople.
391: Paganism outlawed in the Roman Empire.
393: Olympic Games banned as a pagan festival.
395: Goths under Alaric devastate Athens and the Peloponnese.
395: Roman Empire splits into two: Latin west and Byzantine east.
653–658: Arabs occupy Rhodes; sell the remains of the Colossus as scrap metal.
747–843: Icons are banned in the Eastern Church.

827: Arabs establish themselves in Crete, proceed to plunder the rest of the Aegean for over 100 years.

961: Byzantines retake Crete.

1081: Normans from Sicily invade Greek islands.

1088: Monastery of St John founded on Pátmos.

1096: The First Crusade.

1204: The Fourth Crusade: Constantinople taken. Break-up of the Byzantine Empire. Venetians claim the right to the Ionians and other islands.

1210: Venetians take Crete.

1309: Knights Hospitallers of St John arrive on Rhodes, take over and fortify the Dodecanese.

1389: Venetians gain control of much of Greece and the islands.

1453: Ottoman Turks capture Constantinople, rename it Istanbul and make it capital of Ottoman Empire.

1522-37: Rhodes and the other Dodecanese islands invaded and taken over by Ottoman Turks.

1541: El Greco born in Crete.

1649–69: Venetian-Turkish War; ends with Iráklion falling to Turkish forces. Crete is under Ottoman rule.

1797: Napoleon takes the Ionian Islands.

1799: Ionian Republic declared.

1815–64: British rule in the Ionian Islands.

The Struggle for Independence

1821–27: Greece fights Turkey in the War of Independence.

1823: Solomós writes the *Hymn to Liberty*.

1827–29: Aigina (Éghina) the capital of Greece.

1830: Turks cede Euboea (Évvia) to Greeks, but keep control of the Dodecanese.

1834: Athens becomes capital of Greece.

1854–57: Piraeus (Piréas) blockaded by British and French fleets.

1864: Ionian islands, relinquished by Britain, become part of the Greek state.

1896: First modern Olympics held in Athens.

1897: Greece goes to war with Turkey again, but is heavily defeated.

1898: Crete becomes an independent principality within the Ottoman Empire.

1909: Army officers revolt against political establishment in Athens, invite Cretan lawyer Elefthérios Venizélos to form a new government.

1910: Venizélos becomes Prime Minister; his Liberal Party dominates Greek politics for 25 years.

1912–13: Balkans War: Greece takes from Turkey

PRECEDING PAGES: 17th-century map of ancient Greece. **LEFT:** the owl, symbol of goddess Athene's wisdom, appeared on early Athenian coins. **RIGHT:** British troops liberate Athens in 1944.

Crete, Northern and Eastern Aegean islands, and Macedonia. Italy occupies Dodecanese.

1913: King George I is murdered, succeeded by his son, Constantine I.

1924: Greece becomes a republic.

1932: Aristotle Onassis buys six freight ships, the start of his shipping empire.

1940: Greece is neutral in World War II until Mussolini's Italy attacks; Greece aligns with the Allies.

1941: Greece invaded by Nazi Germany.

1943-44: Greece is liberated by Allies, who keep control of the Dodecanese.

1945: Níkos Kazantzákis publishes *Zorba the Greek*.

1946–9: Civil War between Greek government and

Communists opposed to restoring the monarchy.

1947: Dodecanese become part of Greece.

1947–67: Constitutional monarchy in Greece.

1953: Earthquake causes great damage in Ionian Islands: large-scale emigration.

1967–74: Greece ruled by junta of right-wing colonels; King Constantine in exile.

1974: Colonels overthrown; republic established.

1981: Andréas Papandréou's left-wing PASOK party forms first Greek Socialist government.

1981: Greece becomes member of EEC.

1989: PASOK brought down by corruption scandals; out of office for three years.

1996: Papandréou dies; Kóstas Simítis succeeds him and wins re-election. ❑

WAVES OF INVADERS

The history of Greece, and especially its islands, is inextricably linked to the sea. It is a history full of foreign conquerors and occupiers

What distinguishes the course of Greek history from that of her Balkan neighbours is the impact of the sea. The sea diffuses cultures, transfers peoples and encourages trade – and until our own times it was invariably a swifter means of transmission than overland. Nowhere in Greece is the sea as inescapable as on the islands.

The poverty of the arid island soil has forced inhabitants to venture far afield for their livelihood. At the same time, the islands have been vulnerable to foreign incursions whether by Arab pirates, Italian colonists or modern tourists. All have played their part in transforming local conditions; some have had an even wider impact. Phoenician traders, for example, appear to have brought their alphabet to Crete in the early Archaic period, which the Greeks then adopted and changed. At the same time, Egyptian influence was leading island sculptors to work in stone. It is no coincidence that the earliest examples of monumental Greek sculpture are all to be found on the islands.

On Crete, the Bronze Age had produced the first urban civilisation in the Aegean: this was the age of the Knossós and Festós palaces, erected in the centuries after 2000 BC. Other islands such as Santoríni also flourished at this time. Thucydides' account of how King Minos of Crete established his sons as governors in the Cyclades and cleared the sea of pirates certainly suggests considerable Cretan control of the Aegean. The Aegean was not to be dominated by a single sea power for another millennium until the rise of the Athenian empire.

Economic growth

Before this, however, communities of Greeks had begun to flourish on most of the islands, exploiting local quarries and mines, and developing indigenous political systems. Some communities achieved considerable wealth, notably

LEFT: a marble idol from the Early Cycladic era.
RIGHT: an inaccurate artist's impression of the Colossus of Rhodes.

on Sífnos, whose gold and silver mines had made her inhabitants reputedly the richest citizens in the Cyclades by the 6th century BC. Some reflection of this wealth can be seen in the ruins of the marble treasury which Sifniots dedicated to Apollo at Delphi.

It was in the 6th century, too, that the inhab-

itants of Santoríni began to mint their own coinage, a physical manifestation of the island's powerful status in the Aegean. At one point Santoríni's influence was to extend, not only to Crete, Mílos, Páros and Rhodes, but as far west as Corinth and as far east as Asia Minor.

During the 5th century BC, the islands' independence was curtailed as Athens used anti-Persian fears to manipulate the Delian League. This had been formed in 478 BC as an alliance between equal partners to form a strong naval power in the Aegean. But Athens soon controlled the League and used its resources in a series of wars against rivals such as the naval power of Aegina (Éghina).

It was Athenian intrigues with the Corinthian colony on Corfu, however, that led to the Peloponnesian War which was ultimately to cripple – and break – Athens forever.

In the Hellenistic period the islands remained turbulent backwaters, prone to internecine struggles which made them easy prey for their more powerful neighbours. By the middle of the 1st century BC, Rome had established herself in the Aegean; Crete became the centre of a province which included a part of North Africa.

Under Roman guidance roads were laid, aqueducts constructed, new towns and grand buildings erected. Despite this prosperity, the

Aegean as a whole remained in the background in Roman times. Little is known of conditions of life in the islands either then or after AD 395, when they passed into the control of the eastern Roman Empire. Only with the onset of the Arab raids in the 7th century does the historical record become more complete.

With the decline of Roman power in the Mediterranean, the islands faced a long period of instability: for more than a millennium they were attacked by invaders from all points of the compass. From the north, briefly, came the Vandals and Goths; from the south, the Arabs, who established themselves on Crete in 827 and proceeded to plunder the rest of the Aegean

for over a century. From the west came Normans in the 11th century, followed by the Genoese and Venetians; finally, from the east came the Ottoman Turks, who succeeded in dominating almost all of the islands in the Aegean between the 15th and 18th centuries.

Other groups, too, played minor roles – quite apart from powers such as the English, French and Russians, who all shared an interest in the Greek islands. The impact of these various peoples on the islands was complex and tangled, making it awkward to generalise about the historical experiences of the islands themselves. Only by considering the main island groups individually may things fall into place.

The Ionian islands

On the eve of the 1821 Greek uprising, an English traveller to Corfu noted: "The natural weakness and position of the Ionian islands, and all their past history, demonstrate that they must ever be an appendage of some more powerful state; powerful at sea and able to protect them as well as to command." Close to the Greek mainland, vital staging-posts on the voyage from western Europe to the Levant, it was inevitable that the Ionian islands should be a source of constant conflict.

Corfu had suffered brief attacks during the 5th century from Vandals and Goths, the destroyers of the Roman Empire in the West, but it was not until the eastern Empire lost its possessions in southern Italy that the Ionian islands again became vulnerable to invasion. This time the predators were the Normans. At the time when William the Conqueror was establishing Norman control over England, Robert Guiscard, Duke of Apulia, defeated the Byzantine army and its emperor, before dying of a fever at Kefalloniá. His nephew Roger, King of Sicily, occupied Corfu in 1146 and held it for six years. As the Byzantine hold over the islands weakened, the Venetians came in as reluctant allies.

These allies soon proved to have territorial ambitions of their own. The islands were situated on important trade routes to the eastern Mediterranean, and commercial interests led to the desire for political control. After the sack of Constantinople in 1204 during the Fourth Crusade, the islands were divided into fiefdoms among noble Venetian families. Not until 1387 however, were the islands brought under direct

Venetian rule, which continued through a succession of Ottoman attacks down to 1797 when under the new order created by Napoleon's conquests, the islands went to France.

During these four centuries, the Ionian islands were ruled by local nobility and by administrators sent out from Venice. The influence of the Republic was felt in the introduction of cash crops such as olives and currants, in the repressive regime under which the peasants worked and in the Italian language which the nobility affected to speak. At first Venetian rule was energetic – so that, for example, after Ottoman raids had left Zákynthos virtually

and political assassination made life precarious.

The end of Venetian rule was bloodless: when the French invaders arrived, they discovered the fortress guns rusting and the garrison without any gunpowder. Napoleon himself had written in 1797 that "the great maxim of the Republic ought henceforth to be never to abandon Corfu, Zante..." However, British troops managed to establish a foothold in the minor islands in 1809. After Napoleon's defeat this was extended and the new Septinsular Republic was placed under British protection.

Sir Thomas Maitland, the first Lord High Commissioner, in the words of a Victorian his-

uninhabited in the late 15th century, vigorous resettlement policies soon created the basis for new prosperity. Zákynthos had only 36 families in 1485, but 752 families by 1516, and her revenues increased forty-fold in 30 years thanks to the introduction of these valuable crops.

By the 18th century Venice had lost her possessions in the Aegean and the Peloponnese; in the Ionian Sea, the Venetian-held islands were ravaged by pirates operating from Paxos (Paxí) and the Albanian coast; internally, blood feuds

LEFT: Dionýsios Solomós, the Ionian poet whose *Hymn to Freedom* was adopted as the national anthem after Independence. **ABOVE:** a watercolour of Itháki harbour.

BRIBERY AND CORRUPTION

By the end of the 18th century, the Venetians' last remaining stronghold in the Ionian was corrupt. In 1812, the British Whig politician Henry Holland wrote of the Venetian rulers of Corfu: "The governors and other officers sent to the island were usually of noble family and often of decayed fortune; men who undertook the office as a speculation of interest and executed it accordingly. Bribery and every mode of illegal practice were carried on openly; toleration for a crime might easily be purchased; and the laws, in many respects imperfect themselves, were rendered wholly null by the corruption of the judges."

torian, "established a Constitution which, possessing every appearance of freedom, in reality left the whole power in his hands". But it could not satisfy the islanders' desire for freedom from foreign rule, a desire which intensified after the creation of the Kingdom of Greece in 1832. In 1864 Britain relinquished control and the Ionian Islands became part of the modern Greek state.

The Cyclades, Sporades and Saronic Gulf islands

The Cyclades, unlike the Ionian islands, were a commercial backwater: main trade routes passed through Crete and the eastern Aegean islands to Smyrna and Aleppo. While they remained a lure to pirates, they were never of comparable interest to major powers. Until the rise of the seafaring Italian city-states in the 11th century, most trade in the Aegean was in the hands of Greeks.

However, the weakness of the Byzantine navy was underlined by a series of Arab raids against the islands and the Greek mainland. By the 12th century a British chronicler noted that piracy had become the curse of the Aegean: many of the islands were abandoned, while others – Skýros in the Sporades, for example – became pirate lairs.

The sack of Constantinople in 1204, which brought the Ionian islands under Venetian control, also brought new masters to the Aegean. The unimportance of this group of islands to them meant that the Venetians were content to leave the task of occupying them to private citizens. Of these, the most successful was Marco Sanudo, a nephew of the Doge Dandolo, who equipped eight galleys at his own expense and sailed to the Aegean where he founded the Duchy of Náxos in 1207.

Náxos itself became the capital of a fiefdom of some islands, and on it Sanudo built a castle, erected a Catholic cathedral and provided solid fortifications for the town. Other adventurers helped themselves to islands such as Ándhros and Santoríni. The Ghisi family obtained Tínos and Mýkonos, as well as the islands in the Sporades, establishing a dynasty which clashed with the Sanudi until both were overwhelmed by the Ottoman navy in the 16th century.

Traces of the Venetian presence are to be found both in the Catholic communities which survive on Sýros and Tínos. The Duchy of

Náxos lasted over 350 years, and only ended with the death of Joseph Nasi, the Sephardic Jewish favourite of Selim II, upon whom the sultan had bestowed the islands after their capture from the Sanudi.

But the exceptional longevity of the Duchy of Náxos should not be allowed to obscure the turbulence of life in the Aegean in these centuries. Piracy had increased in the late 13th century, with Greek corsairs from Monemvasiá or Santoríni, Sicilians and Genoese – and had led, for example, to the inhabitants of the island of Amorgós to emigrating en masse to Náxos whose fertile interior was relatively inaccessible.

In the 14th century, Catalan mercenaries, brought in for the conflict between Venice and Genoa, ravaged some of the islands and raided others. Ottoman troops landed on Náxos and took 6,000 captives. The Ottoman forces often consisted of recent converts to Islam, and were led by renegade Aegean Greeks such as the notorious brothers from the island of Lésvos, Khair-ed-din and Amrudj Barbarossa.

VENETIAN REMAINS

There is still evidence of the Venetian occupation of the Cyclades, in local family names derived from Italian.

Local rulers began to complain of depopulation: Ándhros had to be resettled by Albanian

mainlanders; Íos, virtually uninhabited, was replenished by families from the Peloponnese. Astypálea was repopulated in 1413, abandoned in 1473 and only inhabited once more after 1570. In the 16th century, the islands suffered a series of attacks by the Turkish navy and by mid-century Venetian influence was on the wane. Within 50 years, most of the islands had been brought under Ottoman rule, though the last, Tínos, only succumbed as late as 1712.

Conditions of life did not improve under

LEFT: detail of an embroidery from Skýros, probably from the 17th century. **ABOVE:** a 1795 watercolour showing the unfinished Temple of Apollo, Náxos.

Ottoman rule. Piracy, famine and fatal disease remained the perennial problems. In the 18th century, the plague decimated the islands on four separate occasions, continuing into the next century, well after the disease had died out in most of Europe. Thus the Ottomans, like their predecessors, were forced to repopulate.

Often the new colonists were not Greeks. Tournefort reported in the early 18th century that most of the inhabitants of Andíparos were descended from French and Maltese corsairs. He also noted that villages on Ándhros were "peopled only by Albanians, dressed still in their traditional style and living their own way, that is to say with neither creed nor law".

It was the Albanians who were to play a major role in the struggle for Greek independence. Waves of Albanians had been colonising the islands of the Aegean since the 14th century. They were concentrated on the Saronic islands – the eminent Koundouriotis family, for example, moved from Epiros to Hydra around the year 1580. By the late 18th century, Hydra, with a largely Albanian population, possessed one of the largest and most powerful shipping fleets in the Aegean, which played no small part in defeating the Ottoman Turks after 1821.

The importance of these islands was underlined by the choice of Aegina (Éghina), for a short time, as the first capital of the new Greek state. Refugees flocked here when it was the seat of government, only to leave again when it was replaced by Náfplion, on the mainland. When Edouard About visited the town in 1839 he reported it "abandoned – the homes that had been built tumbled into ruins, the town once more became a village; its life and activity fled with the government".

The Northeast Aegean islands

Although the east Aegean islands shared the experience of Arab raids with the Cyclades, the two areas developed differently as the rivalry between Venice and Genoa increased after the Fourth Crusade. As allies of the resurgent Byzantine Empire against her Latin enemies, the Genoese were given trading rights in the Black Sea and granted permission to colonise the eastern Aegean.

A Genoese trading company controlled the

mastic plantations of Híos from the beginning of the 14th century. In 1333 Lésvos passed into the hands of the Gatteluso family, who eventually extended their control to Thássos and the other northern islands. However, as in the west Aegean, the power of the Ottoman navies simply overwhelmed these local potentates, and with the fall of Híos in 1566 all the islands of the east Aegean passed into Ottoman hands.

Lésvos had been conquered by the Ottoman Turks as early as 1462, and most of the inhabitants emigrated. In 1453 the inhabitants of Sámos fled to Híos, but returned to the deserted island in the 16th century. Belon du Mans, who

Ottomans brutally suppressed a rather uncertain revolt. Fustel de Coulanges wrote in 1856: "Any person aged more than 32 years whom one meets today on Híos was enslaved and saw his father slaughtered".

It was little consolation to know that the massacre on Híos had aroused the attention of European liberals, and strengthened philhellenic sentiment. Refugees fled westwards, transporting the island's traditional *loukoúmi* industry (the making and selling of Turkish Delight) to Sýros in the Cyclades, whose port of Ermoúpolis became the busiest port in the new Greek state. Other refugees settled in Alexan-

visited the island around 1546, wrote: "It is striking that an island like Sámos must remain deserted. The fear of pirates has rendered her uninhabited so that now there is not a single village there, nor any animals". Despite the islands' proximity to the mainland, they attracted only a small number of Muslim colonisers, and the bulk of the population remained Greek, supplemented by the inevitable Albanian immigrants. Only on Lésvos were Muslim settlers to be found farming the land; elsewhere they stayed close to the towns.

The 1821 insurrection sent shock waves through the islands. Sámos was first; the unrest then spread to Híos where, in 1822, the

dria, Trieste, Marseilles and as far north as Amsterdam.

Elsewhere in the east Aegean, the changes were just as great. The Ottoman authorities were only able to suppress the rising with the aid of Mehmet Ali and his Albanian mercenaries who had as little respect for the local Muslim notables as they had for the Greeks: many Turkish landowners sold up and emigrated to Anatolia, while their properties were bought by middle-class Greeks who became an increasingly powerful force in the aging Ottoman Empire.

By the end of the century the Ottoman hold had become tenuous: Sámos, for example, had maintained a certain autonomy under a traditionally Christian prince. And on Thássos the Oxford don Henry Tozer found in 1884 that there were no Muslims there apart from the governor himself and a few soldiers. Since the people had to pay neither the "head tax" – universal elsewhere in the Ottoman Empire – nor Ottoman trade duties, it is not surprising that they appeared content with their system of government.

The Muslim islanders, on the other hand, continued to leave for the mainland. Even before the Greco-Turkish population exchange in 1923, the Turkish communities on Híos and Lésvos had dwindled away. Their place was filled by a mass of Greek refugees from Anatolia.

> **SCRAP MERCHANTS**
>
> When the Arabs occupied Rhodes from AD 653–658, they broke up the remains of the famous 3rd-century BC Colossus and sold the bronze for scrap.

The Dodecanese

The 14 or more islands, misleadingly known as the "Dodecanese", (*dhódheka* means "12") suffered as elsewhere from the collapse of Roman authority. They were repeatedly attacked and plundered. The Byzantine hold remained firmer here than it did in the west, but after 1204 many of the islands were ceded to Frankish adventurers in return for nominal acknowledgement of Byzantine sovereignty.

By the beginning of the 14th century, Venice had helped herself to those two crucial stepping stones to the East, Kássos and Kárpathos. At the same time, Rhodes was captured from the Byzantine Greeks by the Knights of St John, a military order which, after the loss of Jerusalem in 1187, had been based in Cyprus since 1291. Fulke de Villaret, the first Grand Master of Rhodes, reconstructed the city.

Although the Knights of St John were able to withstand a siege by the Ottomans in 1480, they could not hold off the Ottoman threat indefinitely. In 1521 they were outnumbered by a massive Ottoman force over 100,000 strong, and after a siege lasting five months the starving defenders were forced to capitulate. With the fall of Rhodes, the position of the neighbouring islands was undermined, and by 1537 they had all been incorporated into the formidable Ottoman Empire.

The island's inhabitants were compelled to

LEFT: the sea battle of Sámos, one of the first clashes in the War of Independence; watercolour from 1824.
RIGHT: 19th-century drawing of a Kássos woman.

leave the town of Rhodes and settle outside. But because the Ottomans never made up more than one-third of the population, their overall influence was never that strong. Since the land on many islands was difficult to farm, the islanders looked elsewhere for their livelihoods.

Many became seamen, while on Kálymnos and Sými the tradition of sponge fishing prospered. In 1521, the islanders of Kálymnos paid homage to Suleiman II with sponges and white bread to demonstrate that "sponge fishers do

not cultivate corn, but buy flour – and only of the best quality". During the 19th century, the sponge fishers went international, opening agencies in London, Frankfurt and Basle.

But these developments, typical of the growing Greek middle class, did not lead to union with Greece until late in the day. The islands had been intended for the new Greek state in 1830, but were retained at the last minute by Turkey in return for the mainland island Euboea (Évvia). Liberation from the Ottoman Empire came unexpectedly through the occupation of the islands by the Italians during their war with the Turks in 1912.

At first, the islanders welcomed the Italians. A

congress on Pátmos passed a resolution thanking the Italian nation for delivering them from the Turkish yoke. However, another resolution at the same congress calling for unification of the islands with Greece was less satisfactory to the local Italian commander who broke up the congress and forbade such public meetings.

The Italians did not intend to hold the islands permanently but, with the dismemberment of the Ottoman Empire, their dreams of establishing a foothold in Asia Minor led them to renege on a promise made in 1920 to return the islands to Greece. Mussolini sent groups of reluctant administrators to turn the islands

Strategic Crete

The "Great Island" has had the most violent history of all, thanks to its strategic position, agricultural riches and, not least, its inhabitants' fierce tradition of resistance to foreign oppression. From AD 823, when it was conquered by Arab freebooters out of Alexandria, who made it the centre of the slave trade and a base for pirate raids throughout the Aegean, the strategic importance of Crete has been obvious.

Around 3000 BC, a prosperous civilisation spread its influence throughout the Aegean. The Minoans left proof of their architectural genius in the ruined palaces of Knossós and Festós.

ΣΚΗΝΗ ΕΝ ΚΡΗΤΗ ΚΑΤΑ ΤΟ 1866.

into a fascist colony. But the process was brought to an abrupt halt by World War II. Once Italy surrendered in 1943, the islands were taken over by the Germans who managed, in the course of their brief and very brutal occupation, to exterminate the ancient Jewish population, much against the evident wishes of the islanders, the Italians and even some of their own soldiers.

It is understood that only three survivors of the Jewish community remained on Rhodes. Just a few months after the Jews had been deported, the islands were occupied by the Allies, who finally handed them over to Greece in 1947.

DICTATORSHIP IN ACTION

The Italian occupation of the Dodecanese under Mussolini imposed on the islanders the farcical prohibitions of a totalitarian regime, intent on "Italianising" the islands. An extensive secret police network guarded against nationalist activity; the practice of Orthodox religion was outlawed; the blue and white colours of the Greek flag were prohibited in public; all shop signs had to be painted in Italian – and slogans such as "Viva il Duce, viva la nuova Italia imperiale!" were daubed on the walls of recalcitrant shopkeepers. In the 1930s, many islanders emigrated to the Greek mainland, to Egypt and to Australia.

Though they were daring soldiers, they appear to have preferred commerce to agriculture. They established outposts in the Peloponnese and made contact with the Egyptians.

By 1500 BC, Minoan civilisation had reached its zenith. But then Crete was shaken by a series of disasters: a stupendous volcanic eruption on the island of Santoríni (Thíra) unleashed a tidal wave that damaged settlements along the north coast. Then, barely a generation later, most of the important sites in central and southern Crete were destroyed by fire. But the causes of the wider disintegration of Minoan control remain a mystery. Only Knossós continued to be inhab-

centre of a renaissance of Byzantine culture: Cretan artists such as Domínikos Theotokópoulos, otherwise known as El Greco, helped to enrich the Renaissance in western Europe.

Though the Venetians developed the towns and fortresses on the north coast, they knew how little they were loved by the Cretans. In 1615 a certain Fra Paolo Serpi had warned that "the Greek faith is never to be trusted," and he had recommended that the people "must be watched with more attention lest, like the wild beasts they are, they should find an occasion to use their teeth and claws. The surest way is to keep good garrisons to awe them." Under such

ited as Cretan dominance in the Aegean ended.

In the early 13th century AD, Venice and Genoa tussled to wrest the island away from the waning Byzantine Empire. Although Venice ultimately turned Crete into a prize possession, Byzantine influence remained strong. The old Greek noble families survived, while ties with Constantinople were reflected everywhere in church art and secular literature.

This strong Byzantine tradition became crucial after 1453 when the island gave refuge to exiles fleeing the Turks, and briefly became the

a regime the peasants were probably worse off than under the Turks on the mainland.

Occasionally, as in 1263 and 1571, there were major uprisings which the Venetians harshly put down. After one such revolt, 300 people were executed and many exiled, their villages were burned and razed, their property confiscated and other severe penalties exacted. In 1538 the coasts were laid waste by the pirate Khair-ed-din Barbarossa. On top of all this, the inhabitants faced other – natural – terrors such as the famine which in 1626 reduced the population of the island by one-fifth. In these circumstances it is not surprising that the Venetian presence on the island remained small and that

LEFT: oil painting of the 1866 Cretan Revolt.
ABOVE: Iráklion at the turn of the century.

Roman Catholicism never became widespread. Venice kept its hold on Crete long after most of her other Aegean possessions had been surrendered. But, in 1645, the town of Haniá fell to the Turks and, in 1669, after a siege lasting two years, Iráklion fell too and the entire island came under Ottoman rule. By this time, the Ottoman administration had lost much of its early vigour: in the early 18th century one commentator described Iráklion as "the carcass of a large city... little better than a desert".

In an effort to escape the burdens of Ottoman rule many Cretan families converted to Islam, especially during the 18th century, on a scale

unknown elsewhere in the Aegean. But these converts continued to speak Greek, drink alcohol and had names such as Effendakis and Mehmedakis, which were a bizarre jumble of Greek and Turkish elements. Villages continued to be called by their Greek names even after all their inhabitants had converted.

From 1770, a series of revolts broke out against Ottoman rule. But it was to take more than a century to bring about independence; nevertheless, these insurrections altered the balance of power on the island as many Muslim farmers sold out to Christians before moving, first to the coastal towns, and then, at the turn of the century, away from the island altogether.

These revolts also had a catastrophic effect on the island's economy. Passing through the interior shortly after the 1866–69 insurrection, Tozer noted: "Every village that we passed through, and all that we could see along the hillsides, had been plundered, gutted and burnt." Even today, abandoned villages are not an uncommon sight in the countryside inland.

In 1896, when the next major revolt broke out, the inadequacies of Ottoman rule were so evident that the European powers stepped in. For example, on the whole of the island there was just one short stretch of carriage road which went from from Haniá to Suda Bay; and as William Miller reported in 1897, in Iráklion, the largest town on the island, there were no carriages at all "for the two that used to exist were last employed for the conveyance of the admirals on the Queen's Jubilee last year, on which occasion the bottom of both vehicles fell out, and the distinguished officers had to walk inside the bottomless machines". Troubles in Ottoman Crete in 1897 provoked a wave of sympathy on the mainland. Greek naval forces were sent to the island while the army marched northwards – only to be checked by the Ottoman forces who pushed back down into Greece. This defeat was humiliating for the Greeks, but it proved only to delay the future enlargement of the kingdom for a while.

The following year the island of Crete was made an independent principality under Ottoman sovereignty. The new prince was, significantly, a member of the Greek royal house. The writing was on the wall and within a few years union with Greece had finally been achieved.

A new revolt

In 1909, political change was once again forced through by military means. Junior army officers staged a revolt against the political establishment in Athens and, at their invitation, a new politician with a radical reputation, Eléftherios Venizélos, came to Athens from Crete to form a new government. A consummate diplomat and a man of great personal charm, Venizélos channelled the untapped energies of the Greek middle-class into his own Liberal Party, which dominated Greek politics for the next 25 years. ❑

LEFT: watercolour of urban Cretan costume.
RIGHT: a naïve painting of Elefthérios Venezélos.

THE ISLANDS TODAY

The 20th century has been a political roller-coaster for Greece and its islands, veering between monarchy, military dictatorship and socialist republicanism

The islands did not all become part of independent Greece at the same time. Only the Cyclades, the Sporades and Évvia (Euboea) formed part of the original state in 1830. After a long campaign by the islanders and, more to the point, because they were no longer considered of strategic value, the Ionian islands were ceded by Britain to Greece in 1864.

The other major additions came from war. Crete and the Northeast Aegean islands became part of Greece in 1913 after the Second Balkan War. The Dodecanese islands were freed from Italian occupation by World War II and formally incorporated into Greece in 1948. Since several of the islands were wealthy ports at a time when Athens was still a village, it is scarcely surprising that their influence on developments in the new state was enormous.

In politics, the Hydriot families of Voúlgaris and Koundouriótis, the Metaxás dynasty on Corfu, not to mention the Cretan Elefthérios Venizélos – in many ways the founder of the modern Greek state – all typified the vigour which the islanders brought to the political scene. And their influence did not stop here: Greek literature and music was marked by the Ionian islands' close links with Italy, while Lésvos has produced both the Nobel Prize-winning poet Odysseus Elytis and the naïve painter Theóphilos.

The islands' economic influence has also been profound, especially before the Balkan Wars of 1912–13 added the fertile regions of northern Greece to the impoverished state, and again in recent decades with the increasing flow of tourists. The shipping fleets of the Aegean islands, exports of currants and olive oil from Zákynthos and Kefalloniá, and emigrant remittances from islanders scattered across the globe – from Romania to Australia to Florida – have all helped to bolster the country's economy.

LEFT: a Cretan peasant in traditional dress, around 1950. **RIGHT:** a pelican once started an inter-island feud between Mýkonos and Tínos.

Islands for outcasts

But islands had other uses, too. Límnos, under Turkish rule, was used as a place of exile for political offenders. Henry Tozer, who visited the island in 1884, learned that a former grand vizier had been living on the island for eight years and was "almost forgotten at the capital."

The fortress islet of Spinalónga, off the northeast coast of Crete, after a long career as Venetian outpost and Turkish village, was used as a leper colony until the late 1950s.

The Greek central government also found the islands useful for prisons, both for regular criminals in the large compounds on Aegina (Éghina) and Corfu and, more ominously, at certain times for political opponents. On Aegina, what was built as a mint for the new Kapodístrias government in the late 1820s long served as a prison (its most recent use has been to house wounded wild birds until they are well enough to be released) and the prison on Corfu is still used.

In the 1930s the dictator Metaxás sent his opponents to forbidding islands. During the civil war (1947-49), in which the left-wing forces that had formed a strong resistance to the occupying Nazis were suppressed, the uninhabited island of Makroníssos just off the southeastern coast of Attica was extensively used as a prison camp for political detainees.

The Colonels, who ruled Greece with a heavy, sometimes brutal, hand from 21 April 1967 until 24 July 1974, continued the tradition, incarcerating their political opponents in Makroníssos, Yioúra, and Amorgós as well as the regular prisons on Aegina and Corfu. On

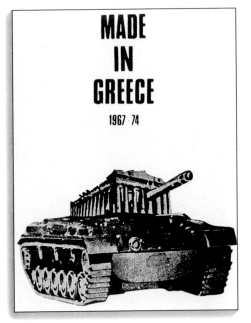

MADE IN GREECE
1967-74

occasions, particularly on Amorgós and Corfu, the islanders managed to circumvent the military security and give the political prisoners some support.

Incoming and outgoing

Since the late 1950s the islands have experienced the erratic but inexorable growth of tourism, a trend initiated when Greek shipowners began to acquire islands for their private use. When Stavros Niarchos and Aristotle Onassis continued their competition by buying the islands of Spetsopoúla just off Spétses in the Saronic Gulf and Skórpios just off Lefkádha in the Ionian Sea, they set an ideal which innumerable tourists have tried to follow in finding their own island paradise.

Mýkonos and Corfu were the first to bring in large numbers of summer visitors, but the trend has spread to virtually all the inhabited islands. If there is a ship going there, then there will be tourists, and the luxury of what they will find is more or less according to the island's accessibility. For both visitors and the islanders themselves, the big change in recent years has been the increasing availability of hydrofoils, the more expensive but far faster vessels introduced over the past 20 years.

The counter to this influx has been a steady flow of emigration from the islands. In the early years of this century the early waves of emigration were from the mainland; large numbers of islanders didn't follow until the 1960s. Several reasons lie behind this failure to emigrate until the latter half of the 20th century. In the first place, would-be emigrants were constrained by the availability of transport and their own awareness of the wider world.

An extreme case of such isolation was to be found in Gávdhos, an islet off Crete. According to Spratt, who visited there in 1865, the inhabitants did not see a boat approach for months on end, and he himself disembarked among naked swimmers who he found were "primitive in their habits and ideas... a mixed and degenerate race". Thus, to some extent, the opportunities for emigration depended upon improvements in transport and communications.

In the second place, several islands prospered after they incorporated into the Greek state. Sýros, for example, became the most important port and manufacturing centre in Greece in the first few decades after 1830. Even after

BACKWARD-LOOKING COLONELS

The military junta that ruled Greece from 1967 to 1974, under the leadership of Colonel George Papadópoulos, was driven by a mixture of self-interest and hazy nationalism. In their attitudes, the Colonels – from peasant or lower middle-class backgrounds – drew on earlier traditions, and symbolised a provincial reaction to a new world of urban consumers. They laid great stress on a return to traditional morality and religion, censored the press and suppressed intellectual debate, and closed the frontiers to bearded, long-haired or mini-skirted foreigners – at least until they realised the implications for Greece's tourist trade.

the rise of Piraeus (Pireás) it remained an important centre where the standing may be gauged by the fine 19th-century villas and warehouses of its capital Ermoúpolis. On other islands, such as Ándhros and Náxos, the late 19th century was a period of rapid exploitation of mineral resources.

By World War I, however, much of this activity had slowed down, and emigration both to Athens and abroad was increasing. In Athens and Piraeus newcomers from islands formed closely-knit communities, each with its own clubs and cafés – islands of familiarity in an ugly urban sprawl. With the collapse of international trade between the wars, the trend was slowed for several decades, but it gathered pace once more with the European "miracle" of the postwar years. Many islanders moved to Italy and West Germany.

Improved communications

By now, the road and rail links between Greece and western Europe had been modernised. So too had links between the islands and the mainland: the first air connection with Athens had been established as far back as 1927 by the Italians, but it was only in the 1960s that aerial links with the Aegean were extended. In the same period, car ferries were introduced. These developments opened up the closed societies of the islands, and the opening continues at speed. The major islands all have airports, and the hydrofoil service has spread to all the major island groups.

Improved communications also opened up the closed island economies – which had survived World War II mostly by subsistence farming – to a new world of export and import. Trucks now can be loaded with agricultural produce on Crete, say, or Pátmos, and then be driven directly up from Piraeus to the sun-starved markets of northwestern Europe. The return flow is consumer delights, clothes, plastic, motorbikes, electronics.

A new balance is slowly being established. In the warm months, at least, the islands are thriving, as you can see in the crowded boats and new construction. The islands are less remote, able to deal with the world at large while still keeping the attraction of being off the beaten track. The bright and ambitious young islanders can now go to work abroad, or study in European and American universities, but more of them return to Greece. They can settle in Athens and visit their island homes just as every Greek retains the tie to home village or, increasingly, settles down to live and work on the island of his birth. A sure sign that the tide has changed is that a fair share of the new buildings you may see are being worked on by Albanians, who have spread even to the islands to find work, just as previous generations of islanders emigrated to work abroad. ❑

POST-JUNTA POLITICS

When the Colonels were driven from power in 1974, a referendum also brought an end to the monarchy. The new Prime Minister was Konstantínos Karamanlís, a hard-line conservative who lobbied for entry into the EEC. Greece became a member in 1981, the same year that Andréas Papandréou led his PASOK party into power as Greece's first socialist government. Financial and personal scandals brought defeat for the socialists in 1989, but without any effective alternative government, PASOK regained power in 1993 and has prevailed ever since, although Papandréou retired in 1995 and died in 1996. His successor is Kóstas Simítis.

LEFT: a poster protesting at the military regime.
RIGHT: a rally supporting Andréas Papandréou's PASOK New Socialist party.

PORTRAIT OF AN ISLAND FAMILY

*The modest tourist boom on Hálki has boosted the island's economy,
but life is still simple and hard for most islanders*

arly evening on Hálki in the Dodecanese and the sun sets behind the crusader castle, high above the village, turning the sands of Póndamos Beach a deep rose colour.

As the tourists enjoy a sundowner in the harbour, or sit out on the newly restored balconies of their holiday villas, Mihaelis Perakis leads his family's donkeys down to drink from the trough in the rocks as he has done for as long as he can remember. He fills his plastic containers from the watering hole for the stock – no taps or easy-fill troughs for them.

Hálki has no rivers or springs, and relies on the water boat to bring supplies for the island families. Daily life revolves around stocking up cans, filling cisterns, known as *stérna*, and making sure the animals – for many families the only form of transport or wealth – are properly watered. Low-key tourism has grown steadily since 1987 and now, with all those extra bodies to shower, shave and refresh, the water system has been improved, but water still has to be treated with great respect.

Ambitious plans

Mihaelis, 28, is a plumber working for Hálki council. His mother, Lefkosia, 50, one of the island's best cooks, has always been in great demand among taverna owners and is now planning to open her own restaurant in the harbour, if the rent is right. Lefkosia's daughter Katholiki (Kiki), 30, helps her mother when she can. But she has just finished her nursing training at the hospital in Rhodes and hopes to work at the local surgery on Hálki. Mihaelis is kept busy with the vagaries of the Greek plumbing system while brother Metaxas, 22, has just completed his army service and also works for the municipality when he's not chilling out in the cafés.

Their father Stavros, 64, known to everyone as Fanos, has his own fishing-boat. When he's not out laying his nets or bringing in the catch he

prepares food and helps his wife in the harbourside taverna. These days EU subsidies for his goats and sheep have helped lighten the financial load, and he still sells meat and wool on Rhodes. But life remains hard on this dry little rock.

Once fertile, the island became barren when seawater seeped into the boreholes. Now the

islanders grow nothing except olives, and goats nibble where a dairy herd once grazed. As the sponge industry declined, Halkians left in droves to seek their fortunes in Florida. Horió became deserted as people moved down to Emborió, the harbour, when the grand old sea captains' houses crumbled. The island's population dwindled from around 3,000 in its heyday to a paltry 300.

In 1987 the Greek government stepped in to bring work to Hálki and under a UNESCO scheme declared it the Island of Peace and Friendship. A hotel was built for foreign tourists in the derelict olive oil factory and local people were given jobs restoring the houses. These

PRECEDING PAGES: a festive gathering at Ólymbos, Kárpathos; *kafenéon* society. **LEFT:** an island family. **RIGHT:** weaving carpets in Santoríni.

days there is a supermarket of sorts as well as the marvellous old *pantopoléon* or grocer's shop run by Petros. The harbour front has been smartened up with new paving and ornate lights thanks to the efforts of the mayor. The islanders have been encouraged to renovate their properties and cultivate gardens. Where there was once scrubby wasteland with rabbits bred for the pot hopping among old tin cans and rubbish, now bougainvillea and geraniums bloom.

The island's income has been given a boost

ARRIVAL OF THE BRITS

Package tourism first came to Hálki when British-based Laskarina Holidays were invited to take over the mansions restored under the UNESCO scheme.

When she's cooking for a taverna she might get two hours' sleep in the afternoon. Some people grab a siesta, but it's often impossible for islanders involved in the busy tourist trade.

Home for the Perakis family is basic by western European standards, quite comfortable by theirs. The kitchen has fitted units and a modern stove – Lefkosia's pride and joy – and there is a simple living room and giant colour TV. They're on the phone now but still have an outside lavatory and shower. Although the

by its steady influx of visitors throughout the season. There are more bars, more tavernas, a handicraft shop, but nothing wild. Trucks and cars replace donkeys, jitneys and mopeds. Teenagers have got gutsy motorbikes to rev up.

Traditional routine

The Perakis family have large flocks now and in summer Lefkosia rises at 4am. She does the housework while it's cool, then feeds the sheep near the house, a traditional neo-classical villa at the back of the village. She gives milk to the lambs, feeds the chickens, ducks and rabbits, then might go up the mountainside to pick *hórta* (wild greens) before going to the taverna.

houses done up for the tourists have en suite shower rooms and loos, many of the islanders still have al fresco arrangements.

Like many islanders, the family work night and day in summer and spend little time at home. In autumn and winter it's different. With no tourists around, it's time to pick olives and make the oil, or go fishing for the local equivalent of whitebait. Fanos catches fish for the family and is part of the island's co-operative, but other fishermen sell their wares from loudspeaker vans around the Rhodes suburbs.

In winter Lefkosia and other island women still bake the family's bread outside in the wood-fuelled oven. Lambs, too are spit-roasted outdoors. It's all very medieval. They have to gather sticks for the fire. It takes an hour to get the oven hot and an hour to cook the bread, but they say it tastes marvellous.

Sometimes the storms are so bad the sea fills the tavernas, so boats are anchored out of the harbour in case they get smashed up. Winters are hard for the young people who don't escape to Rhodes, so they watch videos, play cards or work the machines in the coffee bars. Mihaelis prefers traditional Greek music and dance, particularly Hálki's own fast and furious *soustá*. He is the island's champion dancer, and often leads the circles at village festivals. The *kafenéon* tends to be a men-only domain in winter where fishermen, shepherds and soldiers spin out the hours with blue videos and card schools.

As more tourists visit the island, the local boys and soldiers serving at the barracks have more chance to play *kamáki*, chatting up, and "harpooning" the foreign girls. In summer you'll see the more liberated Hálki girls in the cafeteria. Greek girls have more freedom these days, but parents still keep a watchful eye on them and you'll see fathers whisking protesting daughters home like Cinderella.

In winter some island girls remain indoors and do embroidery or lace-making and learn to run the home. Others might go to college to train for a career. Some local girls fraternise with the soldiers, usually to the horror of the villagers who would prefer them to have husbands from families they know. The girls often see the soldiers as escape routes from a humdrum island life, especially with few Hálki suitors around. The island barracks has national service conscripts from all over Greece and village girls often think if they can land a husband from Athens or another big city, life will be rosy. Dressed in army uniform one girl stole off with a soldier on the early morning ferry. The boatman's son noticed the "soldier" was wearing women's shoes, but didn't give them away. They telephoned her parents from Rhodes who insisted the couple should be married immediately because of the family shame. She was 14. And pregnant.

Tourism may bring work to the island, but the influx of foreigners with Western ideas can lead to problems. The old ways and the new clash head on and young Greeks are the victims in the middle. It may be accepted that boys chase after tourist girls but, if their intentions become more serious, family and neighbourhood close ranks. Parents want their young to marry other Greeks. Not just because of religion: they know the rules and traditions.

"Life is still difficult for women in Greece," says Katholiki Perakis. "My generation wants modern things like bikes and personal stereos, and we want to mix with other people. But our parents and grandparents are years behind and don't understand. I think the gulf will narrow in time and the next generation will be free." ❑

LEFT: an island women bakes bread in a wood-fuelled oven. **RIGHT:** autumn is olive-picking time.

ISLAND ELECTIONS

A tale of passion and intrigue, family strife and private feuds... Island municipal elections usually provoke drama – and often involve drains

The time was clearly ripe when an island shopkeeper, an amiable old soul who liked poetry and had spoken warmly of his son's help in running the business, had the son by the throat and was spluttering with rage. The son, roughly twice his size, managed to break away and retreated into the road, howling. "The election," the old man explained, staring after him, "he just told me who he's voting for."

The candidates' posters had been going up for several days – as soon as the last of the season's charter flights had left. They showed the incumbent mayor wearing a benign and statesmanlike expression. The potential usurper was younger, had a large moustache, and affected the pose of a visionary. Gossip in the *ouzerié* revealed that "hate" would not cover what they thought of one another. The young pretender had once been hounded off the island – a suitcase literally thrown after him into a departing boat – for reasons that were never clear. He was back, they said in the *ouzerié*, for his revenge.

Unruly passions

It would be difficult to exaggerate the passions aroused by island municipal elections. They are run on national party political lines, a passionate matter in its own right in Greece, but are wonderfully exacerbated by real as well as somewhat enigmatic local issues, the power of future patronage, and private feuds. Almost anything is capable of convulsing small, compressed communities of people who, at the time of the year when elections come round, have nothing else to do, are irascible after the strain of the tourist season, and are looking forward to a state-sanctioned opportunity to get cross.

The elections cannot be totally avoided, however much some islanders might wish to distance themselves from the flying fur. Voting is compulsory unless a voter can prove to have been more than 180 km (112 miles) from home

on polling day. Failure to vote may lead to bureaucratic difficulties in, for example, acquiring a passport or having an old one renewed.

A previous election on a neighbouring island had given a foretaste of what might be in store. It had been predicted that the result of that previous election would be extremely close, and

one of the candidates had arranged a secret weapon – 30 registered voters who were living on the mainland but were willing to come back and vote for him. His opponent uncovered the plot and, in collusion with supporters at the mainland port where the returning voters had assembled, managed to have the ferry services to the island cancelled until after voting.

The Englishman telling this tale had been persuaded to fetch the stranded voters, an operation which involved sneaking away in his boat and collecting them under cover of darkness. After numerous complications of an appropriately Byzantine nature, the small boat returned to the island top-heavy with voters and their

LEFT: the Communist party has considerable support in some Aegean islands, such as Lésvos. **RIGHT:** local issues are argued heatedly and publicly.

baggage with minutes to spare. It tottered into the fishing port to the cheers of supporters and the speechless fury of the opposition. The election result was tipped by the imported voters, who supplied a majority of just one vote.

With this incident to draw on, the election committee of the present challenger was approached. "What are the issues?" they were asked through an interpreter, a girl who worked in the shop next door. They went into conference and emerged with a verdict: "Drains." So drains were discussed and, in particular, the mayor's failure to live up to his promises about new ones.

The interpreter became restless and, if her

"No!" The opposition candidate held up an admonishing finger. A lorry had come to a halt outside the campaign office. A gang of workmen climbed down and attacked the cobbles with pick-axes under the noses of the committee. "You see, no problem with drains. New ones."

Two days before voting, the candidates made their speeches – the challenger down on the quay, the incumbent afterwards outside the church. The general idea was that the audience would move on from one to hear the other. A hugely amplified fanfare announced the start. "Ladies and gentlemen," a voice boomed from behind the as yet empty balcony, "I give

translations were to be taken literally, all the committee's replies ended with statements like "…and if you believe that, sir, you are an idiot." When the interpreter stormed out, saying that she could stand no more of their lies, she confirmed the suspicion that she might support the other candidate.

Down the road, the opposition was asked what they thought the election was about. Their spokesman reeled off a list which concerned democracy, a caring society, organised crime, human rights. "But what about drains?" he was prompted by a bystander.

"What about drains?" he echoed.

"Well, the other party says…"

NATIONAL POLITICS

Since 1975, following the overthrow of the military dictatorship, Greece has been a parliamentary democracy headed by a president, elected for a five-year term. The single-chamber parliament has 300 deputies, elected for four years.

Andréas Papandréou's Panhellenic Socialist Movement (PASOK) ruled with a large majority from 1981 until 1989, when it was brought down by a series of scandals. Its major opponents, the right-wing New Democracy party under Konstantínos Karamanlís (later president), was in power for only three years. PASOK has held a comfortable majority since 1993.

you...Dimitris Prevezanos!" Four small boys let off compressed-air hooters to herald the grand entrance.

Dimitris Prevezanos, however, failed to materialise. Another fanfare, another introduction, further hooting – and still no Dimitris. Instead, a water pipe chose that moment to detach itself from a tank above the balcony. Prevezanos supporters, wearing Sunday suits, leapt out of the way.

An enquiry regarding his non-appearance received a simple explanation: "His speech was about drains. Now he must talk about something else. Maybe he can't think of something else."

The mayor did not mention drains, presumably because by then most of the main street and the quay had been dug up, as no one on the island could have failed to notice. He concentrated on broader issues like the new airport building and emphasised his record.

An army contingent arrived on the island for polling day. A man was running a book on the results, with a plastic bag stuffed with bank notes to cover all bets. When asked how much, he winked: four million drachmas. It says something about the island that he felt able to wander off from time to time and leave the bag unattended on a table.

It was a partisan opinion although when, third time lucky, the candidate did appear, he did have something to say about drains. He may have had other topics but the time taken to repair the pipe had to be subtracted from the time available before the incumbent went into action. When he finished speaking, the audience duly filed up the hill to listen to Kostas Papadoulis, the incumbent. The small boys passed their hooters to another set of small boys who would apply them to the task of getting Papadoulis re-elected.

LEFT: the whole village discusses the burning issues of the election. **RIGHT:** the posters urge: "Vote PASOK".

The bets were settled at 8pm when red flares announced that the result was known: Papadoulis was back in office for four years. He was carried shoulder-high around the village while a disappointed Dimitris Prevezanos was said to be packing for a further spell of exile, this time self-imposed, on the mainland.

The following morning, father and son resumed normal relations and – to almost nobody's surprise – the work on the drains ran into "technical difficulties" and ceased. They were not completed for the next big event on the calendar, Easter, and only just in time for the second, the charter flights which signalled the beginning of the tourist season. ❏

DEBUNKING THE BOUZOÚKI

Like the islands themselves, Greek music has been influenced by many other cultures, which gives it a richness and complexity that's worth seeking out

The visitor is ambling along some majestic harbour at sunset, with the sea breeze between the masts of the yachts and caiques, and looking forward to a meal of fried octopus, washed down perhaps with a little *oúzo*. What better way to complete the image than with background music on the *bouzoúki*? After all, isn't *bouzoúki* music the quintessence of all things Greek?

Well, no. Those plinkety-plink soundtracks for Manos Hatzidakis' *Never on Sunday* and Mikis Theodhorakis' *Zorba the Greek*, sold *ad nauseam* in cover versions from resort souvenir stalls, have effectively closed foreign minds to the possibility of anything else of value in Greek music.

What the big record companies push on inexperienced foreigners, in catalogue sections cynically labelled "*Touristiká*", is merely the shabby, melted tip of the iceberg, a snapshot of a brief period in the early 1960s which coincided with Greece's arrival as a mass-tourism destination. While the original compositions, arrangements and recordings had some merit, the offcut remixes – watered down for western tastes and sporting such titles as *Disco Bouzouki My Love* (*sic*) – are another matter.

Diverse influences

Greece amply deserves the cliché image of a musical crossroads and collecting-basket, with a range of cosmopolitan influences inside a deceptively small country.

The great *bouzoúki* myth has overshadowed the genuine Aegean music hidden away behind the tacky *skyládhika* (roadhouse-type dives) with their over-miked amplification. The real thing has an altogether cleaner sound – gentler and nobler than the commercialised pap. Acoustic *nisiotiká* or island music, especially in the Cyclades (of all Greek territories the least

affected by foreign occupation), is very much *sui generis*, with only a vague resemblance to some Italian folk material.

The rhythms, often in unconventional time-signatures, are lilting and hypnotic; the melodies, traditionally executed on violin, clarinet and some sort of fretted lute, are exquisite.

The lyrics, tokens of a more innocent time, grapple with eternal island concerns – the sea that took a loved one, the island mother who wonders if her sons will ever return from foreign exile, the precious days when the endless fishing can be laid aside and clean clothes can be donned for the festival of the Panaghía – but occasionally verge on the poetically surreal, as in the popular *Mes Sto Egeou ta Nisia*.

These days, the various artists of the Náxos-born Konitopoulos clan are the best you'll hear, but particularly prized are 1950s and 1960s recordings of the mother-daughter team from the Dodecanese, Anna and Emilia Hatzidaki. In the Ionian islands, the Italian heritage is evi-

PRECEDING PAGES: a cornucopia of cards; musicians on Kárpathos playing *lýra* and lute. **LEFT:** a music shop selling both traditional instruments and amplifiers. **RIGHT:** the ubiquitous *bouzoúki*.

dent in Neapolitan-style *kantádhes*, sung by choirs, and often accompanied by mandolin, violin and guitar tuned to western harmonics and seven-tone scales.

Compositions and instrumentation of Asia Minor and the northern mainland (the *sandoúri* or hammer dulcimer, or brass bands on Lésvos) enrich the repertoire of the northeast Aegean islands and the Dodecanese. Meanwhile traces of North African and Arabic music can be discerned in the long vocal introductions to Cretan songs. Across the mainland,

> **SCALE MODEL**
>
> The note-order in a Greek mode will not start with do–re–mi (C–D–E) as in western scales, but do–do sharp–mi (C–C#–E).

the gypsies' contribution to instrumental music – especially the clarinet – has been pervasive if unacknowledged, and especially in the mountainous spine of the north Píndhos, much is shared musically with southern Albania (historically northern Epirus).

Earliest influences

Ancient Greek music was monophonic – without harmonies – and its scales were simple, probably much like a contemporary ecclesiastical chant. Traditional Greek music is still pentatonic (five notes make up the scale) and modal, a system adopted later by all peoples of the Middle East, via Byzantine chant – though

it should be said (in response to Greek ultra-nationalists, who claim credit for originating absolutely everything) that the folk music of many other people the world over is also pentatonic.

Greece's lyrics were never divorced from music, as they were in the West, where tune were composed for existing stanzas or opera librettos commissioned separately. Since antiquity, when poetry was sung, both have been inseparable. Instrumental music remains a relative rarity, while the solo voice is still used for dirges, "table" songs and epics.

Rhythms – and blues?

Western metre generally was limited to two, three or four beats to the bar, a box out of which not even Beethoven dared venture. The Greeks, on the other hand, seem to have matched their musical rhythms to the cadences of their poetry, from the age of the Homeric hexameter onwards. Western jazz musicians have only recently begun to appreciate and use the catchy 5/8, 7/8, 9/8 and even 11/8 time signatures of modern Greek folk music.

The composer Mimis Plessas, a former jazzman who now accounts for a fair portion of Greek movie soundtrack music, relates an interesting account of a jam session with the American jazz trumpeter Dizzy Gillespie in 1953. Being Greek, Plessas had no trouble fingering a nimble 7/8 folk rhythm on the piano – and promptly lost Dizzy. "I can't do it – something's missing," said the great jazzman. Less convincingly, Plessas has said: "Imagine the field cry of the black man transported to Greece – that's what Greek music is."

Plessas was not the first individual to have simplistically found similarities between the American blues and Greek song – especially *rembétika*, the genre foreigners are most likely to be exposed to, and gravitate towards. In its original form, this was the clandestine music of a particular segment of the Anatolian refugee population who flooded into Athens, Piraeus and Thessaloníki after the disastrous 1919–22 Greco-Turkish war, and the subsequent compulsory exchange of religious minorities between the two nations.

It is superficially similar to the blues in its origins and preoccupations – poverty and social exclusion, disease, the allure of drugs and idleness, faithless women, thwarted love – and its practitioners and lyrics were similarly persecuted and censored throughout the 1920s and 1930s.

Westernising Greeks despised, and still despise, its "Oriental" roots, but one can safely say that *rembétika* existed in some form around the east Aegean coast and the Black Sea for decades before that. On one occasion, an expatriate Soviet novelist, on exposure to the music, delightedly exclaimed that a nearly identical style, played on *balalaïka*, had flourished in the harbour dives of Odessa before the 1917 Revolution.

By the 1950s, however, *rembétika* became "domesticated" and incorporated into the canon of mainstream Greek music; in 1953 Manolis Hiotis nailed the coffin of the pure rembetic style by adding a fourth string to the *bouzoúki*, allowing it to be tuned tonally rather than modally – and giving rise to *laïkó* and *elafrá*, the urban "popular" music you hear on the radio today.

This can be seen as one aspect of the progressive post-war westernisation of Greece, now under American tutelage, with the Greek musical scene arrayed in two opposing camps: adherents of folk-derived styles opposed to those who spurn ethnic roots in favour of imported jazz/cabaret, symphonic and rock models.

The state of the art

Communist Theodhorákis himself, after his *Zorba* outing of 1965, shunned Byzantine/rembetic/folk bases completely in favour of quasi-classical, western-symphonic works and film music. In general, the political Left has historically condemned "decadent", apolitical, escapist styles such as *rembétika* and *laïkó*, attempting at one point to "raise mass consciousness" with recycled *andártika*, wartime resistance songs.

More thoughtful musicians have attempted to bridge the high-low culture gap with hybrid styles: the strongly rooted *éntekhno* of Yannis Markopoulos, where folk instruments and themes are used within large-scale compositions of great emotive power; a whole succes-

sion of guitarist-composers, led by Dionysis Savvopoulos, who challenged the hammerlock of the vulgarised *bouzoúki* with modern lyrics as well, giving rise to Greek folk-rock; and numerous revivalists, such as Haïnidhes and Loudhovikos ton Anoghion, who countered the rock-drum-kit-and-electrification debasing of live folk performances with updated and rearranged standards which were not ashamed to acknowledge instrumental debts to surrounding cultures.

Genuine *rembétika* enjoyed a brief revival after the fall of the junta, which had tried to ban it like much else, but the fad – most pro-

nounced among urban intellectuals – has now waned, and the flood of well-produced re-issue recordings is now principally aimed at a foreign audience, many first primed to the music by Stavros Xarhakos' soundtrack to the 1983 film, *Rembétiko*.

But "pure" *laïkó* and *nisiotiká*, despite being looked down on by educated Greeks (especially overseas students), refuses to die. It's a tale often repeated in Greece, where the westernised, cultural elite keep busy attempting unsuccessfully to banish "low-class" habits. Unruly multiculturalism continues to be the the the nemesis of nationalists and reformers in search of an illusory "purity". ❑

LEFT: music ensemble, the Ionian islands.
ABOVE: a concert in Zákynthos, where choirs sing Neapolitan-style *kantádhes*.

PERILS OF THE CATERING TRADE

Many people from abroad have dreamed of opening a restaurant or bar in
Greece – but the dream is often shattered by labyrinthine legislation

A few years ago the British popular press revelled in the case of a London grandmother who invested her £30,000 life savings in a restaurant on Rhodes and looked forward to a happy and prosperous retirement. Instead, she found herself locked up in a police cell with the prospect of spending the next five months there unless she bought off the sentence for the equivalent of £1,000.

The first lesson for any foreigner wishing to follow Mrs Molly Huddleston's example by starting a business on a Greek island is that the Greek legal process can all too easily begin rather than end with a spell in prison. Detailed prosecution, defence, litigation and so forth take place later, often much later. A knowledge of the law and the resolve to remain meticulously on the right side of it are therefore desirable starting points – although the process can often feel like shadow-boxing with an opponent of stupefying complexity.

False assumptions

So where had Mrs Huddleston gone wrong? It was her belief that visitors to the island might occasionally enjoy "traditional British food" after so much Greek, and that is what she provided. Cucumbers and tomatoes are optional ingredients in a British salad, but she had forgotten (or perhaps never known) that in Greece the contents of a salad are defined by law. Mrs Huddleston's salads were either light on the cucumbers and tomatoes, or omitted them altogether – a serious matter.

Furthermore, while Mrs Huddleston was aware of the fixed price for a baked potato, she rashly assumed that she could charge a little more if she filled them with chilli sauce, a dish popular with her more discerning customers. That, too, went into the policeman's notebook.

Mrs Huddleston's misfortune was not a flash in the pan – the work, of a bad-tempered policeman with a grudge or a hangover. At the same

LEFT: taverna tables await the tourists. **RIGHT:** the classic Greek salad is strictly regulated by law.

time, at the other end of the Aegean Fat Ronnie, a young American chef, had given up his job at a prestigious New York hotel to pursue the ambition of opening his own restaurant. He had never seen a Greek island, but the enthusiastic description by a Greek friend who knew the islands – and of a restaurant that happened to be

for sale on one of them – made up his mind.

The friend was a lawyer, so Ronnie, by nature a cautious fellow, avoided some of the pitfalls into which naïve foreign investors might plunge. The sale of bars and discos, in particular, is seldom cut and dried. The owner will probably open negotiations asking for a large lump sum for "goodwill", a percentage of turnover in perpetuity, and "rent". Buyers anxious to secure a place in paradise should not accept that all property transactions are concluded along such lines and should seek legal advice.

But this may not be cut and dried either. On the smaller islands, there are probably no more than a couple of local lawyers and they will each act for one half of the population against the other. Being lawyers, they will respectively be at or near the top of ferociously polarised municipal politics and the make-or-break powers of patronage flowing from them. The foreign buyer ought to find out who the vendor's lawyer is (anyone would be able to tell them!) and proceed forthwith to the other one.

Lobster tale

Fat Ronnie had astutely, if unknowingly, overcome potential difficulties in that direction, but he was nevertheless faring no better (and possibly rather worse) than Mrs Huddleston in

Rhodes. Within a fortnight of opening, he had logged no fewer than 107 separate offences which, in addition to violation of the notoriously demanding cucumber legislation, included the extraordinary business of a consignment of lobsters which, although still alive and kicking, were deemed by the inspectors to be "not fresh".

A bemused Ronnie tried to find out what it all meant. The 107 offences? Prison, undoubtedly, until and unless he bought off the sentence or, as Mrs Huddleston was proposing, appealed quickly to the European Court of Human Rights. The "not fresh" lobsters? If he couldn't produce a suitable receipt showing the precise date when he bought them, it was assumed that they were not within the prescribed definition of "fresh" and therefore his menu lied when it said they were.

The condemned lobsters were actually still alive when Ronnie had to destroy them under official supervision. At that point, Ronnie was seriously reconsidering the wisdom of starting his own business in Greece.

Another couple, a Greek man and English woman, tried twice to set up restaurants on islands. Their first attempt involved fixing up rented premises at considerable expense which, as soon as the restaurant opened, were found to have been in violation of the building code for restaurants. The owner knew this, but was happy to have his premises refurbished. As soon as the couple left, he rented them to a fellow-islander for an *ouzerié*.

They tried again on another island, this time with a pizzeria. They made it through the bureaucratic hassle, acquired all the required papers – but when they opened, they discovered that the islanders wouldn't sell them provisions. They stayed the season, buying their supplies in Piraeus, but then returned to Athens where they now operate, quite successfully, a very good restaurant.

The wisdom of business

One quickly concludes from these horror stories that the Greeks don't want foreigners working their turf – but reconsider what "foreigner" means and where the term is used. These stories are all based on the fact that the islands are small, close-knit communities which consider anyone not born on their island (including Greeks) as foreigners. They earn most of their annual income in the few summer months and are threatened by the idea that someone, anyone, from outside is going to take away their livelihood.

So potential competitors, wherever they come from, are likely to feel the full weight of the Greek mountain of legislation. Even if all the legalities are surmounted, potential competitors are likely to feel the weight of local non-cooperation, if nothing else. Before catatonic paranoia sets in they ought to remind themselves that the laws were drawn up by Greeks for Greeks. The fact that foreigners become entangled is nothing more than incidental.

Fat Ronnie had originally planned to serve French and Italian food, but the inspectors rejected his draft menu because, without special dispensation, restaurants must have a preponderance of Greek dishes on the menu in the interest of cultural integrity. The law was brought in, commendably, to inhibit the fast-food, sausages and chips blight that has ruined so many places pandering to the tastes of mass tourism.

The government's good intentions in both respects, making sure that visitors are not over-charged and that the tourist areas are not reduced to anonymous cultural slag heaps, unfortunately have a tendency to backfire.

Learning the rules

If you are not Greek and want to set up a restaurant on a Greek island you need a good island lawyer. In fact, no foreigner should attempt to do business anywhere in Greece without high calibre legal support. With good legal advice it is possible for you as a foreigner to set up shop on the more level playing field now at least theoretically established by the European Union.

One of the many things the lawyer will do is explain that the regulations which can be misused locally against potential competition were, in fact, drawn up to protect the customer. Greek salads, for example, were defined by law because some restaurants served tourists supposed Greek salads either short on or missing tomatoes, cucumbers, feta or olives, all basic ingredients for a Greek salad.

In 1997 there was much publicity when the Minister of Development, Vaso Papandreou, was eating in an island restaurant and noticed

that the waiting staff issuing strange orders to the kitchen. The waiters were saying the equivalent of "meatballs f" and meatballs g", which turned out to mean a smaller serving for the foreigners and a larger serving for the Greeks. Legal protection for the foreign tourist is a very good idea.

Even before finding a lawyer, however, you should know very well where you are going. If you want to conduct any kind of business on a Greek island it would be a sensible idea for you first to spend a few years living there getting to know your neighbours. Even better, marry one of the islanders. ❑

NON-COMPETITORS WELCOME

The antipathy felt towards would-be restaurateurs from abroad does not apply where there is no fear of competition. Foreigners who wish to pursue a career on an island writing books or poetry or painting – anything, in fact, that the islanders themselves would not normally be doing – will be made to feel tremendously welcome. Moreover, the island economies depend on the annual influx of foreign waitresses and barmaids. Greek men are fiercely protective of their own interests when it comes to filling well-paid summer jobs, but they will concede that it is sometimes necessary to employ women, and they would rather have foreign women in those menial positions than their own.

LEFT: a cafeteria on Hydra. **RIGHT:** tile style.

EATING YOUR WAY ROUND THE ISLANDS

Traditional Greek food is better than its reputation, especially if you ignore what's offered for tourists and seek out traditional local dishes

Anyone who has experienced tourist menus of chicken and chips, microwaved moussaka and "ros-beef" can be excused for believing that Greece isn't the place for culinary delights. So for a taste of real Greek cooking follow the locals down to the back-street tavernas. The food at traditional family-run places with plastic tablecloths more than compensates for lack of fancy décor. If communication is a problem, go in, take a look at what's cooking and point at what you want. Ordering this way is accepted practice.

You'll soon find there's more to Greek cuisine than kebabs and *taramosaláta*. Vegetables like fresh green beans, okra or butter beans, cooked in olive oil and tomato; hearty fish soups; cheese and spinach pies with a feather-light filo pastry; rich casseroles of rabbit, octopus even snails; courgette flowers stuffed with rice and fried in batter – the islands offer dishes for all tastes. There are plenty of options for vegetarians because of the many fast days in the Orthodox calendar. But fish is very expensive (and sold by weight, not per portion).

Regional variations reflect island history and many dishes have strong Italian and Turkish influences from past occupations. You'll find pastas and pilafs, plus vegetable recipes like *briam* and *imam baïldi*, their Turkish names absorbed into Greek menus.

From the cabbage *dolmádhes* of Kálymnos, the *sofríto* casseroles of Corfu to the *froutála* omelettes of Ándhros, every island has its speciality. Some may seem strange – sea urchins or boiled sheep's heads are not for the faint-hearted – but most island food is delicious. If all else fails, *horiátiki,* the classic Greek village salad (*above*), with feta, olives, chunky cucumber and tomato, takes some beating.

▷ **APPETISERS**
A selection of *mezédhes* or starters (clockwise from top left): Cretan potatoes baked with herbs; *taramosaláta*; *dolmádhes* stuffed with mince and savoury rice; pickled octopus.

◁ **HARD CHEESE**
Besides salty feta, Greece has a wide range of cheeses, both soft and hard, creamy and sharp, made from goats' and sheep's milk. Crete in particular supplies a wide variety.

AND SOMETHING TO DRINK?

△ **TEMPTING TENTACLES**
Charcoal-grilled octopus is a common sight and a perfect appetiser with an ouzo.

◁ **EATING AL FRESCO**
The informal taverna is the commonest form of eaterie, often with tables outside and music at night. For a wider menu, with more oven-baked dishes, look for an *estiatório*, or a *psistaría*, which specialises in spit-roasts and grills.

PICK YOUR PRODUCE
me islands have to
port fresh fruit and veg
cause they can't grow
eir own, while others have
h market gardens.

MORE *MEZEDHES*
ockwise from top centre:
opittákia, triangular
ese pies; *loukánika*,
me-made sausages with
ves; bean and sausage
sserole; *bourekákia*, filo
ls stuffed with spinach.

You can drink anything in Greece from cocktails to local firewater. If you prefer wine, retsina (white wine flavoured with pine resin, *above*) is an acquired taste, ranging from lightly to heavily scented. It's usually better from the barrel, but brands like Kourtaki and Rhodian CAIR are fine.

Popular inexpensive wines include Cambas, Boutari and Lac des Roches, available in reds, whites and rosés, but if you want something better try Emery's crisp white Villare, Tsantalí Agiorítiko in white and red, Boutari Grand Reserve or the Carras label. Try local wines from the barrel or Greek boutique labels such as Hatzimihaëlis or Skouras. Amstel and Heineken beers are widely available, bottled and draught.

After dinner try Greek brandy, Metaxa, which comes in three starred grades. The *kafenéon* (coffee bar) or *zaharoplastéo* (pastry shop) will serve up Greek coffee – *skéto* (without sugar), *glykó* (sweet) or *métrio* (medium). If you want instant, ask for "Nescafe" which has become the generic term.

◁ **TURKISH DELIGHT**
Special *souvlákia* sold in Drapetsona, Piraeus, are made to recipes brought by refugees from Asia Minor in the 1920s. Skewered meat and tomatoes are served on a bed of pitta bread.

▷ **STRONG STUFF**
Ouzo, the national drink, is made from aniseed and turns milky when water is added. It's usually drunk with olives or other starters (*mezédhes*).

CRUISING ROUND THE ISLANDS

Greeks have sailed between the islands for thousands of years. Today it is possible to follow in their wake, on anything from day-trips to all-inclusive luxury cruises

H aving more than 50 inhabited islands means having ships to serve them, and Greece has a long shipping tradition. Anyone who has ridden over the Aegean, with the prows of the white ships rivalling the dazzling sun itself, knows the affinity Greeks have for their ships. The giants of the past, such as Aristotle Onassis and Stavros Niarchos, are no

longer with us, and their successors keep a much lower profile.

They are here, though, hundreds of Greek shipping companies operating out of one square kilometre of office blocks clustered together in the port city of Piraeus. They are centred on the seafront of Aktí Miaoúli, where international bankers in pinstriped suits rub shoulders with burly crewmen and dusky banana vendors.

The owners remain emotionally, even mystically, committed to their business. Few satisfactions can equal that of gazing out of one's air-conditioned headquarters seven floors above Aktí Miaoúli and watching one's ship come in, slowly coming to moor along the quay. The same feeling must have prompted the great 18th-century captains of Hydra and Spétses to build their *arhontiká* facing out to sea.

The transporting of goods to and from the Greek islands is fundamental to the economies of all the Greek islands. For visitors to the country, however, the most interesting aspect is the pleasure of being cargo, the joys of cruising.

Which cruise to choose?

The most frequent voyages in Greece are one-day cruises, most of them operating out of Piraeus or the Flísvos harbour in Fáliron just outside Athens and taking you to the islands of Aegina, Hydra and Póros, with a guide and a packed lunch.

There are also three, four, seven and 14-day cruises, most of them operating out of Piraeus but some one to three-day cruises visit Santoríni and some of the eastern Cyclades islands from Iráklion. Small companies such as Pleasure Cruises Shipping operate one-day cruises to Póros, Hydra and Aegina, while slightly larger companies such as Golden Sun Cruises operate one, three, four and seven-day cruises.

The longer cruises are dominated by Royal Olympic Cruises, whose liners are the jewels in the Greek passenger shipping fleet. They are floating hotels, with swimming pools, boutiques, and a choice of restaurants and entertainment. Royal Olympic's three-day cruises start from Piraeus, taking in Mýkonos, Rhodes,

---

ONE-DAY WONDERS

A typical one-day cruise from Piraeus or Fáliron is an excellent introduction to Greek islands, combined with a relaxing day on board shiip. You will visit the 5th-century BC Temple of Aféa in Aegina, one of the finest in all Greece; in Póros you will pass through the narrow straits with the town's white houses towering above the ship on one side and the extensive expanse of lemon-tree forest on the other; in Hydra you will visit that beautiful little town ringed around the harbour. There are also one-day cruises from Iráklion, Crete, to Santoríni. Sailing into that remarkable crater is one of the most extraordinary experiences in the world.

Kusadasi (Ephesus) in Turkey, Pátmos, and back to Piraeus. The four-day cruises go Piraeus, Mýkonos, Kusadasi, Turkey, Pátmos, Rhodes, Iráklion, Santoríni, Piraeus. All these are on either Royal Olympic's *Triton* or the new *World Renaissance*.

Six seven-day cruises are available on the *Stella Solaris*, the *Stella Oceanis*, the *Odysseus*, the *Orpheus* or the new *Olympic Countess*. The focus varies between the Aegean islands, the Ionian Sea, Egypt, Israel, Turkey, and they also visit Yalta and Odessa in the Black Sea.

Three 14-day cruises are available on the *Stella Solaris* covering more of the eastern Mediterranean and the Black Sea. The 21-day cruise on the *Stella Solaris* is in fact three of the seven-day trips end to end, covering all the territory more thoroughly.

This is far and away the best way to see the most interesting ports in the eastern Mediterranean and Black Sea in full comfort with good food to satiation.

> **MARITIME HQ**
>
> In the 19th century the centre of Greece's shipping industry was the island of Sýros. Now it is Piraeus, which is home to more than 600 shipping firms.

Politics at sea

As with all things Greek, there is a political dimension, hinging on the word *cabotage*. Cabotage is an international legal term meaning, as far as the Greek shipping companies are concerned, that they have the monopoly of carrying goods and passengers between Greek ports. Many foreign ships cruise Greek waters with passengers they bring from outside, and return to some port outside Greece, but cabotage has protected the Greek shipping companies from foreign competition in Greek waters for years.

A couple of years ago the American ship *Marco Polo* was greeted with vociferous demonstrations by ship workers coming down from Athens (but most certainly not by the local merchants) when it docked in Náfplion.

This nautical monopoly disintegrated when the European Union decreed that cabotage, for EU ships at least, would end on the last day of 1998. Henceforth the market will be wide open, which should mean that existing Greek ships will be improved and brand-new ships will be

brought into service to stave off competition.

Royal Olympic Cruises – created by the merger of Epirotiki and Sun Lines – is a major result of this trend. The company has already introduced two new ships designed to carry about 1,000 passengers, just the size needed for cruising the Greek islands.

Greek governments are fond of imposing regulations, often impenetrable, usually expensive, upon every aspect of life they can dream of, and this certainly includes Greek shipping. Many Greek

ship-owners have responded to this by registering their ships in another country. This was fine for international routes but, with cabotage in force, foreign-registered ships could not cruise between the Greek islands. Now, with the end of cabotage, the Greek ship-owners can threaten their government with flags of convenience if maritime legislation is not adjusted in their favour.

Much of the problem has to do with labour, a major issue of concern as Greece struggles to join the single European currency. It will be interesting to see how supportive of Greek cruise companies the political powers will decide to be. ❑

PRECEDING PAGES: Kastellórizo harbour at dawn; the Mýkonos ferry sails into Sýros. **LEFT:** *Stella Solaris* off Santoríni. **RIGHT:** cruising into Pátmos.

THE SAILING SCENE

Sailing is a rewarding way of exploring this country of islands, whether
in your own yacht, in a chartered boat or as part of a flotilla

While the package holidaymaker and the ubiquitous backpacker are forced to rely on the ferries and their often impenetrable timetables in order to travel among the islands, the yachtsman can enjoy a remarkable degree of independence – except, of course, from the winds. Sailing around Greece is not over-complicated by bureau-

cracy, but some paperwork, unfortunately, is unavoidable.

To sail into Greek waters in your own yacht, you need customs clearance in one of 28 designated entry ports (the list can be obtained from tourist boards or your country's national sailing authority) to obtain a Transit Log for yachts over 12 metres (39 ft), or a Temporary Duty-Free Admission booklet for smaller yachts. Usually, both these documents are valid for six months and enable a crew to sail freely throughout the country.

A visiting yacht should be officially registered in its country of origin and its skipper should make sure that each member of the crew has a valid passport. It's worth writing out a crew list with passport numbers so that any official check can be made easier.

Chartering, now a fundamental part of the sailing scene in Greece, began throughout the islands in the mid-1970s, the idea of an enterprising group of British boat-owners who decided that they had had enough of miserable English summers and wanted holidays in the sun. This type of sailing is increasingly prevalent and has done much to encourage the development of marinas and improved facilities (for example, the extensive provision of fresh drinking water). At the same time, the increase in numbers in recent years has seen a spread of poorer quality boats.

But most reputable charter companies supply yachts that are renewed every five years or so. They are designed for holidays in the sun and equipped to a luxurious standard with deep freezes, deck showers, snorkeling equipment and even a pair of gardening gloves to handle the anchor chain.

Making the right choice

It's important to match experience with the correct type of charter. Inexperienced sailors should select a flotilla holiday where a group of yachts cruise as a fleet, under the instructive eye of a lead boat crew. If you are an experienced sailor, you may want to arrange a "bare boat" charter, in which you act as your own skipper. If you can afford a crewed charter, you can simply relax on deck and leave all the sailing, boat handling, cooking and bureaucracy to paid hands.

Whether you're taking your own yacht to Greece or chartering, the choice of sailing areas is large and your choice should take account of varying local weather conditions.

The recognised sailing season is from April to October when the skies are clear, and temperatures rise into the 80s and 90s Fahrenheit (25° to 35°C) in July and August. Winds throughout the Aegean Sea tend to be from the north. The most talked-about weather phenomenon is the *meltémi*, which can affect the entire

Aegean and Ionian, and can reach Beaufort Force 7 to 8 in mid-summer. It is an unpredictable wind. Usually it rises in the early afternoon and calms with sunset, but it can arrive without warning and blow for as little as one hour or for as long as one week. Yachtsmen must take care not to be caught on a lee shore, and should be aware that the *meltémi* can cause an extremely uncomfortable steep, short sea.

In the northern Aegean the *meltémi* blows from the northeast and, further south towards the Cyclades, predominantly from the north. Recently, the strong midsummer northerlies that blow down the Turkish coast have per-

up-to-date information whenever you need it, as you also can from VHF channels 16 and 25. Virtually every Greek evening newscast is followed by a weather report which someone can translate for you, and the port authorities will be well informed.

The Saronic Gulf and the Ionian Sea offer the gentlest sailing conditions, mainly because the islands are relatively close to each other and because the *meltémi* in the Ionian is usually far weaker than it can be in the open Aegean. The Ionian is blessed with a northwest wind called the *maéstros*, nowhere near as strong as the *meltémi*. The *maéstros* tends to blow only

suaded some charter companies to classify the Dodecanese as the most difficult waters in which to sail.

Sailing in the Dodecanese has the additional problem of the nearby Turkish border. The Turks insist that anyone sailing in their waters must clear customs at one of their ports of entry. The border is policed at sea and it is therefore unwise to enter Turkish waters unless you intend to enter Turkey officially.

Weather reporting in Greece is generally good. If you have a weather fax you can get

FLY THE FLAG

All charter vessels must sail under the Greek flag, even if the yacht is hired from, say, a British-based company. It is wiser to charter from one of the larger companies, which will prepare the charter agreement and is better organised at helping you through the process of leaving the marina. Keep the boat's papers, including the crew list, accessible: you may have to present them to the port authorities when you dock in a new harbour. If you are going to "bareboat" charter, at least two of the crew must have sailing qualifications, and you will need to take them with you to satisfy the authorities that you can be trusted in Greek waters.

LEFT: running repairs aloft. **ABOVE:** a flotilla of yachts moored at Póthia in Kálymnos.

in the afternoon when the heat of the Greek mainland accelerates the wind off the sea. Occasionally a hot, southerly *sirócco* wind, sometimes carrying red dust from North Africa, will blow hard but it doesn't last long.

Despite this extravagant variety of local winds, Greek seas are often quite windless and yachtsmen should sometimes be prepared to motor. Whatever the conditions, you should always protect yourself against the sun and the increased glare off the water – which can produce temporary blindness.

But the greatest appeal of the Greek islands is the solitude offered by their remoteness. The

green islands of the Ionian are, perhaps, the yachtsman's first choice for a number of reasons. The shelter among the many islands offers safe cruising, but if you want more lively conditions, a trip in the open waters to the west of Lefkádha (Léfkas) and Kefalloniá will provide marvellous sailing. Easy anchorages and safe village moorings are within a few hours' sail of each other throughout the Ionian islands. The time to sail the Ionian is definitely during spring and autumn months: August sees Italian yachtsmen pouring over from Italy, clogging up the numerous but small harbours.

The Saronic Gulf is a favourite haunt of cruising yachts because it is so close to Piraeus. The little island of Angístri, off Aegina, has some lovely beaches; Póros, Hydra and Spétses have attractive town harbours as well as quieter coves; and the east coast of the Peloponnese is unjustly underrated. In mid-season it will be difficult to find a berth at the town quays where, almost without exception, mooring is stern or bow to the quay and as close as possible to the quayside tavernas.

Moving east from the Saronic Gulf, the influence of the *meltémi* becomes stronger and it is not until you travel north of the Sporades, still affected by the *meltémi*, that you find less travelled cruising grounds among the great inlets and peninsulas to the east of the deep bay which has Thessaloníki at its head. There are fewer villages and towns along this coast and you should be prepared to anchor, sometimes in depths of 30 metres (100 ft) or more.

(For further information and useful addesses, see the *Travel Tips* listings section at the end of this book.) ❑

MARINAS AROUND THE ISLANDS

The biggest concentration of marinas in Greece is on the coast of Attica near Athens and Piraeus. But because of the commercial shipping and general traffic in and out of the capital, it is not an area of peace and beauty. Zéa Marina, in Piraeus, is large and crowded; Mikrolímano, the home of the Greek deep-water racing fleet, is cleaner and prettier; and Kalamáki, 8 km (5 miles) away from central Athens, is the largest.

Other major marinas among or near Greek islands are at Thessaloníki, where there is an excellent development at Kalamariás; at Gouvía, about an hour's sail north from Corfu town; and at Corfu itself. Corfu's own marina is

more convenient than Gouvía, ideal for a city tour and for bunkering water and fuel. The recently enlarged marina at Lefkádha is right in town, just off the canal. And there's a large marina at Mandhráki in Rhodes, which is more suited to larger yachts.

All these marinas make excellent staging posts for yachts which need to re-stock with food and water. There are, of course, charter bases in all these locations, which normally means there are repair and chandlery facilities on hand.

There's more about marinas in the Greek National Tourist Office's free booklet *Sailing the Greek Seas*.

Island Hopping

The pleasures of travelling from one island to another using Greece's interlinking ferry routes are numerous. There is the never-ceasing view – a bas-relief pattern in blue of low, mysterious mountains. A chance to mingle with the Greeks themselves who pile on board with food, children and, as often as not, a *bouzoúki* or two. Plus, a unique opportunity to visit other islands not on the itinerary – 15 minutes closely observing a port from the top deck can reveal much about a place and its people. A bustle of activity takes place within view – reunions, farewells and the redistribution of a virtual warehouse of goods. Is that a piano being loaded on board? Is that crate of chickens really being exchanged for blankets? Without thorough checking, however, it is easy to fall prey to the worst aspects of island hopping in the form of missed connections, being stranded, or – a particularly Greek pastime – sailing straight past a chosen island and then having to make a two-day journey to reach it again.

To travel the ferries wisely, it helps to remember three basic facts. First, ferry journeys can be long. Second, they can be frustrating. If your ship reaches the small remote island you are trying to reach in the middle of the night, it is your responsibility to wake up and get off. For this reason, seasoned island-hoppers travel with an alarm clock. However, a hasty departure in darkness has deposited more than one independent traveller on the wrong island altogether.

Third, weather is a factor. The wind called the *meltémi* is a fact of Greek life, although recent reports indicate that *el Niño* has weakened it somewhat. Don't bank on it. When the winds are too strong the ships are delayed or kept in port. If you are depending upon the ferries to take you back to Athens for your international flight, leave at least one full day's leeway. Athens has its pleasures; missing your flight home does not.

The best known ferry routes are the main Cyclades circuit (Santoríni, Íos, Náxos, Páros and Mýkonos) and the Argo Saronic Gulf route (Aegina, Hydra, Póros). Another route is to the major Dodecanese islands; travelling between Rhodes, Kós, Kálymnos, Léros and Pátmos is easy. Less well known, and therefore more satisfying, are the western Cyclades islands (Kýthnos, Sérifos, Sífnos and

Mílos) and three of the four Sporades islands (Skiáthos, Skópelos, Alónissos). These routes exist as much to serve domestic needs as they are to serve tourists and they operate all year round, albeit at a reduced level. Both Rhodes and Kós in the Dodecanese are hubs for several satellite islands. And there are also the Ionian islands, where it is easy to travel between Lefkádha, Itháki and Kefalloniá.

Bookshops in Athens sell a monthly guide called *Hellenic Travelling*, an expensive but highly informative source of information about most ferry sailings. A map is useful when studying it, for some of the listings give the name of the port where the

ferry docks, rather than the name of the island.

In recent years the hydrofoils have been playing an increasing role in inter-island travel. They now go to all the islands mentioned above in much less time than is taken by the ferries. This is great, particularly if your time is limited, but there are disadvantages. The hydrofoils are considerably more expensive and provide practically no view; it is like travelling in a high-speed water-borne bus. And hydrofoils are not immune to the weather, for they are less able to bear high waves than ferries. They have also been known to stay in port through a scheduled departure simply because there were not enough passengers to justify the trip. There is no way to escape the uncertainties. ❑

LEFT: sailing into harbour. **RIGHT:** relaxing on a ferry.

MANAGING THE TOURISTS

*Mass tourism has brought massive problems to Greece. Diverse remedies
have been attempted, but there is still some way to go*

Greece is essentially a small, jagged hump of rock and grey-green vegetation supporting an indigenous population of 10 million. Yet every summer, nearly as many foreign tourists descend on the country. By the early 1990s, more than eight million tourists visited the mainland and islands, pumping more than $3 billion a year into the economy.

Tourism had been either the second-largest or the largest foreign-exchange earner for Greece since the early 1970s. In recognition of this pivotal role, Greece's first Ministry of Tourism was founded to address long-neglected crises in the industry.

Growing pains

Greece's limited infrastructure and tourist facilities were both stretched to their limit. Popular islands teemed with hundreds of thousands of summer visitors. Streets that had been constructed for a donkey and two passers-by became rivers of slow-moving gawkers. Hotels were booked up far in advance, disappointing foolhardy travellers who arrived without a reservation.

Arid islands, supplied by tanker, had to ration water. Beaches were packed with sun-worshippers lying only inches apart. Nude sunbathers searching for the ultimate sybaritic experience appeared increasingly on family beaches. Native islanders, whose pleasures and priorities centred around the church and the community, were not amused.

Still less popular were thousands of young backpackers who arrived on the most crowded islands without pre-booked accommodation. They often had barely a drachma to their names, pushed up the local crime rate, and ended up sleeping on rooftops or beaches with nothing but the stars for cover.

Ferryboats to many islands were consistently overcrowded at high season. The craft themselves – often retired from more demanding

LEFT: tourists flock to the beaches in their thousands.
RIGHT: another charter flight arrives in Skiáthos.

North Sea or Baltic services, pending relegation to Southeast Asia, or the wrecker's yard – were nothing to write home about, either. Seats on island-hopping aeroplanes had to be booked two months in advance, and Athenians with island homes found they had to reserve their seats in spring for the entire summer.

Theoretical remedies

Even before tourism became the largest global industry, studies predicted a future onslaught of young, low-income tourists, part of an estimated 2 billion travellers ranging around the globe by the year 2000, spoilt for choice in destinations.

The official Greek response, a consensus hammered out by the disparate elements of the Greek tourism industry convened by the first Tourism Minister Nikos Skoulas, was to emphasise quality clientele over quantity. Penniless backpackers were to be actively discouraged; upmarket, specialised tourism, involving high per-arrival spending, was to be promoted;

and the necessary infrastructure projects funded and built. It was further proposed to designate Greece as a "marine tourism country", to highlight the inland, monumental heritage, and to develop a higher level of professional services.

An immediate step taken was to forbid admission of charter-flight passengers without an accompanying room reservation, in a move to quash "hooliganism" among young tourists. This measure principally affected the British, roughly one in four arrivals. Athens also put a theoretical halt to licensing accommodation categories – mostly C-class hotels, and B-class rooms – on islands where there was an over-

PLANS FOR GROWTH

As part of the Skoulas tourism initiative, a dozen new full-service marinas were planned, and existing ones improved, with the help of the European Union's Integrated Mediterranean Programmes. Schools of tourism management were established, and a massive, coordinated overseas publicity campaign was undertaken, replete with some forgettable or ambiguous slogans ("Wherever you go, Greece awaits you"). New small-craft airports were opened on the smaller islands, bringing the Greek total to 36, and the domestic monopoly of Olympic Airways and its subsidiary, Olympic Aviation, was declared over.

supply, while simultaneously granting more permits for the construction of A- and luxury-class hotels, with generous incentives for supplementary facilities such as golf courses, tennis courts and convention halls.

But with the connivance of seat-only operators, the accommodation requirement was easily circumvented. The required vouchers soon became dummies, or were valid only for the first night, and in any case could not be enforced for EU nationals after 1993. Local bribes frequently neutralised national or urban controls on hotel building permits.

Reality bites

Ministry planners failed to recognise that, amid the early-1990s recessions, disposable income was unlikely to be available abroad to patronise all those grandiose projects. Poor accommodation distribution still plagues Greece. In early 1998 there were nearly 1 million licensed beds in hotels and *dhomátia*, with several provinces (such as Sámos and Iráklion) suffering from vast excess capacity, rarely full even in August, while other spots remain undersupplied.

Restored spas on Lésvos, a new marina on Híos (the one on Sámos has languished unfinished since 1991), the long-awaited restoration of Maniot towers as accommodation, all seemed like shuffling deckchairs on the *Titanic*, so inadequate were many aspects of Greece's chaotic infrastructure.

The nadir came in 1993, as the independent tourism ministry was reabsorbed into the economics ministry, and members of AITO, a group of independent British tour operators such as Laskarina and Sunvil, aired their grievances in *The Sunday Times*. The last straw was the sudden disappearance in mid-season of a critical ferry link, owing to a Byzantine wrangle between rival shipping companies and subsidising bureaucrats. With no subsequent improvement in boat or hydrofoil reliability, nor any Greek ministerial support for the AITO position, the islands concerned (Astypálea and Kastellórizo) were simply dropped from Laskarina's brochure.

The result: opt for a quality holiday on an offbeat, unspoiled island without an international airport – just what the ministry had encouraged – and there was no guarantee that you'd ever get there.

Hopes and prospects

Currently, a two-week, cheap-and-cheerful studio package, including flight, goes for about £350; a higher-quality package costs £400-450. For £100-200 more (or even the same price), British sunseekers can sample the exotic delights of Cuba, The Gambia, Goa or Florida. Individuals who love Greece, who have a connection with a particular place, and who speak a bit of the language, will continue to return regularly, but the country hasn't been trendy since the 1970s.

> ### NUMBERS UP
>
> Greece has seen a modest increase in tourism numbers in recent years – due to more "shoulder-season" bookings in spring and autumn.

The tourism industry's main task involves luring back significant numbers to what Greece does better or uniquely: clean seas, a high degree of personal safety, characterful inland villages, low-impact sports (venues for scuba diving, for instance, previously limited by the archeology lobby, steadily increase). The other is to work on the "product's" weak points: unreliable transport; aging, brutalist-modern hotels and *dhomátia*; and indifferent cuisine.

The overcrowded-ferry abuses of 1996, when captains were fined for loading boats to double safe capacity, should never recur since the introduction of mandatory computerised booking and ticketing for all major domestic sailings. More progressive shipping lines such as Minoan and ANEK voluntarily instituted the practice years ago, and are among those companies ordering purpose-built, state-of-the-art boats rather than relying on cast-offs from northern Europe.

In 1997 the National Tourist Organisation finally had a stab at producing the first universal, semi-reliable, impartial printed ferry schedule, intended for overseas distribution. Several private competitors to Olympic Airways have emerged since the deregulation of the Greek skies, and if (as is perennially threatened) Olympic goes under and is inadequately "reorganised", these more efficient carriers may find themselves with a suddenly enlarged flight network.

Extensive restoration projects on the islands and mainland appeal to connoisseurs, but much more could be done with Greece's ample supply of medieval ruins. The level of cuisine in many resorts remains abysmal; locals retort that higher standards would be pearls before swine, and rail against the "supermarket tourists" who, having paid cut-rate fare and lodging, rub salt in the wound by self-catering, even without a kitchen. Cooking in hotel rooms is manifestly obnoxious, but offenders would probably splash out on taverna fare if it was more often worth paying for.

Some Greek tourism authorities still live in hope of a magic bullet which would simultaneously banish all cheapskates and lager-

louts, and bring malleable big-spenders rolling in. A wiser strategy, as Americans remain largely absent following the terrorism scares of the 1980s, and more Germans stay home because of economic uncertainties, would be to diversify the visitor portfolio. Already appreciative and relatively well-behaved central Europeans drive down to the north mainland, or fly in on packages; the Russian *nouveaux riches* have been arriving too. Weekend breaks and shopping visits by (horrors) Turks to the border islands could be more actively encouraged.

With the big plans becalmed, the only certainty is that improvement will come in multifaceted increments. ❑

LEFT: queues at the charter terminal at Iráklion airport. **RIGHT:** tourism meets archeology at Knossós.

Sea, Sun, Sand and Sex

The arrival of nubile package tourists presents a challenge to local lads, and
on some islands seduction has achieved the status of competitive sport

When the airport was built on Skiáthos in the mid-1970s, it put the island within three or four hours of direct flight from northern Europe. The number of visitors multiplied many times over, and the lifestyle of the islanders adapted rapidly.

Before the airport, Skiáthos was typical of small, relatively inaccessible Aegean islands.

The unmarried men on the island might have assumed that unattached women were old dears who shrouded themselves in black and hobbled about on sticks. If other types existed, they were without exception under lock and key.

But the Northerners disgorged from charter flights seemed to arrange matters differently. Some of them travelled as couples – but not enough, it was observed, to preclude a surprisingly healthy surplus of single women who, moreover, welcomed male company, not least local fishermen.

The lexicon of modern tourism is four "Ss", the belief or hope that a beach in a hot country will produce the desired result: Sea plus Sun plus Sand equals Sex. With probably the best beaches in Greece, Skiáthos was inevitably going to be the setting for many such erotic expectations. The tourist industry boomed and gave the island a reputation as "the straight Mýkonos".

One of those early arrivals was a woman, now respectably middle-aged, who was to return year after year. Her annual pilgrimage began in Australia. What was it that made the immense journey worthwhile? "At home," she said, "I worked in an office and was one in a million. Here, everyone got to know me. I walked down the street and waved back to them, felt like a queen."

Was that the only reason? Australians are commendably candid and straightforward: "No, I used to come for what all the single women were after – sex."

Traditional word, new meaning

The local response to this interesting turn of events was, if not a lexicon of their own, a password: *kamáki*. To the older fishermen, it was simply what they called the trident used for spearing octopus. To the younger ones, the word referred to the pursuit and conquest of foreign females. Fumbling island novices couldn't believe their luck. *Kamáki*, some decided, could be played as a divine game, in the way gods clocked up merit by doing good works. In the modern idiom, they played for points, as in bridge or billiards.

The rules of the game, with local variations, are supposed to be secret, but lips can be loosened by vanity (or perhaps a mischievous sense of humour). It can be revealed here that on Skiáthos points are awarded on a scale of one to 10.

An Englishwoman is worth just one point, while Germans and Norwegians are joint second-to-last and worth two. The criteria, *kamáki* contestants take pains to emphasise, are not concerned with individual or national

---

Left: a hopeful Greek boy entertains a visitor.
Right: unambiguous T-shirts for sale in Páros.

performance. They reflect availability. The English are the single largest group of visitors to Skiáthos; Germans and Norwegians are roughly equal, next in line. At the time of writing, the highest score possible on the island ("six, maybe seven") was invested in an 18-year-old Canadian girl who, the *kamáki* set were fascinated to learn, was a serving member of the Royal Canadian Mounted Police. The theoretical maximum of 10 points, which few expected ever to achieve, lay in the rarified realm of "North Korean and Eskimo" women.

Reversing the roles

While male-orientated hedonism in Thailand or the Philippines attracts criticism from certain quarters, *kamáki* reverses the roles and the female victims, if any, are willing. Occasional casualties among the men are caused by hectic preparations for the opening of the *kamáki* season. Serious contestants will spend the spring lifting weights. The modern idea of Adonis, on the evidence of the past few years, is not only muscular but blond. Very blond.

The climax of spring training is the ritual anointing of heads with peroxide bleach, but stubbornly swarthy scalps may become piebald when the dark roots reappear.

But on the whole the results would seem to be satisfactory. "The boys are beautiful," said an American woman reminiscing about happy times spent on a number of Greek islands. "Personally, I've only been to bed with a couple of them, but I love looking at them. Women feel they're a long way from home, nobody would know, so… It helps if the boy can speak English but, if he can't that's okay too."

She recalled that on the morning after the two occasions she remembered best, she was asked for a photograph of herself.

If the nomination of the *Kamáki* King at the end of the summer season is at all contentious, the collection of photographs is introduced as evidence and influence the island jury. Failing photographs, letters (written on flights home with time to kill?) do almost as well.

But it must be acknowledged that, while the majority of *kamáki* contestants have picked up basic conversational English over the years, their proficiency may not extend to reading or writing letters in return. ❏

WRITING THE GREAT NOVEL

Many authors – and would-be authors – decide that a Greek island is the perfect place in which to write a book. Some even achieve it

Bring a woman, Lawrence Durrell advised Henry Miller in 1938, promising that in other respects his Greek island, lacking the more tiresome distractions of 20th-century society, was the perfect place to finish a novel. "We could sail and bathe in mornings, have a fine sunny lunch with wine, then a long afternoon siesta, bathe before tea and then four

hours' work in a slow rich evening." At the time, Miller was keen to finish a book and might have wondered about the efficacy of Durrell's idea of a hard day at the office.

Miller did finish the book (it was *Tropic of Capricorn*) and, although the extent to which it materialised on Corfu is unknown, the achievement ought to stand as a benchmark for the permanent presence that has since imposed itself on nearly every Greek island – writers wrestling with great works.

Most of them would have thrown a beach towel in with a typewriter or wordprocessor and decamped to their island expressly to write a book; others might have arrived for other rea-

sons but been inspired by the amount of writing going on around them.

On one island, a book on local history had been in production for more than 20 years. It was by a clever Englishwoman who led a semi-reclusive existence in a primitive cottage high on a mountain. She would descend to the village once a week on a moped to do her shopping; otherwise nobody saw much of her. It was said that she'd come to the island to forget an unhappy love affair at Oxford.

The expatriate colony once published a little book about the island, and in it was an article by her which demonstrated convincingly the rigour of a trained historian. The article is probably as much as anyone will ever know about a project which had occupied most of her adult life. That year, she destroyed the manuscript. Asked why, she shrugged and said nothing.

Conspiracy of distraction

During the tourist season, a conspiracy of distraction forever drives a wedge between writer and great work. Durrell's invitation to Miller sets out some of them: the weather is magnificent and the sea so congenial that there is always a plausible excuse to dive in and remain there for some time.

Durrell's "fine sunny lunch with wine" is another of the yawning man-traps set for the island writer, especially the "with wine". By any criterion, expatriates who settle on islands are slightly odd. That makes them excellent company; it also means that, on the whole, they drink a bit.

Credit is extended everywhere to resident writers. The trusting and hospitable Greeks revere Homer and are willing to regard anyone who can type with two fingers as a potential heir. The less flattering explanation is that in winter there is no way off most islands except by boat, and creditors are likely to be lining the quay. Either way, their generosity can be a lifesaver because even writers who are in a position to have their banks at home send them money are often caught short.

Somewhere· on the island there will be a

wholesaler or a grocer who sells *oúzo* and brandy from the barrel – bring your own bottle. Short-term visitors are unlikely to have the time to find out who or where they are; expatriates, on the other hand, can find them blindfolded. Wine sold in huge bottles is commensurately cheap, and etiquette requires that, once opened, the bottle must be finished at one sitting.

One writer on the island discovered that, by reversing Durrell's timetable and applying himself in the mornings, he could turn out a slim volume of poetry per decade. Over lunch at his special table in a taverna below his house, he would discuss with another writer their respective great works. He was working on his third volume and was fairly confident that it would be ready by the turn of the millennium.

Bottle count

These were definitely lunches "with wine", and he would mysteriously arrange the bottles in a straight line on what seemed to be a constant compass bearing. (Greek waiters don't clear empty bottles; it is their way of keeping track of the ever-increasing numbers.)

A visit to the poet's house revealed that the view from the terrace bore down directly on the taverna and, in particular, on to "his" table. Concerned that too grand a lunch on the Durell model might jeopardise work on volume three, the poet's wife had acquired a powerful pair of binoculars and turned the terrace into an observation post. From here she monitored the growing line of bottles that had been emptied by her husband and passing acquaintances, and if the situation appeared to be getting out of hand, she would descend imperially either to speak on the virtues of moderation or, *in extremis*, to march him off by the ear. The studied arrangement of the bottles, then, was a smokescreen. "He thinks that I can only see one," his wife revealed. "In that belief he is mistaken."

Whatever cloud may have been hanging over the third volume of poems, the first two were accomplished facts. Moreover, they were on sale in the local bookshop, a vindication for any writer whose credentials are called into question. Very few island writers are in a position to dispel doubt so triumphantly. Very few, indeed,

LEFT AND RIGHT: sunshine, sea, a typewriter and a bottle or two are all you need…

are on sale anywhere or, deep in their hearts, expect to be. It is enough merely to be writing a book, regardless of the outcome.

In the winter months, when all but one or two of the bars and tavernas are closed and the sea is too cold for swimming, there is nothing for the expatriate colony to do. It would be inconceivable, for example, to squander the need to call at the post office and at the bank by doing both on a single outing, even if post office and bank happened to be close neighbours.

Corfu cannot have had many visitors when Miller dropped in on Durrell in 1938, but Durrell's own literary output from his island base

proves that it can be done, if only by observing the sanctity of those four hours, either in the slow rich evening or, for a certain kind of poet, in the morning.

Less dedicated writers are more inclined to use the great novel to assuage Puritan misgivings about months of bone-idleness. It soothes the conscience and enhances the fun: after all, 150,000 completed words are a better memento of an island visit than a suntan or stamps registered in one's passport. All too often, of course, the great novel is never actually published – or indeed finished. But the possibility of its being completed provides the perfect excuse to return to the island for one more try. ❏

ISLAND WILDLIFE

The diverse island landscapes support a diverse collection of flora and fauna.
Birds in particular, both resident and migrant, bring delight to ornithologists

Arrive at a Greek island in the heat of summer and you may feel you've inadvertently stumbled upon a little-known outpost of the Sahara. Arid brown countryside sheds clouds of dust each time the hair-dryer winds blow, dead tumbleweeds roll, and the only surviving plant life is in carefully nurtured village window-boxes.

Visit in spring, however and the picture is entirely different. Green leaves and coloured flowers cover the plains, hillsides and even areas of waste ground become gardens.

The first seedlings and new leaves sprout shortly after the first rains of autumn. Growth gathers pace through the cool but sunny winters then, a few weeks into the new year, the flowers start to open in the far southeast. Rhodes, Kárpathos and eastern Crete are followed in succession by western Crete, then the Peloponnese and the eastern Aegean. Spring arrives in the Ionian islands and Thássos as summer appears in Rhodes.

As the plants lead, so other wildlife follows. Insects increase, and the insect-eaters flourish; food-chains gear up for a spring and early summer of proliferation.

Plants a-plenty

Before mankind first settled in the region, the Greek islands had a mixture of some woodland, some tall, dense, impenetrably shrubby *maquis* vegetation, and much *garigue*. The latter is familiar to Hellenophiles who enjoy the countryside – low shrubby bushes, which are often spiny and resist both the grazing of animals and the bare legs of walkers. Mixed together with the shrubs are fragrant herbs, colourful annuals and, enjoying protection from those spines, fragile orchids.

It is a myth that man and his flocks destroyed a verdant Greek Eden of continuous woodland: some larger islands had their own quota of

plant-munching animals – such as deer – long before any human arrivals. It was this that led to the flora's evolution of discouraging defences such as spines, bristles and foul tastes, which armed it well for the comparatively recent introduction of the domesticated sheep and goat. (See also *Insight on Wild Flowers* on pages 92–3.)

Reclusive mammals

Wild mammals occur on the islands, but most of them are secretive. Crete has its ibex-like wild goat or *agrími* (also called the *krí-krí*), a rare inhabitant of the White Mountains. With fears of its demise from over-hunting, some animals were transferred to the island of Dhía, near Iráklion, where they flourished and overpopulated – eating the rare native plants.

Elsewhere, the largest mammals are the badger, and the jackal of the eastern Aegean, but the one you are more likely to see is the stone-marten. This resembles a dark brown ferret, long, slim, agile and fast-moving. They are sighted both during the day and in headlights as

---

PRECEDING PAGES: goats on the Cretan mountains; donkeys in midwinter. **LEFT:** dolphins sometimes perform for ferry passengers. **RIGHT:** a European bee-eater conforming to its job description.

they cross roads at night. They are frequent victims of the taxidermist's art, and many tavernas have a stuffed marten on the wall or a dusty shelf.

Most other mammals are small: rats (only common on Corfu), mice and shrews, and a variety of bats that can move from island to mainland and vice-versa.

PYGMY PONY

On Skýros there is a very small wild horse, a unique breed very similar to the horses carved on the frieze of the Parthenon.

The National Marine Park north of Alónissos is an important haven for the Mediterranean monk seal – the most endangered of all the world's seals. About 50 of a total world popu-

anywhere there is a salty coastal pool, but visit Lésvos to see them nesting in quantity.

Much smaller, but most colourful, are the crested pink, white and black hoopoe, the bright blue and brown roller, and the multi-coloured bee-eater. For many ornithologists, the most excitement comes from seeing the raptors – hawks, falcons, eagles and vultures, although the most frequent species is the common buzzard.

The larger species inhabit mountain areas, where gorges and cliffs provide secure nesting

lation of only 500 live here. Between islands, look out for common dolphins speeding alongside ferries.

Twitchers' territory

While the mammal-watcher may find himself under-employed, the bird-watcher should not be. The spring migration brings a variety of species north from Africa. Their final destination may be much further north, but the Greek islands may be their first landfall after the Mediterranean crossing. Some of the larger birds are most spectacular. Both black and white storks migrate through Greece, and nest on the way. Individual flamingos may turn up

and the requisite isolation. Golden eagles may be the most romantic, but vultures are undoubtedly the most spectacular. Griffon vultures, sometimes in flocks of up to 20, patrol the skies, soaring effortlessly on broad wings the size of a door and a half. The scarcer lammergeier has narrow wings, the ultimate flying machine in its search for bones – or tortoises – to drop onto rocks and break open.

Reptiles and insects

The most abundant reptiles are lizards, some 21 species, of which the Balkan green lizard is perhaps the most conspicuous. Bolder and more stockily built is the iguana-like agama, sometime called the Rhodes dragon, though it's also found in Corfu and several Aegean islands. This greyish rough-skinned lizard, when disturbed, often stays around for a few minutes to check out the danger.

Tortoises occur on many islands, though surprisingly not on the largest, Crete. Once gathered in tens of thousands for the pet-trade, they now lead safer lives wandering noisily through the underbrush. Their freshwater aquatic relatives, the terrapins, favour streams with bare muddy banks for sunbathing, but are wary and disappear quickly.

Marine loggerhead turtles are decreasing in

Aegean islands – they usually have a zigzag pattern down the spine, and move rather lazily.

Mosquitoes may seem the commonest insects at night, but Corfu is noted for its springtime fireflies, little flashing beacons that drift over damp fields and hedges after dark. Look for paler lights in the hedgerows and you may see glow-worms. During the day, butterflies are obvious, often in great quantity and variety. Some of the large hawk-moths may be seen during the day – the hummingbird hawk-moth, like its namesake, relies on superfast wingbeats to hover at flowers as it feeds.

Noisier are the huge, glossy blue-black

numbers as their nesting beaches are lost to tourism. They used to breed until recently on Crete and Sámos – now they are restricted to a few semi-protected beaches on Kefalloniá and Zákynthos.

Snakes often cause alarm, but most are harmless, and all prefer to be left alone. Locals tend to overreact and attack any snake they see, though this is actually the best way to increase the chance of being bitten. Poisonous vipers do occur in some of the Ionian, Cycladic and east

carpenter bees which spend much of their time looking for suitable nesting sites, usually a hollow cane. Noisiest of all is the cicada, an overgrown aphid, which perches – usually on a pine tree – and keeps up a deafening racket. Despite their size and volume, they are surprisingly hard to see. African locusts are really giant grasshoppers, though they never pillage in devastating swarms this side of the Mediterranean.

Praying mantids keep their barbed forearms in a position of supplication until an unwary insect moves nearby – then the mantis becomes a hungry atheist. Even the male of the species is devoured as he romances the female, his protein helping to nourish the next generation. ❏

FAR LEFT: the Mediterranean monk seal is a protected species. **LEFT:** a European roller. **ABOVE:** a griffon vulture soars. **RIGHT:** the once-endangered tortoise.

THE ISLANDS IN BLOOM

The Greek islands are at their most abundant in spring and early summer, when every hillside and valley is decorated with glorious colour

Greece in spring is a botanist's dream and a gardener's despair. Some 6,000 species of wild plant grow in Greece and the islands, and in the spring (March to May) visitors may enjoy a magnificent cornucopia of flowers and fragrances.

Hillsides resemble giant rock gardens, while brilliant patches of untended waste ground outdo northern Europe's carefully tended herbaceous borders with ease. Winter rains, followed by a bright, hot, frost-free spring, produce a season's flowers compressed into a few, spectacular weeks before the summer's heat and drought become too much. By late May or June the flowers are over, the seeds for next year's show are ripening, and greens are fading to brown to match the tourists on the beaches.

SUMMER SURVIVAL

Except in the cooler, higher mountains, most plants go into semi-dormancy to survive the arid summer. The first rains of autumn, which could be in early September, but may be late November, tempt a few autumn bulbs into flower but also initiate the germination of seeds – plants that will grow and build up strength during the winter in preparation for the following spring when their flowers will again colour in the waiting canvas of the hills and valleys.

The richness and diversity of the flora are due in part to the islands' location between three continents – Europe, Asia and Africa – partly to the Ice-Age survival in temperate Greece of pre-glacial species, and partly to the wonderful variety of habitats. Limestone, the foundation of much of Greece, is a favoured home for plants, providing the stability, minerals, water supply and protection they need.

▷ **THE HILLS ARE ALIVE**
Sunshine, colour and quantity mark the spring flowering of the islands, as here in the mountains of Crete in mid-April.

△ **A GOOD REED**
Not bamboo – but it has similar uses. The giant reed (*Arundo donax*) can even be made into pan-pipes.

▽ **CUP OF MANY COLOURS**
Ranunculus asiaticus is an unlikely buttercup, with poppy-sized flowers in shades of white, pink, orange, red – and occasionally yellow.

▽ **SCARLET MEMORIAL**
The startling reds of *Anemone coronaria* mark the arrival of spring and in myth represent the spilt blood of the dying Adonis.

▽ **HANDY BUSH**
The long flowering period of the native oleander makes it popular in garden and as an ornamental roadside crash-barrier.

BEETLES, BEES AND BUTTERFLIES

The profusion of flowers and plants provides food for an equal profusion of insects. Butterflies are conspicuous from spring to autumn, including the swallowtail (*above*) whose equally colourful caterpillars feed on the leaves of common fennel. Its larger, paler and more angular relative, the scarce swallowtail, despite its name, is even more abundant.

Look for clouded yellows and paler cleopatras, reddish-brown painted ladies and southern commas, white admirals, and a myriad of smaller blue butterflies.

Butterflies, bees and day-flying hawkmoths tend to go for flowers with nectar, while beetles and flies go for the pollen. Some bugs even use the heat accumulated in the solar cup of many flowers in order to warm up their sex lives.

The leaves of plants feed armies of insect herbivores, which themselves are eaten by more aggressive insects. Some of the omniverous Greek grasshoppers and crickets are as happy munching through a caterpillar, or even another grasshopper, as the grass it was sitting on.

◁ **FIRE FENNEL**
According to legend, fire was brought to earth by Prometheus hidden in the smouldering stem of a giant fennel (*Ferula communis*).

▽ **NATURAL FOOD**
Wild artichokes are painfully spiny to prepare for the pot, but their flavour is much prized by Greek country folk over the spineless cultivated variety, and their market price increases accordingly.

ISLANDS OUT OF SEASON

The onset of winter and the disappearance of the tourists brings a sudden and dramatic change to the smaller Greek islands

It is only when the charter flights have finally returned to base that the real character of a small island staggers out of its unseasonal hibernation. The larger islands are capable of absorbing a deluge of visitors without having to adopt a totally different identity. A visitor arriving in Crete in October would not discover, as could happen on a smaller island, that the police station had just closed and would not re-open until needed again late in the spring.

It is difficult to exaggerate the disfiguring impact when an island with a population measured in hundreds is swamped by 10 times as many people, all at the same time. How would Britain, say, with a population of 60 million, cope with 600 million visitors in one go?

Quick change

Understandably dazed by the whole thing, the islanders have to find their feet again when everyone goes away. Superficially, the change into winter uniform is swift. Migrant waiters and kitchen staff pile on to departing ferries to look for winter jobs on the mainland. Awnings over pavement cafés are rolled up and stowed; the chairs and tables stacked and dragged away. Most of the shops are closed and padlocked.

A good sign that the islanders are feeling themselves again after the grinding hours they have put in during the season is the resumption of the evening promenade, an almost formal ritual in which small groups file from one end of the locally prescribed route to the other, and back again. Overtaking is apparently not allowed. Among them are the elderly and handicapped who are seldom seen in public during the season.

Winter visitors who join the throng are bound to attract curious glances from the traffic going in the opposite direction. The process of acceptance as an honorary member of the community is a ritual in itself. First, perhaps, a half-cocked eyebrow; later, a nod; then ultimately, triumphantly, a stop for a chat.

LEFT: even the Cyclades see snow in winter.
RIGHT: stormy weather over Tínos.

The promenade is a chance to observe all kinds of island machinery in motion. Orthodox priests, symbols of a former propriety that doesn't stand a chance against the summer heathens, reassert their magisterial presence among the faithful. Office-holders and petitioners in the schismatic world of island politics fall into step beside the mayor for a mobile conference.

If the municipal elections are in sight, the plotting that goes on during the promenade will explode into campaigns which sound like the rumble of impending civil war. The party manifestos may commend or deplore, as the case may be, the state of the village drains, but the winner's powers of patronage are such that the outcome is regarded, not unrealistically, as a matter of economic life or death.

Visitors can skip politics, however, and still feel that they are part of local life. There are any number of religious festivals involving processions through the streets, the mayor and priests conspicuously linked in secular-clerical solidarity at the head of an enthusiastic brass band.

The locals have to buy food and other supplies, so there is never any difficulty getting hold of provisions. But the smaller islands are seldom self-sufficient, and if they have to rely on ferries – which are not nearly so frequent during the winter, and are likely to be cancelled in bad weather – there may be temporary shortages of most fresh produce.

Power failures which last more than a day cause a commotion because the bakeries can't function. The lesser kind go unnoticed (although not by wintering writers with wordprocessors).

The fishermen sail at dusk and return at dawn but, for the rest of the male population, the longer nights are the cue to bring out playing cards. Officially, no money changes hands, but passers-by can't fail to notice scraps of paper and meticulous accounting. In reality, there is a massive redistribution of the summer takings, although by the following spring most of the money is supposedly back where it started.

Winter visitors

Landlords don't expect to earn rent in winter, so when a visitor comes along out of season the negotiations are flexible. Prime accommodation on the sea may be worth a slight premium while the water is still at a tolerable temperature, although after September and before May there is hardly a beach that couldn't be annexed and occupied as private property.

If outdoor conditions are an important criterion, the southern islands are generally warmer. All over the Aegean, however, the winter wind will sometimes cut through to the bone, and houses that were not built specifically for the summer trade are more likely to have some form of heating. Tenants would be expected to pay for the fuel they use.

It is worth asking about vacant farmhouses; these have the added advantage that neighbours are always popping around with eggs, a bottle and an extra glass. This agreeable way of life can be had for a reasonable rent, not excluding lavish consumption of drink and cigarettes.

An insider's view

The English novelist Simon Raven spent the winter of 1960 on Hydra looking into "what goes on when winter comes, when the last epicene giggle has hovered and died in the October air". He decided he was among a bunch of atavistic pirates who, happily preoccupied by making money during the summer, reverted in winter to the old distrust of strangers who used to come only to spy on their illicit booty.

Hydra has since become accustomed to having a few foreigners stay on and, assuming the islanders never saw what Raven wrote about them, he would probably feel more comfortable among them now. The one impression formed then which he would not wish to change now is that only in winter could his eye make out what the island was really like. ❏

WINTER ENTERTAINMENT

An island's *ouzeriés*, those basic drinking establishments where a request for a cocktail would draw a blank stare, stay open through the winter for the locals. Some of the island's tavernas and posher bars may keep their doors open too, although probably on an informal rota as if the owners were sharing the workload, or some may just open at weekends. Even a disco may re-open unexpectedly, but that could last for just a night or two and on the next it might just as inexplicably close down again. On investigation you may discover that the owner found it more profitable to spend the night out in his fishing boat.

LEFT: an ancient provider of winter warmth on Ikaría.
RIGHT: January storm clouds over Hydra harbour.

ΑΓ. ΑΘΑΝΑΣΙΟΣ Λ.Μ. 49

·ΗΛΙΑΣ Λ.Μ

PLACES

A detailed guide to all the island groups, with their principal
sites clearly cross-referenced by number to the maps

The poet Odysseus Elytis once said: "Greece rests on the sea." It's an observation that few countries could claim with such authority. Some 25,000 sq. km (10,000 sq. miles) of the Aegean and the Ionian seas are covered by islands, the exact number of which has, in characteristic Greek fashion, been the topic of discussion and dispute. There may be 3,000 islands and islets, of which 167 are inhabited; there may be only 1,000, of which less 60 are inhabited.

The frame of reference that defines a populated place is open to interpretation. Does a tiny outcrop, bare save for one shepherd and six goats, constitute an uninhabited island? Can an island totally deserted except for pilgrimages made annually to a small chapel at its summit claim to be inhabited?

The reality matters much more to foreigners than to Greeks, who are interested in sea and sky rather than in facts and figures. What is indisputable, however, is the sheer variety of landscape and experience to be found lurking behind the familiar images.

This is what we attempt to show here, islands with an ancient past and a modern outlook, the complex choice and the pure simple pleasures. In order to accommodate everything that is implied in the phrase "a Greek island" we have devoted space to tiny islands such as Ághios Efstrátios and Télendhos, as well as the well-known giants like Crete and Rhodes and the holiday favourites such as Corfu and Mýkonos. We do not ignore the familiar, popular islands, of course, but we explore them with typical Insight thoroughness, to search out the true heart of the place behind the tourist clichés.

So welcome aboard the ferry – and try not to be fazed by variations in spelling you will encounter. We have tried to be consistent in the way we spell place names, but when it comes to transliterating their language into Roman characters, the Greeks themselves are notoriously variable. Where there is more than one version of a place's name, we have indicated options. But be prepared to see different versions again on notices or road signs. For more on the Greek language, see the *Travel Tips* section at the back of this book. ❑

PRECEDING PAGES: Mýkonos harbour; fishing boats and the church – two important features of island life; lunchtime on Hydra. **LEFT:** passengers disembark from an Aegean ferry.

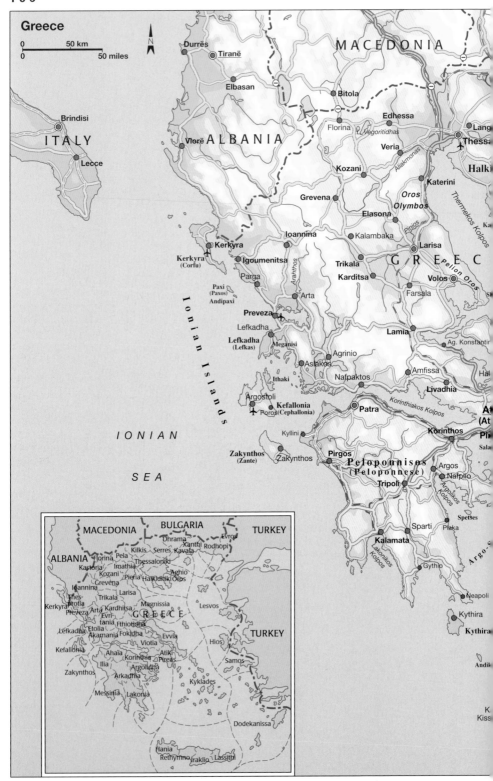

Greece

0 — 50 km
0 — 50 miles

N

ITALY

Brindisi

Lecce

ALBANIA

Durrës
Tiranë

Elbasan

Vlorë

MACEDONIA

Bitola

Edhessa
Florina LL Vegoritidhas

Veria

Kozani

Grevena

Lang
Thessa

Halk

Katerini

*Oros
Olymbos*

Elasona

Ioannina

Kerkyra
Kerkyra
(Corfu)

Igoumenitsa

Parga

Paxi
(Paxos)
Andipaxi

Preveza

Lefkadha

Lefkadha
(Lefkas)

Meganisi

Astakos

Ithaki

Argostoli

Kefallonia
Poros (Cephallonia)

Arakthos

Kalambaka

Pinios

Trikala

Karditsa

Arta

Agrinio

Nafpaktos

Larisa

G R E E C

Volos

Pellon Oros

Farsala

Lamia

Ag. Konstantin

Amfissa

Livadhia

Patra

Korinthiakos Kolpos

Kyllini

Zakynthos
(Zante)

Zakynthos

Pirgos

Peloponnisos
(Peloponnese)

Tripoli

Korinthos

At
(At
Pir

Sala

Argos
Nafplio

*Argolikos
Kolpos*

Spetses

Plaka

Ha

Aliakmonas

Thermekos Kolpos

Ka

Si

I o n i a n   I s l a n d s

I O N I A N

S E A

Sparti

Kalamata

*Messiniakos
Kolpos*

Gythio

Argo-

Neapoli

Kythira

Kythira

Andik

K
Kiss

MACEDONIA

BULGARIA

TURKEY

Dhrama
Xanthi
Kilkis Serres Kavala Rodhopi

Evros

ALBANIA Florina Pela
Kastoria Imathia
Kozani
Ioannina Grevena Pieria

Thessaloniki

Aghio
Halkidhiki Oros

Ios
Thes-
protia Trikala
Kerkyra Ptolia
Preveza Arta Kardhitsa
Evri-
tania Fthiotidha
Lefkadha Etolia
Akarnania Fokidha
Kefallonia
Ahaia
Ilia Korinthia
Zakynthos Arkadhia
Messinia Lakonia

Larisa

Magnissia

Lesvos

G R E E C E

Viotia
Atiki-
Pireas
Argolidha

Evvia

Hios

Samos

TURKEY

Kyklades

Dodekanissa

Hania
Rethymno Iraklio Lassithi

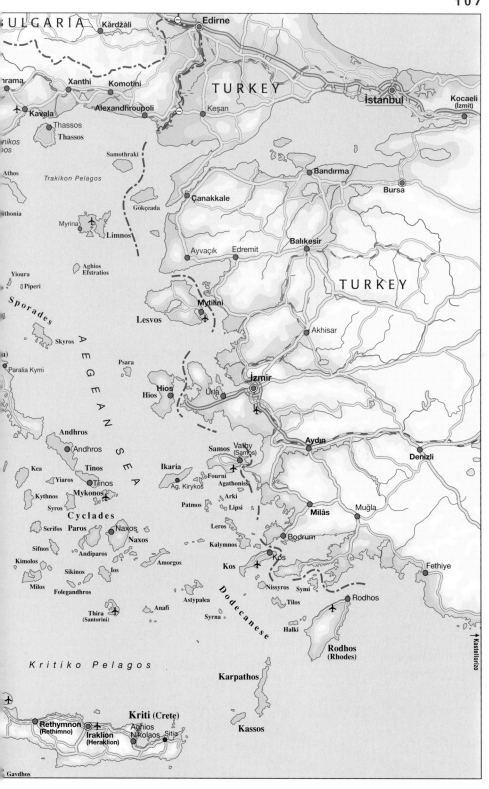

BULGARIA   Kǎrdžàli   Edirne

Drama   Xanthi   Komotini   TURKEY

Kavala   Alexandhroupoli   Keşan   İstanbul   Kocaeli (İzmit)

Thassos
Thassos

nikos
os

Athos   Trakikon Pelagos

Samothraki

Bandırma   Bursa

Çanakkale

Gökçeada

ithonia

Myrina   Limnos   Ayvaçık   Edremit   Balıkesir

Yioura   Aghios Efstratios

Piperi

TURKEY

Sporades   Mytilini

Lesvos   Akhisar

a)
Skyros

Paralia Kymi   Psara

AEGEAN SEA

Hios   Urla   İzmir
Hios

Andhros
Andhros   Samos   Vathy (Samos)   Aydın   Denizli

Kea   Tinos   Ikaria   Fourni
Yiaros   Tiinos   Ag. Kirykos   Agathonissi
Kythnos   Mykonos   Arki
Syros   Patmos   Lipsi   Milâs   Muğla
Cyclades   Leros
Serifos   Paros   Naxos   Bodrum
Naxos   Kalymnos
Sifnos   Andiparos   Kos
Kimolos   Amorgos   Kos   Fethiye
Sikinos   Ios
Milos   Nissyros   Symi
Folegandhros   Astypalea   Tilos   Rodhos
Thira (Santorini)   Anafi   Syrna   Dodecanese   Halki

Kritiko Pelagos   Rodhos (Rhodes)

Karpathos

Kastellorizo

Kriti (Crete)
Rethymnon (Rethimno)   Aghios Nikolaos   Sitia   Kassos
Iraklion (Heraklion)

Gavdhos

ATHENS STOPOVER

Noisy, dirty, sometimes smelly, often spectacular, always exhilarating, Athens can be simply exhausting. But if you have a day or two to look around, there's plenty to see

Map on page 110

Since Athens was suddenly elevated, unprepared, to the status of capital of the new Greek state after the War of Independence, it has grown haphazardly, and too fast. It never had a chance to mellow into venerable old age. Old and new have not blended too well; you can still sense the small prewar city pushing through the huge sprawl of today's modern capital.

Occasionally, you come across what must have been a country villa, ensconced between tall office buildings, its owner still fighting against the tide, its windows hermetically closed against pollution and the roar of the traffic. Traffic in Athens has to be seen (and heard) to be believed. Not only do there seem to be more motorcycles than in any other city in Europe, but the central squares are filled with temporary barricades and huge cranes supporting the underground construction of the city's metro. Athenians are quietly optimistic that this new system may actually be operating in time for the Athens Olympic Games in 2004.

But branching off from the frenzied central arteries are the minor veins of the city, relatively free from congestion. Most apartment blocks have balconies and verandahs, and there you can see the Athenians in summer emerging from their afternoon siesta in underpants and nighties, reading the paper, watching the neighbours, watering their plants, eating their evening meal. The hot weather makes life in the open air a necessity; this in turn means gregariousness – it is no accident that there is no word for "privacy" in Greek – though nowadays the pale-blue flicker of television draws more and more people indoors.

There is a constant struggle to catch up with the West while clinging to the old traditional ways. Tavernas, competing with pizza and fast-food shops, try to keep up a semblance of local colour. Arranged marriages are still going strong, but the matchmaker is now competing with a computer service. Doughnuts and *louloúria*, popcorn and *passatémpo*; a priest, majestic in flowing black robes, licking an ice-cream cone or riding a motorbike – unthinkable 10 or 15 years ago. It is coexistence…but the edges are still jagged.

Ancient Athens

If your sightseeing time in Athens is limited, it makes sense to start with the sights that are universally recognised as symbols of Ancient Greece, the monuments dating from Athens' golden years, the 5th century BC. Seen from the right angle driving up the **Ierá Odhós** (the Sacred Way), the **Acropolis ❶** still has a presence that makes the grimy concrete of modern Athens fade into insignificance. Climb up in the early morning, when the crowds are thinnest, and a strip of blue sea edged with grey hills marks the horizon

LEFT: a Classical survivor in modern Athens. **BELOW:** the city seen from the Acropolis.

The Tomb of the Unknown Warrior, by Syntagma Square, is guarded by Evzónes, soldiers in traditional mountain costume. Ernest Hemingway described them as "those big tall babies in ballet skirts".

(Mon–Fri, 8am–6.30pm summer; 8.30am–4.30pm winter; Sat–Sun, 8.30am–2.30pm; free Sun).

The **Propylaia**, the battered official entrance to the Acropolis built by Mnesikles in the 430s BC, was cleverly designed with imposing outside columns to impress people coming up the hill. Parts of its coffered stone ceiling, once painted and gilded, are still visible as you walk through. And roped off on what was once the citadel's southern bastion is the small, square temple of **Athena Nike**, finished in 421 BC.

Until the year 2000, the Acropolis will look like a stonemason's workshop, much as it must have done in the 440s BC when the **Parthenon** was under construction as the crowning glory of Pericles' giant public works programme. Some of his contemporaries thought it extravagant: Pericles was accused of dressing his city up like a harlot. In fact, the Parthenon celebrates Athena as a virgin goddess and the city's protector. Her statue, 12 metres (39 ft) tall and made of ivory and gold plate to Phidias's design, used to gleam in its dim interior. In late antiquity it was taken to Constantinople, where it disappeared.

Conservators have lifted down hundreds of blocks of marble masonry from the Parthenon to replace the rusting iron clamps inserted in the 1920s with noncorrosive titanium (rust made the clamps expand, cracking the stone). The restorers also succeeded in identifying and collecting about 1,600 chunks of Parthenon marble scattered over the hilltop, many blown off in the 1687 explosion caused by a Venetian mortar igniting Ottoman munitions stored inside the temple. When they are replaced, about 15 percent more of the building will be on view. New blocks cut from near the ancient quarries on Mount Pendéli, which supplied the 5th-century BC constructors, will fill the gaps.

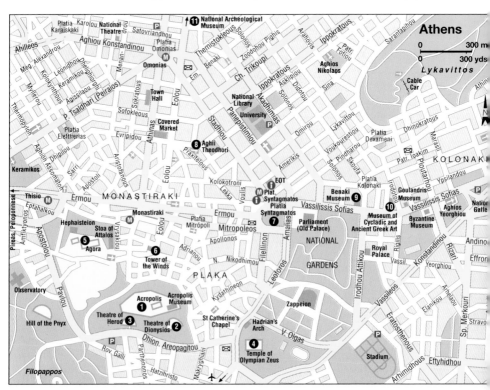

The **Erechtheion**, an elegant architecturally complex repository of ancient cults going back to the Bronze Age, is already restored. Completed in 395 BC, a generation later than the Parthenon, it once contained the supposed tomb of King Kekrops, a mythical founder of the ancient Athenian royal family, and also housed an early wooden statue of Athena.

The Caryatids now supporting the porch are modern copies. The four surviving originals were removed to the **Acropolis Museum** to prevent further damage from the *néfos*, the ochre blanket of atmospheric pollution that often hangs over Athens. There were originally six Caryatids: one was taken by the Ottomans and lost, another is in the British Museum in London, thanks to Lord Elgin. Their four sisters stare out from a nitrogen-filled case, scarred but still impressively female. The coquettish *koraï* reveal a pre-classical ideal: if you look closely, you can make out the traces of make-up and earrings, and the patterns of their crinkled, close-fitting dresses (Mon 11am–6.45pm; Tue–Fri, 8am–6.45pm; Sat–Sun 8.30am–2.30am; free Sun).

On the south side of the Acropolis lies the **Theatre of Dionysios ❷**. The marble seating tiers that survive date from around 320 BC and later, but scholars are generally agreed that plays by the likes of Aeschylus, Sophocles, Euripides and Aristophanes were first staged here at 5th-century BC religious festivals. A state subsidy for theatre-goers meant that every Athenian citizen could take time off to attend (Mon–Sat, 9am-2.45pm; Sun 9am-1.45pm). Herod Atticus, a wealthy Greek landowner who served in the Roman senate, built another theatre on the south slope of the Acropolis in the 2nd century AD, as a memorial to his wife. The steeply-raked **Theatre of Herod ❸** is now used during the Athens Festival for performances of classical drama, opera and ballet.

Map on page 110

In Ottoman times, the Erechtheion was used by the city's Turkish military commander as a billet for his harem.

BELOW: eating outdoors in the Pláka.

Also in the 2nd century the Roman Emperor Hadrian, a fervent admirer of classical Greece, erected an ornate **arch** marking the spot where the classical city ended and the provincial Roman university town began. Little of this Roman city can be seen beneath the green of the **Záppion Park** and the archeological area behind the towering columns of the **Temple of Olympian Zeus ❹**, but recent excavations in the corner of the Záppeio indicate that many Roman buildings stood in this area, at least as far as the stadium built by Herod Atticus. Work on the Temple of Olympian Zeus had been abandoned in around 520 BC when funds ran out, but Hadrian finished the construction and dedicated the temple to himself (Tue–Sun, 8.30am–2.45pm).

As the Acropolis was mainly used for religious purposes, so the ancient Greek **Agora ❺** was employed for all public activities – commercial, political, civic, educational, theatrical, athletic. Today it looks like a cluttered field of ruins. If archeologists had their way, the whole of Pláka would have been levelled. But the reconstructed **Stoa of Attalos**, a 2nd-century BC shopping mall, is a cool place to linger among scents of ancient herbs replanted by the American excavators. The **Hephaisteion**, the Doric temple opposite, will help you appreciate that the Parthenon is truly a masterpiece (Tue–Sun, 8.30am–2.45pm). Across from the Agora, one corner of the **Painted Stoa** has been exposed in Adrianoú Street. This building gave its name to Stoicism, the stiff-upper-lip brand of philosophy that Zeno the Cypriot taught there in the 3rd century BC.

A 1st-century BC Syrian was responsible for the picturesque **Tower of the Winds ❻**, a well-preserved marble octagon overlooking the scanty remains of the Roman Agora. It is decorated with eight relief figures, each depicting a different breeze, and once contained a water-clock (Tue–Sun, 8.30am–2.45pm)

BELOW: the Theatre of Dionysios.

City streets

The heart of the modern city lies within a triangle defined by **Platía Omónias** Omónia Square) in the north, **Platía Syntagmátos (Syntagma Square)** ❼ to the southeast and **Monastiráki** in the south. Except for three small cross-streets, no cars are permitted in this area, which has taken on a new lease of life. **Ermou**, once a traffic-clogged mess, is now a long pedestrian walkway with reinvigorated shops, enlivened by pavement buskers and push-carts. Many buildings have been refurbished, while the new lighting makes this an attractive area to wander in the evening in search of the perfect taverna.

Map on page 110

The entire area is a huge sprawl of shops, more upmarket towards Syntagma Square. **Monastiráki** has a market selling a weird assortment of objects, where kitsch-collectors will find much to interest them. The old **covered market**, a 19th-century gem roughly half-way between Monastiráki and Omónia squares, is the city's main meat and fish market, crowded with shoppers milling between open stands displaying fish, seafood and any variety of poultry and meat you can imagine, all being loudly praised by vendors.

The Pláka is the place to find leather goods of all kinds.

The **Pláka**, the old quarter clustering at the foot of the Acropolis, has been refurbished and restored to its former condition (or rather to a fairly good reproduction of it), the garish nightclubs and discos have been closed down, motor-vehicles prohibited (for the most part), houses repainted and streets tidied up. It has become a delightful, sheltered place to meander in. You might almost imagine yourself in a village, miles from the urban monster below. It is full of small beauties, too: look out for the Byzantione churches, the Old University, the fragmented ancient arches and walls.

Byzantine Athens is scantily represented: a dozen or so churches, many dating

BELOW: the towering Acropolis is impressive from any angle.

Map on page 110

from the 11th century, can be tracked down in the Pláka and others huddle below street level in the shadow of the city's tall, modern buildings. They are still in constant use: passers-by slip in to light a yellow beeswax candle, cross themselves and kiss an icon in near-darkness before returning to the noise outside. One of the handsomest is **Ághii Theodhóri** ❽, just off Klafthmónos Square. It was built in the 11th century on the site of an earlier church in characteristic cruciform shape with a tiled dome and a terracotta frieze of animals and plants. The **Church of Sotíra Lykodhímou** on Filellínon Street dates from the same time but was bought by the Tsar of Russia in 1845 and redecorated inside. It now serves the city's small Russian Orthodox community; the singing is renowned.

Athens museums

The newly re-opened **Benáki Museum** ❾, at the northeast corner of the National Garden, houses a wonderfully eclectic collection of treasures from all periods of Greek history – including jewellery, costumes and two icons attributed to El Greco in the days when he was a young Cretan painter called Domenico Theotocópoulos (Tue–Sun, 8.30am–3pm). Near the Benáki is another museum with a world-renowned private collection on display. The **Museum of Cycladic and Ancient Greek Art** ❿ features the prehistoric white marble figurines which were dismissed as barbaric by turn-of-the-century art critics but include Picasso and Modigliani among their admirers. They come from graves in the Cycladic islands but scholars are still uncertain of their purpose. The nearby **Byzantine Museum**, a mock-Florentine mansion built by an eccentric 19th-century duchess, contains a brilliant array of icons and church relics.

Crammed with badly-labelled treasures from every period of antiquity, the **National Archeological Museum** ⓫ should be visited early in the morning before the guided tours turn the echoing marble halls into a deafening Babel. Not to be missed are the Mycenaean collection, the Thíra frescoes and the major bronze sculptures (Mon 12.30–7pm, Tue–Fri, 8am–7pm, Sat–Sun, 8.30am–2.30pm; free Sun and public holidays).

Athens by night

The night is long in this city. Athenians fiercely resist sleep, or make up for lost nighttime sleep with a long afternoon siesta (caution: *never* telephone an Athenian between 2pm and 6pm). Cafés and bars stay open until the small hours; bars and pubs here are unlike those of other European capital: they are larger, they have tables, provide music (usually loud) and serve food (usually expensive) as well as drinks.

Three o'clock in the morning, and the traffic still won't give up. Groups linger on street-corners, goodnights take forever. The main streets are never entirely deserted. Perhaps this is one of the reasons why Athens is a safe city to walk in at night, except for the occasional bag-snatcher, for real violence is rare. The "unquiet generation" finally goes to bed; verandahs and balconies go dark, cats prowl, climbing jasmine smells stronger – and all the conflicting elements in the patchwork city seem momentarily resolved in the brief summer night. ❑

ABOVE: an icon attributed to El Greco, in the Benáki Museum. **BELOW:** a Plaka taverna sign.

Coping with Piraeus

There's no point in pretending that Piraeus (Piréas) is the kind of place anyone wants to spend much time in – unless that person happens to work in one of the air-conditioned shipping offices overlooking the harbour. But it is possible to idle away a few hours while waiting to catch a ferry, even if there are few echoes of *Never on Sunday* these days. (Low life moved to Athens during the puritanical colonels' dictatorship. Since then, successive mayors have been elected on a "smarten up Piraeus" ticket.)

The basic rule about Piraeus ferries is to get there one hour before sailing time so that you have half an hour to find the right quay before the boarding deadline: unlike other kinds of transport in Greece, ships really do leave on time. But, unless it's high summer or you require a berth, don't worry about getting tickets in advance: you can pick them up from one of the dockside agencies.

An express bus runs direct to Piraeus from both terminals at Athens airport and stops outside the Port Authority (OLP) passenger building on Akti Miaoúli Street – a useful place to know since you can leave luggage in the café upstairs free of charge between 6am and 7.30pm. (The other passenger terminal on Provlis Tselepis Quay, where the Mýkonos boat comes in, is more crowded and the staff there less accommodating.) Unencumbered, you can now get equipped for the islands and take a look around Piraeus and its environs.

Drakopoulos' bookstore on Dheftéras Merarchías has a good selection of English paperbacks, maps and island guides, as well as useful items such as toothpaste and stationery. For a meal, the Do-Nut shop nearby offers something for every stage of the day, from breakfast to *patsás* (tripe soup) – a traditional late-night dish for those arriving back in Piraeus in the early morning. Nuts and fresh fruit for the voyage are on sale at the stall next door. For something lighter, try the *ouzerié* round the corner on Filonos Street.

The radical cosmopolitan atmosphere for which Piraeus was famous 2,500 years ago still flourishes – the port and its industrial suburbs are left-wing strongholds – but few remains survive. A stretch of elegant 4th-century BC wall runs beside the coast road beyond the Pasalimáni yacht harbour, and an amphitheatre backs on to the archaeological museum on Philhellínon Street, which is well worth visiting if there's time.

Its prize exhibits are two bronze statues found by workmen digging a drain in Piraeus: a magnificent *kouros* (6th-century BC figure) of a young man, and a 4th-century helmeted Athena, looking oddly soulful for a warrior goddess. Both may have come from a shipment of loot overlooked by Greece's Roman conquerors in the 1st century BC.

Pasalimáni is crowded with medium-sized yachts – a floating campsite in summer – but towards the Flying Dolphin hydrofoil terminal you may see huge, old-fashioned two and three-masters as well as sleek motor-yachts moored. Further round the headland are cafés and fish restaurants overlooking the Saronic Gulf. ❑

RIGHT: Piraeus is constantly busy with cruise liners, ferries and cargo ships.

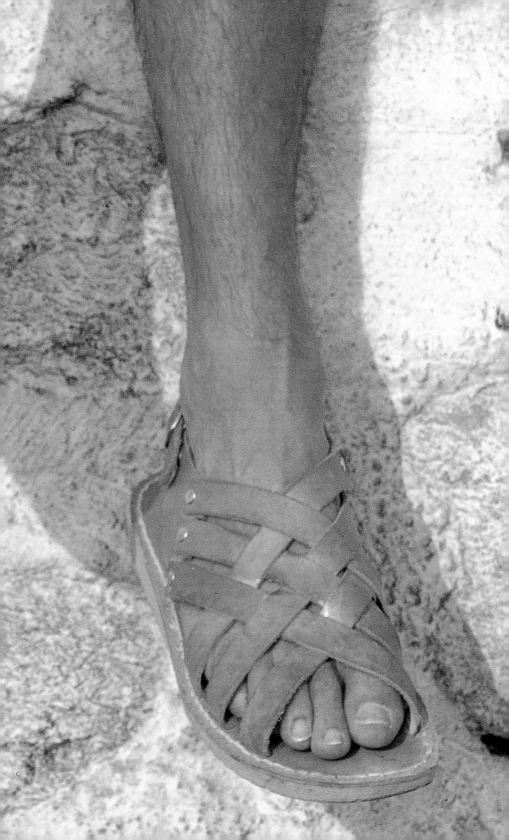

THE IONIAN ISLANDS

Corfu, Paxí, Lefkádha, Itháki, Kefalloniá,
Zákynthos, Kýthira

The islands of the west coast are known in Greek as the *Eftánisa* – the seven isles. However, the seventh island, Kýthira, lies off the southern tip of the Peloponnese and, although it is linked by history, culture and architecture, it remains quite isolated from the other six islands.

During the 8th and 7th centuries BC, wanderers from Corinth settled on the most northerly of the Ionian islands, bringing with them a distinct culture. Two centuries later the secession of Corfu from Corinth brought about the beginning of the Peloponnesian War. Over the years the Ionians have had many warrior landlords, but it is the long period of Venetian rule that has left the most indelible mark on the islands.

Artists, craftsmen and poets were often sent to Venice for their education, bringing back to the islands a cosmopolitan and international perspective. Even today, thanks to good air and sea links with Italy, the islands have a distinctly Italian flavour – and that doesn't only apply to the many pizzerias that jostle for space with tavernas on many a harbour promenade.

It is the heavy rainfall which makes the Ionians among the greenest of Greek island chains. Olive groves and vineyards are reminders that agriculture, rather than the dubious riches of tourism, still claim a part in the economy. But it is this same unsettled weather that has ruined many a traveller's holiday: from mid-September until mid-May, rains can wash out any beach outing suddenly and without warning. Fortunately, escape is never far away. The Ionians' links with the mainland are very good, and several coaches daily at the height of the season make the journey from Athens to Corfu (allow at least 10 hours), via a connecting ferry service. It's also possible to reach Kefalloniá or Zákynthos by bus and ferry from Athens.

Today the Ionians are threatened not by invaders (other than tour companies) but by earthquakes. A series of quakes has at various times beset the islands, the most recent and serious being in 1953. Casualties were great and the beautiful Venetian-built capitals of Kefalloniá and Zákynthos were flattened.

Reconstruction began almost immediately. The residents of Argostóli in Kefalloniá put up makeshift buildings which still remain, in order to resume busy, industrious lives. Zakynthians, however, elected to recreate their Venetian city on a grand scale, using original plans and grids. These contrasting attitudes to tragedy tell an island tale. ❑

PRECEDING PAGES: footloose and fancy-free; spring flowers bloom in an Ionian olive grove. **LEFT:** an excursion to the Melissáni Cave, Kefalloniá.

CORFU

Few islands have been as exploited and developed for tourism as Corfu. Yet, away from the package-tour resorts, there is much to savour in this beautiful green island

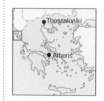

Map on page 124

A catalogue of bloody invasions and changing foreign rule chequers the history of Corfu (Kérkyra). Today, the Corfiots reap the benefits of all those battles. With a rich inheritance of olive trees dating from Venetian rule, they prosper from agricultural wealth and a thriving tourist trade.

The island known as Corcyra was colonised by the city-state of Corinth early in the 8th century BC and, basically, remained under Corinthian control for the next 150 years. In the 5th century BC, Corcyra prospered as an independent city-state, siding with Athens in the Peloponnesian War. After the Macedonians, the Romans ruled the region, but the Corfiots sided with Antony against Octavian in the sea battle of Actium in 31 BC which ended Antony's (and Cleopatra's) attempt to take over Rome. Octavian, when he became Emperor Augustus, had Corfu's temples destroyed in punishment, but thereafter the island seems to have fallen into a long and comfortable existence under Roman control.

Byzantine rule followed, with considerable instability at first, but all the Ionian islands were enjoying a period of prosperity when Normans based in Sicily moved against the Byzantines in the 11th century. This began a long series of changes, during which the island was ruled by the Venetians, the Byzantine Despotate of Epirus, the Kingdom of Naples, and the Venetians again, this time for 411 years, ending in 1797. The French ruled the island from 1797 until 1799, after which the Russians and the Ottomans, perennial enemies, cooperated as guarantors of the so-called Septinsular Republic until 1807. This was followed by French rule again until 1814, when the British took over until relinquishing the island to Greece in 1864.

One look at the architecture of Corfu town, or at any one of the churches on the island, will tell you how much this history has left its mark upon Corfiot life. The Corfiots are vibrant and full of fun, not much addicted to hard work, and (usually) warmly hospitable to the several hundred thousand visitors, many of them British, who come to the island each year.

A multicultural capital

Corfu town, also known as **Kérkyra ❶**, occupies a peninsula on the east coast. In the north are the **Old Port**, where the ferries from the mainland dock, and the **Old Fort**, dating back to the 8th century (Tue–Fri, 8am–7pm; Sat, Sun 8.30am–3pm). **Kanóni**, overlooking the picturesque Pontikoníssi island is at the southern point. In between lie the beautiful Italianate buildings of Corfu town. It is wonderful to wander down these narrow streets to encounter open squares, Venetian, French and English buildings, narrow passageways, churches, leather shops, restaurants, ice-cream stands, jewellery shops, and all the regular

LEFT: an elegant passage in Corfu town. **BELOW:** a memorial to a Venetian dignitary.

grocery stores and bakeries of a busy people. The 16th-century **New Fort (Néo Froúrio)** is in far better condition than the Old Fort (daily, Apr–Oct).

A large open space, referred to in Greek as the *spianáda*, was kept between the Old Fort and the town so attackers would have no cover. Today this esplanade gives the city a wide field of green on which, of course, the Corfiots play cricket. The two 18th/19th-century apartment buildings facing the esplanade and modelled after the rue de Rivoli in Paris are known as the Liston, referring to the "listed ones" – those members of the aristocracy who were listed in a Golden Book (*Libro d'Oro*), and thus had sufficient social standing to walk beneath the arcades. You may prefer to sit at one of the Liston cafés and drink a glass of the locally produced ginger beer.

A few blocks back in the streets behind the Liston is the 16th-century **Church of Ághios Spyrídon**, the island's guardian saint after whom many of the men are named Spyros. Ághios Spyrídon was a 4th-century Cypriot bishop whose remains were taken to Constantinople in the 7th century and then, in the 15th, smuggled back to Corfu, where he is credited with saving the island from sev-

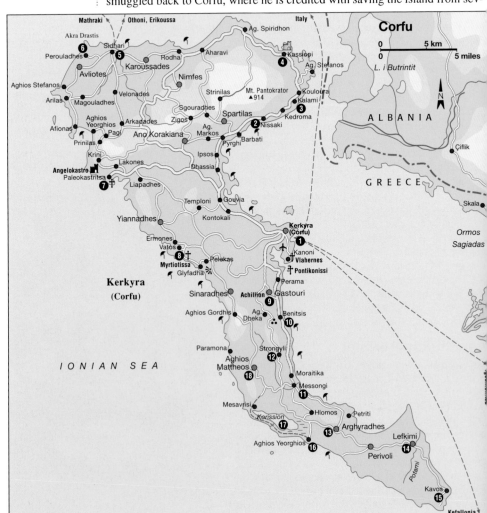

eral disasters. His casket, prominently displayed in the church, is visited frequently and carried around town four times a year.

Whatever else you may do in town, don't miss Medusa in the **Archeological Museum**, to the south of the esplanade (daily 8.30am–3pm). This is a massive, charming, gorgon pediment from the 6th-century BC Temple of Artemis in the ancient city of Paleopolis. There is nothing else like it in Archaic Greek art.

The north of the island

Along the coast road north of Corfu town is **Kontokáli**, once a village but now given over to serving the tourist trade. For all the large numbers, its small main street is quite pleasant and the restaurants plentiful. The coast all along the wide bay is filled with hotels, restaurants and stores offering virtually anything that could be of interest to the tourist trade. The best beach along this coast is the farthest, at **Barbáti**, before the mountains drop more sharply down to the sea.

If you have rented a car, the roads in the hills around **Mount Pantokrátor** can be idyllic, with views over cypresses towering dark green over silver-green olive trees. At **Nissáki 2** there is a small beach down from the road where the wonderful crystal-clear aquamarine water can be seen more easily.

The coast along the island's northeastern bulge after Nissáki is particularly beautiful, notably the small coves of **Kalámi 3**, **Kouloúra** and **Ághios Stéfanos**. Farther up the coast is **Kassiópi 4**, once a small fishing village and now a busy resort. The Roman emperor Nero gave a song recital here in AD 67, but the ruined Angevin castle on the headland is the oldest building here. There are several wonderful pebble beaches. For the night crowd, discos and bars are here in force.

Map on page 124

The White House at Kalámi, where Lawrence Durrell wrote "Prospero's Cell" is now a pleasant taverna.

BELOW: the Esplanade in Corfu town, where cricket is played.

Map
on page
124

There are salt marshes along the northern coast after Kassiópi and the beaches are not developed. **Aharávi** appears as an unappealing crossroads on the main road, but the village closer to the sea is quiet and pleasant. **Ródha** is full-tilt tourist development without judgement, although there are some good restaurants and bars. **Sidhári ❺** is headed in the same direction. There are some quiet beaches in the northwest below the pleasant village of **Perouládhes ❻**. The resort of **Ághios Stéfanos** on the northwest coast is on a human scale, and you can arrange trips here (and from Sidhári) to three of the small islands off Corfu, **Mathráki, Othoní** and **Eríkoussa**.

The most famous beaches are on the west coast, beginning with the wide bay of **Ághios Yeórghios**. The small village of **Kríni** leads to the 13th-century Angevin castle of **Angelókastro**, after which are the beautiful double bays of **Paleokastrítsa ❼**, once idyllic, now swamped. The best view of Paleokastrítsa is from the mountain above it at the Bella Vista café outside the village **Lákones**.

The smaller bay of **Ermónes** is up-market, but can be crowded. The small, rocky coast at **Myrtiótissa ❽** is popular with nudists, just before the long stretch of sandy beach at **Glyfádha**. Another highly developed, popular sand beach is further south, at **Ághios Górdhis**.

The south of the island

To the south of Corfu town, inland near the village of Gastoúri, is the pretentious **Achillíon ❾**, built in the late 19th century for the Empress Elisabeth of Austria. It used to house a casino and has also been used for European Union meetings, but it now functions as a museum (daily 8.45am–3.30pm). **Benítsis ❿**, on the coast road heading south, is heavily developed, with plenty of night life and day action. The main street in **Moraítika** is one line of restaurants/bars/shops, but the beach is good. **Messongí ⓫** is marginally more pleasant.

But as with the north, the inland roads open up another country. Taking the road high up to **Ághios Dhéka**, the journey south is best enjoyed meandering down along the road through **Strongylí ⓬**. The east coast then begs for reconsideration by the time you reach **Arghyrádhes ⓭**. Coastal villages such as **Boúkaris** and **Petrití** feel a refreshing million miles away from the dismally over-subscribed resorts up the coast.

The administrative centre of the southern part of the island is **Lefkími ⓮**, but the big package tour centre is **Kávos ⓯** on the east coast near the southernmost tip of the island. If you are an unredeemed adolescent fond of uninterrupted alcohol, junk food and carnival games, go here; otherwise, stay clear.

The western coastal section going north towards **Ághios Yeórghios ⓰** boasts long stretches of sandy beaches, which have a windswept, barren appeal. The marshland surrounding **Lake Korissión ⓱** indicates that it is not going to be as exotic as its name, but the long, flat stretches of land and still water are atmospheric. North of charming **Ághios Matthéos ⓲**, the scenery again returns to hilly splendour and the beaches get busier. Picturesque roads wind through pretty villages across the slim waist of the island, and wind their way back to Corfu town. ❑

ABOVE: the Achillíon palace is stuffed with over-the-top statuary. **BELOW:** Theotókos Monastery near Paleokastrítsa.

Working the Land

The silver olive trees that grace the Ionian landscape play more than just a picturesque part in island life. For thousands of years the olive and its oil have formed a staple part of not only the Greek diet, but the Ionian economy as well.

But for most island farmers agricultural produce is for domestic use only. And the traditional, non-mechanised farming methods employed to produce it are forced on them by the islands' hilly terrain.

A typical farming community is a disorganised scatter of 20 to 100 houses closely packed together with small yards containing chickens and the occasional pig (being fattened for Christmas). Most remote villages now have road communications and at least one telephone, but running water can often be a problem, especially at the height of summer.

A village on any Greek island that is farmed in the traditional way can usually be identified by the irregular fields which form its territory – an unusual visual aspect resulting from the system of splitting up the land to form inheritances and marriage dowries.

A remote village has probably three types of farmers. First, there's the large-scale goatherder with 100 to 500 animals, who purchases food such as maize and animal-feed cake. He concentrates on producing kids or lambs for the peak periods of Easter and the New Year. The second is the small-scale farmer, who simply wants to keep his household supplied with bread, pulses (lentils, broad beans and chick peas – the staple diet of winter) and vegetables. Finally, there's the single, elderly woman who owns a few goats and a few acres, and works them on her own.

Once the bitter winds of winter arrive, most small-scale farmers collect branches from wild bushes like the strawberry tree and bring them down from the hills by donkey for feed. In some remote villages the proportion of elderly people is quite high, and it is not unusual to see 80-year-olds scaling mulberry trees.

In spring, they take their animals to graze in fields away from the village. As the season progresses the ubiquitous vegetable gardens begin producing tomatoes, potatoes, beans, and aubergines. These crops supplement the diet well into the summer but involve the investment of much time, labour, and effort.

In June the work in the fields is back-breaking, for the harvest is reaped by hand with a sickle or scythe. The cut crop is laid out in the fields to dry, then (if grain) carried back to be threshed. Threshing is now usually done by machine but in some islands it is still done by walking a team of hired mules or donkeys over the strewn crop to smash the husks with their hoofs. Then it is winnowed and sieved.

These traditional farming methods are quickly disappearing. The exodus of the youth from the villages to the towns or the mainland to find work, plus competition with other European Union farmers, have meant that methods must change. The number of fields over-grown with scrub bear witness to this fact. However, this difficult but picturesque way of life does still exist; to witness it, you just need a sharp eye and a willingness to climb a few hills. ❑

RIGHT: gathering *horta* – wild greens

SOUTHERN IONIAN ISLANDS

Everything here, from architecture to food, has been influenced by the Italians, who continue to arrive in large numbers every August. Yet every Ionian island has its own character

Map on page 130

Paxí (or **Paxós**), the smallest of the seven main islands of the Ionian archipelago, is a three-hour boat trip from Corfu. It is hilly and green, with rugged cliffs, several littoral caves, and several good, although not sandy, beaches, all interspersed with groves of olive trees. The gnarled, twisted trunks of these trees, and their leaves like silver coins tossed in the breeze, are landmarks of the island, and represented the major source of income before the coming of tourism. Paxí's olive oil is regarded by many as the best produced in all Greece, and has won many international medals.

The pleasures of a stay on Paxí are simple. There is little in the way of organised entertainment, and although each year the island becomes more popular, the unpredictable Ionian weather means that ferries and smaller craft occasionally cannot land at all, unintentionally preserving a tranquil and low-key atmosphere.

The boats dock at the small main town, **Gáïos ❶**, set around one main square and sheltered from the winds by the two islets of **Ághios Nikólaos** and **Panaghía**. Ághios Nikólaos has a 15th-century windmill and Venetian castle on it, and Panaghía has a monastery. Gáïos itself has narrow old streets, a few grand 19th-century buildings with Ventian-style balconies and shutters, and several tavernas.

The island has one main road, which meanders north from Gáïos to Lákka and passes through the attractive harbour village of **Longós** on the eastern coast. There are rooms to rent here, and some good tavernas, but better swimming on this coast is to be had at the adjacent Levrehió beach.

The most photographed site is the little horseshoe bay at **Lákka ❷** with the Byzantine Church of Ypapántis and two beaches. Rooms can be rented here, and there are several restaurants. There will, almost certainly, also be many yachts.

The eastern coast of the little island of **Andípaxi** (Antípaxos) is gentle and rolling, with sandy beaches; the western coast is wilder and more dramatic. Only 100 or so people live permanently on Andípaxi, but many people know it and visitors come down from both Paxí and Corfu for the day. Two tavernas are open during the summer. A day spent in Andípaxi is made all the more pleasurable by sampling the locally produced red or white wine.

Lefkádha

Lefkádha (Lefkáda, Léfkas) has several advantages as an island to visit. It can be reached by road from the mainland, over a floating drawbridge across the Lefkádha canal; it is large enough to provide considerable room and variation; it is comfortably devel-

LEFT: inside the church of Ághios Dionýsios in Zákynthos town.
BELOW: tourists in Gáïos, Paxí.

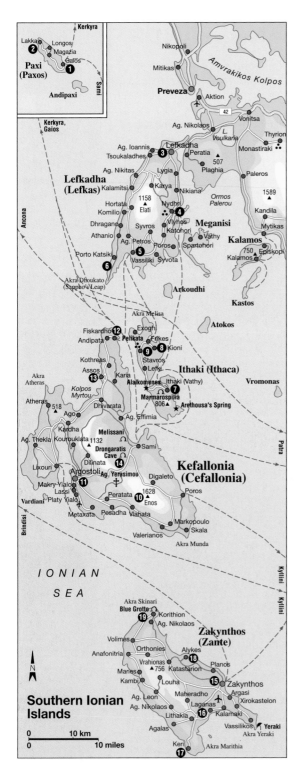

Southern Ionian Islands

0   10 km
0   10 miles

oped along the eastern coast; and it has beautiful beaches along the northern and western coasts.

Lefkádha town ❸ faces the canal and provides extensive and very safe mooring for a number of yachts. The pedestrian-only main street is lined with shops where you will find anything you are likely to need, from yacht supplies to pharmacies, shoe stores to the post office. There are also some extraordinary churches, all dating from the last years of the 17th and first years of the 18th centuries. They look for all the world like Baroque churches lifted from Italy, shrunk en route, and set down in Lefkádha. The first, and oldest, you will see is the **Church of Ághios Spyrídon** on the main square.

The east coast is green and gentle, though the mountains are close enough to provide dramatic background. Many of the island's olive groves and vineyards are along this protected coast, where there are hotels and rooms for rent and calm water beaches all the way through **Lygiá** and **Nikiána** down to the tourist boom town of **Nydhrí ❹**, 20 km (12 miles) south of Lefkádha town on the northern edge of the deeply indented Vlyhó Bay.

Thirty years ago Nydrí was a tiny fishing village where Aristotle Onassis used to come over from his private island of **Skorpiós** for dinner; now it is full of yachts and package tourists. Five km (3 miles) further south is **Vlyhó**, much calmer and more pleasing, but the shallow water in the bay is uninviting. The road climbs after Vlyhó, and the elevated view back over Vlyhó toward Nydrí is lovely.

On the south coast there is a good pebble beach below **Póros**, but the most dramatic cove is the narrow, curved bay of **Syvóta**. The muddy shore by the village does not invite swimming here, but there are some good tavernas. The road continues over the mountain to **Vassilikí ❺**, 40 km (25 miles) south of Lefkádha town, a fine little harbour and a great long beach, the goal for many windsurfers.

Boats run from here to the beautiful beaches on the west coast, rounding the island's most famous landmark at the tip of the peninsula, the rocky headland known as **Sappho's Leap**.

Map on page 130

The best known of the west-coast beaches is **Pórto Katsíki ❻**, now accessible by road and usually packed. Farther up the coast is a beautiful stretch of beach known as **Káthisma**, also accessible by road but so long that you can walk off and leave most of the crowd behind. **Ághios Nikítas** is another tiny, once beautiful fishing village now utterly overwhelmed by the summer crowd. In high season it is a place to avoid.

Another long stretch of beach runs a couple of kilometres north of Ághios Nikítas; it is not as pretty as Káthisma and not developed. More beaches, notably below the village of **Tsoukaládhes** which can be reached by car, are strung out along this northwestern coast, but most of them can be reached only by boat.

From **Ághios Ioánnis** at the edge of the mountain there is a continuous stretch of beach all the way past the old windmills and around the shallow saltwater lake known as the Yíra to the lighthouse at the canal entrance. Most people go to the section of beach at Ághios Ioánnis, where the water can be seen from the road and there are some restaurants, but if you want more privacy you can stop anywhere along the road by the Yíra and walk over the dunes to the sea. Across the canal at the entrance is the island's 14th-century fort of Santa Maura, on the mainland since the canal was dredged in 1905. Behind Ághios Ioánnis on the edge of the mountain is the 17th-century **Monastery of Faneroméni**, which has beautiful views down over the beach at Ághios Ioánnis, the windmills, the Yíra, Lefkádha town, and the canal.

The main trip inland is to the mountain village of **Karyá**, 14 km (9 miles)

The church of Ághios Menás in Lefkádha town has a unique clock tower made of steel girders.

BELOW: fishermen in Lefkádha harbour.

southwest of Lefkádha town. The route passes through several villages with medieval architecture in the upland plains before reaching Karyá, which has traditional architecture and a huge plane tree in the village square. The village is known for its embroidery, and you will still see some women wearing the traditional dark costumes.

Itháki

In 1939 Itháki had a population of around 15,000; now it is nearer 3,000, thanks to mass emigration – particularly to Australia and South Africa – following the 1953 earthquake.

The archeological evidence that this actually was the ancient home of Odysseus, the wandering hero of Homer's *Odyssey*, is not conclusive, but everyone who lives on the island has no doubt. Most boats dock at the main town, **Vathý ❼** (meaning "deep"), at the end of a deeply inset bay. The town was badly damaged by an earthquake in 1953 but much has been rebuilt in the old style. The many tavernas and bars along the waterfront are particularly attractive in the evening. There are two pebble beaches near town, and several others you can reach by boat for day excursions.

Near Vathý are three sites associated with Odysseus: **Arethousa's Spring**, the **Cave of the Nymphs**, and ancient **Alalkómene**. The walk from Vathý to Arethousa's Spring is a 1½ -hour walk, somewhat arduous but with beautiful views. On arriving home after his epic voyage, Odysseus is supposed to have waited for his son Telemachos here before returning to his palace to eject his wife's suitors. The unimpressive Cave of the Nymphs above Dexiá Bay (where he is said to have landed) is where Odysseus supposedly hid the 13 tripods that had been given him by the Phaeacians (ancient Corfiots, according to modern Corfiots).

BELOW: Itháki's capital, Vathý.

The ruins locally known as the **Castle of Odysseus**, on the site of the ancient city of Alalkomene, are 5 km (3 miles) west of Vathý, on the road between

Dexiá Bay and the little port of **Píso Aetós**. The archeologist Heinrich Schliemann believed he had found Odysseus' palace here but, although subsequent excavations have uncovered evidence of a settlement dating back to 1400 BC, there is nothing to link it to Odysseus.

Itháki is actually two peninsulas joined by an isthmus barely wide enough for the island's main road. In the northern half, the two lovely little port villages of **Fríkes** and **Kióni** ❽ on the east coast are ideal places to stay, if you can find a place. Kióni is the more attractive but Fríkes is open to tourists longer and has better tavernas. Both have beaches a short walk away.

The route north across the isthmus from Vathý, along the coast to the villages of **Léfki** and **Stavrós** ❾, is particularly beautiful. The medieval Church of the Dormition of the Virgin (**Kimisís tis Theotókou**), in the small village of **Anoghí** below Stavrós on the inland road, has a wonderful iconostasis and Byzantine frescoes. **Moní Katherón**, 3 km (2 miles) further south, has a magnificent view back toward Vathý.

Stavrós is a pleasant but undistinguished town above the nearby **Pólis** beach. The name means "city" but there are no signs of a city here in this beautiful bay. Remains of the island's oldest settlement are on Pilikáta Hill in Stavrós. They are not much to see but do date from the 3rd millennium BC and constitute a more substantial claim to being Odysseus's castle. For the most beautiful view on the island, go on past the little hill village of **Exoghí** (the name means "out of the earth") to the chapel. It would be difficult to find a more beautiful vista anywhere in the Ionian Islands, or anywhere at all. Another road from Stavrós leads to the village of **Platrithiás**, which also has Mycenean remains, known as Homer's School, and a path to the undeveloped pebble beach in Afáles Bay.

Map on page 130

Stavrós is one of several places in Itháki claiming to be the site of Odysseus's castle, and marks its claim with this bust of the Homeric hero.

BELOW: relaxing at Vathý harbour.

*Argostóli's museum
tells the recent
history of the island
and its earthquakes
in photographs.*

BELOW: an overview
of Kefalloniá.

Kefalloniá

Kefalloniá (Cephalonia) is the largest and most mountainous of the Ionian Islands, with a population famous throughout Greece for being of independent mind. The island is dominated by the towering **Mount Énos** (Aínos) , at 1,628 metres (5,340 ft) the highest mountain in the island group and covered with, reasonably enough, Cephalonian fir.

The capital town of **Argostóli** ⓫, almost totally destroyed by the 1953 earthquake, has been rebuilt in a utilitarian, rather than a graceful style. Buildings are squat, square and unlovely, giving a vague impression of a frontier town from a cowboy film. Nevertheless, the town has a rough and ready charm centred around the main *platía*. Sights to see include the **Historical and Folk Museum** in the Korghialénios Library (Mon–Sat, 9am–2pm), which contains folk costumes, rustic farming implements, Byzantine icons and some moving photographs of Argostóli before and immediately after the earthquake.

The west coast of this section of the island below Argostóli has some wonderful beaches, beginning at **Lássi** with **Makrý Yialó** and **Platý Yialó**, and continuing all the way down the coast. The beaches near Lássi can become heavily populated, but they are so large that there is always room. Sea water flows into the unusual so-called "swallow holes" (*katavóthres*) near Argostóli and reappears on the eastern side of the island near Sámi at Karavómylo. Although now just a trickle, before the 1953 earthquake the flow was strong enough to power flour mills.

Inland from Argostóli, in the area known as Livathó above the village of **Peratáta**, is the island's Venetian capital, **Ághios Yeórghios**, inhabited from the 13th century until it was damaged by an earthquake in the 17th century. The ruins, particularly of the castle on the top of the hill, are in relatively good condition and worth seeing.

There are many fish farms along the road on the east side of the Argostóli Gulf, and the west side is not particularly inviting. **Lixoúri** can be reached by frequent ferries from Argostóli. Built since 1953, the town itself is rather dull, but it has some comfortable hotels and restaurants. The first beach to the south, Lépedha should be passed up for the beaches of **Mégas Lákkos** and **Xi**, beautiful stretches of red sand backed by cliffs. The only problem here is that when there is a southerly wind the beaches tend to collect seaweed. Between them is **Kounopétra**, the huge boulder that was so unstable that it rocked until the 1953 earthquake set it still. There is a fine pebble beach at **Petaní** in the northwest of this peninsula.

The island's most famous resort is the small port of **Fiskárdho** ⓬, on the northern tip. The name is a corruption of the name of the Norman leader, Robert Guiscard, who captured the island in 1082 but died here in 1085. There is good anchorage here for the many – very many – visiting yachts. In high season the village is packed. There are wonderful small pebble beaches, many of them decorated with cypress trees, all around this northern part of the island. Ferry boats run from Fiskárdho to both Lefkádha and Itháki.

The north of the island has not been much damaged by earthquake, as you can see in the picturesque village

Map on page 130

of **Ássos ⓭**, which sits on the isthmus leading to a hill rising sharply out of the sea. The large Venetian fort on the hill's summit was built in the last decades of the 16th century. South of Ássos, still on the east side of the large Gulf of Mýrtos, lies the dramatically beautiful beach at **Mýrtos**. If you swim here when the swell is high you should treat the undertow with considerable respect.

The road from Argostóli to **Sámi** on the east coast is more interesting than the town itself, from where ferries head off for several destinations. Just north of Sámi is **Karavómylo**, where the sea water from the *katavóthres* near Argostóli reappears after passing through the island. **Melissáni**, 2 km (1 mile) north of Sámi, is an underground lake with part of its roof open to the sky. When the sun shines down on the waters the colours are magnificent.

The large **Drongaráti Cave ⓮**, just west of Sámi, is an emormous chamber with multicoloured stalactites and stalagmites, among which space has been arranged for concert performances. **Aghía Effimía**, north of Sámi, is a fishing village now being developed. All along the coast, from Sámi down to Póros the mountain drops steeply to the sea and there are little coves that are incomparable but accessible only by boat.

Kefalloniá is noted for its honey (thyme-scented), quince jelly, rabbit stew and a local speciality called riganáta – feta cheese mixed with bread, oil and oregano.

Zákynthos

Zákynthos or Zante is yet another beautiful island with green mountains and plains, Venetian architecture, stunning beaches, wonderful tourist development, and tourist development run amok. Much of the large harbour town of **Zákynthos ⓯** was rebuilt after the 1953 earthquake in the same style, so it may appear like a movie set. The boats dock by Plateí Solomoú, named after Dionýsios Solomós, the 19th-century Greek poet who wrote the words to the Greek

BELOW: the church is reflected by contemporary island life.

Map on page 130

The reason they build their houses so lowe [in Zákynthos] is, because of the mani-fold Earthquakes which doe as much share this Iland as any other place in the World.

— THOMAS CORYAT, 1612

BELOW: Zákynthos town seen from the *kástro* of Bóhali.

national anthem. The 17th-century **Church of Ághios Dionýsios**, the island's patron saint, with its campanile, are on the left of the harbour as your boat approaches, and the 14th-century **Church of Ághios Nikólaos tou Mólou** is on the right. Take the time to visit the **Museum of Post-Byzantine Art** facing the sea along the square (Tue–Sun, 8am–2.30pm). The museum has beautiful works of the Ionian school formed by Cretan artists who fled the Ottoman occupation of Crete and met Ionian artists strongly influenced by the Italian renaissance. Some of the 17th and 18th-century paintings are superb.

In medieval times the people lived above the present town in the area known as **Bóhali**, within the walls of the large *kástro*. Construction began in the 14th century, when an Italian dynasty from Naples ruled the island, and continued under the Venetians. The walls provide fine views of the green inland plain and mountains as well as the hotels in Laganás Bay to the south.

All-night partying

The main destination for most visitors is the long beautiful white sand beach adjoining **Laganás ⑯**, along which has grown an agglomeration of hotels and restaurants and bars and fast food joints and discos. If you like to party all night then this is the place. The explosive tourist development at Laganás Bay is relatively new. For centuries, perhaps millennia, the gentle beaches here have been major nesting grounds for loggerhead turtles, which come here every summer to lay their eggs (*see facing page*). The Sea Turtle Protection Society patrols the beach to protect the nests and operates an information booth to tell visitors about the gentle creatures which may well startle you exceedingly as you swim. A long stretch of isolated beach to the east has been bought by the Greek World Wide Fund for Nature to try to provide undisturbed nesting areas.

The more beautiful parts of Zákynthos are to be found at the island's edges. The southeast peninsula below Zákynthos town past **Argási** has some wonderful beaches along the east coast, culminating in the beach at **Yeráki** at the southern tip. This is also a protected turtle nesting ground so visitors cannot stay on the beach after sunset.

At **Kerí ⑰** on the southeast peninsula there are incomparable views of the sea and the harbour from which boats can take you along the little beaches and grottoes along the west coast. The beaches on this island defy superlatives. The shoreline above **Kámbi**, on the southwest coast, has Shipwreck Cove, where an old wreck rests in the sand between towering cliffs. Inland from the west coast lies the sprawling village of **Volímes**, noted for its weaving and for the honey and cheese you can buy from roadside stalls.

Two beach resorts on the island's north coast, both quieter than those to the south, are **Tsiliví** and **Alykés ⑱**, the latter being particularly good for windsurfing. The island's most northerly resort is **Ághios Nikólaos**, which has a hotel, a couple of tavernas and a small sandy beach. From Ághios Nikólaos you can take a boat trip to the **Blue Grotto ⑲**, on the northern tip of the island, where two sea caves interconnect and the sunlight on the brilliantly clear water reflects blue on to the walls. ❑

Turtles v. tourists

The loggerhead turtle crawls out of the sea onto the moonlit beach of her birthplace, the island of Zákynthos. She has crossed the length of the Mediterranean to return, at last, to this spot. Summoning all her strength, the 90 kg (200 lb) reptile carefully selects a place in the sand where she digs a nest with her rear flippers. Into it she lays 100 soft eggs, each the size of a ping-pong ball, covers them with soft sand and returns exhausted to the sea to rest in the shallows. Then she swims away – unaware that her labour may have been in vain. For here on Zákynthos, tourism is threatening these ancient creatures with extinction.

The survival of the loggerhead (*Caretta caretta*) is endangered before she even reaches the beach. In the early evening, the shallow coastal waters are filled with female turtles resting after their long journey to the island. It has been estimated that nearly half of them may be maimed or killed by pedalos or the propellers of speedboats taking out waterskiers and para-gliders. Carelessly discarded litter from the 30,000 tourists creates another hazard, as turtles suffocate trying to swallow plastic bags which they mistake for jellyfish, a favourite food.

For the female turtle, the hazards increase when she slips ashore. Disorientated by the glittering lights of hotels and the strange noises coming from the tourists and tavernas, she may scurry back to the seas, uncertain where to deposit her eggs. Those that try to continue their labours may suffer the indignity of ignorant spectators brandishing torches and flashing camera lights, frightening the turtles back into the sea where the eggs may be released never to hatch.

The eggs that are successfully laid are often doomed by motorcyclists, horse riders and car drivers who speed across the sand, packing it down so that it is impossible for the hatchlings to emerge. Beach umbrellas are unwittingly driven into nests, piercing the eggs. Tamarisk trees, planted in haste to shade sunbathers, pose another problem as hatchlings become tangled up in the tree roots. Even the innocent sandcastle builder may create holes which become shallow graves for the young turtles.

Hatching takes place from early August to late September – the time of year when most of the tourists arrive. The 6-cm (2½-in) hatchlings may emerge from their hazardous 50-day incubation and, instead of heading instinctively to the light on the horizon line at sea, frequently wander confused up the beach to the dazzling lights of the hotels and bars. This error brings death from exhaustion or from dehydration.

For thousands of years Zákynthos has hosted the greatest concentration of nesting turtles in the Mediterranean. The Laganás bay coastline was once a favourite spot but, confused by the combination of boats, buildings and noise that tourism has brought, the turtles have abandoned the busy sands. The majority now nest in the more secluded beaches of Sekánia and Dáfni, where there is barely room for the activities of the bewildered reptiles. Only 800 turtles now breed on Zákynthos, barely half the number to be found here 15 years ago. ❑

RIGHT: the loggerhead runs countless risks.

KÝTHIRA

Geographically nearer to Crete than to the Ionian group, this is one of Greece's quietest islands. Most visitors are Greeks from Athens – or Greek Australians returning home

BELOW: a native of Kýthira.

In legend Kýthira, suspended off Cape Maléa in the Lakonian Gulf, was one of the birthplaces of Aphrodite (the other, stronger contender is in south-western Cyprus). Essentially a bleak, thyme-covered plateau slashed by well-watered and vegetated ravines, the island forms part of a sunken land bridge between the Peloponnese and Crete, from where many Venetian refugees arrived in the 17th century.

And an in-between sort of place it is, in many respects: it has two names (Tserigo was its Venetian alias); a history of Venetian and British rule like the bona-fide Ionian islands, but today governed from Piraeus along with the Argo-Saronics; an architecture that's a hybrid of Cycladic and Venetian; and a pronounced Australian flavour, courtesy of remittances and personal visits from 60,000 emigrants Down-Under – and ubiquitous eucalypts.

Kýthira (also spelt Kýthera and Kíthira) frankly does not put itself out for outsiders. Accommodation is expensive and oversubscribed, good tavernas are thin on the ground. Habitually rough seas, which can play havoc with daily ferries from Neápolis on Cape Maléa, prompted the construction of an all-weather harbour at Dhiakófti in 1997, though local politics kept this from being fully operational until 1999. Despite all that, Kýthira seems increasingly popular as a haunt of trendy Greeks, thanks to regular hydrofoils and flights from Athens – plus the **Hóra ❶** (also known as **Kýthira**), one of the finest island capitals of the Aegean.

The imposing, flat-roofed mansions of the lower town date from the 17th to 19th centuries. The Venetian **kástro** overhead is of earlier vintage. Still intact is an elaborate domed cistern system, while up top a few rusty cannon guarding a Venetian church seem superfluous, given the incredibly steep drop to the sea at **Kapsáli**. This is the yacht and alternative hydrofoil berthing, and where most tourists stay, though its beach is mediocre.

The best beaches

Much better beaches lie east of Hóra at **Halkós**, south of **Kálamos** village, and at **Fyrí Ámmos**, east of Kálamos, with sea-caves to explore. North of Fyrí Ámmos, and easier to get to, more excellent beaches dot the east coast: **Kombonádha**, **Kaladhí** with a rock monolith in the surf at one end, and two – **Asprógas** and **Paleópoli** – to either side of Kastrí Point with its Minoan settlement, which was explored by Heinrich Schliemann in 1887.

The beachy strip ends at the fishing anchorage of **Avlémonas ❷**, where seemingly half the island's population turns up for weekend lunches at the main fish taverna. The diminutive octagonal Venetian fort at the harbour mouth is scarcely more than a gun

emplacement. There's a better, 16th-century castle, complete with a Lion of St Mark, at **Káto Hóra**, just outside the attractive village of **Mylopótamos ❸**, with a waterfall and abandoned mill in a wooded canyon. Like similar ones in the Cyclades, the Káto Hóra fortress was not a military stronghold but a civilian refuge from pirates, with derelict houses inside the gate.

Some 2.5 km (1½ miles) west of Káto Hóra, perched above the surf-lashed west coast, the black-limestone cave of **Aghía Sofía ❹** is the best of several namesake caves on Kýthira. A 13th-century hermit adorned the entrance with frescoes of Holy Wisdom personified, and three attendant virtues, though the inner cave was never inhabited, being too remote and dry. (Locals insist that Aphrodite slept there, but today the only endemic life is a minute white spider.) About one-sixth of the cave, and marvellous stalactites and stalagmites, are open for visits (Jun–Sep; Tue, Thu, Sat, Sun, 10am–2pm; Wed, Fri 4–8pm).

Capital of Kýthira after 1248, the ghost village of **Paleohóra ❺** in the northeast of the island failed the pirate-proof test in 1537, when the notorious Barbarossa spotted and sacked it. The ruins, including six frescoed (and locked) churches, cover the summit of a high bluff plunging to the confluence of two gorges which unite as Kakí Langádha, reaching the sea at a small lake.

Potamós ❻, 2 km (1¼ miles) north of the Paleohóra turning, is Kýthira's second village, most notable for its Sunday-morning farmer's market.

Aghía Pelaghía, the former ferry port with a scruffy beach, has come down in the world since **Dhiakófti** commenced working. More rewarding is **Karvás ❼**, the northernmost and prettiest of the ravine oasis-villages that Kýthira abounds in. This valley meets the sea at **Platiá Ámmos** beach; pebbly **Foúrni** cove lies adjacent. ❑

So many Kythirans (possibly 60,000) have emigrated to Australia that the post office in Hóra contains a Sydney telephone directory.

> Map on page 139

BELOW: Kapsáli harbour seen from Hóra high above.

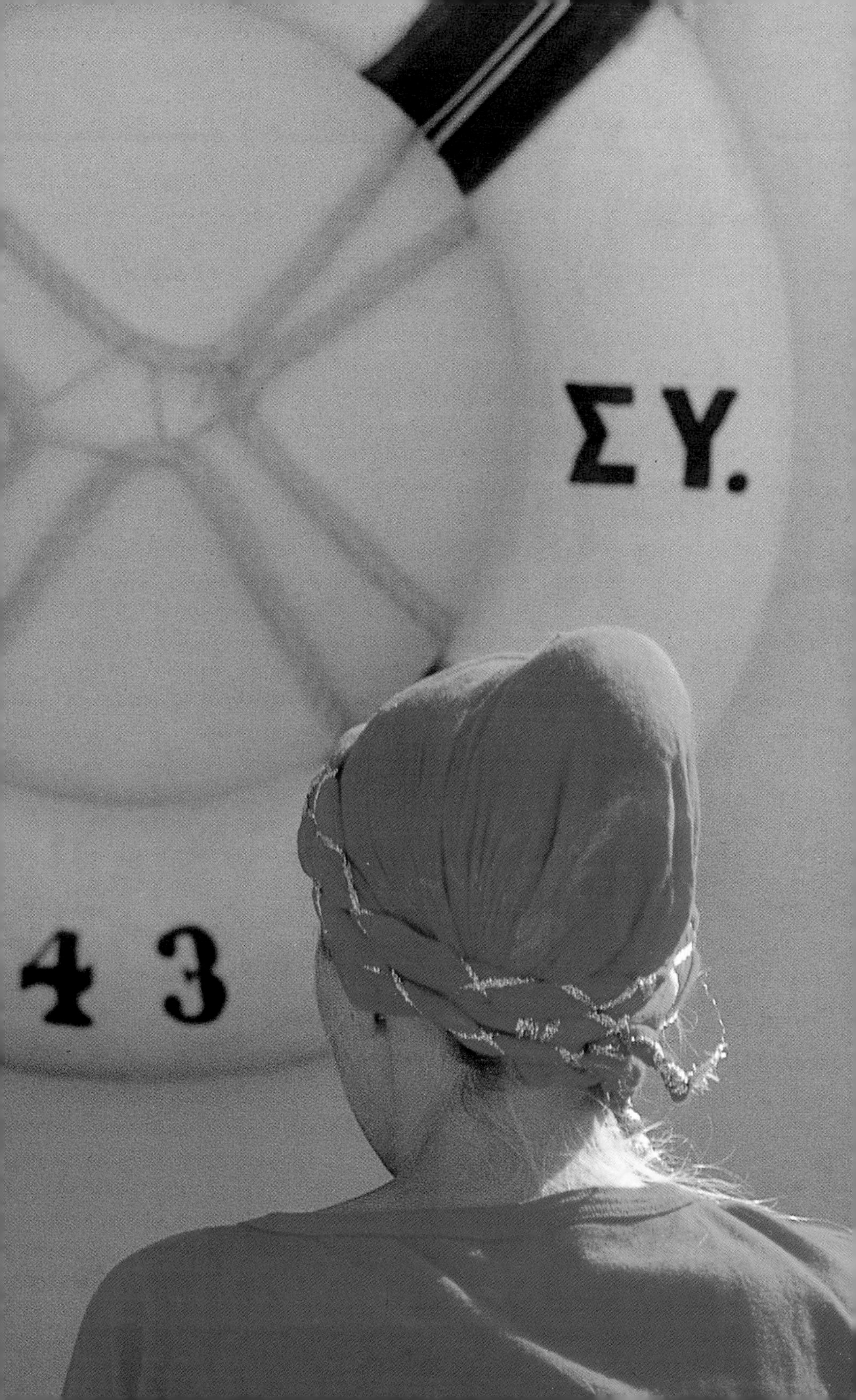
ΣΥ.
43

ISLANDS OF THE SARONIC GULF

Salamína, Aegina, Póros, Hydra and Spétses

The five islands of the Saronic Gulf might best be described as "commuter" islands. As they are within a short ferry ride (or even shorter hydrofoil trip) from Piraeus, the temptation is to treat the islands as an extension of the mainland or, more specifically, suburbs of Athens.

Entrepreneurs have been quick to exploit the proximity. The one-day cruise from Piraeus calling at Aegina, Hydra and Póros is a very popular atraction for tourists visiting Athens (rivalled only by Delphi as the most enjoyable day spent out of town). When the cruise ships mingle with the ferries, the hydrofoils and the regular scheduled caiques, there is often a virtual traffic jam on the waters, and foreigners easily outnumber Greeks at most Saronic ports.

In spite of all this, these are Greek islands, not Athens suburbs – distinctive in character, rich in history and, behind the crowds and chi-chi boutiques, remarkably attractive. Salamis (Salamína) is renowned for the epoch-making battle in 480 BC which decided the outcome of the Persian Wars. Aegina (Éghina) is the site of the Temple of Aféa, one of the most important antiquities located on any Greek island.

Póros has been immortalised by Henry Miller in one of his books, and Spétses by John Fowles in one of his. Not to be outdone, since the 1960s Hydra (Ydhra) has attracted artists, film-makers, well-heeled Athenians, trendy French and Italians, movie stars and other international celebrities.   ❏

PRECEDING PAGES: passengers on a ferry in the Saronic Gulf; donkeys patiently awaiting tourists at Hydra harbour. **LEFT:** octopus drying on the washing line.

ARGO-SARONIC ISLANDS

These five islands are all within easy reach of the mainland, and popular with Greek day trippers. Nevertheless, they are distinctive, rich in history and remarkably attractive

Map on page 148

Salamína

This low, flat island (also called Salamis) is popular with Athenians but offers little interest to visitors. It is the largest of the Saronic Gulf islands, but so close to Athens that most Greeks regard it as part of the mainland. The most fun to be had might well be the half-hour journey from Piraeus; the tiny caique laden with commuters reading tabloid newspapers threads its way between huge liners destined for more exotic locations.

Salamína is best known for the 480 BC ancient naval battle in which the outnumbered Athenian ships routed Xerxes' Persian fleet, the Greek ships being the "wooden walls" that the oracle of Delphi had predicted would save Athens. Today the island is decidedly not posh. Its appeal is that it is not much developed and can be reached so quickly, just a few minutes' ride across from **Pérama** to the port of **Paloúkia**, a town with a strong naval presence and a couple of waterside tavernas.

Most of the inhabitants live in the island's capital, **Salamína** (or **Kouloúri**) **❶**, which has an archaeological and a folk museum. Boats also leave regularly from Piraeus harbour for Selínia, Paralía Kakís Víglas, Peráni, and Peristéria on the east coast. The island's pride, the late 17th-century **Faneroméni Monastery**, is on the northwest coast, 6 km (3½ miles) from Salamína town. The pleasant village of **Eándio ❷** on the west coast has a good hotel. From here you can go down to the southeast coast of **Peráni** and the small but very pretty little harbour of **Peristéria**.

Aegina

Aegina (or Aigina or Éghina) is close enough to be within easy reach of the mainland and far enough to retain its island identity. About an hour and a half by ferry from Piraeus, or half an hour by the hydrofoil, Aegina has had little trouble attracting visitors. Long a favourite Athenian retreat, it remains more popular among weekend smog evaders than among foreign tourists or Greeks from elsewhere.

Aegina's main produce is pistachio nuts, which you can buy at shops and stands along the harbour street. Shaped on the map like an upside-down triangle, Aegina's south is marked by the magnificent cone of **Mount Óros**, the highest peak in the Argo-Saronic Islands, visible on a smog-free day from the Acropolis in Athens. The centre and eastern side of the island is mountainous; a gently-sloping fertile plain runs down to the western corner where Aegina town overlays in part the ancient capital of the island.

For a brief time (from 1826 until 1828) Aegina served as the first capital of the modern state of Greece. **Aegina town (Éghina) ❸** has several 19th-

LEFT: the massive church of Ághios Nektários, Aegina. **BELOW:** traditional pottery made in the traditional way.

century buildings constructed when the country's first president, Ioánn Kapodístrias (1776–1831), lived and worked here. The **Archeological Museu** (Tue–Sun, 8.30am–3pm) in the town displays a number of interesting artifact The modern harbour, crowded with yachts and caïques, is next to the ancien harbour, now the shallow town beach north of the main quay, towards th ancient site of **Kolóna**.

Further north from the port stands the **Kolóna** ("column"), all that remains the Temple of Apollo built in 520–500 BC. It was superseded by a late Roma fortress, fragments of which survive on the seaward side. Although from the se the position of the temple looks unimpressive, the view from the hill in la summer is very pleasant. There is a small museum on the site and the reco structed mosaic floor of an ancient synagogue (Tue–Sun, 8.30am–3pm).

The island's most famous ancient site is the **Temple of Aféa** ❹, in th northeast, above the often packed summer resort town of **Aghía Marína**. Th temple stands at the top of a hill in a pine grove commanding a splendid vie of the Aegean. Built in 490 BC, in the years after the victory at Salamis, it ha been called "the most perfectly developed of the late Archaic temples in Eur pean Hellas". It is the only surviving Greek temple with a second row of sma superimposed columns in the interior of the sanctuary. It is also beautiful an quiet, one of the most impressive ancient Greek temples you will see (Mon–Sa 8.15am–7pm, 5pm in winter; Sun 8.30am–3pm).

On the way to the Temple of Aféa you will pass by the **Monastery of Ághic Nektários**, the most recent Orthodox saint. Across the ravine from the larg monastery is the abandoned medieval city known as **Paleohóra** ("old town" where the islanders came to live after the island was sacked by pirates in the la

9th century. They were too open by attack down in the port, and lived up here until early in the 19th century. Most of the 38 churches left standing are in utter disrepair, but you can see the remains of many frescoes.

The west coast of the island is quite gentle, with a good sand beach at **Marathóna**, but better reasons to head this direction are to enjoy a meal in one of the many fish tavernas along the harbour at **Pérdhika ❺** or to go on by small hired boat to swim at the beautiful beach on the little uninhabited island of **Moní**.

Angístri is the small island facing Aegina town. It was originally settled by Albanians, but today is largely colonised by Germans, who have bought most of the houses in the village of **Metóhi**, above the port of **Skála**. The larger boats stop at Skála and the smaller boats from Aegina stop at the more attractive **Mylos**. The island is not much developed but there are several hotels. The most attractive beach is on the southwestern coast by the small islet of **Dhoroúsa**.

Lemonódassos, opposite Póros on the mainland, is a huge lemon grove with 30,000 trees – and a taverna selling delicious fresh lemonade.

Póros

Póros is separated from the Peloponnese by a small passage of water which gives the island its name – the word *póros* in Greek means "passage" or "ford". As you sail down the passage from the northern entrance, the channel opens ahead and **Póros town ❻** comes into view. It is almost landlocked and one of the most protected anchorages in the Aegean. Your first glimpse of the town will be of the white houses and bright orange rooftops, with a clock tower on top of the hill. The effect is disarming. On the mainland opposite, the village of **Galatás** makes a wonderful sight, with its white steps and dark alleys, and extensive lemon groves. Sailing through Póros is so impressive that

BELOW: the unique two-storey Temple of Aféa.

"Suddenly the land converges on all sides and the boat is squeezed into a narrow strait from which there seems to be no egress... To sail slowly through the streets of Póros is to recapture the joy of passing through the neck of the womb. It is a joy too deep almost to be remembered."

– HENRY MILLER
The Colossus of Maroussi, 1942

BELOW: the Flying Dolphin hydrofoil sails right into Póros town.

ferry captains often call out to passengers to hasten deck-side so as not to miss the extraordinary illusion that they are actually sailing through the streets of the town.

The town is built around several hills, one crowned with the blue and white clock tower. The climb to the tower is revealing – melons, grapes and flowers overhang domestic verandas. Staircases which begin with promise are apt to end in a villa-owner's market garden. This disregard for tourism is also evident along the harbour, where pride of place is given to a busy meat market.

Although a number of hotels have been built on Póros, and prominent Athenians have owned vacation houses here for decades, the island has never been fashionable like Hydra or Spétses, but during summer it gets every bit as crowded as Aegina. In 1846 the Greek naval station was established on the peninsula just before the narrow stream separating the small section of Póros town from the main part of the island. The site is now used for training naval cadets. This area contains several fine family mansions with well-tended gardens and can be a refreshing place to stroll on a hot summer afternoon.

The main sight near the sea on Póros is the **Monastery of Zoödóhos Pighi** (Virgin of the Life-Giving Spring) ❼ on a wooded hillside (20 minutes from town by bus). Only a few monks still live there today. Noteworthy is a wooden, gold-painted iconostasis dating from the 19th century.

In front of the monastery, a road encircling the heights to the east climbs through the pine woods to the ruins of the **Sanctuary of Poseidon**, in a saddle between the highest hills of the island. From here came much of the stone used in building the Monastery of the Panaghía on Hydra. The temple was excavated at the turn of the century and little remains, but its setting is rewarding.

Hydra

The island of Hydra (or Ydhra, once Ydrea, "the well watered") now appears as a long, barren rock. But the harbour and lovely white and grey stone buildings built up around the town are incomparable, attracting the artistic and the fashionable since the 1950s and many, many more ever since. It is one of the few places in the country that has reined in the uncontrolled growth of cement construction, and retained its original beauty.

Map on page 148

The heart of the island is its harbour-town, also called **Hydra (Ydhra)** ❽. All round the picturesque bay, white stone houses climb the slope accented by massive grey *arhontiká*, the houses built by the shipping families who made fortunes in the 18th and 19th centuries. Along the quay are the colourful shops of the marketplace, with the clock tower of the **Monastery of the Panaghía** in the centre. Much of the stone used in building this 18th-century monastery was taken from the ancient Sanctuary of Poseidon on the island of Póros.

Tourism to Hydra was given a boost by the 1957 film "Boy on a Dolphin", starring Sophia Loren, which was set on the island.

The harbour, girded by a little thread of a breakwater, forms a soft and perfect crescent, its two ends flanked by l9th-century cannons. The town has many good tavérnas and restaurants, as well as highly popular bars and discos. Some of the well-preserved and imposing *arhontiká* are open to visitors. The Athens School of Fine Arts has established a branch in the huge mansion built by Admiral Tombazis, which hosts artists of international acclaim. A Merchant Navy Training School occupies the Tsamádos House and across the way are the Hydriot Archives.

The higher reaches of the town and the hills beyond remain surprisingly untouched, charming and full of Greek colour. Narrow alleys and steep staircases lead from one quarter to the next. The uniformity of white walls is broken

BELOW: a 19th-century bridge at Vlyhós, Hydra.

Map
on page
148

Greece's national heroine of the War of Independence was a Spetsiot woman called Laskarína Bouboulína, who took command of her husband's ships after he was killed by pirates. Her house is behind the Dápia.

BELOW: reflections of Spétses.

again and again by a century-old doorway, a bright blue window frame, a flig of striking scarlet steps, or a dark green garden fence.

An hour's walk upwards and inland leads to the **Convent of Aghía Efprax** and the **Monastery of Profítis Ilías**, while the **Zoúrvas Monastery** is to k found in the extreme east.

Island beaches, however, are less impressive. **Mandhráki ❾**, northeast (town, has the only sand beach, but the southwest is more interesting. A wide pa goes along the coast to **Kamíni** and **Vlychós**, with its early 19th-century arche stone bridge. There are some good tavérnas in both Kamíni and Vlychós, ar water taxis available if you've had too much good fish and wine.

Spétses

Spétses (or Spétsai) is the southernmost of the Argo-Saronic Gulf island In antiquity it was known as Pityoússa, "pine tree" island, and it is still by fi the most wooded of the islands in the group. It also has more sandy beache Tourist development here is more extensive than on Hydra but less than (either Póros or Aegina, and in recent years responsible planning has helpe keep the island's charm.

Although **Spétses town ❿** has its share of bars and fast-food places, tl **Paleó Limáni** (Old Harbour) still radiates a gentle grace, its own particula magic that is apparent to even the short-term visitor. The 18th-century Italiai style mansions (*arhontiká*) one sees in this part of the town are now the proj erty of wealthy Athenian families who return to the island every summer.

Like Hydra, Spétses was one of the main centres of activity during the Gree War of Independence, using its fleet of over 50 ships for the Greek cause. Tl

island is distinguished for being the first in the arcl ipelago to revolt against Ottoman rule in 1821 an the fortified harbour, still bristling with cannons, no surrounds the town's main square, the **Dápia** (a nam sometimes applied to the whole town).

Although Spétses's fleet declined after the War (Independence, with the emergence of Piraeus as tl main seaport, the traditions of shipbuilding continu unabated. The small museum in the imposing *arhoi tikó* of Hadzighiánnis Mexís, a major shipowner i the late 18th century, contains coins, costumes, shi models, weapons and other memorabilia from tl island's past.

Outside the town to the northwest is **Anarghýric and Korghialénios College**, a Greek impression of a English public school. John Fowles taught here an memorialised both the institution and the island in h 1966 novel *The Magus*. The school no longer operat< and the buildings are used only occasionally as a coi ference centre or for special programmes. This sectic of town is less posh than the Old Harbour and h< some fine small tavernas.

The town beach by the Church of Ághios Mámas an the small beach in the Old Harbour are unattractive i contrast to the beautiful beaches of **Aghía Marína Ághii Anarghyrí**, **Ághía Paraskeví** and **Zogeri** going around the wooded southern coast of the islan from the east to the west

Pipe Dreams

A note you're likely to see behind your bathroom door warns: "Throw your paper in the bin provided." A slightly more precise instruction you might see is: "Don't put anything down the toilet you haven't consumed first." It's a sobering thought after *kalamária* and a few ouzos.

Seasoned Hellenophiles know all about Greek plumbing and observe the no-paper rule, thus avoiding clogging, flood and hysterics from landladies. They also know that it's a good idea to carry tissues or *hartopetsétes* (napkins) nabbed from taverna tables, just in case. The cramped cubicles at the back of Kostas's or Yeorghios's seldom bear close inspection, with their overflowing bins, floors awash and no loo roll. *In extremis* the brand-name cry of "Softex" is a nationally recognised distress signal.

Squat-over loos are common, especially in public conveniences. You might even come across a hole in the floor over the sea for instant and natural flushing. Some toilets can be grim: for reasons known only to themselves, some Greeks prefer to ignore the pan altogether and use the floor instead.

But in the main, toilet facilities in most tavernas and restaurants are adequate, with soap, towels and the ever-present bottle of *hloríni* (bleach). But perhaps the biggest mystery of all is why the Greeks go in for bathroom fittings that are straight out of a 1970s *Homes and Gardens*.

Visit the remotest of islands, the poorest of village rooms and you can be sure that *tó loutró* (the bathroom) will be sumptuously equipped and decorated. Colours outmoded in most countries (avocado, rose pink or even hard-to-clean maroon) are all the rage. Patterned tiles, the more garish the better, are a must, as are the bidet, shower with backless chair but no curtain, fancy taps and mirror-fronted bathroom cabinet.

The fact that there's rarely a shower tray, just a hole in the uneven floor down which you have to urge the water with the loo brush, and the door won't shut because it has been warped by the water, is neither here nor

there. Sometimes even running water seems optional. But the matching suite is essential.

"Can we drink the water?" is a normal tourist question. "Where can we *find* the water?" is a specifically Greek inquiry. Lack of fresh water is a giant problem for many islands so you may have to drink bottled, and wait patiently for the waterboat to arrive. When the boat comes in there's usually a mad scramble as families with hosepipes fill their wells, jugs and containers. You too may have to make daily trips to the pump or village tap. Most countries take H_2O for granted, but in arid Greece in high summer water is a precious commodity and conservation is the key.

Some islands have Heath Robinson water systems that rely on pumps and bewildering pipework. Pondering over pressure, bores, cisterns, pumps and ball-cocks, one visitor asked a Greek plumber why he couldn't put paper down the pan. What was the secret of Hellenic plumbing?

The workman scratched his head, sipped his coffee and finally revealed: "The pipes. She is different size from the rest of Europe. *Ti na kánoume?*" (What can we do?) ❑

RIGHT: a traditional village tap.

THE CYCLADES ISLANDS

Ándhros, Kéa, Tínos, Kýthnos, Sýros, Mýkonos, Sérifos,
Sífnos, Andíparos, Páros, Náxos, Mílos, Folégandhros,
Síkinos, Íos, Amorgós, Santoríni, Anáfi

The Cyclades fix in the mind memories and dreams of sun-drenched seascapes. The white cube houses, justly famous, have inspired many modern architects, Le Corbusier among them. The beaches are dazzling, the food fresh, fellow-travellers companionable, and the ferry connections so organised that short holidays can take in more than one "paradise".

For many people the Cyclades are Greece; other island chains are mere distractions from this blue Aegean essence. Of the 56 Cycladic islands, 24 are inhabited. The scenic highpoint is probably Santoríni. Southernmost of the Cyclades, dramatic Santoríni was created by a volcanic explosion about 3,500 years ago, and there is nothing like it. The spiritual centre remains Apollo's ancient Delos: "Cyclades" means a cycle around Delos.

There are two basic ferry routes. The first, eastern and central, takes in elegant Ándhros and religious Tínos, includes Mýkonos, Páros and Náxos – the back-packers' (and everyone else's) beat – calls briefly at undeveloped islets like Donoússa and Iráklia, and concludes in spectacular Santoríni. The second, western, arches by Kýthnos, Sérifos, Sífnos and Mílos; these are somewhat less popular, with different cultural attributes. Off both ferry routes, Kéa attracts Athenian weekenders.

The Cyclades were inhabited as early as 6000 BC. In the third millennium a fascinating culture flourished, with beautiful arts and crafts and lively commerce, as anyone who visits the Goulandris Museum of Cycladic Art in Athens will appreciate. This modern museum (on Neofytou Douka Street) is the world's first devoted to Cycladic art, which is most famous for its glittering marble female figurines.

And high culture continued to the Roman decline, with buildings, statues and poetry. Although this vast backdrop of culture and history might not be evident amidst the hedonistic jet-setters of Mýkonos or youthful merry-makers of little Íos, it is never very far away. One sunset over the Vale of Klíma, the marble-strewn valley in Mílos where the Louvre's Aphrodite (Venus de Milo to the Latinate) was discovered, is all that's needed.

As Greece's Nobel laureate poet, Odysseus Elytis, wrote: "Íos, Síkinos, Sérifos, Mílos – each word a swallow to bring you spring in the midst of summer." ❑

PRECEDING PAGES: have backpack, will travel; the elaborate dovecotes of Tínos.
LEFT: view from a church on the rim of Santoríni's crater.

THE CYCLADES

From the hectic night-life of Mýkonos and Íos to the rugged beauty of Mílos and Sérifos, and the unspoilt seclusion of tiny Kímolos and Anáfi, there is something for all tastes among these islands

Map on pages 162–3

Ándhros

The red Ándhros soil makes everything glow sienna at sunset, especially on its bare northern heights. Ándhros was settled centuries ago by Orthodox Albanians (a few still speak Albanian); their stone huts of the north contrast with the whitewash and red tile of the other villages. Golden eagles and long-haired goats may be spotted here too. Farmland is divided by painstakingly built stone walls, unusual for the pattern of triangular slates incorporated into them. From **Kalyvári**, the northernmost hamlet, roads appear as no more than chalk marks, and a diaphanous blue haze unfolds in the late afternoon to blur the distinction between sky and sea.

The port town, **Gávrio**, is only that. **Batsí ❶**, 6 km (4 miles) south, is a pleasant Cycladic "fishing" town: whitewash, cafés, beaches, packaged tours, and development at the outskirts. On the east coast, **Ándhros town (Hóra) ❷** remains remarkably unspoiled. Many of the shops look as they did 50 years ago. This is because so many rich Athenians have weekend houses here – less than three boat hours from Athens – that tourism has not been assiduously pursued. The Goulandris shipping family has created the excellent **Modern Art Museum**, a few steps north of the main square (Jul–Sep, Wed–Mon, 10am–2pm and 6–9pm). Works by modern Greek artists as well as European Modernists are featured. Entrance is free, and the sculpture garden, tiny and exquisite, is imbued with a modernist sense of play. The prize exhibit in the **Archeological Museum** (Tue–Sun, 8.30am–3pm), indeed one of the prize exhibits in all Greece, is the famous Hermes of Ándhros, a 2nd-century copy of Praxiteles' statue.

LEFT: looking down on Mýkonos.
BELOW: the Flying Dolphin hydrofoil arrives at Batsí, Ándhros.

Between Batsí and Ándhros town runs a long, deep valley, with terraces all the way up its sides toward the island's highest mountain range, which rises to 994 metres (3,260 ft). Sycamores, mulberries and walnut trees flourish amid acres of pine. Feeding all this verdure, a series of springs whirls down from the mountaintops, most notably at **Ménites**, where **Panaghía Koúmoulos** is sited. The spring is considered sacred; possibly there was a big temple to Dionysos here.

The **Monastery of Zoödóhos Pighí** ("Life-giving Spring") also claims to be on a sacred spot. Situated in the hills northeast of Batsí, the monastery is looked after by a diminishing group of nuns guarding a library of precious sacred manuscripts. Adjacent is a fountain on the eponymous spring.

Three km (2 miles) to the west, about an hour's walk from Gávrio, the remarkable Hellenistic tower of **Ághios Pétros** remains a mystery: what is it doing here? Turn off the main road at the "Camping Ándhros" signs south of the port, then follow the

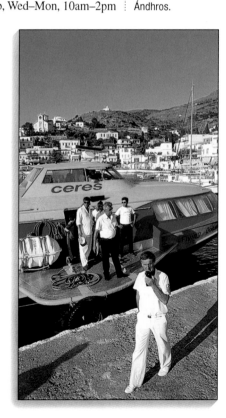

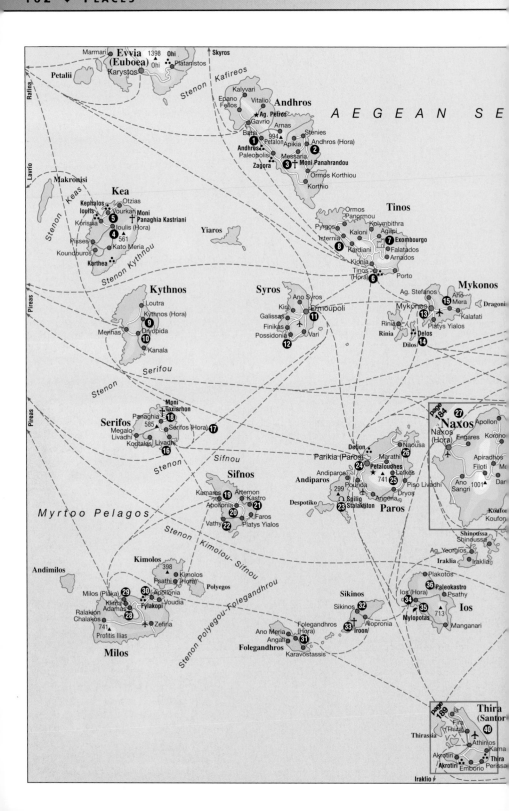

A E G E A N   S E

Marmari Evvia 1398 Ohi
(Euboea) Ohi Platanistos
Karystos Skyros
Petalii
Stenon Kafireos

Kalyvari
Epano Vitalio Andhros
Felos
Ag. Petros
Gavrio
Arnas
Batsi 994 Stenies
① Petaloh Andhros (Hora)
Andhros Apikia ②
Paleopolis Messaria
Zagora ③ † Moni Panahrandou
Ormos Korthiou
Korthio

Makronisi
Kea Otzias
Kephalos Vourkari Moni
Ioulis ⑤ † Panaghia Kastriani
Korissia Ioulis (Hora)
④ 561
Pisses Kato Meria
Koundouros
Karthea

Ormos Tinos
Panormou
Pyrgos Kolymbithra
Agapi
Isternia Kaloni ⑦ Exombourgo
⑧ Kardiani Falatados
Kionia Arnados
Tinos Porto
(Hora) ⑥

Yiaros

Kythnos Syros Mykonos
Loutra Ano Syros Ag. Stefanos Ano
Kythnos (Hora) Kini Ermoupoli Mykonos ⑮ Mera
⑨ Galissas ⑪ ⑬ Dragoni
Dryopida Finikas Kalafati
Merihas ⑩ Possidonia Vari Rinia Platys Yialos
Kanala ⑫ Rinia Delos
Dilos ⑭

Serifou
Stenon
Moni
Taxiarhon
Panaghia ⑱
Serifos 585 Serifos (Hora) ⑰
Megalo
Livadhi
Koutalas Livadhi
⑯
Stenon Sifnou

Myrtoo Pelagos

Sifnos
Kamares ⑲ Artemon
Apollonia Kastro ㉑
⑳ Faros
Vathy ㉒ Platys Yialos

Naxos
page ㉗ 184
Naxos Apollon
(Hora) Engares Korono
㉖ Naousa
Marathi Apiradhos
Deljon ㉔ Filoti Mo
Parikia (Paros) Petaloudhes Lefkes
Andiparos 741 ㉕ Piso Livadhi
㉓ Pounda Ano Dan
Despotiko Angeria Sangri 1001
Spilig Dryos Koufor
Stalaktiton Paros Koufon

Shinoussa
Shinoussa
Ag. Yeorgios
Iraklia Iraklia

Stenon Kimolou- Sifnou

Kimolos
398 Kimolos
Psathi (Hora) Polyegos
Andimilos Plakotos
Milos (Plaka) ㉙ Apollonia Sikinos Plakotos
⑳ Voudia Ios (Hora) ㊱ Paleokastro
Klima Fylakopi Sikinos Psathy
Ralakion Adamas ㉜ Ios
Chalakos ㉘ Zefiria ㉞ ㉟
741 Mylopotas 713
Profitis Ilias Folegandhros Manganari
Milos Ano Meria (Hora) Alopronia
Angali ㉝ † Iroon
Folegandhros ㉛
Karavostassis

Thira
page 189 (Santor
Ia
Fira
Thirassia Thira ㊵
Athinios Kama
Akrotiri Thira
Akrotiri Emborio Perissa

Iraklio

Cyclades

↑
N

0   10 km

0   10 miles

Samos

Ikaria

Perdiki

Ploumari

Fourni

Armenistis   Evdilos

Therma

Christos   Ag. Kirykos

Amalon   1037 ▲   Fourni

Plaghia

Karkinagri

Patmos

Kambos
Patmos

Patmos ●

Patmos

I r a k i o n   P e l a g o s

noussa

Donoussa

Kinaros

Levitha

Amorgos

Tholaria   822 ▲

Eghiali

Potamos

Moni Panaghia
③⑨ **Hozoviotissa**

Katapola   Amorgos (Hora)

Myti   **③⑦**   **③⑧**

Minoa

Arkessini

Kos

Astypalea   Vathy

r p a t h i o

Analipsis

e l a g o s   Astypalea

Kalymnos   *Kos*

Moni
Anafi   **Panaghia**
(Hora) **Kalamiotissa**
④② ● ✝ ✝

98
os   **④①** **Zoodohos Pighi**

Ághios Pétros road. South of the Paleópolis/Hóra road is the most spectacular of Ándhros's 13 Byzantine monasteries, **Panáhrandou ❸** ("Wholly Immaculate") ; 1,000 years old, it retains ties with Constantinople. The round trip on foot lasts about 3 hours (2 hours by donkey) from **Messariá**, a green valley town with the Byzantine Taxiárhis (Archangel) church.

Paleópolis, the ancient capital, doesn't give much hint of its past; but the Hermes statue in the archeological museum was discovered here. From the road 1,000 steps descend to a fine beach. A bit further south, the **Zagora** promontory is the site of a walled city-state that flourished in the 8th-century BC, Homer's time. It is fenced and excavation work has stopped.

Ándhros has many beaches; the easiest to get to are **Nimbório** south of the port, the string of beaches between Gávrio and Batsí, and **Yiália** (near Steniés, north of Ándhros town) – plus a number of lovely remote coves such as **Ághios Péllos**.

Kéa

In the last century there were a million oaks on well-watered Kéa, and many still give shade. Olive trees, however, are lacking; since ancient times, the island has been noted for its almonds. Kéa's main town, **Ioulís (Hóra) ❹**, rides a rounded ridge overlooking the island's northern reach; it was a spot chosen precisely for its inaccessibility from foreign marauders. Kéa (popularly Tziá and anciently Kéos) is now popular with Athenians. Kéa-bound boats leave from Lávrio, some 50 km (30 miles) from Athens, and land at **Korissía**, locally called **Livádhi**.

Hóra's **Archeological Museum** (Tue– Sun, 8.30am–3pm) doesn't contain much, but it's free. The **Lion of Kéa**, a 15-minute walk northeast of Hóra, is carved from granite; it is probably early Archaic. In legend it represents a lion brought in to eat evil Nereids. The smiling, maneless beast is almost 6 metres (20 ft) long.

The jagged west coast has many sandy spits, some inacessible. **Písses** and **Koúndouros** are just two of the resorts that have sprung up to accommodate Athenian escapees. Close to Korissía is the bay-

According to legend, the water from the spring at Ménites turned to wine each year on Dionysos's feast day. Today the nearby Sariza spring does the next best thing, supplying sparkling water that is sold in bottles throughout Greece.

BELOW: ploughing the red earth in Ándhros.

side village of **Vourkári** ❺, with **Aghía Iríni** church, a Minoan excavation and an ancient road. A short distance to the north, **Cape Kéfala** is the site of the oldest Neolithic settlement in the Cyclades.

Almost all Keans live in Hóra. The rest of Kéa is made up of resorts, of which the busiest, **Otziás**, in the north, has the pick of beaches. Each 15 August, pilgrims make their way to **Panaghía Kastrianí Monastery** to the northeast. The remains of four old Ionian cities – Koressia, Ioulis, Kartheia and Poiessa – testify to Kéa's one-time political importance. The first two are near their modern namesakes. Poiessa is near **Písses** and Kartheia near **Póles**, south of Káto Meriá.

Tínos

Tínos receives many thousands of tourists – but they are mostly Greeks here for the church, the **Panaghía Evangelístria** (Our Lady Annunciate). In 1823, the nun Pelaghía dreamt of an icon; it was duly unearthed and the church was built to house it. The icon's healing powers have made **Tínos town (Hóra)** ❻ the Lourdes of Greece. Women fall to their knees upon arrival, and crawl painfully to the church (the marble steps leading to it are carpeted). Healing miracles often occur. On her feast days – 25 March (Annunciation) and 15 August (Assumption), thousands of Greeks pour off the boats, including many gypsies in glittery clothes, for the procession of the little icon. The church complex is full of marble, precious votives (especially silver boats), and contains several museums. Religion is the point here, not antiquity.

The site of Poseidon's temple at **Kiónia** beach, one of the few ancient sites, is neglected, though there is still one non-Christian figure to be found among the clutter of icons, man-sized candles and plastic holy water bottles that are for sale

in the church quarter: a beatifically stark rendering of Poseidon's sea-nymph wife Amphitrite.

Map
on pages
162–3

Amidst the religious paraphernalia are also locally-produced jewellery and marble sculptures. Tínos is renowned for the latter – especially the fanlights – and there is still a marble-sculpture school in the village of **Pýrgos**. This is the place to see Tiniot artists at work or hanging out in cafés on the all-marble square. The owner of the biggest marble shop, Lambros Diamandopoulos, repairs marble belfries all over Greece.

Tínos's other hallmark is Greece's most elaborate dovecotes. There are hundreds of them inland, a tradition started by the Venetians. Their pattern of triangular windows is echoed over doorways and in fences and window-shapes. It is a pliant symbol, which seems to represent anything from the shape of a sail to, certainly in Tínos's case, the Trinity.

For a sombre reminder of the Ottoman conquest, visit the peak of **Exómbourgo ❼**, 643 metres (2,110 ft) high, with its ruined fortress. Tínos was the last island to fall to the Turks, in 1723. A bus ride to Exómbourgo and beyond will also reveal some weird, mushroom-shaped, wind-sculpted rocks, especially above **Vólax** village, famed for its basket weaving, and a proliferation of chapels, many newly constructed.

The marble carvers of Tínos are famous throughout Greece for their intricate craftsmanship. Watch them at work in the village of Pýrgos.

Kolymbíthra in the north is Tínos's best beach. **Ághios Sóstis**, near **Pórto** on the south coast, is also a long decent stretch of beach, lightly commercialised.

Of the several monasteries to see, **Katapolianí**, near **Istérnia ❽**, is exceptional. Abandoned by monks, it is inhabited by a shy farm family who will heave the old door away from the chapel's entrance for the infrequent visitor. The bay of **Isterníon** is a fabulous hike from Istérnia. Take the marble steps to a dirt path which, after 10 minutes of dust and goat blockades, leads to a marble-cobbled path down to the sea. An asphalt road and caiques go there too. Beautiful **Kardianí**, the village southeast of Istérnia, is the island's most spectacularly set – though arcaded **Arnádos** gives it competition.

BELOW: doorways and dovecotes in Tínos.

Kýthnos

After iron mining operations ceased, Kýthnos lost its prime source of income. Foreign tourism has not supplemented it, but Athenian tourism has helped. Kythniots today are mainly dairy and livestock farmers. Elderly residents and visitors frequent the thermal baths at **Loutrá** (the island's medieval name was Thermia), on the northeast coast; therefore Kýthnos is very quiet. It is also quite barren. Bowers of blossoms cultivated in family gardens provide the only colour against the dun-coloured, flat landscape.

Mérihas on the west coast has most of the accommodation on Kythnos. In summer, a "taxi-boat" runs from Mérihas to **Episkopí**, **Apókrisi** and **Kolóna** beaches. Landlocked **Kýthnos (Hóra) ❾** 6 km (4 miles) northeast of Mérihas, is exquisite. Whereas most Cycladic towns crawl spider-like over the area, Hóra follows a rectangular plan. Wood-beamed arches span across narrow streets to join two sides of one house. In the passages underneath, the rock pavements are playfully decorated in whitewash with fish,

Much of Kýthnos's electricity is supplied by a "wind park" just east of Hóra and a "solar park" on the road to Loutrá.

stylised ships, or flowers. There is a small, sweet-smelling oleander-filled main square. The fields at the back of the town rise gently away from the ravine to the south, dotted with farmhouses and tile-roofed chapels.

A walk to Loutrá (5 km/3 miles from Hóra) goes through the rural central plain. Cows sedately cross the road, udders swinging, and long-haired sheep cluster under the rare tree. The hot springs at Loutrá have coloured the soil reddish. Above Loutrá, at **Maroúla**, excavations have revealed the earliest known settlement in the Cyclades – from before 4500 BC. **Bryókastro** (Ancient Kythnos), a two-hour walk from Hóra, is a seaside ruin where the foundations of the old town are visible. A nearby islet fortress, glowering in the direction of Hydra and the Peloponnese, has also been excavated.

A stream bed splits **Dryopída ❿** (the medieval capital) into two; the chambered Katafíki cave here is linked in legend with the Nereids. The town itself presents an appealing red-roofed spectacle, especially when seen from above.

Sýros

The braggadocio in Sýros's tourist literature must be forgiven: when Sýros ceased to be Greece's premier port in the late 1800s, it lost a lot of status, too. The island remains the capital of the Cyclades, but when Piraeus sapped its steam as a trade centre, Sýros was cut off and left, as one Greek guide says, "a grand but old-fashioned lady who lives on her memories of the good old days and on her half forgotten glories." This is a shame, for with its excellent inter-island ferry links and low-key but useful facilities, Sýros can be a pleasant and rewarding place to stay.

Shipyards dominate the capital, **Ermoúpoli ⓫**. Sýros calls itself the "Man-

BELOW: worship of the sun god Apollo on a Cycladic beach.

chester of Greece", which doesn't help its resort image, but shows how proud Syrians are of their industrial importance. Although little at first seems appealing about Ermoúpoli, the scent of roasting octopus and the lights of the quayside tavernas give it a festive air at night. And one of Greece's greatest *rembétika* musicians, Markos Vamvakaris, was a Syrian; his music remains popular in the tavernas. Behind the harbour itself a few grace-notes appear: the area called **Ta Vapória** ("the ships"), uphill from the shopping streets, is where you'll find many 19th-century neo-classical mansions (a few doubling as cheap hotels).

The marble-paved, plane tree-shaded main square, Platía Miaoúlis, is lined with imposing buildings in somewhat shabby condition. The Apollon Theatre, adjacent to the Town Hall, is modelled after La Scala in Milan; its recent renovation is still a point of pride. The tradition of the Saturday night stroll – young men on the prowl, fathers displaying marriageable daughters, women in new clothes, excited children – keeps the square lively. As you poke around the back streets, Ermoúpoli reveals itself as the most elegant neo-classical town in Greece.

The port is dominated by two hills, each capped by a church. On the lower, **Vrontádo**, stands the Greek Orthodox **Church of the Resurrection** (Anástasis). On the higher is **Áno Sýros**, the medieval Catholic quarter, dominated by **Aghíos Yeórghios** church and Capuchin monastery (adjacent is a British World War I cemetery). Ermoúpoli is one of Orthodox Greece's most Catholic towns.

Fínikas, a beachside town in the southwest, is named after the Phoenicians, probably Sýros's first inhabitants. The island's south is softer and greener than the thinly populated north and has good beaches, namely **Possidonía** ⓬ and **Vári** as well as Fínikas. At **Possidonía** (also known as Dellagrázia) there is a

The name Sýros may be derived from Osiris, the Egyptian god of corn and the dead. Ermoúpoli was named by its founders, refugees from Híos, in honour of Hermes, the god of commerce.

BELOW: a stormy day on Sýros.

Pelican Power

A nyone who visits Mýkonos returns with clear-cut memories. The string of windmills on the horizon? The sun-bleached cubic houses? The beaches, the bodies, the bars? Perhaps. But for many one of the most enduring memories of Mýkonos is Petros the Pelican. How did the island come to have such a high-profile mascot?

There are conflicting versions of the story. Mykoniots questioned on the subject of Petros would agree on only two points. First, the original Petros is dead and the bird who now sticks his formidable beak under the elbows of the fishmongers is Petros Two. Second, Petros One went missing once, and kidnapping was suspected by the islanders of nearby Tínos.

As for the rest of the Petros story, rumours run rife. Petros One is said to have died at least three different ways. He caught pneumonia and was taken to a Thessaloníki doctor, who put him down. Or someone strangled him. Or someone tried to bed the poor bird.

The record has now been set straight, and the man to do it, Bo Patrick, sits quietly each afternoon in his Little Venice photo gallery, and at night behind his bar (Bo's) near the town hall. He has a superb moustache, and squints deeply and thoughtfully at anything beyond the range of the doorway.

Born on Lésvos, Patrick spent much of his childhood and working life (mainly in television production) in America. He returned to Greece in the early 1970s. This time he came to Mýkonos, settling into his dual role as photographer and barkeeper.

Bo's skills and the fact that he got to know Petros One very well over the years resulted in a book. *Whitewash and Pink Feathers* tells the tale in detail, gleaned from older islanders and then sieved for the facts – not an easy task when dealing with any kind of Greek myth, ancient or modern. For seekers of the truth, and for anyone who has wondered about the origins of this handsome bird, here is the result of Patrick's research into the Petros story.

Four pelicans were travelling from the Black Sea to their winter home in Egypt when a storm drove them off course and grounded them on Mýkonos. Three of the birds perished, but Petros survived and was adopted by a local fisherman, Theódoros. He lived on the quayside and appeared to bask in the attention, drawing visitors to the then yet-to-be-discovered island.

One day, Petros followed a boatload of Mykoniot schoolchildren to Tínos. A malevolent Tiniot fisherman clipped the bird's flight feathers, which turned Petros from a visitor into a hostage. The Tiniot refuted Mýkonos's claim to the bird, saying he was theirs. One day, Theódoros came over to the island and the bird leapt to his shoulders. Ownership was established, a deal was struck and Petros went home to Mýkonos again, to much joyous celebration. (Today, Tínos has its own pelican, friendly but not as famous.)

In 1985, Petros was hit by a car and died. The following year, Petros Two arrived from Munich, donated by a German travel baron and dedicated to the lovers of Mýkonos.

All is now well, as pink feathers litter the quayside once again. ❑

LEFT: Petros Two, in Mýkonos since 1986.

series of churches. Pythagoras's teacher, Pherekydes, the inventor of the sundial, was from here, and several caves bear his name. Up the west coast, **Galissás** and **Kíni** are emerging beach resorts. During the rule of the Colonels, political prisoners were interned on **Yiáros**, the empty island to the north.

Mýkonos

If it weren't for Mýkonos's twisting dazzles of architecture, its plentiful beaches and chapels, and its reputation for shopping and sexy nightlife, this small blue and white island would be a dreary place. It is rocky and treeless, and there are no ancient sites. Yet people are irresistibly drawn here by the thousand. Why?

The Alefkándra district, known as Little Venice because of its balconies jutting out over the sea, is the artists' quarter of Mýkonos.

Mýkonos has made itself glamorous. Otherwise unprosperous, it has turned its ruggedness into a tourist-pleasing package that works – incidentally making it more expensive than the other islands.

Mýkonos town ⑬ has its legends, however, which include the bars, transvestite shows, fur and jewellery shops, and restaurants serving Lobster Thermidor. The most innocent-looking grandmother can be a hustler, charmingly unburdening a load of grapes on you and then demanding twice the going price. But even the smoothest of the locals is not truly in form until haggling begins for the fishermen's catch, for which they have to contend with Petros the Pelican. Later in the day, it's back to the tourists again. Luxury liners shimmer on the horizon while passengers are shipped ashore for shopping sprees, then horn-blasted reluctantly back, laden with sheepskins and gold bracelets.

It is possible to eschew all this and still enjoy Mýkonos. The **Folklore Museum** (Mon–Sat, 5.30–8.30pm; Sun 6.30–8.30pm) and the **Archeological Museum** (Tue–Sun, 8.30am–2.30pm), at different ends of Mýkonos's quay, are full of interesting objects. And the town is the prettiest and most solicitously preserved in the Cyclades, with its wooden balconies loaded with flowers, red-domed chapels and billows of whitewash. The odd-shaped **Paraportiani** (Our Lady of the Postern Gate) is probably Greece's most photographed church. **Little Venice**, a row of buildings hanging over the sea at the north, is the least frenetic part of town.

BELOW: the windmills above Mýkonos town.

Caiques start from Mýkonos town for **Dílos** ⑭, the sacred island that is the centre of the Cyclades (*see page 164*). Or one can strike inland to **Áno Merá** ⑮ 7 km (4 miles) east, the only real village on the island, which is largely unspoilt by tourism. Its main attraction is **Tourlianí Monastery**, with red domes and an ornate marble tower. It houses some fine 16th-century icons and embroideries. On the road leading to Panórmos Bay and Fteliá beach lies the 12th-century Paleokástro convent (indefinitely closed because of a collapsed roof.)

Mýkonos is famous, indeed notorious, for its all-night bars and all-day beaches. For bars, you must inquire – the scene changes all the time. For beaches, **Paradise** is straight nude, **Super Paradise** gay nude, and both are beautiful; **Kalafáti**, reached via Áno Merá, is quiet; **Platýs Yialós** and **Psárrou** are popular with families. And the reservoir lake in the island's centre attracts thousands of migrating birds – the feathered kind.

Map on pages 162–3

Ancient Delos

The tiny island of Dílos (Delos in ancient times) is nirvana for archeologists. Extensive Greco-Roman ruins occupying much of Dílos' 4 sq. km (1½ sq. miles) make the site the equal of Delphi and Olympia.

The voyage southwest from Mýkonos may be only 45 minutes but, as the caique heaves and shudders in the choppy sea, it can seem 10 times that long. Take a sweater or wear several layers as the sea breeze can be very stiff. Having accomplished these preliminaries it's then best to forget the physical and concentrate your mind on the metaphysical.

It was on ancient Delos that Leto, pregnant by Zeus, gave birth to Apollo. Delos, at that time a floating rock, was rewarded when four diamond pillars stretched up and anchored it in the heart of the Cyclades.

On arriving at Dílos, you should orient yourself to avoid getting lost among the ruins. Most of these occupy the two arms of a right angle. Ahead of you (the southern arm) are the theatre and mainly domestic buildings.

To the left is the sanctuary to which pilgrims from all over the Mediterranean came with votive offerings and sacrificial animals.

For nearly 1,000 years, this sanctuary was the political and religious centre of the Aegean and host to the Delian Festival every four years. This, until the 4th century BC, was Greece's greatest festival. The Romans turned it into a grand trade fair and made Delos a free port. It also became Greece's slave market where as many as 10,000 slaves were said to be sold on one day.

By the start of the Christian era, the power and glory that was Delos was waning and soon afterwards the island fell into disuse. During the next two millennia the stones were silent; then, with the arrival of French archeologists in the 1870s, they began to speak.

Follow the pilgrim route to a ruined monumental gateway leading into the Sanctuary of Apollo. Within are three temples dedicated to Apollo – there is also a temple of Artemis – and parts of a colossal marble statue of Apollo which was destroyed when a massive bronze palm tree fell on it. Close by is the Sanctuary of Dionysos with several phalli standing on pedestals and Dionysiac friezes. Upstanding is a marble phallic bird symbolising the body's immortality.

Continue to the stunning Lion Terrace where five anorexic, archaic lions squat, apparently ready to pounce. Below this is the Sacred Lake and the palm tree which marks the spot of Apollo's birth.

Most visitors delight in that part of Dílos which was occupied by artisans rather than gods. Their houses, close to the port, are a regular warren of narrow lanes lined by drains from 2,000 years ago, with niches for oil lamps which illuminated the streets. The main road leads to the theatre which seated 5,500. It is unimpressive but there are superb views from the uppermost of its 43 rows. Close to the theatre are grander houses surrounded by columns and with exquisite mosaics on their floors.

A word of warning: it is a good idea to stamp your feet loudly when exploring little-trafficked areas, to warn the snake population of your approach. They tend to nip at passing ankles when startled. ❏

LEFT: one of the guardians of the Lion Terrace.

Sérifos

A long tail of land slashes out to enclose **Livádhi** ⑯, the harbour of Sérifos. With a half a dozen each of tavernas, hotels, disco-bars and shops, Livádhi is a pleasant place to stay, with good beaches on either side. **Sérifos town (Hóra)** ⑰ clings closely to the mountain above and has a precipitous beauty emphasised by the starker, taller mountains. Buses ascend to Hóra regularly, but the long flights of old stone steps (a half-hour climb) make for a more authentic approach.

Map on pages 162–3

Hóra has two parts: Káto (Lower) and Áno (Upper). The upper is the more interesting; its ridge leads in the west to the old ruined **Kástro**. The view of the gleaming bay and other islands is spectacular. The beach that looks so inviting to the southwest, called **Psilí Ámmos**, really is.

The road is paved as far as the fortified Byzantine **Taxiárhon Monastery** ⑱ to the island's extreme north. The scenic walk there from Áno Hóra's main square follows a wide fieldstone path. Numerous small bays with tiny, empty beaches lie below. Habitation is sparse, and there are just a few small farms along the way. After a good hour's walk, the village of **Kallítsos** appears at the far side of a steep valley. Marigolds and palm trees grow between the older houses; some abandoned stone huts straddle the palisade of rock overlooking the sea. Though there are no tavernas, a fresh-water fountain along the main cement path refreshes.

Makários, the monk who looks after the Taxiárhon monastery on Sérifos, has lived there alone since 1958.

The paved road cuts westward from here, leading to the Taxiárhon in about half an hour. The monastery sits directly on the roadside, opposite a small chapel and cemetery. The resident monk, Makários, one of Sérifos's two parish priests, will show you the ornate icon-screen and such rare treasures as lamps from Egypt and Russia and an ivory inlaid bishop's throne. Makários also fishes and raises livestock.

BELOW: a miller inside a working windmill.

The rustic villages of **Galáni**, **Pýrgos** and **Panaghía** focus the magnificent valley beyond the Taxiárhon. You can cross this valley by one of two footpaths around the hill that bisects it, or stick to the road. The original, 10th-century **Panaghía** (Virgin) church is infamous for its 16 August feast-day (Xílo Panaghía), when lads and maidens used to rush in pairs to be the first to dance around the church's olive tree: the first couple to complete the dance would be allowed to marry during the year. Jealousy and feuding resulted, and when the island's youth started beating off unwanted competition with switches, a priest put a stop to the fighting. Now the priest is always the first to circle the tree.

Sérifos abounds in beaches, most of them accessible only on foot, and so unspoiled. **Megálo Livádhi** in the southwest is the island's second port (buses cross to it in the summer only). Once a mining centre, it is now rather forlorn.

Sífnos

Resplendent with olive trees, bougainvillea and wind-bent juniper, Sífnos may well be the greenest of the Cyclades, as often touted. The island's villages are flawlessly pretty and the valleys surrounding them are filled with dovecotes and monasteries. Indeed,

Sífnos is famous throughout Greece for its ceramics, particularly simple everyday pottery made to traditional designs from grey and red clay.

BELOW: Hrysopighí monastery, Sífnos.

even the island's harbour, **Kamáres** , has a pleasant aspect. Its mouth is narrow, formed by opposing mountain ridges that look like two dusty-flanked dinosaurs backing towards each other unawares.

Sífnos's central range of mountains softens as it meanders south; towards the empty north, it spreads into sand-coloured pyramids. The main road strikes through a steep, deep valley from Kamáres 5.5 km (3½ miles) to **Apollonía** ⑳, the capital. Countless terraces cascade from the mountain tops; the pale soil makes it look as though a golden nectar were poured down over them, cooling in ridges along the way.

Sífnos was and is a potter's isle. In Kamáres, Fáros, Platýs Yialós and especially isolated Hersónisos, potters still set out long racks of earthenware to dry in the sun. Weaving and jewellery-making are the other crafts, the jewellery-making dating from times when Sífnos was rich in gold and silver. There are fine examples of local weaving in Apollonía's **folklore museum** (a notice on the door tells you where to find the curator).

Connected to Apollonía, **Artemón** (the towns are named for the divine twins Apollo and Artemis) is Sífnos's richest town, with mansions and old churches. The chief church, the **Kóhi** ("nook"), in whose courtyard cultural events are held in summer, is built over a temple to Artemis. Down the block a plaque marks the house of mournful poet John Gryparis (1871–1942).

The oldest community is **Kástro** ㉑, the former capital perched 100 metres (300 ft) above the sea and 3 km (2 miles) east of Apollonía. Kástro's layout of concentric streets sets it apart from other settlements. Catalans and Venetians once ruled the town; the walls they built are still in evidence, as are some remains of an ancient acropolis. Most of the buildings are from the 14th century.

The big Venetian building in the centre of town is the **Archeological Museum** (Tue–Sat, 9am–3pm; Sun 10am–2pm; free).

Sífnos's south shore settlements make tranquil beach-side bases. **Fáros**, on a clover-shaped bay, abounds in tiny churches. Sífnos's prettiest spot may be **Hrysopighí** ("Golden Wellspring") **Monastery**, built in 1653 on an islet reached by a footbridge. It is no longer in monastic use and basic rooms can be rented in summer.

The adjoining beach of **Apókofto** ("cut-off") is lovely and sheltered, with a popular taverna. **Platýs Yialós** is crowded in summer and deserted in winter. A beach settlement with rooms, here backpackers feel most at home. Public notices primly advise that camping on the beach (there is a campsite) and nude bathing are prohibited, and that "cleanliness is the key to civilisation". Many glorious walks into the island's interior begin around this area.

A paint-blazed footpath leads from **Kataváti** just south of Apollonía to remote **Vathý** ㉒, a potter's coastal hamlet provided with a road only in 1993. Caiques make the trip from Kamáres in the summer, and there are tavernas and private rooms on the beach. Its sandy-floored bay is edged by a number of small coves, yet it is a man-made feature that makes Vathý so visually stunning: **Taxiárhis** (Archangel) **Monastery**, poised as though ready to set sail.

Andíparos

Once, 5,000 years ago, this small, pretty island was joined to Páros. A narrow channel now separates the two, plied by frequent car ferries and excursion boats bringing visitors to its famous cave, **Spílio Stalaktitón** (the Cave of the Stalactites) ㉓. At the entrance to the cavern stands the Church of Ioánnis Spiliótis

Map on pages 162–3

Hrysopighí Monastery has an icon with allegedly miraculous powers: it once destroyed the stone bridge to the islet, saving the monastery from pirate attack; then later saved Sífnos from plague (1675) and locusts (1928).

BELOW: the main attraction on Andíparos.

UNDERGROUND TOURISM

The Cave of the Stalactites, the principal attraction on Andíparos, was first discovered during the reign of Alexander the Great, around 330 BC, and has been attracting visitors ever since. Despite the predations of souvenir hunters, who have broken and removed stalactites for centuries, it is still a fantastic spooky chamber, full of weird shapes and shadows.

Almost as impressive as the stalactites and stalagmites are the inscriptions left by past visitors, including King Otho of Greece and Lord Byron. The oldest piece of graffiti has sadly been lost – a note from several individuals stating that they were hiding in the cave from Alexander the Great who suspected them of plotting his assassination. Another inscription (in Latin) records the Christmas mass celebrated in the cave by the French Marquis de Nointel in 1673.

In summer buses and boats run to the cave from Andíparos town, or it is a two-hour walk. Then you descend more than 70 metres (230 ft) from the cave entrance to the vaulted chamber, surrounded by stalagmites and stalactites. There are concrete steps now, and electric lighting, but the effect is still breathtaking. The entire cave is really twice as deep, but the rest has been closed as too dangerous. (Open daily, 9.45am–4.45pm.)

(St John of the Cave). Buses run from **Andíparos town** to the cave, but most day-trippers bypass the pretty village, so it is relatively easy to find rooms here outside of August (the newer houses belong to Athenians).

Andíparos measures only 11 km by 5 km (7 miles by 3 miles), so there are no impossible distances. The beachside campsite on **Diapóri** bay faces a calm, shallow channel between two islets; at their end rise two sea rocks, the Red Tower and the Black Tower, visible from Parikía. The little ferry passes two islets; on one, Saliagos, British excavators in 1964 revealed a neolithic (before 4000 BC) settlement, including a fat female figurine now in the Parikía museum. The other belongs to the Goulandris family, who established Athens's eponymous museum.

The ancient world's most rollicking poet, Archilochus (c680–640 BC), was from Páros. He was fond of a drink, and often performed "with wits thunderstruck with wine".

Good beaches and bars have lured to Andíparos some of Páros's former business. **Ághios Yeórghios**, on the south coast, has two tavernas and faces the goat island of **Despotikó**. South of the cave the **Faneroméni chapel** stands alone on a southeastern cape.

Páros

The two open-air cinemas in **Parikía** ❷❹ (also called Páros) have amazingly good fare. Townspeople, tourists and laid-over boat passengers sit gazing at a screen under the stars, and somehow the experience feels supremely Greek. Reading Greek subtitles is a also good way to pick up a few handy phrases – more so at least than in Parikía's many bars and crêperies. If you arrive at this heavily trafficked island in August, however, expect to sleep either under those very same stars or expensively; the cheaper rooms go fast, though in the evening they are empty – everyone is taking in the famous nightlife. Parikía is as pretty

BELOW: Náousa, Páros, is now a fashionable village.

as Mykonos, but not so labyrinthine. The four main things to see are the beautiful 6th-century **Ekatontapylianí church** ("Our Lady of a Hundred Doors"), the **Archeological Museum** (Tue–Sun, 8.30am–2.30pm), the ancient **cemetery** (next to the post office) and the Venetian **Kástro** in the centre of town, built wholly of classical marbles. Páros has the world's most translucent marble; you can still visit the ancient tunnel-quarries in **Maráthi** and pick up a chip.

The island is loaded with beaches. **Hrysí Aktí** (Golden Beach), on the east coast just north of **Dhryós** (which also has a good beach), is a perennial favourite. **Léfkes** ❷, the Turkish capital, is the largest inland village. There are several 17th-century churches, the two most prominent edged with an opaline-blue wash. Léfkes ("Poplars") makes a good base for walking excursions, as the area is full of monasteries.

In beautiful **Náousa** ❷, on the north coast, the little harbour's colourful boats seem to nudge up right against the fishermen's houses. Though the village has become fashionable, with upmarket boutiques and restaurants, the harbour is sacrosanct. Caiques leave from here for several fine beaches; the world windsurfing championship is often held on Santa Maria beach.

One of the best walks from Léfkes is over the Byzantine cobbled road leading to **Píso Livádhi**, where a fold of rich Aegean blue separates Páros from the high, dark crags of **Náxos** ❷ (*see page 184*).

In the west is the much-visited **Valley of the Butterflies**, or **Petaloúdhes**, a big well-watered garden with huge trees. The black and yellow butterflies – moths actually – are colourful and countless in summer (open Jun–Sep, daily 9am–8pm). A big road goes there, but no bus. The bus does, however, go to **Poúnda**, from where the small ferry sails to Andíparos.

Map on pages 162–3

The summer visitors to Petaloúdhes, southwest of Parikiá, are not butterflies but Jersey tiger moths.

BELOW: a Greek Orthodox wedding on Páros.

Mílos

Mílos is a geologist's paradise. The colors and shapes of rocks, caves, cliffs, coastline and hot springs make it eerily beautiful. Snaking streams of lava formed much of the island's coastline. The lava dripped into caves and thickened as it hit the sea, thrusting up weird rock formations that take on animal shapes when caught in the purple shadows of the setting sun. The island has always been extensively mined, once for obsidian, now for bentonite, perlite, barite and china clay. The gaping quarries disfigure the landscape.

Modern Miliots are possessed of a quiet sophistication and worldliness. They have graciously adapted to the thin stream of tourism the island receives, concentrated in **Adamás** ㉘, the port, and Apollónia, a fishing village in the northeast. On the map, Mílos resembles a bat in flight; almost all the island's total population of 4,500 is in the eastern wings; the western wing is wildly beautiful. One way to kill time while waiting for a boat in Adamás would be to take a hot springs bath, if they were open, but the tiny entrance door in the concrete wall near where the boats dock is locked. Inside the **Aghía Triádha** church in Adamás, Cretan-style icons dominate. Links have always been strong between Mílos and the "great island": Cretan refugees founded Adamás in 1853, though ancient tombs have been opened here too.

The island's capital, **Pláka** (also called **Mílos**) ㉙ has both an **Archeological Museum** (Tue–Sun, 8.30am–3pm) and a **Folklore Museum** (Tue–Sat, 10am–1pm and 6–8pm; Sun 10am–1pm). The latter, set in an old house, is packed with diverse exhibits from rock specimens and goat horns to samples of native weaving. A hike to the **Panaghía Thalássitra** ("Mariner Virgin"), the chapel above Pláka (follow signs for Anna's Art Dresses) and the old **Kástro**

Greek Street in London is named after the Miliot ghetto in Soho, populated by refugees from Mílos in the 17th century.

BELOW: the west coast of Mílos, with Andímilos islet in the distance.

walls gives a splendid views of the bay-bound Mílos and, on clear days, as far as Páros. The escutcheon on the church is of the Crispi family, who wrested Mílos from the Sanudi in 1363.

Southwest of Pláka lies the verdant **Vale of Klíma**, on whose seaside slope the ancient Miliots built their city. Excavations undertaken by the British School in Athens in the late 1800s uncovered a Dionysian altar here, and remains of an ancient gymnasium. There is even a Roman mosaic. Follow the catacombs sign, and detour on to the track to the **theatre**. It is very well preserved, probably because of its Roman renovation.

Near the theatre, a marble plaque marks the spot where a farmer unearthed the Aphrodite of Mílos (Venus de Milo) in 1820. The statue was probably carved in the 1st century BC – of Parian marble since Mílos lacks good stone. Mílos was long famous for producing superb statuary, wrought by succeeding generations of a family called Grophon. Other examples of Miliot sculpting include a (copied) bust of Asclepius in the British Museum and a Hermes in the Berlin Museum. More can be found in the Archeological Museum in Athens.

Below the theatre lies one of the island's prettiest villages, **Klíma**, with brightly painted boathouses lining the shore. Further down the road from Pláka to Adámas are the only **Christian catacombs** in all Greece. Carved into the hillside, they are the earliest evidence of Christian worship in the country. The 291 tombs – which probably held 8,000 bodies – have all been robbed, yet the site remains moving. Though cheerily lit by tiny electric lanterns, the frescoes and religious graffiti are hard to discern, and only the initial 50 metres (360 ft) are open to the public.

Ten km (6 miles) northeast from Adámas lies the rubble of the ancient city of Fylakopí, whose script and art resemble that of the Minoans. It flourished for a thousand years after 2600 BC. The famous flying fish fresco is now in Athens, but many objects are in the Pláka museum. All around Fylakopí are strewn flakes of obsidian, which was used for sharp tools before bronze became common; visitors came to Mílos for it from 7000 BC.

Mílos's polychrome geology is especially impressive here. Next to the site glitters the **Papafránkas Cave**, where precipitous stone steps take you down for an atmospheric swim. The multicoloured sea rocks offshore, **Glaronísia**, can be reached by cruise boat from Apollónia.

Apollónia ㉚, a restful base in the northeast, is a popular resort with a tree-fringed beach. It is a good starting point for several short walks that give the full measure of Mílos's strange beauty. A short distance west along the coast (follow the town beach), four volcanic boulders do a ring dance atop a crest of sandstone; the feeling of movement is undeniable, though the rocks were petrified here centuries ago.

Kímolos

This tiny island – 35 sq. km (14 sq. miles), with a population of 800 – is an alluring presence for anyone who has been staying in Apollónia on Mílos. The distance between the two is just under a nautical mile. Kímolos's chalky cliffs, mined for Fuller's earth and

The Venus de Milo was entrusted to the French Consul in Istanbul (she probably lost her arms in transit), to keep her safe from the Turks. He promptly shipped her off to France, where Louis XVIII put her on display in the Louvre. She has been there ever since.

BELOW: Kímolos, seen from the coast of Mílos.

Most of the Cyclades islands that grew their own grain have windmills but, unlike this one in Síkinos, most of them have fallen into disuse.

BELOW: the steep terraced slopes of Folégandhros.

tufa building blocks, turn a velvety rose at sunset and then seem to disappear in the evening haze. The caique takes only 20 minutes to cross the narrow channel from Apollónia to **Psáthi**, Kímolos's landing. Some ferries to Mílos also stop here. **Hóra**, the one town, is a 20-minute walk up from the quay. The 14th-century Venetian **Kástro** above Hóra, sadly in an advanced state of decay, looks down on a row of windmills, of which one still grinds. The most interesting church is **Ághios Ioánnes Hrysóstomos**, built in the14th-century and well restored.

Kímolos, once a pirates' hideout, today provides refuge from the more crowded islands. Although blessedly undeveloped, it has several beaches at Alykí, Klíma, Prássa, Bonátsi and Ellinikó, all within easy walking distance. Offshore from Ellinikó is Ághios Andréas, now an islet. Excavations there have revealed a significant and fascinating Mycenaean settlement. Prássa has a reasonable shingle beach and some rooms to rent.

Folégandhros

The vaulting steepness of Folégandhros's coast has deterred outside invasion over the centuries and so lent the islanders security. Despite its tiny size – 32 sq km (12 sq. miles) populated by barely 500 people – its role in very recent history has not been insignificant: many Greeks were exiled here during the country's 1967–74 military rule. Its ancient and early Christian ties with Crete were strong, and many paintings of the Cretan School can be found in its churches today. In myth, a son of King Minos founded the island.

Folégandhros abounds with bays, wild herbs and grapes. **Karavostássis**, the port, **Angáli**, at the waist of the island on the west shore, and **Ághios Nikólaos**

above it are the little-developed beaches. The recent spate of construction solved a summer "no rooms" problem; the campsite at **Livádhi** in the south provides a useful backup.

There are buses to the capital, **Folégandhros** or **Hóra ❸**, a magnificently sited medieval town with an inner **kástro** high above the sea. **Hrysospiliá**, the "golden cave" near Hóra, gapes over the sea. It is rich with stalagmites and stalactites. Excavations show this was a place of refuge in the Middle Ages. It's only accessible to good climbers, who can get there by caique from Hóra.

The island's second village, **Áno Meriá**, comprises stone houses and farms; the surrounding hills are dotted with chapels. Historically, Folegandrian supplications were for rain – and still are, for on no other Cycladic island are wells and cisterns so closely guarded.

Síkinos

Rocky Síkinos, despite the usual variety of harbourside lodgings, couldn't be less like its larger neighbour, Íos. Although connected to Piraeus and other Cyclades twice or thrice weekly by ferry, and by caique to Íos and Folégandhros in summer, Síkinos so far seems to have shrugged off tourism. It also escapes mention in the history books for long periods of time, but there are antiquities and churches to be seen.

The three beaches, **Aloprónia** (also the port), **Ághios Nikólaos** and **Ághios Yeórghios** to the north face Íos. From Aloprónia harbour there's a regular bus or an hour's hike to **Síkinos town ❷**, which consists of the simple village (**Hóra**) and the medieval **Kástro**, with its wonderful village square arranged for defence. The abandoned convent of **Zoödóhos Pighí** sits above the town.

Map on pages 162–3

BELOW: Síkinos through a ruined Kástro doorway.

Perhaps even barer than Íos, Síkinos is a sparse island with few obvious diversions. One site of note, the **Iroön** , near the village of **Episkopí**, stand on what was once thought to have been a temple to Apollo; this is now reckoned to be an elaborate Roman tomb, incorporated into a church during medieval times. Síkinos's old Greek name, Oenoe, testifies to the fact that the island once produced a celebrated wine (*oinos*), but not any longer.

Íos

Little Íos has ethos; it is a state of mind. A tiny island with few historic attractions, it has drawn the young and footloose since the 1960s. The current lot, a weak echo of their hippie forbears (who encamped here year-round), flock here to live cheaply, drink and dry out in the blistering sun.

The centre of Íos's nightlife shifts constantly about the tiny capital town **Hóra** (also called **Íos**) ❸. In order to ensure his corner of the market, the owner of the Íos By Night club cooks up a Miss Íos contest each Friday. The prize i 5,000 drachmas and a bottle of "champagne". (Mr Íos contests are also held, but only by default, when no girls can be persuaded to participate.)

People still sleep on the beach at **Mylopótas** ❸, although this is now less common. Boutique shopping is minimal. But one thing people are sure to spend money on while here is drinking. Nightclubs stud the hill above Íos harbour with another large cluster of bars in the Hóra. Homemade music strummed or well-travelled guitars and drugs, former stock items on Íos, aren't much in evidence any more. After the sun sets, Íos resembles a downmarket, younger Mýkonos. At around 11pm, beach stragglers break the quiet ready for night-time revels (a bus runs regularly between beach and harbour via Hóra). Once

BELOW: a midnight Easter service.

Map
on pages
162–3

ensconced inside a bar, they could be anywhere in the western world, with few Greeks in sight.

The permanent effects of the tourist invasion have been twofold: Íos is no longer poor, and traditional life has virtually disappeared. Hóra is the only town; there are no smaller villages to keep up the old ways. As one elderly resident recounts, weddings were once week-long feasts for all. Now, unless they are held in winter, they last an evening, as everyone is too busy tending tourist-related enterprises.

Íos is not devoid of natural beauty or charm; even the bleary-eyed can see it. The harbour is one of the Aegean's prettiest. The hilltop Hóra, capped by a windmill, blazes with the blue domes of two Byzantine churches. Its layout and the palm trees that flank it look almost Levantine. Buses are frequent, and there is a long marble stairway from the port. The flat plain north of the harbour is filling up with new houses and at least one villa complex has been constructed on the main road.

Íos has many good swimming beaches, including the nude beaches north of the harbour. There are summer caiques to **Manganári Bay** in the south and **Psáthy** in the east. A half day's walk northeast ends at **Aghía Theodóti**, with beach and seasonal camping. A traditional *panaghíri* (saint's festival) is held at Theodóti church on 8 September, the only festival in which the entire island still participates.

Beyond the church are the remains of **Paleokástro** ㊱, an elevated fortress containing the marble ruins of what was the medieval capital. At a lonely spot toward the northern tip, behind the cove at **Plakótos**, is a series of prehistoric graves, one of which the islanders fiercely believe is Homer's.

BELOW: *tsouréki,* traditional Easter sweet bread.

Amorgós

The spine of mountains – the tallest is Krikelas in the northeast, at 822 metres (2,696 ft) – precludes expansive views unless you're on top of them. The south-westerly harbour town of **Katápola** ❸ occupies a small coastal plain. Trees overhang the quayside and thick orchards fringe the town. Unfortunately, new development is encroaching on the older Cycladic structures as Amorgós gets more summer tourist traffic each year.

Three important ancient cities once thrived here. At **Minóa** (just above Katápola) are very scant ruins of a gymnasium, stadium and temple to Apollo. **Arkessíni**, in the far southwest, comprises a burial site and a well-preserved Hellenistic fortress. **Aigialis** (Eghiális), above Amorgós's second northeastern harbour, was also an ancient colony; now only the ruined fortress is visible. As Semonides of Amorgos wrote around 650 BC, "The generation of men is like that of leaves."

The elevated **Hóra** (or **Amorgós town**) ❸, accessible by a regular bus service, is a cluster of whitewashed houses and numerous churches around a 13th-century Venetian castle, and a regulation row of windmills.

The island's two most famous churches are outside Hóra. **Ághios Yeórghios Valsamítis**, 4 km (2 miles) southwest, is on a sacred spring once believed to cure lepers and now watering someone's market garden; this church's pagan oracle was finally closed only after World War II. Half an hour east of Hóra, clinging to the side of a 180-metre (590-ft) cliff, the spectacular 11th-century Byzantine **monastery of the Panaghía Hozoviótissa** ❸ – one of the most beautiful in Greece – is home to a revered icon of the Virgin from Palestine. For the mirac-ulous story of the chisel and vision of the church's building, take a copy of the church pamphlet.

BELOW: Panghía Hozoviótissa monastery on the cliffs of Amorgós.

Below the monastery, **Aghía Ánna** beach beckons. To the southwest lie empty, secluded coves for bathing and sunning; a line of windmills edges the ridge above. The coastal ledges are covered with wild thyme and oregano, which release their pungent bouquet when crushed underfoot. A Hellenistic watch-tower looking towards Anáfi marks the island's south-ernmost point, below Arkessíni.

The north of the island is characterised by high-perched villages, excepting **Eghiális**, a small anchor-age with accommodation and good beaches nearby. Some ferry boats, plus caiques from elsewhere on Amorgós, put in here. Beyond it is **Tholária**, surrounded by Roman tombs. Sheer rock faces notwithstanding, Amorgós is full of tiny, hidden beaches. Locally produced maps name them all and provide valuable information, couched in comic Eng-lish and German, about places like the former "valley of the old useless, doomed donkeys".

Anáfi

In legend, Apollo conjured up Anáfi to shelter Jason and the Argonauts when the seas grew rough and they risked losing the Golden Fleece. Apollo's shrine was built here in thanksgiving. Divine intervention has never again been reliable. Earthquakes originating on its volatile neighbour **Santoríni** ❹ (*see page 180*) usually shivered through Anáfi, causing tidal waves and maelstroms of volcanic detritus. Anáfi's appearance has probably not altered much since then: it still looks like a rough boulder heaved up out of the sea and kept in place only by the goodness of a tenacious god.

However, a different god is involved now: **Zoödóhos Pighí** ("Lifegiving Wellspring") **Monastery ⑪** was erected over the old shrine in the island's southeast corner. Extensive courses of marble masonry in its walls are believed to be remnants of the old temple. Above the monastery, improbably soars the smaller monastery of **Panaghía Kalamiótissa**, high on a pinnacle that is Anáfi's most distinctive feature. Fewer than 300 people live on the island today, surviving mainly by fishing and subsistence farming. Summer tourism, mostly German, has boosted the economy only slightly, and the island makes few concessions. It is served by a twice-weekly caique from Santoríni and several ferries from Piraeus.

The south-facing harbour, **Ághios Nikólaos**, has rooms available in summer. A short bus ride or half-hour walk up, the main town, **Hóra** (or **Anáfi**) ⑫, offers a wider choice and finer setting, and life in the quiet streets has so far been unaltered by tourism. A ruined Venetian **kástro** reigns overhead. Feast days on Anáfi – 10 days after Easter and 8 September – are occasions for all-out dancing.

Hikes eastward lead first to the beach at **Klisídi** (with seasonal taverna) and then to half a dozen more, all superb, before reaching the two monasteries. The interior is virtually empty, except for the rubble of another Venetian castle above central Roúkounas beach. Goat paths amble aimlessly; follow them, for Anáfi remains a hawk-haunted place for solitude. ❑

Map on pages 162–3

THE BACK ISLANDS

The so-called "Back Islands" near Náxos were once thickly populated. Now **Donoússa**, **Iráklia**, **Shinoússa** and **Koufonísi** have populations of 100 to 200 each, while **Kéros** is completely uninhabited. For Iráklia, Shinoússa and Koufoníssi there are ferries twice or thrice a week, and smaller boats from Náxos. Donoússa has ferry connections four times a week, and is served by caiques from Náxos, Páros and Santoríni in summer. No boats go to Kéros. A stay on any of the Back Islands means, at least out of season, accommodation with local families and a very low-key existence. Water is scarce on all of them.

Hilly Donoússa is covered with vineyards; views from the harbour take in the barren Makáres islands and the grand profile of Náxos. Iráklia has two settlements: the harbour, Ághios Yeórghios, and Hóra, just over an hour's hike above. Shinoússa's hilltop Hóra has a medieval fortress at its back; Messariá is a tiny beach settlement on the north coast. Koufoníssi (its neighbour, Káto Koufoníssi, belongs mainly to goats) has an actual hotel, and an east coast beach with a seasonal taverna. Kéros was a third-millenium BC burial site. Much of the Cycladic material in great museums comes from here, and if you put in to Kéros, the police will want to know why.

BELOW: the Mílos-Síkinos ferry arrives.

NÁXOS

Mountainous Náxos is still a fairly well-kept secret, where tourism has been slow to develop. But it offers lush green valleys, even in the height of summer, and sweeping sandy beaches

Naxian marble has always been prized. It was used for the famous lions of Delos (see page 170).

BELOW: the Portára gateway at the unfinished temple of Delian Apollo.

Náxos is the largest, most heroic, most magnificent of the Cyclades. High mountains, long beaches, inaccessible villages, ruins, medieval monasteries, and fascinating history make any visit here too short. Hemmed in by the Cyclades' highest mountains, the interior recalls the more forbidding parts of the Peloponnese. **Mount Zas** – or Zeus, who was born in a huge bat-filled cave here – is 1,001 metres (3,284 ft), but not difficult to climb. **Hóra** (**Náxos town**) ❶ is a labyrinthine chaos of Venetian homes and castle walls, post-Byzantine churches, Cycladic to medieval ruins, and garden restaurants.

Hóra is divided into sections whose place names reflect the port's long Venetian occupation. The **Catholic Cathedral** at the east of the town demarcates the Fontana section. The residential Borgo quarter behind the main *platía* is splendidly Cycladic. Higher up, within the walled **Kástro**, live descendants, still Catholic, of the Venetian overlords; look for their coats of arms over doorways. The former French School, built into the ramparts, now houses the **Archeological Museum** (Tue–Sun, 8.30am–3pm). Just north of Hóra is the Grotta area, with the remains of a Cycladic settlement (c2500 BC).

On an islet (connected by a causeway) to the north of Hóra's ferry dock, a colossal free-standing marble door frame marks the entrance to the **Temple of**

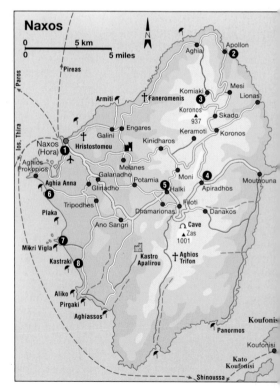

Delian Apollo of 530 BC. It was never completed, despite the efforts of Lygdamis, Naxos's energetic tyrant. If it had ever been finished, it would have been Archaic Greece's largest temple.

Map on page 184

On the northern shore of Náxos is the resort town of **Apóllon ❷**, a one-time hippie enclave three hours from Hóra by the daily bus. A huge 6th-century BC *kouros*, probably bearded Dionysos, lies on the hillside above it, abandoned when the marble cracked. (Another cracked *kouros* reposes in a splendid garden 10km/6 miles east of Náxos in Melanés, near the road to Kourohóri.)

The rest of the island is a sumptuous wilderness, ripe for exploration by anyone with the time and stamina (or hired means of transport) to do it justice. The rural villages of Náxos are numerous and unpredictable, with reception to foreigners varying enormously from one to another. Olive and fruit trees grow densely around them, concealing Byzantine churches and crumbling Venetian manors. Four villages on the road back from Apóllon to Hóra are particularly worthy of attention: Komiakí, Apíradhos, Filóti and Halkí.

The gigantic kouros at Apóllon, left unfinished in around 600 BC, weighs 30 tonnes and is 10.5 metres (35 ft) long.

Komiakí ❸, the highest village on the island, is extremely attractive, has wonderful views over the surrounding terraced vineyards, and is the original home of the local *Kitrón* liqueur. **Apíradhos ❹** was originally settled by Cretan refugees in the 17th and 18th centuries – the dialect is noticeable. The town, whose streets are marble, even looks Cretan. Its little **Archeological Museum** (open daily: if closed, ask someone for the guard) contains some rough-carved reliefs that are unique and uninterpretable. In the school a teacher has set up a museum of local minerals.

Filóti, on the slopes of Mount Zas, is Naxos's second largest town. If you are there for the three-day festival which starts on 14 August, don't bother trying to stay sober. Near Filóti a bad road leads (14km/9 miles) southeast to the Heímarros Tower, strongly built in the 3rd century BC.

BELOW: relaxing at midday.

The Trageá valley, from Filóti to Halkí, is all olive trees, amid which are several Byzantine churches – numerous walks are possible here. **Halkí ❺**, the Trageá's main town, has several fine churches, the best being **Panaghía Protóthronis** (First-Enthroned Virgin), actually 500 years older than its official foundation date, 1052. The Annunciation fresco over the sanctuary is a masterpiece. Next to the church is the 17th-century Grazia tower. Many such towers, which the Venetian lords built to guard their holdings, can be seen throughout fertile Náxos.

Goats and migrating birds are southeastern Naxos's chief inhabitants. On the way to Halkí a good road branches off to **Moní**, whose restaurants are justly popular for their mountain views. On the way to Moní the road passes the **Drosianí**, or Church of the Dewy Virgin, which has rare early medieval frescoes.

It is only in the last 10 years that Náxos has become known for its beaches. Some of the best in all the Cyclades are on the west coast of the island, facing Páros. **Ághios Yeórghios** south of the port is the most popular. **Aghía Anna ❻**, partly nude, is a good beach for rooms; **Mikrí Vígla ❼** beyond it has a good taverna; and **Kastráki ❽**, the furthest south, offers blissful solitude. ❑

SANTORÍNI

Santoríni's whitewashed villages cling to volcanic cliffs above beaches of black sand. It is an island shaped by geological turmoil, and one of the most dramatic in all Greece

Map on page 189

Entering the bay of Santoríni on a boat is one of Greece's great experiences. Broken pieces of a volcano's rim – Santoríni and its attendant islets – form a multicoloured circle around a bottomless lagoon that, before the eruption, was the island's high centre. When the volcano blew (c1500 BC), Minoan ships sank, earthquakes followed, and sunsets were affected globally for years. The island's long crescent, formed of petrified lava, seems at sunset to reflect fire from Hades.

Thíra (or Thera) is its ancient and official name. Greeks however prefer its medieval name, Santoríni, after Saint Irene of Salonica, who died here in 304. **Firá** (or **Thíra**) **❶**, the capital, sits high on the rim, its white houses (many barrel-vaulted against earthquakes) blooming like asphodels. The town is largely pedestrianised, its winding cobbled streets terraced into the volcanic cliffs. Firá has an **Archeological Museum** (Tue–Sun, 8.30am–3pm; free Sun) and a cultural festival every September. The **Mégaron Gýzi Museum** (daily May–Sep, 10.30am–1.30pm and 5–8pm) is housed in a beautiful 17th-century mansion that was spared in the 1956 earthquake. The collection includes engravings, documents, paintings and prints featuring Santorinian landscapes, pre-quake photographs and island maps from the 16th to the 19th century.

Despite August's rock 'n' roll atmosphere, for most of the year Firá is quiet. Although it is packed with jewellers, boutiques and cave-like discos, it has the power to charm. A sunset drink at a cliffside café – contemplating the rust-and-purple striated cliffs, blue bay, twinkling lights and sensual white lines of its architecture – remains unforgettable. Some boats put in below Firá at **Skála Firá**, but most dock at **Athiniás**, 10 km (6 miles) further south.

Ancient Thíra

To the east of Firá, the land smoothes out into fertile fields. A few bare hills push up again in the southeast. On one of them sits **Ancient Thíra ❷**, inaccessible for safety. Founded by Dorians in the 9th century BC, it was occupied by 5,000 Romans until an earthquake knocked it down for good. The foundations of the ancient buildings are still clear. In his *Gymnopédies,* the composer Eric Satie imagined the dances that were performed here by naked boys in honour of Apollo.

In the south, **Akrotíri ❸**, a Minoan town preserved in volcanic ash like Pompeii, continues to be excavated under a roof built to protect the remains. The town clearly had comfortable two-storey houses, good plumbing and attractive little squares, and a walk through it brings the past to life. No bones have been found, which implies that the inhabitant, though they had to leave in a hurry, knew of the coming eruption.

LEFT: the churches of Ía. **BELOW:** white houses, purple sea.

You don't need to walk up the 600 steps from Skála Firá to Firá, or charter a donkey: there is also a cable-car.

BELOW: Santoríni shopkeeper.

But if you want to see the beautiful frescoes, pots and furniture that have been found there you must, to the islanders' chagrin, go to Athens' Archeological Museum. Near Akrotíri on Red Beach, a taverna set in caves serves sweet, lava-nurtured Santoríni wines in dented tin jugs.

Santoríni's population swells from 9,000 to 70,000 in summer, and most of the visitors congregate in the capital. Though Firá is most developed, many other places offer plentiful accommodation. Ía (Oía) ❹, on the island's northernmost peninsula, is perhaps Greece's most photographed village. Ía has been beautifully restored since, in 1956, a severe earthquake sent a layer of lava sliding down over the houses. Afterwards, people dug their way back inside their homes. Life is marginally quieter here than in Firá, with fewer bars and tavernas, and earlier closing hours.

A steep walk down twisting stone steps from the western end of town ends at **Ammoudiá** beach, overhung by houses. Beautiful cave houses, rented out by the National Tourist Organisation (EOT), are a specialty of Ía. The gentle hike along the caldera's edge from Ía to **Imerovígli** (north of Firá) allows you to experience the cruel reds and purples of the petrified lava and the island's tempestuous geology. The volcano is only dormant, not extinct; it still emits gas and steam at 80°C (175°F) and earthquakes are always a disturbing possibility.

Every year there are more places available to stay and eat in **Kamári** ❺ and **Périssa** ❻, busy resorts on the east coast. Périssa has the main campsite. Both have roasting hot black pebble beaches (at Périssa the strand is 8 km/5 miles long). They make a good starting point from which to climb to Ancient Thíra (if you don't take a taxi or bike) and then Mount Profítis Ilías, the next hill inland. The museum in **Profítis Ilías Monastery** exhibits tools and even complete

workshops of the various crafts practised here by the monks since time immemorial. Homemade wine and liqueur are still set out for guests. But remember, monks are not obliged to keep regular hours for tourists. The hours that Profítis Ilías is open to the public tend to be erratic: try to ascertain whether the monastery is open before setting out on your climb.

It is also possible to walk to the monastery from **Pýrgos** ❼, an island village on the central plain. Yellow wheat sheaves, grapevines twisted into wreaths Santoríni-style, tiny thick-skinned tomatoes (grown without water for concentrated flavour), and riots of spring wild flowers – all growing out of angry-looking pumice soil – make up the island's gentler side. Small caves used as toolsheds, barns and sometimes even as homes, occasionally yawn up from wide stretches of grassy fields.

The last stretch of road before tiny **Monólithos**, near the airport (a 45-minute walk from Firá), is lined with hollowed-out sandstone formations that emit eerie piping noises when the wind rushes through them. There's quite a good beach here too. Monólithos itself has three of the island's best tavernas. Buses run frequently, or you can take a taxi or tour for wine tastings at one of Santoríni's wineries. (Bus transportation on the island is unexpectedly good, with regular services augmented by excursion buses to places like Akrotíri.)

The blazing whiteness and sensual lines of Cycladic architecture are doubly disarming in Santoríni, against the smoky purple banks of the old lava, and from every portside passage there is a sombre, fantastic view to be seen of the ocean-bound volcano with "Burnt Islands" at its centre. Lights twinkle across the strait on the islet of **Thirassía**, sparse in vegetation and inhabitants, as though from some lost planet. ❑

Map on page 189

Volcanic Santoríni is believed by many to be the origin of the lost kingdom of Atlantis, which was swallowed up by the sea.

BELOW:
Firá at night.

MIXING PIETY WITH PLEASURE

Greek religious festivals – and there are many – celebrate saints' days and other events in the religious calendar with devotion and high spirits

Greek island life is punctuated throughout the year by saints' days and religious festivals or *panighýri*. As there are around 300 saints in the Orthodox calendar, there is an excuse for a party most days of the year.

Easter is the most important festival (often preceded by a pre-Lenten carnival). It's a great time to visit, with traditional services marking the Resurrection everywhere from humble chapels to mighty monasteries. Colourful, noisy and potentially dangerous – in Kálymnos they throw dynamite to ensure Christ has truly risen – it's like Firework Night and Christmas rolled into one.

During Holy Week, or *Megáli Evdhomádha*, churches are festooned in black. On Maundy Thursday monks on Pátmos re-enact the washing of Christ's feet at the Last Supper. On Good Friday the *Epitáfios*, or bier of Christ, is decorated by the women and paraded through the streets at dusk (*above*) as they sing hymns.

On Easter Saturday the churches are decked in white. On the stroke of midnight everything is plunged in darkness as the priest lights the first candle from the holy flame to represent the light of the world, and intones: "*Hristós anésti* [Christ has risen]". This is the signal for all the congregation to light their candles. Fireworks explode, rockets soar, dynamite sometimes shatters windows, and everyone plays conkers with their red-dyed eggs. Families then break the Lenten fast with Easter soup made from lamb's offal with lemon, rice and spring onions.

On Easter Sunday there's great rejoicing as a lamb or kid is barbecued outdoors over charcoal with the usual music and dancing. There are often parties on Easter Monday and in some islands an effigy of Judas is filled with fireworks and burned.

▽ **AFTER MIDNIGHT**
In the early hours of Easter Sunday, crowds head home in candlelit processions. Families mark the sign of the cross over their door with their candle to bring good luck.

▷ **SCARLET SHELLS**
Hard-boiled eggs, dyed red to symbolise the blood of Christ, are cracked in a game like conkers on Easter Day.

◁ **EASTER TWISTS**
A sweet, twisted bread called *tsouréki* is made for Easter in various shapes, often with a red egg in the centre.

◁ MONDAY MAYHEM

"Clean Monday" is the end of the pre-Lenten carnival, with exuberant celebrations on some islands, including kite-flying and flour fights.

▽ STEPS TO SALVATION

Devout women crawl in penance to the church of the Panaghía Evangelístria on Tínos at the feast of the Assumption in August.

◁ MOUNTAINTOP MASS

Saints' days are celebrated by *panighýri* (festivals) at hundreds of small chapels throughout the islands. Left: Cycladic islanders honour Aghía Marína, the protector of crops, on 17 July.

△ ALL DRESSED UP

In Ólymbos, the remote mountain village on Kárpathos, the eldest daughter or *kanakará* wears her traditional costume and dowry of gold coins for major festivals.

◁ EASTER PARADE

Priest and villagers join in traditional chants in an Easter procession on Páros.

CELEBRATING ALL YEAR ROUND

Greeks mix piety and pleasure with gusto for all their festivals from the most important to the smallest fair. The biggest religious festival after Easter, the Assumption of the Virgin (*Panaghías*) on 15 August, draws Greeks home from all over the world.

Following the long liturgy on the night of the 14th, the icon of the Madonna is paraded and kissed. Then there's a communal feast – and the party can go on for days. The celebrations are spectacular in Kárpathos, with dazzling costumes, special dances and traditional songs.

Every month there are festivals on the islands for everything from sponges to snakes, and national holidays like *Óhi* or "No Day" (28 October), with patriotic parades to mark the Greeks' emphatic reply to Mussolini's surrender ultimatum.

Celebrations begin the night before feast days and everyone in the community takes part from babies to grannies. Patron saints are honoured with services followed by barbecues, music and dance. The picture above shows the feast of Ághios Dimítris on Síkinos in October, which is conveniently when the first wine is ready to drink.

THE SPORADES AND ÉVVIA

Skiáthos, Skópelos, Alónissos, Skýros and Évvia

The Sporades – in English, "sporadic" or "scattered" – are a group of four islands in the northwest Aegean. Évvia, lying stretched along the Greek mainland to the south of the Sporades, is Greece's second largest island, after Crete.

Mainlanders have long recognised Skiáthos's beaches as the best in the Aegean and made an annual pilgrimage. They are now outnumbered by foreigners, and the fact that there are shops that sell nothing but expensive fur coats and will accept any conceivable credit card is a forecast of what to expect.

In spite of a rich history, Alónissos is the least developed island in terms of tourism while Skópelos, more recently and self-consciously the senior partner among the trio, is a compromise. Skýros, the largest and in many ways the most interesting of the Sporades, is detached from the others. It is like a scaled-down version of Crete, with an independent spirit and a deeply entrenched local culture impervious to the events that constantly swirl around it. Évvia, Greece's second largest island after Crete, has not been spoilt by tourism. Its diverse landscape and rich history make it almost a microcosm of the whole country.

While hopping between Skiáthos, Skópelos and Alónissos is very easy, and Évvia has many connections to the nearby mainland, Skýros involves a longer trip; but they all are connected now by hydrofoil. Skiáthos alone among them has an international airport with several (charter) flights daily in summer, mainly from Britain, Germany and Scandinavia, and domestic connections. Skýros has an airport but, apart from a feeder service from Athens, it is reserved for the Greek Air Force. Ferries and hydrofoils run to all the islands from Vólos and Ághios Konstandínos on the mainland.

The islands are what's left of a mountain range which snapped away from the mainland in a geological convulsion and "sank". They lie within a narrow band where prevailing winds and other factors produce reliable rainfall and lush vegetation, notably pine forests. The rains do not intrude in summer. Instead, the *meltémi*, a northerly wind, helps to hold temperatures down a little.

The traditional trade route between the Mediterranean and the Black Sea via the Bosphorus passes the Sporades. Since antiquity, bad weather has brought unexpected and often unwanted callers, including distressed invasion fleets (for example, Xerxes) and pirates. Yet major archeological sites are surprisingly few.

World War I produced a postscript to the strategic location: it was on a convoy heading for Gallipoli that the poet Rupert Brooke died. Skýros rose into view, and it was here that they buried him. ❑

PRECEDING PAGES: three Orthodox priests; three beach bums on "Banana Beach", Skiáthos. **LEFT:** the Karababa Turkish castle near Halkídha, Évvia.

THE SPORADES

Map on page 200

Once exclusive resorts for the rich and famous, the Sporades now attract Greek and foreign holidaymakers alike, whether for the nightlife of Skiáthos or the quieter charm of Alónissos

Skiáthos

The scythe of **Koukounariés** is used as evidence on thousands of picture postcards that the Aegean can produce the kind of beach normally associated with the Caribbean. Propriety would prevent as many postcards from featuring **Krassí ❶** (colloquially "Banana Beach") because it caters for nudists. The fact that no one cares whether bathers at Banana Beach strip off or not is typical of the easy-going, relaxed nature of the people of Skiáthos as a whole.

The island has beaches for all occasions, not least because some among the supposed 60 will always be sheltered wherever the wind is coming from. Koukounariés and Banana are near neighbours at the end of the twisting, busy 18-km (11-mile) coast road from the town; there are dozens along it and several more beyond, many with a taverna or at least a kiosk selling drinks and sandwiches. A path leading down from the road usually promises a beach at the end; with luck it won't be as crowded as Koukounariés.

Round-the-island boat trips pass the rocky and otherwise inaccessible northern shoreline where the only human construction is the **Kástro ❷**, the abandoned 16th-century capital once connected to the rest of the island by a single drawbridge. For 300 years the islanders huddled on this wind-buffeted crag, hoping the pirates would pass them by. During the last war Allied soldiers hid out there, waiting for evacuation by a friendly submarine. Nowadays it is an obligatory stop for the excursion caiques after they have dipped into three technicolour grottoes and dropped anchor at **Lalaria**, a cove famous for its smooth, round stones, and before proceeding to a beach taverna for lunch.

A moped or hired car is necessary to follow the unpaved roads looping through the mountains. They provide stunning views as well as the chance to pop into monasteries which, with the Kástro, are more or less the only buildings of historic interest. Of these, the grandest and closest to town is **Evangelistría**, with the **Panaghía Kehrías** and **Kounístra** also worth a visit should the beaches pall.

The bluff above the under-used beach at the end of the very busy airport runway has produced fragments suggesting a prehistoric settlement, but neither it nor the rest of the island has ever been properly excavated. Fires set by the Nazis destroyed most of the pretty pre-war town.

But **Skiáthos ❸**, the port village, makes up in liveliness what it may lack in architectural merit. In fact, its nightlife is probably the most important consideration after the beaches for the type of visitor which Skiáthos attracts in intimidating numbers in August. The preferences of the fast-living set change con-

LEFT: Skiáthos has beaches to rival the Caribbean.
BELOW: an ancient citizen of Skýros.

stantly, but it is not difficult to spot which places are in vogue at any particular time, whether one's preference is for beer and blues, wine and Vivaldi or tequila and 1950s rock and roll. The lights are brightest but also the tackiest along **Papadhiamántis**, the road that bisects the two hills on which the town stands, and along the *paralía* or waterfront. The atmosphere is a bit classier and quieter around **Polytéhniou** and the cobbled alleys above the port.

Expect restaurants, with international flavours as well as Greek, rather than tavernas and be prepared to pay accordingly, especially along the seafront. Plate-smashing and other forms of sociable anarchy are at a safe distance out of town; to the fury of taxi drivers and the regular bus operators, the tavernas concerned lay on special transport from the main dock.

Skópelos

Skópelos's traditional stone farmhouses (kalívia) all have distinctive outdoor ovens where the island's famous plums were dried to become prunes.

An enduring image of Skópelos, for anyone who has been there in August, is the way in which the famous local plum is picked, examined, wiped and, before being popped into the mouth, given a final polish with the thumb. And who, on sailing or driving along the coast between Glóssa and Skópelos town and knowing a particular local tale, would not be on the look-out for the spot which best fitted the dénouement?

It seems that a rampaging dragon had proved itself to be invulnerable to conventional weapons. The local priest, one Reginos, was implored to direct a sermon at the beast, the islanders having heard enough of them to think that it might do the trick. Finding itself as bored as they had been, the dragon reared away and fled until it could go no further. The pious Reginos followed doggedly and, on cornering his quarry on a clifftop, prepared to deliver another one. Despairing at the

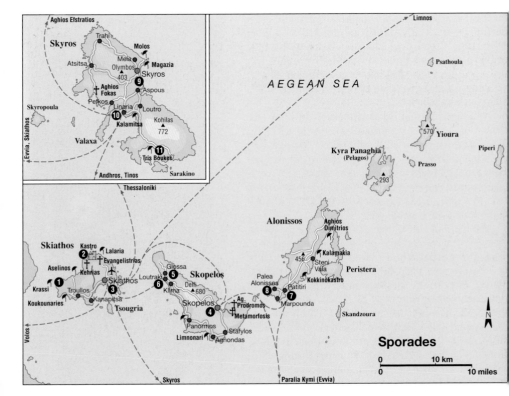

prospect, the dragon dived off, and the impact on landing created one of the indentations which are characteristic of the deeply rugged coastline.

Visitors waiting in Vólos rather than Ághios Konstandínos for passage to Skópelos (the alternative is to fly to Skiáthos and catch a Flying Dolphin hydrofoil or ferry from there) could usefully call at the archeological museum to look at the contents of a grave discovered on the island fairly recently. The gold crown and ornate weapons almost certainly belonged to Stafylos, a Minoan who colonised Skópelos and then went on to be crowned its king.

The island's distinguished past is not so much demonstrated by prominent historical sites as by the exceptionally fine houses in **Skópelos town** ❹, a handsome amphitheatre around a harbour lined with bars and tavernas under mulberry trees. Skópelos escaped earthquakes and Nazi vindictiveness and is therefore the most "authentic" and traditional of the three northern Sporades (Skýros being in a class by itself). Slate roofs, wooden balconies, hand-painted shop signs and flagstone streets give it a serenity and dignity rarely found in Skiáthos in season. On the other hand, beaches are not the island's forte. It has far fewer than Skiáthos and Alónissos – mostly on the south and west coasts – though nudists are welcomed at **Velánio** just beyond the family beach at **Stáfylos** (where the king's tomb was found). As compensation, Skópelos offers forested hills for spectacular walks to 40 monasteries and 360 churches, 123 of which are tucked among the houses above the port, which in turn is crowned by a Venetian castle planted on ancient foundations.

Glóssa ❺, the island's other town, is something of an oddity in that the people who live there have a pronounced dialect which, together with houses whose features are not like other island architecture, suggests that at some time they immigrated from Thessaly. They seem to have made themselves welcome: other islanders refer approvingly to their "exaggerated hospitality".

The main road on the island runs south from the port of **Loutráki** ❻, where Glóssa used to stand before it moved up the mountain for safety's sake, along the west coast, then loops back to Skópelos town. It is an attractive run which includes a number of hamlets, beaches and **Panórmos**, where there are a few remains of a city which probably existed in 500 BC. The wise money is on the dragon having made its desperate departing leap somewhere around Panórmou Bay. Now yachts park in one of its fjordlike inlets and tavernas ring its shores. Further south along the coast road, **Agnóndas** is a tiny harbour with beachside tavernas that are popular with locals.

Alónissos

This island is full of ghosts whispering what might have been. On the hill above **Patitíri** ❼, the last port on the Vólos/Ághios Konstandínos ferry and hydrofoil routes, is the **Hóra**, also called **Paleá Alónissos** ❽, the former capital destroyed by an earthquake in 1965. This compounded the blow the islanders had already suffered when all their grapevines withered and died from phylloxera only a few years earlier.

Alónissos seems to have been ever thus: the previous capital, Ikos, literally disappeared when the

BELOW: Skiáthos harbour.

The annual Skýros carnival takes place just before Lent, but in fact has its roots in a pre-Christian pagan festival.

BELOW: a boat under construction, with lovely Skópelos town beyond.

ground on which it stood toppled into the sea. The submerged remains of the capital, off **Kokkinókastro** beach, are an important part of the Sporades Marine Park, a conservation area which may be explored with a snorkel but not with scuba tanks (this is a general rule in protected parts of the Aegean to prevent pilfering and damage).

Of the famous wines which were once shipped all over ancient Greece in urns stamped "Ikion", there is no longer any trace. Yet in 1970, paleolithic evidence was found which could mean that Alónissos was singled out for habitation before any other island in the Aegean, perhaps as early as 100,000 BC, and it was considered a prize over which Philip of Macedon and the Athenians fought bitterly.

The way the island has adjusted to its unrealised potential and bad luck is something for which many visitors should be grateful. Its people are laid-back and charming, its atmosphere cheerful and unpretentious. It is also the least developed of the Sporades, a much quieter island surrounded by an interesting collection of islets. Some of them are off-limits to tourists and fishermen alike, protected areas within the Marine Park reserved for the endangered monk seal and other rare fauna. **Yioura**, for example, is home to a unique breed of wild goat and also has a cave that is full of stalactites and stalagmites which it pleases the islanders to believe was once occupied by a protective cyclops. It and **Pipéri** may not be visited, but caiques leave Patitíri on calm days for excursions to the closer islets of **Peristéra** and **Kyrá Panaghía**, where sheep roam and there are a couple of monasteries to glimpse.

The fishing round Alónissos is excellent too, and many of the swordfish which provide some of the best eating in the Sporades are taken in the waters

around the island. In the absence of proper roads, apart from the one to **Stení Vála**, caiques are the most practical form of transport. There is a fleet of them waiting every morning at Patitíri to take bathers to the beach of their choice. The terrain is rugged and walking accordingly quite demanding, but motorbiking is much safer here than on the winding roads of Skiáthos and Skópelos.

The path from Patitíri up to Paleá Alónissos is steep, but the old town is served by a bus and is well worth a visit. Thanks largely to the efforts of foreigners who spied a bargain and bought up the old ruins, it is fast coming back to life. Boutiques are springing up in once-abandoned courtyards and there are several bars and tavernas commanding stunning views, as well as providing restorative drinks and delicious food.

Skýros

The main character in Skýros's Carnival goat dance, staged just before Lent, is a *yéros* (old man) who wears a mask made out of goat skin and by shaking his hips rings the many sheep bells hanging from his waist. The second figure is the *koréla*, a young man dressed and behaving as a woman. Foreign visitors enjoying the spectacle ought to know that the third figure (the *frángos*), a buffoon who has a large bell strapped to his back and blows into a seashell, represents, well, a foreigner. Islanders might politely point out, however, that he is specifically a western European of the 17th century.

Visitors should not take the mockery to heart. Skýros does not have to put up with so many of them that their presence becomes intrusive, and in many ways the island goes on in its own sweet way as it has always done. The Greek Air Force, for instance, has taken over what was once a lovely beach at the north-

Skýros has some unique miniature horses, which have been bred exclusively on the island since ancient times. They may be the same breed as the horses depicted on the Parthenon frieze.

BELOW: the Faltaïts Museum above Skýros town.

Map on page 200

The Faltaïts Museum in a mansion north of town, is the family home of Manos Faltaïts, an artist, poet and sociologist with a deep love of Skyrian traditions. His collection presents the life of the island through folk art and crafts, books, costumes and photographs. (Daily 10am–1pm and 5.30–8pm.)

BELOW: Manos Faltaïts. **RIGHT:** carnival characters.

ern edge of the island, but nobody will be aware of their presence except on the rare occasion when a pilot buzzes the **Magaziá** beach on the northeast coast below Skýros town. The Skyrians are more interested in the quietly growing strength of their summer season, and their own way of life.

Older islanders will still wear traditional clothes as a matter of course, and behind their characteristic pebbled entrances the cubist houses contain amazing collections of craft work and other prized objects, many of them originally piratical booty. Carved wooden furniture passed down though the generations is often rather too small to be practical, which the islanders themselves seem to acknowledge by hanging a lot of it on the walls. The Skyrians also produce wonderful pottery, which you can find in a couple of shops along the main street up in town and from two producers down in the Magaziá area near the Xenia Hotel in Skýros town.

Skýros town ❾ is on the northern half of the island on the east coast, high above the long sand beach at the Magaziá. Life in the town is played out all along the meandering main street, which runs from the telephone exchange (OTE) past the raised, largely ignored square to the northern edge of town where a statue of a naked man representing Immortal Poetry (in memory of Rupert Brooke) commands the view. A side street wanders up to the **kástro**, the old Byzantine/Venetian castle on the heights from which, in legend, Theseus was thrown to his death.

The beach below town runs from the Magaziá all the way down to **Mólos**, and there are some more stretches of beach, although not as attractive, farther along the northeast coast near **Polýhri**. On the west side of the island there are pleasant sandy coves at **Linariá ❿**, just past the port, and **Péfkos**. The central section of this part of the island is wooded, as is the northern coast from just past the airport down to the little bay of **Atsítsa** which has, as required, a little taverna by the water.

Skýros was probably originally two islands, the halves joining near where there is now a road linking Linariá, the main port, with the little village of **Aspoús** on the way to Skýros town. The southern sector of the island is mountainous and largely barren, and visitors are unlikely to venture below **Kolimbádha** unless they are heading for **Pénnes** beach or at **Trís Boúkes ⓫**.

Trís Boúkes, the site of **Rupert Brooke's grave**, is about a 30-minute drive from Kolimbádha, and Pénnes another 15 minutes more over a reasonably well-tended, wide dirt road. The beaches at **Paghiá** and **Skloúka** just north of Kolimbádha are lined with a growing number of summer homes but have none of the appeal of the beaches in the north of the island. The real appeal of the southern part of Skýros is from the sea, for cliffs along most of the coast from Pénnes all the way around to Achílli Bay near Aspoús fall straight down into the sea. These cliffs are inhabited by a few wild goats and seemingly innumerable Eleanora's Falcons, which can be seen darting around the heights all the way over to Skýros town. Excursions by boat can be arranged at Linariá, where the Flying Dolphins and the island-owned ferry land. ❑

ÉVVIA

*Greece's second largest island is largely unspoilt by tourism,
and little known by outsiders. Although it is barely separated
from the mainland, Évvia has a rich, independent history*

BELOW: fishing in
Halkídha harbour.

On the map, Évvia (Euboea) looks like a large jigsaw puzzle piece just slightly out of position. The island's main town, Halkídha, is close enough to the mainland for an elderly drawbridge and a new suspension bridge to make easy connection. Aristotle is supposed to have been so frustrated in trying to understand the tides here in the narrow channel, which are highly irregular and sometimes quite fast, that he killed himself by jumping into the waters.

In antiquity the two most prominent cities were Chalcis (modern Halkídha) and nearby Eretria, both of which became powerful trading cities, establishing colonies in Syria, the Aegean islands, Italy, and Sicily. After the Persian wars Evvia came under Athenian control, from which it revolted in 411 BC. Thereafter it was under either Athenian or Theban rule until the Macedonians arrived in 338 BC, then the Romans in 194 BC. This evolved into Byzantine control, which lasted until the Venetians captured the island in 1210. The Venetians ruled the island for over 250 years, until it was taken by the Ottoman Turks in 1470. Evvia became part of Greece in 1830, after the Greek War of Independence.

Halkídha (Halkís, Chalkís) ❶ is now an industrial town, but the **kástro** with its mosque and **Church of Aghía Paraskeví** are worth visiting, as is the **Archeological Museum** in the new town (Tue–Sun, 8.30am–3pm). There is also a synagogue, built in the middle of the 19th century and still used by the small Jewish Romaniote community. **Erétria ❷** to the south is a crowded summer resort town where the ferries land from Skála Oropoú on the mainland. This is a town to pass through (as is Halkídha), but the small **Archeological Museum** here is very good (Tue–Sun, 8.30am–3pm).

The road south along the gentle coast is dotted with villages and summer homes until just before **Alivéri** where it turns inland. From **Lépoura** to the north the main road goes through the hamlet of **Háni Avlonaríou**, with the large and unusual 14th-century Church of Ághios Dimitríos, before continuing through often beautiful hilly farmland to drop down on the east coast to **Paralía** (or Stómio), where a small river reaches the sea. The wide new road then runs along the shore through **Platána** to the harbour at **Paralía Kými** and the boat to Skýros.

In general, the southern part of the island is drier and less green. The turning for the south is at **Lépoura**. On the main road between **Almyropótamos** and **Polypótamos** along the narrowest part of the island, there are views from the road down to the sea to both the east and the west. Near the village of **Stýra ❸** are the ruins of three buildings of huge stone known locally as Dragon Houses (*dhrakóspita*). These remains are of great age but unknown date.

Neá Stýra, 4 km (2½ miles) away on the coast, is a

resort town with direct ferry connections (40 minutes) to the small port of Aghía Marína on the west coast of Attica. **Marmári**, another resort/port village farther down the coast, has frequent ferry boat connections with Rafína (1 hour 15 minutes). The main town in the south is the prosperous town of **Kárystos** ❹ with its long beach. Both ferries and Flying Dolphins from Rafína stop here.

North of Halkídha the small village of **Stení** ❺ on the slopes of **Mount Dhírfys** (1,743 metres/5,718 ft) is a favorite goal for Athenians seeking clean air and grill restaurants. **Prokópi** ❻, on the main road, was built beside the Keréa River on land bought from the Ottomans by the Englishman Edward Noel in the 1830s. The Noel-Bakers, his descendants, manage a conference centre in the old family home. The town was settled after 1923 by refugees from Asia Minor who brought with them the relics of an 18th-century saint named St John the Russian, canonised in 1962. The saint's relics are in the unattractive cement church in the central square.

Prokópi is famed for its honey, which you can buy in the village in a variety of flavours, including thyme, orange-flower and pine.

Límni ❼ on the west coast is a pretty and convenient 19th-century town, though the nearby beaches are unimpressive. A long stretch of truly outstanding beach is farther north, after the ancient but still functioning baths at **Loutrá Edhipsoú** ❽, from **Gregolímano** and **Aghios Yeórghios** all the way around the triangular point of the peninsula.

The east coast is mountainous, dropping sharply to the sea, but there are a few beaches, such as **Angáli**, **Paralía Kotsikiás**, **Psaropoúli** and **Ellinká**, of which the last is the smallest and prettiest.

The famous bronze statue of Poseidon poised to throw a trident, now in Room 15 of the Archeological Museum in Athens, was found in 1928 in the sea off **Cape Artemesion** (Ákti Artemíssio) on the northern coast. ❑

Map on page 207

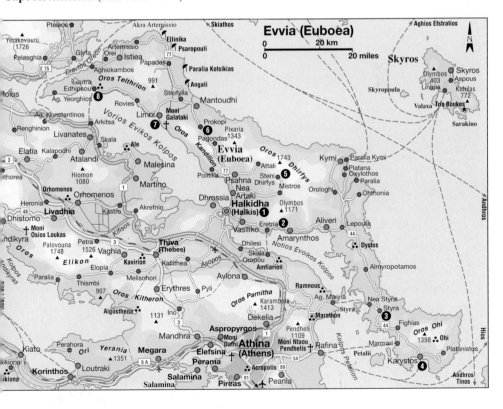

THE NORTHEAST AEGEAN

Thássos, Samothráki, Límnos, Ághios Efstrátios,
Lésvos, Psará, Híos, Ikaría, Sámos

The islands of the northeast Aegean have little in common other than a history of medieval Genoese rule. The northerly group, comprising Thássos, Samothráki and Límnos, has few or no connections with the south Aegean; indeed Thássos belongs to the Macedonian province of Kavála, and Samothráki to Thracian Évros. This close to the mainland, and with a short summer season, the Greeks' own affection for these convenient islands takes precedence over foreign package tourism. Except for marble-cored Thássos, these isles – as well as Lésvos – are of volcanic origin, their gentle slopes thinly covered by lava-tolerant oak trees.

Lésvos, Híos and Sámos to the southeast once played leading roles in antiquity, colonising across the Mediterranean and promoting the arts and sciences, though little tangible evidence of ancient glory remains. All three islands served as bridges between Asia Minor and the rest of the Hellenic world and were, in fact, once joined to the coast of Asia Minor until Ice-Age cataclysms isolated them. Turkey is still omnipresent on the horizon, just 2 km (1 mile) away across the Mykale straits at Sámos. Politically, however, the two countries are often light years apart, something reflected in absurdly inflated fares for the short boat trip across.

Híos, Sámos and Ikaría are rugged limestone and schist, forested with pine, olive and cypress. Delicate spring and autumn wildflowers, especially on Sámos, heighten their appeal, and numerous small mammals and birds thrive, having migrated over from Anatolia before the rising sea marooned them. Beaches, fairly evenly distributed across the group, vary from long shores of fist-sized pebbles to sheltered, sandy crescents.

As ever, transport to, betweeen and on the bigger islands varies with the population and level of tourism. Samothráki has a skeletal bus service and overpriced ferries from Alexandhroúpoli; Thássos by contrast has frequent buses and regular car ferries from Kavála and Keramotí. Límnos and Lésvos have regular flights and sailings from Piraeus and Thessaloníki, plus each other; Híos is linked daily with Athens and Lésvos, less regularly with Sámos or Ikaría, and – unlike northern neighbours – not at all by charter to northern Europe. Ikaría is similarly remote, though like adjacent Sámos is connected to certain Cyclades. Sámos itself could rank as an honorary Dodecanese island: it has ferry and hydrofoil links with all isles from Pátmos to Kós, and receives far more international charters than runner-up Lésvos. ❏

PRECEDING PAGES: a grim reminder of the 1822 massacre on Híos; tomatoes strung up to dry in Pyrghí, Híos. **LEFT:** baptism is a community event.

THÁSSOS, SAMOTHRÁKI AND LÍMNOS

Map on page 216

Greece's most northerly islands do not see much package tourism, but they offer more than enough by way of ancient ruins, empty beaches and picturesque villages

Thássos

Just seven nautical miles (12 km) from mainland Macedonia, Thássos – always a favourite retreat of northern Greeks – has recently welcomed a cosmopolitan assortment of foreigners. Yet the island seems relatively unspoiled, with package tourism well quarantined. Mountainous, almost circular Thássos is essentially a giant lump of marble, mixed with granite and schist, crumbling into white beach sand at the island's margins. Lower elevations, covered in vast olive plantations, remain attractive, but "the Diamond of the North" (*Dhiamándis tou Vorrá*) had its lustre severely dulled by forest fires in 1981, 1985, 1989 and 1993, which were deliberately set by developers after cheap building land. Thássos is now three-quarters denuded of its original pine forest, which survives only in the northeast. Elsewhere, only the inland villages and a thin fringe of surrounding vegetation were saved. The bus service around the coastal ring road is adequate, though most visitors rent motorbikes or cars (Thássos is small enough for a long-day tour). The east and south coasts have the better beaches; the west coast has access to most inland villages.

Thássos' past glory is most evident at the harbour capital of **Liménas** (or **Limín**, also known simply as **Thássos**) ❶, where substantial remnants of the ancient town have been excavated; choice bits of the ancient acropolis overhead are nocturnally illuminated. The biggest area, behind the picturesque fishing harbour which traces the confines of the ancient commercial port, is the **agora**. The nearby archeological museum is closed until the year 2000 for a major overhaul to accommodate a backlog of finds.

Beginning at the **Temple of Dionysos**, a path permits a rewarding walking tour of the ancient walls and acropolis. First stop is the Hellenistic **theatre** (currently closed for re-excavation). Continue to the **medieval fortress**, built by a succession of occupiers from the masonry of a temple of Apollo. Tracing the course of massive 5th-century BC walls brings you to the foundations of a **temple of Athena**, beyond which a rock outcrop bears a **shrine of Pan**, visible in badly eroded relief. From here a vertiginous "secret" stairway plunges to the **Gate of Parmenon**, the only ancient entry still intact, at the southern edge of town.

The first village clockwise from Liménas, slate-roofed **Panaghía** ❷, is a large, busy place where life revolves around the *platía* with its plane trees and four-spouted fountain. **Potamiá**, further down the valley, is far less architecturally distinguished: visitors come mainly for the sake of the **Polygnotos Vaghis**

LEFT: Hóra (Samothráki) at sunset. **BELOW:** off-season sewing.

Museum (Tue–Sat, 9am–1pm, summer also 6–9pm; Sun, 10am–2pm), featuring the work of that locally-born sculptor. Beyond, the road plunges to the coast at Potamiá Bay.

Skála Potamiás, at its south end, is all lodging and tavernas, with more of that to the north at Hryssí Ammoudhiá. In between stretches a fine, blond-sand beach. There are even better strands at Kínyra, 24 km (15 miles) from Liménas, but most one-day tourists schedule a lunch stop at one of the several tavernas of Alykí ❸ hamlet, architecturally preserved thanks to adjacent ruins: an ancient temple and two atmospheric Byzantine basilicas. The local topography of a low spit, sandy to the west, nearly pinching off a headland is strikingly photogenic. So too is the Convent of Arhangélou Mihaïl 5 km (3 miles) to the west, high above a barren coast – but mainly from a distance; it has been renovated rather hideously since 1974.

At Limenária ❹, now the island's second town, mansions of departed German mining executives survive. More intriguingly, perhaps, it's the starting-

Locally-made honey, candied walnuts and tsípouro, the fire-water of northern Greece, are favourite souvenirs of Thássos.

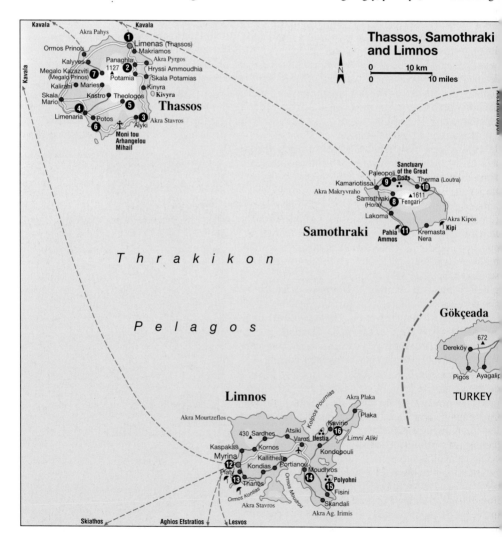

Thassos, Samothraki and Limnos

0   10 km
0   10 miles

Thassos

Samothraki

T h r a k i k o n

P e l a g o s

Gökçeada

Limnos

TURKEY

point for a safari up to hilltop **Kástro**, the most naturally pirate-proof of the inland villages. Beyond Limenária, there's little to compel a stop other than side roads up to the villages from their *skáles*, relatively recent – and scraggly – shore settlements built once the seas had been cleared of marauders.

Theológos ❺, actually reached from the over-developed resort of **Potós ❻**, was the island's Ottoman capital, a linear place where most houses have walled gardens. **Mariés** sits piled up at the top of a wooded valley, just glimpsing the sea. By contrast **Sotíros** enjoys phenomenal sunsets, best enjoyed from its central taverna under enormous plane trees. Of all the inland settlements, **Megálo Kazazvíti** (officially **Megálo Prínos**) ❼ has the grandest *platía* and the best-preserved traditional houses, snapped up and restored by outsiders. Ground-floor windows still retain iron bars, reminders of pirate days.

Map on page 216

Unlike the elitist Eleusinian Mysteries, the Samothracian cult of the Kabiri was open to all comers, including women and slaves. But, as at Eleusis, the details of the rites are unknown, for adherents took a vow of silence.

Samothráki

Samothráki (or Samothrace) raises forbidding granite heights above stony shores and storm-lashed waters, both offering poor natural anchorage. Homer described Poseidon perched atop 1,611-metre (5,000-ft) **Mount Fengári**, the Aegean's highest summit, watching the action of the Trojan War to the east. Fengári and its foothills occupy much of the island, with little level terrain except in the far west. Its southwest flank features scattered villages lost amid olive groves varied by the occasional poplar. North-facing slopes are damper, with chestnuts and oaks, plus plane trees along the numerous watercourses. Springs are abundant, and waterfalls even plunge directly to the sea at **Kremastá Nerá** in the south. Only the west of the island has paved roads, and a rudimentary bus service.

Tourism is barely developed, and the remaining islanders prefer it that way. In its absence the population has dipped below 3,000, as farming can only support so many. Boats and occasional hydrofoils dock at **Kamariótissa**, the functional port where rental vehicles are in short supply.

Hóra or **Samothráki ❽**, the official capital 5 km (3 miles) east of Kamariótissa, is more rewarding, nestling almost invisibly in a circular hollow. A cobbled commercial street serpentines past sturdy, basalt-built houses, many now unused. From outdoor seating at the two tavernas on Hóra's large *platía*, you glimpse the sea beyond a crumbled Byzantine-Genoese fort at the edge of town.

Samothráki's other great sight lies just outside the ancient capital **Paleópoli ❾**, 6 km (3½ miles) from Kamariótissa along the north-coast road. From the late Bronze Age until the coming of Christianity, the **Sanctuary of the Great Gods** was the major religious centre of the Aegean. Local deities of the original Thracian settlers were easily syncretised with the Olympian gods of later Aeolian colonists, in particular the Kabiri, or divine twins Castor and Pollux, patrons of seafarers (who needed all the help they could get hereabouts).

The sanctuary ruins (Tue–Sun, 8.30am–3pm) visible today are mostly late Hellenistic, and still eerily impressive, though overgrown. Obvious monuments include a partly re-erected temple of the second initiation; the peculiar round *Arsinoeion*, used for sacri-

BELOW: the hamlet of Kástro, Thássos.

fices; a round theatre area, for performances during the summer festival; and the fountain niche where the celebrated Winged Victory of Samothrace, now in the Louvre, was discovered.

Some 6 km (3½ miles) further east, hot springs, cool cascades and a dense canopy of plane trees make the spa hamlet of **Thermá (Loutrá)** , the most popular base on the island, patronised by an uneasy mix of the elderly infirm and young bohemian types from several nations. Hot baths come in three temperatures and styles – including outdoor pools under a wooden shelter – while cold-plunge fanatics make for **Gría Váthra** canyon to the east. Thermá is also the base camp for the climb of Mount Fengári, a six-hour round-trip.

The villages south of Hóra see few visitors, though they lie astride the route to **Pahiá Ámmos** ⓫, the island's only sandy beach. From **Lákoma** village, it's about 8 km (5 miles) by rough dirt track to the beach, where a single seasonal taverna operates. Beyond Pahiá Ámmos, you can walk to smaller **Vátos** nudist beach, but you'll need a boat – or to drive completely around Samothráki – to reach the gravel beach of **Kípi** in the far southeast.

Límnos

Dominating the approaches to the Dardanelles, Límnos has been occupied since Neolithic times, and always prospered as a trading station and military outpost, rather than a major political power. The Greek military still controls nearly half the island's extent, including half of the huge airport, belying an otherwise peaceful atmosphere. The volcanic soil dwindles to excellent beaches, or produces excellent wine and a variety of other farm products. The surrounding seas yield plenty of fish, thanks to periodic migrations through the Dardanelles.

Most things of interest are found in the port-capital, **Mýrina** ⓬, or a short distance to either side – luckily, since the bus service is appalling. Volcanic stone has been put to good use in the older houses and street cobbles of Mýrina, while elaborate Ottoman mansions face the northerly town beach of **Romeïkós Yialós** with its cafés. The southerly beach of **Tourkikós Yialós** abuts the fishing port and contains half a dozen seafood tavernas.

Mýrina's admirable **Archeological Museum** (Tue-Sun, 8.30am–3pm) holds finds from the island's major archeological sites. Public evidence of the town's Ottoman period is limited to an inscribed fountain and a dilapidated mosque behind a supermarket, both near the harbour end of the long market street. Festooned engagingly over the headland above town, the ruined local **kástro** is worth climbing up to for sunset views.

The road north from Mýrina passes the exclusive **Aktí Mýrina** resort en route to good beaches at **Avlónas** and **Ághios Ioánnis**. In the opposite direction lie even better ones at **Platý** ⓭ and **Thános**, with tiered namesake villages on the hillsides just above. Continuing southeast from Thános brings you to **Nevgátis**, acknowledged as the island's best beach.

Sadder relics of more recent history flank the drab port town of **Moúdhros** ⓮ – two Allied cemeteries maintained by the Commonwealth War Graves Commission. During World War I, Moúdhros was the

The 4th-century BC statue of Victory (Athena Nike) was discovered in 1863 by a French diplomat, Charles Champoiseau, who immediately sent it to Paris. The Greek government has long demanded its return, but so far has had to settle for a plaster copy.

BELOW: a figure near Thermá, Samothráki, points to the coastal campsite.

principal base for the disastrous Gallipoli campaign. Of roughly 36,000 casualties, 887 are interred outside Moúdhros town on the way to **Roussopoúli**, while 348 more lie behind the village church at **Portianoú**, across the bay.

The major archeological sites on Límnos are all a long trip away, in the far east of the island. **Polyóhni** , southwest of Roussopoúli, was a fortified town even older than Troy, but was destroyed by an earthquake in 2100 BC and never rebuilt. **Ifestía** on the north coast was the ancient capital and the largest city on the island until the Byzantine period. The foundations of a temple of Hephaistos and a Roman theatre are visible. Across the bay at **Kavírio** was a sanctuary to the Kabiri, the Great Gods. Not much remains to be seen except the stumps and bases of columns.

A tiny wedge of land south of Límnos, **Ághios Efstrátios (Aï Strátis)** is without doubt the most desolate spot in the Northeast Aegean – all the more so since a 1967 earthquake devastated the single village. Owing to junta-era corruption, reparable dwellings were bulldozed and the surviving inhabitants (nearly half were killed) provided with ugly, prefabricated replacement housing on a grid plan. This, plus two dozen surviving old buildings on the left, is what you see if you disembark the regular ferries stopping here on the Rafína-Límnos-Kavála route, or (in summer) the small ferry based in Límnos – together these constitute Aï Strátis's lifeline, as all supplies must be imported.

Fish are the only thing in local abundance. There's little arable land aside from the valley partly clogged by the prefabs. The inevitably sad settlement can muster perhaps 200 permanent residents. There are a couple of taverna-cafés and a single pension for the rare tourist. None of the beaches, within 90 minutes' walk to north or south, is likely to contain another soul. ❑

Map on page 216

In the Polyóhni ruins archeologists discovered a hoard of gold jewellery from the 3rd millennium BC. It is now on display in Athens.

BELOW: an old boat-builder's yard on Límnos.

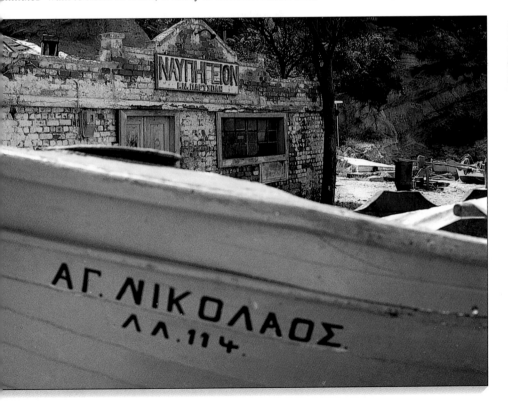

LÉSVOS, HÍOS, IKARÍA AND SÁMOS

These were some of Ancient Greece's wealthiest islands, and there are many impressive relics of their former prosperity, as well as reminders of their dramatic, more recent history

Map on page 222

Lésvos

Greece's third largest island, measuring 70 by 40 km (44 by 24 miles) at its extremities, remote, fertile Lésvos is the antithesis of the *nisáki* or quaint little islet. Between far-flung villages lie 11 million olive trees producing 45,000 tonnes of oil every year. Shipbuilding, carpentry, ouzo-distilling and pottery remain important, but none rivals the olive, especially since it complements the second industry of tourism. Nets to catch this "black gold" are laid out in autumn, as soon as the tourists leave.

With its thick southern forests and idyllic orchards, Lésvos was a preferred Roman holiday spot. The Byzantines considered it a humane exile for deposed nobility, while the Genoese Gateluzzi clan kept a thriving court here for a century. To the Ottomans it was "The Garden of the Aegean", their most productive, strictly governed and heavily colonised Aegean island.

Following 18th-century reforms within the empire, a Christian land-owning aristocracy developed, served by a large population of labouring peasants. This quasi-feudal system made Lésvos fertile ground for post-1912 Leftist movements, and its habit of returning Communist MPs since the junta fell has earned it the epithet "Red Island" among fellow-Greeks. The years after 1912 also saw a vital local intelligentsia emerge, but since World War II Lésvos's socio-economic fabric has shrunk considerably with emigration to Athens, Australia and America. However the founding here in 1987 of the University of the Aegean brought hope for a cultural revival.

Mytilíni ❶, the capital (its name a popular alias for the entire island), has a revved-up, slightly gritty atmosphere, as befits a port town of 30,000. It's interesting to stroll around, though few outsiders stay. Behind the waterfront, assorted church domes and spires enliven the skyline, while Odhós Ermoú one street inland contains an entire bazaar, from the fish market to a clutch of excellent but pricey antique shops. On the headland to the northeast sits the medieval **kástro** (Tue–Sun, 8.30am–3pm), with ruins from various eras. Behind the ferry dock is the **Archeological Museum** (Tue–Sun, 8.30am–3pm) featuring Hellenistic mosaics depicting scenes from Menander's comedies and interesting grave *stelae*.

More noteworthy is the **Theophilos Museum** (Tue–Sun, 9am–2pm, 5–8pm, free Sun) which contains over 60 paintings by locally-born Theophilos Hazimihaïl, Greece's most celebrated naïve painter. The **Thériade Museum** at **Variá**, 4 km (2½ miles) south of town

LEFT: a priest observes a card game in Híos. **BELOW:** a beach in the Gulf of Yéra, southeast Lésvos.

Lesvos, Hios, Ikaria and Samos

Lesvos

Hios

Ikaria

Samos

AEGEAN SEA

TURKEY

İzmir

0   10 km
0   10 miles

N

(Tue–Sun, 9am–2pm and 5–8pm), was founded by another native son who, while an avant-garde art publisher in Paris, assembled this collection, with work by the likes of Chagall, Picasso, Rouault and Léger.

The road running northwest from Mytilíni follows the coast facing Turkey. **Mandamádhos ❷**, 37 km (23 miles) from Mytilíni, offers a surviving pottery industry and, at the outskirts, the enormous **Monastery of the Taxiárhis** with its much-revered black icon. At **Kápi** the road divides; the northerly fork is wider, better paved and more scenic as it curls across the flanks of Mount Lepétymnos, passing by the handsome village of **Sykaminiá ❸**, the birthplace of novelist Stratis Myrivilis.

You descend to sea level at **Mólyvos** (sometimes known by its ancient name, **Míthymna**) **❹**, the linchpin of Lésvos tourism and understandably so: the ranks of sturdy tiled houses climbing to the medieval castle are an appealing sight, as is the stone-paved fishing harbour. But its days as a colony for bohemian artists and alternative activities are over, with package tourism dominant since the late 1980s. **Pétra ❺**, 5 km (3 miles) south, accommodates the overflow on its long beach, while inland at the village centre looms a rock plug crowned with the **Panaghía Glykofiloússa** church. At its foot the 18th-century **Vareltzídena Mansion** (Tue–Sun, 8.30am–3pm) is worth a look, as is the frescoed church of **Ághios Nikólaos**.

The Theophilos Museum in Mytilíni contains the largest collection of works by Greece's most famous naïve painter.

From Pétra, head 17 km (11 miles) south to **Kalloní ❻** and the turning for **Límonos Monastery ❼**, home to small ecclesiastical and folklore museums, before continuing west towards the more rugged half of the island, with its lunar volcanic terrain. Stream valleys foster little oases, such as the one around **Perivolís Monastery**, 30 km (19 miles) from Limónos (daily 8am–7pm), dec-

BELOW: the harbour of Mytilíni.

Map on page 222

Lésvos claims to produce the finest olive oil in all Greece. The olives are harvested in November and December, and pressed within 24 hours of being picked.

orated with wonderful frescoes. Beyond 10 km (6 miles), on top of an extinct volcano, the **Monastery of Ipsiloú** contemplates the abomination of desolation – complete with scattered trunks of the "Petrified Forest", prehistoric sequoias mineralised by volcanic ash.

Sígri , 90 km (56 miles) from Mytilíni, is a sleepy place flanked by good beaches, and very much the end of the line, though it has recently become an alternate ferry port. Most prefer **Skála Eressoú** , 14 km (9 miles) south of Ipsiloú, for a beach experience. In particular numerous lesbians come to honour Sappho, who was born here.

Southern Lésvos, between the two gulfs, is home to olive groves rolling up to 968-metre (3,176-ft) Mount Ólymbos. **Plomári** on the coast is Lésvos' second town, famous for its oúzo industry. Most tourists stay at pebble-beach **Ághios Isídhoros** 3 km (2 miles) east, though **Melínda** 6 km (4 miles) west is more scenic. **Vaterá**, with its 7-km (4½-mile) sand beach reckoned the best on the island, lies still further west, reached by a different road. En route, you can stop for a soak at the restored medieval spa outside **Polyhnítos** , 45 km (28 miles) from Mytilíni. Inland from Plomári, the remarkable hill village of **Aghiássos** nestles in a wooded valley under Ólymbos. Its heart is the major pilgrimage church of **Panaghía Vrefokratoússa**, which comes alive for the 15 August festival, Lésvos' biggest. Local musicians are considered among the island's best; they're evident at the pre-Lenten carnival as well, celebrated here with gusto.

Híos

Although Híos (often spelt Chíos) had been important and prosperous since antiquity, the Middle Ages made the Híos of today. After the Genoese seized control here in 1346, the Justiniani clan established a cartel, the *maona*, which controlled the highly profitable trade in gum mastic. During their rule, which also saw the introduction of silk and citrus production, Híos became one of the wealthiest and most cultured islands in the Mediterranean.

In 1566 the Ottomans expelled the Genoese, but granted the islanders numerous privileges, so that Híos continued to flourish until March 1822, when poorly armed agitators from Sámos convinced the reluctant Hiots to participate in the independence uprising. Sultan Mahmut II, enraged at this ingratitude, exacted a terrible revenge. A two-month rampage commanded by Admiral Kara Ali killed 30,000 islanders, enslaved 45,000 more, and saw all settlements except the mastic-producing villages razed. Híos had only partly recovered when a strong earthquake in March 1881 destroyed much of what remained and killed 4,000.

Today Híos and its satellite islet Inoússes are home to some of Greece's wealthiest shipping families. The catastrophic 19th century ensures that **Híos town** or **Hóra** (pop. 25,000) seems off-puttingly modern at first glance. But scratch the ferro-concrete surface and you'll find traces of the Genoese and Ottoman years. The most obvious medieval feature is the **kástro**. Moated on the landward side, it lacks a seaward rampart, destroyed after the 1881 quake. Just

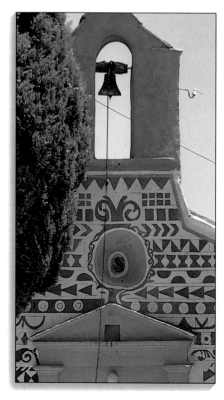

inside the impressive **Porta Maggiora** stands the **Justiniani Museum** (Tue–Sun, 9am–3pm), a worthwhile collection of religious art rescued from rural churches. Off a small nearby square is the Muslim cemetery with the tomb of Kara Ali – the massacring admiral, blown up along with his flagship by one of Admiral Kanaris's fire-boats in June 1822. Still further inside lies the old Muslim and Jewish quarter with its derelict mosque and overhanging houses. Christians were required to settle outside the walls.

The lively bazaar extends south of central **Platía Vounakíou**, with Aplotariás as its backbone – fascinating alleyways between this street and Venizélou culminate in a wonderful *belle époque* meat-and-produce gazebo. Also on Platía Vounakíou, the intact **Mecidiye Mosque** now serves as a Byzantine Museum (Mon–Fri, 9am–2pm), merely a warehouse for various lapidary fragments; the "real" archeological museum is closed indefinitely for repairs.

Heading south out of Hóra you pass through **Kámbos** ⓮, a broad plain of high-walled citrus groves dotted with the imposing sandstone mansions of the medieval aristocracy, standing along narrow, unmarked lanes. Many were destroyed by the earthquake, while a few have been restored as accommodation or restaurants. Irrigation water was originally drawn up by *manganós* or water-wheel; a few survive in the centre of ornately paved courtyards.

The onward road heads southwest towards mastic-producing southern Híos, with its 20 villages collectively known as the *mastihohoriá*, built as pirate-proof strongholds by the Genoese during the 14th and 15th centuries. Each village is laid out on a dense, rectangular plan, with narrow passages over-arched by earthquake buttresses, and the backs of the outer houses doubling as the perimeter wall.

Map on page 222

The sailors of Híos were such skilled navigators that, it is claimed, Christopher Columbus came to study with Hiot captains before his voyages.

BELOW: stringing tomatoes to dry in Pyrghí, Híos.

Most of the houses in the mastic village of Pyrghí are incised with black and white geometric patterns called xystá.

BELOW:
scraping resin off
a mastic tree.

Pyrghí , 21 km (13 miles) from Hóra, is one of the best-preserved *mastihohoriá*. A passageway off its central square leads to Byzantine **Ághii Apóstoli** church, decorated with later frescoes. In Pyrghí's back alleys, tomatoes are laboriously strung for drying in late summer by teams of local women. Some 11 km (7 miles) west, **Mestá** ⑯ seems a more sombre, monochrome labyrinth, which retains defensive towers at its corners. Several three-storeyed houses have been restored as accommodation. Such quarters are typically claustrophobic, though, and guests will appreciate the nearby beach resorts of **Kómi** (sand) and **Emboriós** (volcanic pebbles).

With your own car, the beautiful, deserted west coast with its many coves is accessible via **Véssa**. Between **Kastélla** and **Elínda** bays, a good road snakes uphill to **Avgónyma** ⑰, a clustered village well restored by returned Greek-Americans. Just 4 km (2½ miles) north perches almost-deserted, crumbling **Anávatos**, well camouflaged against its cliff. Here in 1822, 400 Hiots leapt from it to their deaths rather than be captured.

Some 5 km (3 miles) east, **Néa Moní** ⑱ (daily 8am–1pm and 4–8pm, 4–6pm winter) forms one of the finest surviving examples of mid-Byzantine architecture, founded in 1049 by Emperor Constantine Monomachus IX on a spot where a miraculous icon of the Virgin had appeared. It suffered heavily in 1822 and 1881, first with the murder of its monks, plus the pillage of its treasures, and then with the collapse of its dome. Despite the damage, its mosaics of scenes from the life of Christ are outstanding. The outbuildings have lain in ruins since the events of the 19th century. By the gate, an ossuary displays the bones of the 1822 martyrs together with generations of monks. The paved road eventually takes you to castle-crowned **Volissós** ⑲ in the northwest. To either side of this half-

UP A GUM TREE

The mastic bushes of southern Híos are the unique source of gum mastic, once the basis for many products: it was popular in Istanbul as chewing gum and was allegedly used to freshen the breath of the sultan's concubines; the Romans had their toothpicks made from mastic because they believed it kept their teeth white and prevented tooth decay; the "father of medicine", Hippocrates, praised its therapeutic value for coughs and colds; and lately some practitioners of alternative medicine have been making even more ambitious claims on its behalf.

The first stages of the mastic production process are basically unchanged since ancient times. The villagers set off from the *mastihohoriá* on late summer mornings, some on donkeys, some in pick-up trucks. They make incisions in the bark of the trees, which weep resin "tears". These are carefully scraped off and cleaned of leaves or twigs.

In the final stage, the raw gum is sent to a central processing plant where the "tears" are washed, baked and formed into "chiclets". Some 150 tons of mastic are produced annually, most of it exported to France, Bulgaria and Saudi Arabia for prices of up to $35 a kilo.

empty village are the island's finest beaches – and visible scars from a series of 1980s fires which burnt two-thirds of Híos's forests.

Despite provincial appearances, the peaceful, green islet of **Inoússes** (Oinoússes), some 16 km (10 miles) north of Híos harbour by regular caique, is actually the wealthiest territory in Greece, home to the Livanos, Lemos and Pateras shipping families. Appropriately, a marine academy that trains many seamen for Greece's merchant fleet stands at the west end of the quay, with a small private maritime museum in the centre of the single town. Small but decent beaches lie to either side.

The tiny islet of **Psará**, 71 km (44 miles) to the west of Híos, derives its name from the adjective *psarós* or "grey" – and a grey place it is, especially since 1824, when 14,000 Ottoman troops landed here to avenge continued harassment of their shipping by Psaran Admiral Kanaris, who commanded the third largest Greek fleet after those of Hydra and Spétses. Some 27,000 islanders died – many blowing themselves up in a ridge-top powder magazine rather than surrender – and only about 3,000 escaped. The Ottomans burned any remaining buildings and vegetation.

Today about 350 inhabitants remain on melancholy Psará, its bleakness relieved only by occasional fig trees and one cultivated field in the west. Besides the lone port village, there's just a deserted monastery in the far north. Six beaches lie northeast of the port, each better than the one before, though all of them catch tide-wrack on this exposed coast. Just a few tourists trickle over from Híos, either on the thrice-weekly Miniotis Line ferry from Híos town, or on a summer-only caique from Volissós of similar frequency; ferries call rarely from Sígri on Lésvos.

Map on page 222

"The Massacre of Chios", an 1824 painting by Delacroix depicting the slaughter of 1822, caused controversy in Europe and won much sympathy for the Greek cause.

BELOW: washing mastic in the Hóra processing plant.

Ikaría

This narrow, wing-shaped island is named after the mythical Ikaros (Icarus), who supposedly fell into the sea nearby when his wax wings melted. One of the least developed large islands in the Aegean, Ikaría has little to offer anyone intent on ticking off four-star sights, but appeals to those disposed to an eccentric, slightly Ruritanian environment. During the military regime of the colonels, the island served as a place of exile for hundreds of communists. The locals thought they were the most noble, humanitarian folk they'd ever met, and still vote Communist in droves – not quite what Athens intended.

Apparently impervious to the irony, the Greek Air Force has adopted the doomed aviator Ikaros as its patron.

Ághios Kírykos ⑳ is the capital and main southerly port. It is little more than a sleepy fishing village, its tourist facilities geared to the clientele at the neighbouring spa of **Thermá**. Taxis are far more reliable than the bus for the spectacular 41-km (25-mile) drive over the 1,000-metre (3,300-ft) Atherás ridge to **Évdhilos ㉑**, the north-facing second port, a small, relaxed resort.

Another 16 km (10 miles) takes you past **Kámbos**, with its sandy beach and ruined Byzantine palace, to the end of the asphalt at **Armenistís ㉒**. It is only here that foreigners congregate, for the sake of excellent beaches – Livádhi and Mesaktí, just east – though the surf can be deadly.

Nás, 4 km (2½ miles) west, is named for the *náos* or temple of Artemis Tavropolio on the banks of the river draining to a popular pebble cove. **Yialiskári**, a fishing port 4 km (2½ miles) east, is distinguished by its photogenic jetty chapel. There are few bona fide inland villages, as the proud Ikarians hate to live on top of each other, and keep plenty of room for orchards between their houses. Above Armenistís are four hamlets lost in pine forest, collectively known as **Ráhes**. At **Hristós**, the largest, people cram the café-bars all night,

BELOW: sailing the Aegean in style.

sleep until noon, and carry belongings (or store potent wine) in hairy goatskin bags. The surrounding countryside completes the hobbit-like image with vertical natural monoliths and troglodytic cottages for livestock made entirely of gigantic slate slabs. Dirt roads are abysmal, especially towards the south coast, where the few hamlets are more easily reached by boat.

Foúrni, one of a mini-archipelago of islets southeast of Ikaría, lives from its thriving fishing fleet and boatyards. Seafood dinners figure high in the ambitions of arriving tourists, who mostly stay in the main, surprisingly large port town. A road links this with Ághios Ioánnis Hryssóstomos in the south and idyllic Hryssomiliá in the far north, the only other habitations, but path walking (where possible) and boat-riding are more relaxing ways of getting around. The best of many beaches are at **Kámbi**, one ridge south of the port, or at **Psilí Ámmos** and **Kálamos** on the north.

Sámos

Almost subtropical Sámos, with vine terraces, cypress and olive groves, surviving forests of black and Calabrian pine, hillside villages, and beaches of every size and consistency, appeals to numerous package tourists. A half-dozen wild fires since 1986 have not yet done for its natural beauty, and only the east has been thoroughly commercialised. Impassable gorges, the Aegean's second highest mountain and beaches accessible only on foot hold sway in the far west.

Natural endowments take precedence over man-made ones, as evidence of ancient glory is sparse, and Sámos has an identity problem owing to a 16th-century depopulation and later recolonisation. First settled in the 13th century BC, by the 7th century Sámos was a major maritime power thanks to its innovative

Map on page 222

In July 1912, a Dr Malahias declared Ikaría liberated from the Turks. For three months it was an independent republic with its own money and stamps.

BELOW: the remote chapel of Yialiskári, Ikaría.

One column is all that remains of Polykrates' great temple to Hera. He planned it to be the largest temple in Greece, but it was never completed.

BELOW: *kouros* in the Archeological Museum, Vathý.

triremes, still shown on local wine labels. A "golden age" ensued under the rule (538–522) of Polykrates, a brilliant but unscrupulous tyrant who doubled as a pirate. Wealth, however accumulated, supported a luxurious capital of 60,000, and a court attended by the likes of philosopher-mathematician Pythagoras, the astronomer Aristarchus and the bard Aesop. Decline ensued with Polykrates' death at the hands of the Persians, and the rise of Athens.

Heavily commercialised **Pythagório**  occupies the site of Polykrates' capital, three of whose monuments earned Herodotus' highest praise: "I have spoken at greater length of the Samians because of all the Greeks they have achieved the three greatest constructions." From the immense harbour mole constructed by ancient slaves (the first of the great constructions), you watch Mount Mykale in Turkey majestically change colour at dusk.

The 1,040-metre (3,200-ft) **Evpalínio Órygma** (Eupalinos' Tunnel) an aqueduct built by Polykrates through the hillside northwest of town, is the second construction, and one of the technological marvels of the ancient world. Surveying was so good that two work crews beginning from each end met with no vertical error and a horizontal one of less than one percent. You can visit much of it (Tue–Sun, 9am–2.30pm), along the catwalk used to remove spoil from the water channel far below. The ruins of the third construction, the **Hera Temple** (**Iréon**) ㉔, lie 8 km (5 miles) west of Pythagório, past coastal Roman baths and the airport. Polykrates' grandiose commission was never actually completed – and Byzantine builders dismantled it for cut stone.

Vathý or **Sámos town** ㉕, built along a deep inlet on the north coast, is the capital and main port, founded in 1832. Tourism is less pervasive here, though many do call at the **Archeological Museum** (Tue–Sun, 8.30am–3pm), one of the best in the provinces, with a rich trove of finds from the sanctuary of Hera. Given pride of place is a 5-metre (16-ft) nearly intact *kouros* (male statue), the largest ever found. The small-objects collection in a separate wing confirms the Middle-Eastern slant of worship and clientele at the temple: orientalised ivories and locally cast griffin's heads.

Áno Vathý, the large village clinging to the hillside 2 km (1 mile) southeast, existed for two centuries before the harbour settlement. A stroll will take you through steep cobbled streets separating 300-year-old houses, their overhanging second storeys and plaster and lath construction more akin to northern Greece and Anatolia than the central Aegean.

The first stop of note on the north-coast road is **Kokkári** ㉖ after 12 km (7½ miles), a former fishing village now devoted to tourism. The original centre is cradled between twin headlands, and windsurfers enjoy the long, westerly pebble beach. Overhead loom the wooded crags of **Mount Ámbelos** (1,150m/ 3,800ft), a favourite of hikers. Paths go up directly from behind Kokkári, while cars climb a road just past Avlákia to the thriving village of **Vourliótes** ㉗, with several tavernas on its photogenic square. The monastery of **Vrondianí**, 3 km (2 miles) east, co-hosts the island's liveliest festival (7–8 September).

The coastal highway continues west, sometimes as a sea-level corniche route, to **Karlóvassi** ㉘, 34 km

(21 miles) from Vathy. It's a sprawling, somewhat dishevelled place, little touristed and lumped into four districts. **Néo**, the biggest, has cavernous, derelict warehouses down by the water, vestiges of the leather-tanning trade which thrived here before 1940. **Meséo** is more villagey, as is **Áno** (or Paleó), lining a vegetated valley behind the sentinel church of Ághia Triádha. **Limín**, just below Áno, has most local tourist facilities, including a ferry service.

The shore west of here has some of Sámos' best beaches, including sand-and-pebble **Potámi**, visited by most of Karlóvassi at weekends. Beyond here, you must walk to a pair of remote, scenic beaches at **Seïtáni**. Karlóvassi lies roughly halfway around an anti-clockwise loop of the island. Head south, then east through an interior dotted with small villages of tiled, shuttered houses and stripy-domed churches. There are few special sights, just the routine of older men drinking coffee, the central spring providing water for gold-chain Lotharios washing small Japanese cars, contractors mixing cement or the last few itinerant greengrocers with laden donkeys (pickups are the norm now).

At the **Ághii Theodhóri** junction, choose southwest or east. The former takes you through **Marathókambos** and its port to **Votsalákia**, Sámos' fastest-growing beach resort. Better, more secluded coves lie further west along the road curling around the base of **Mount Kérkis** (1,433 metres/4,725 ft), which forms the west end of the island. The refuge of several hundred *andártes* between 1943 and 1948, it's usually climbed from Evangelístria convent on the south or Kosmadhéï on the north – either way a full day's outing.

Returning to Pythagório, schedule stops in **Pýrgos** for a can of local honey, and just below Mavratzéï, at the **monastery of Megális Panaghías**, with the best frescoes on Sámos, from after 1586. ❑

> **Map on page 222**

Pythagório (formerly Tigáni) was renamed as recently as 1955, to honour the great Samian Pythagoras – an irony, since the mathematician exiled himself in disgust at the greed of the tyrant Polykrates.

BELOW: boat maintenance at Pythagório harbour.

THE DODECANESE

Rhodes, Kárpathos, Kássos, Hálki, Kastellórizo, Alimiá, Tílos, Sými, Níssyros, Kós, Psérimos, Astypálea, Kálymnos, Télendhos, Léros, Lipsí, Pátmos, Arkí, Agathoníssi

The term "Dodecanese" is relatively new to the Greek vocabulary. For the four centuries that these far-flung islands were ruled by the Ottomans, they were known, incongruously, as the southern Sporades. At the beginning of the 20th century, in response to the withdrawal by the Young Turks of historic privileges granted by various sultans, 12 islands (*dhódheka nisiá* in Greek) jointly protested. Their rebellion failed, but the name stuck – hence the Dodecanese (*Dhodhekánisos* in Greek).

In fact, there are and always have been more than 12 islands in this archipelago. Depending on how you count, the chain consists of 14, 18 or (including every desert islet) even 27 islands. The only point of agreement is that the number of principal inhabited islands is never lower than 12.

The 19 islands included in these chapters are divided into three sections. Rhodes appears separately, for it is the capital and main transport hub of the province. The collective term "Southern Dodecanese" has been coined to include the islands immediately around Rhodes, which are easiest reached from overseas by an initial charter flight into the mother island, followed by a feeder flight or ferry – even to distant Kastellórizo, the proverbial "inset" island, rarely included on maps of Greece.

"Northern Dodecanese" islands, on the other hand, use Kós as a touchdown point, though some, such as holy Pátmos, are also easily reached from Sámos in the northeast Aegean. Seasonal hydrofoils based on Rhodes, Kálymnos and Sámos fill in the gaps between aircraft and conventional boats.

The Dodecanese were Greece's final territorial acquisition in 1948. Before that they were ruled (briefly) by the British; before that, there was a two-year occupation by the Germans, who had succeeded the Italians on their capitulation in late 1943. They in turn had ruled since 1912 with delusions of recreating the Roman Empire, leaving rashes of Art Deco follies on each island to mark their passing. The Italians had taken over from the Ottomans, who had ousted the Knights of St John in 1523 and (except for Rhodes and Kós) administered these islands mostly with benign neglect. Thus, to walk the streets of Kós or Rhodes is to witness a cultural patchwork: a minaret on one corner, an Italian villa on another, facing each other across an expanse of excavated Hellenistic foundations, all overshadowed by the fortifications of the crusading Knights. ❏

PRECEDING PAGES: waiters welcome a visitor from abroad; twilight at the entrance to Mandhráki harbour, Rhodes. **LEFT:** old man, old book.

RHODES

Map on page 244

According to the ancient Greeks, Rhodes is "more beautiful than the sun". Even today's brash resorts cannot dim the appeal of its benign climate, entrancing countryside and unique history

T he capital of the Dodecanese and fourth largest Greek island, Rhodes (Ródhos) has long been on the package-tour trail. It's a reduced-VAT port, thronged from May to October by Scandinavians in search of Valhalla via cheap booze. Stylish Italians swarm the streets in August, and the British beer-and-bouzoúki brigade also abound, propping up the hundreds of bars in town and the built-up outskirts. Rhodes spells fun for the young, free and single.

But far from the madding crowds in Neohóri (Rhodes New Town) and the serried ranks of umbrellas and sunbeds on the northern beaches, you can still find a more unspoiled island light years away from the "No Problem, No Aids" T-shirts and tawdry knick-knacks of the resorts. Frequent bus services run down both coasts from beside the "New Market", but it's worth hiring a car, jeep or powerful motorbike if you really want to explore deserted beaches, remote monasteries and castles perched above citrus groves.

Patchwork history

The legacy of ancient Greeks, crusading knights, besieging Ottomans and colonial Italians forms a fascinating patchwork in Rhodes town, from castle turrets to the ancient street-plan. There are temple pillars and Byzantine churches, mosques with minarets, plus the twin bronze deer guarding the waters of Mandhráki harbour where perhaps the Colossus once stood.

This wondrous statue depicting Apollo Helios, the work of local sculptors Kharis and Lakhis, stood over 30 metres (100 ft) tall. Impressive by any standards, legend made it even more so by describing it as standing astride the harbour entrance. But to do so it would have to have been over ten times its original size, an impossible engineering feat. Wherever it actually was, the monument stood until it collapsed in an earthquake in 226 BC. The bronze was sold for scrap in the 7th century AD.

Under the Byzantine empire, Rhodes was governed by the Genoese – until the Knights of St John, who had fled Jerusalem via Cyprus, captured the city in 1309, beginning a rule that lasted 213 years, under 19 Grand Masters. They substantially refortified the city, and raided Ottoman shipping. Finally, in 1522, Sultan Süleyman the Magnificent took the city after a six-month siege that pitted 100,000 warriors against 650 knights. The Grand Master and 180 surviving brethren surrendered and were allowed safe conduct to Malta. The Ottomans held the island for 390 years. Churches were converted to mosques, and Christians were banned from living within the city walls.

In 1912, Italy occupied Rhodes while at war with Turkey, and embarked on a massive archeological

LEFT: medieval windmills on Mandhráki harbour.
BELOW: the Apollo temple at Monte Smith.

construction program. During World War II, when Italy capitulated in 1943, the Germans took over. Rhodes was liberated by the Allies in 1945, and the Greek flag hoisted in 1948 when the Dodecanese became united with Greece.

These days, the island is still under siege – by tourists. Present-day **Rhodes town (Ródhos)** ❶ divides neatly into the New Town, Neohóri, settled by Greeks in Ottoman times, and the Old City. The contrast is marked: fast food, designer clothes and techno-beat versus cobbled streets and a village feel.

The bronze deer guarding the port recall the time when the island was plagued by snakes. The Delphic oracle suggested the introduction of stags, who did the trick by spearing the serpents with their antlers.

The New Town

Here, smart shops abound, peddling Lacoste, Trussardi and Benetton. Inexpensive umbrellas are big business and you can have any logo embossed. Watch the world go by and the yachts bobbing from one of the pricey, touristy pavement cafés at **Mandhráki** port. Marginally cheaper are cafés inside the **covered market (Néa Agorá)** Ⓐ among fishmongers, butchers and wonderfully heaped-up produce. Cheap *souvlákia* and fresh orange juice are available, plus there's a good bakery.

Mandhráki's quay buzzes night and day with caricature artists, popcorn vendors, sponge-sellers and touts hawking daily boat trips. Excursion boats leave by 9am for the island of Sými, calling first at Panormítis Monastery, or down the east coast to Líndhos. Hydrofoils depart from the base of the jetty, while full-sized ferries leave from the commercial harbour, a 15-minute walk east.

Mandhráki, guarded by the round bastion-lighthouse of **Ághios Nikólaos (St Nicholas' Fort)** Ⓑ, is also an established port of call on the international yachting circuit, with local charters too. By the harbour entrance stands a cluster of Italian Art Deco: the Governor's House with its Gothic arches, the **church of the**

BELOW: selling boat excursions on Mandhráki quay.

Annunciation (Evangelismós) **C** next door, and across the way the post office, town hall and municipal theatre in quick succession. Opposite the theatre, the **Mosque of Murad Reis D** stands beside one of the island's larger Muslim graveyards. On the other side of this is the **Villa Cleobolus**, where Lawrence Durrell lived from 1945 to 1947. A stroll along the waterfront from here brings you to the grandly named **Hydrobiological Institute** (ie, the aquarium; daily 9am–9pm) at the island's north cape, with live specimens in the basement.

Inland Neohóri thumps with nightlife, revellers spilling out of the bars onto the pavements in high season. A sign reading "A balanced diet is a drink in each hand" represents the prevailing philosophy. There are said to be over 200 bars packed into an area measuring less than a square kilometre. Orfanídhou in particular is informally dubbed "Skandi Street" after the new Vikings.

In the municipal gardens beneath the Old City walls, there are *Son et Lumière* performances (**Íhos kai Fos E**) every evening, re-enacting the siege of Süleyman the Magnificent. Pay as you enter – but check with the box office that the performance for that night is in your language.

Some 2 km (1 mile) southwest of Mandhráki, **Monte Smith** – more correctly, Ághios Stéfanos hill – offers panoramic views over the town. This was the site of Rhodes' Hellenistic acropolis, with a stadium, a heavily restored *odeion* and evocatively re-erected columns of an Apollo temple dating from the 3rd century BC. In the far south of the new town, *en route* to Líndhos, **Rodíni Park**, home of the ancient rhetoric school, turns up modern babble during August with a wine festival every evening (8pm–midnight; entrance fee includes unlimited wine). The grounds with their gardens, lakes and bridges were refurbished in 1996, and incorporate some rock-cut Hellenistic tombs.

Maps:
Area 244
City 241

Monte Smith, the hill to the west of town, is named after the British admiral Sir Sidney Smith who kept watch from here for the Napoleonic fleet in 1802.

BELOW: in the Archeological Museum.

Rhodes City

The most famous item in the Archeological Museum is the marble Aphrodite dating from the 1st century BC, the inspiration for Gerald Durrell's "Reflections on a Merine Venus".

BELOW: the courtyard of the Knights' Hospital.

The Old City

The medieval walled town, with its ramparts, 11 surviving gates and narrow cobbled streets, is so well preserved a visitor half expects to bump into a Crusader. Recognized as a UNESCO heritage site, its monuments are now getting some long-needed maintenance. Many of the streets follow their right-angled ancient predecessors: in the maze-like Ottoman quarters, it's easier to get lost.

Step through the northernmost **Liberty Gate (Pylí Eleftherías)** into **Platía Sýmis** to view the foundations of an Aphrodite temple. The adjacent **Platía Arghyrokástrou** is flanked by the Inn of the Order of Auvergne and the **Decorative Arts Collection** (Tue–Sun, 8.30am–3pm), with costumes, ceramics and carved woodwork gathered from old houses across the archipelago. Just opposite stands the **Byzantine Museum** (Tue–Sun, 8.30am–3pm), situated in the former Knights' cathedral, now known as **Panaghía Kástrou**. Much of its collection of icons and frescoes rescued from rural chapels has moved to the Palace of the Grand Masters *(see below)*.

Next stop is the 15th-century **Knights Hospital ❻**, now the **Archeological Museum** (Tue–Sat, 8.30am–6pm). Among the badly labelled and displayed exhibits is the famous, sea-eroded Aphrodite Thalassia, Durrell's Marine Venus, the star of the Hellenistic statuary gallery.

From here the **Street of the Knights (Odhós Ippotón) ❼** leads in medieval splendour straight uphill to the Palace of the Grand Masters. Italian-restored, and preserved from commercialisation, the thoroughfare houses the inns of the Knights as they were divided by linguistic affinity. The Inn of France, emblazoned with heraldry of several Grand Masters, is the most imposing.

The **Palace of the Grand Masters ❽** itself (Mon 12.30–7pm, Tue–Fri

am–7pm, Sat–Sun 8am–3pm) was almost completely destroyed when a muni-
ions store in the nearby church of St John exploded in 1856, killing 800. Dur-
ng 1937-39 it was hastily rebuilt by the Italians as a holiday retreat for King
'ictor Emmanuel and Mussolini, neither of whom ever used it. Traipse up the
randiose staircase to ogle the ostentatious upper-floor decoration, including
Iellenistic mosaics transferred here from Kós. The ground floor houses an
xcellent medieval exhibit (Tue–Sat, 8am–2.30pm) which, with its displays on
ne Knights' tenure and sacred art transferred from Panaghía Kástrou, is certainly
ne best museum on Rhodes.

The main commercial thoroughfare is **Sokrátous ❶**, a "Golden Mile" packed
vith fur and leather shops, jewellers, lace and embroidery stalls, and every
ther kind of tourist paraphernalia imaginable. Sokrátous links **Platía Ippokrá-**
ous and its ornate fountain with the pink **Süleymaniye Mosque ❷** at the top
f the hill. It's currently shut and under scaffolding, as are most Ottoman mon-
ments here. The old town still has a sizeable Turkish minority, though since
948 they deliberately keep a low profile. One such monument that's still work-
ng, and esteemed by Orthodox and Muslim alike, is the **hamam** (Turkish baths,
igned as **Dhimotiká Loutrá**; erratic hours) on Platía Ariónos.

The other local minority which dwelt here, the Jews, was deported to
.uschwitz by the Nazis in June 1944. Few returned, and their **synagogue** on
imíou is essentially maintained as a memorial. Behind the *hamam* on
.ndhroníkou, the Nélli Dhimóglou folk dance troupe offers potted folklore in
ne **Nélli Dhimóglou Theatre ❸** (Mon–Fri, 9.20pm). For other nightlife,
rowing numbers of pubs and bars are appearing in the Old City, albeit at a
)wer decibel level than in Neohóri.

Map
on page
241

*The magnificent
walls of the Old City
date from the 14th
century and are up to
12 metres (40 ft) thick
in places. The only
way to get on to them
is on an organised
walk. Tours start at
the Palace of the
Grand Masters (Tue
and Sat, 2.45pm).*

BELOW: the
Museum of
Decorative Arts.

The West Coast

Rhodes' west coast is the damper, windier, greener side of the island, with agriculture on a par with tourism. Scrappy shingle beaches have failed to slow hotel construction at **Ixiá** and **Triánda**, busy resorts that blend into each other and Neohóri. A road leads inland 5 km (3 miles) from Triánda to the site of **ancient Ialyssós** ❷ (Tue–Fri, 8.30am–6pm, Sat–Mon, 8.30am–3pm), better known today as **Filérimos**, after the Byzantine monastery established here. Of the old city, only a Doric fountain and some Hellenistic temple foundations are evident. The restored Gothic **monastery**, with its vaulted chambers, original fish-mosaic floor and rampant bougainvillea is the main attraction.

Kremastí, back on the coast, is famous for its annual festival of the Virgin (15-23 August), but is otherwise eminently avoidable. The airport lies between here and **Paradhíssi** village, often resorted to for solace when homeward charters get delayed (a common occurrence). Just past Paradhíssi, another inland turning leads to a famous Rhodian beauty spot, the **Petaloúdhes** or "Butterfl

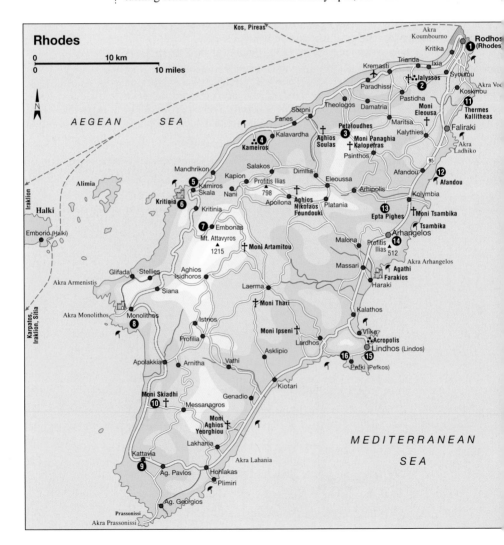

Valley" ❸. The access road crosses the canyon about halfway along its length. Head upstream or downstream, along paths and over bridges, past the *Liquidambar orientalis* (sweet-gum) trees on which Jersey tiger moths roost during summer. Black and yellow when at rest, they flash bright red wing-tops in flight. From the top of the valley, about 6 km (4 miles) inland from **Soroní** on the coast road, a dirt track leads to the **monastery of Ághios Soúlas** which has a major festival on 29–30 July featuring donkey races.

Map on page 244

The other big tourist attraction of the west coast, 32 km (20 miles) from Mandhráki, is **Kamíros (ancient Kameiros)** ❹, excavated in 1929. Though no single monument stands out, it's a remarkably complete Doric townscape, without the usual later accretions. Unusually, there were no fortifications, nor an acropolis on the gently sloping hillside.

Back on the coast **Skála Kamírou** (also **Kámiros Skála**) ❺ is a small port with heavily touristed fish tavernas, and afternoon ferries for the tiny island of Hálki opposite. **Kritinía** ❻ castle just overhead, one of the Knights' rural garrisons, is today a dilapidated shell but merits a visit for the views out to sea.

Filérimos monastery, an Italian restoration of the original, has many 14th-century wall-paintings and mosaics.

The interior and far south

Inland, at the base of 1,215m (3,985ft) Mount Attávyros, **Émbonas** ❼ is the centre of the Rhodian wine industry. Products of the private Emery winery are considered the best. Numerous meat-orientated tavernas serve lunch and "Greek Night" suppers to coach tours. The road skirts the base of the mountain through conifer forest en route to the attractive village of **Siána**, famous for its honey and *soúma* – a strong grape-distillate spirit that's deceptively smooth. Some 4 km (2½ miles) further, flat-roofed **Monólithos** ❽ village

LEFT: a Petaloúdhes butterfly salesman. **BELOW:** the modern Trianda Hotel.

gives access to the eponymous castle perched on a narrow pinnacle, with a 200-metre (655-ft) sheer drop all around.

Inland Rhodes is the perfect antidote to the tourist extravagances of the coastal resorts, its rolling hills still partly wooded despite fires started by arsonists since the late 1980s. The late Byzantine church of **Ághios Nikólaos Foundouklí,** 3 km (2 miles) west of **Eleoússa,** has good frescoes. You can continue west to densely shady **Mount Profítis Ilías** (798m/2,618ft), and descend by cobble trail to the village of **Salakós,** where "Nymph" brand spring water is bottled.

Alternatively, from **Apóllona** on the mountain's south side, a rough track (jeeps only) leads directly to **Láerma,** and thence through pines to the Byzantine **monastery of Thári,** reinhabited in 1990 by monks who oversaw the cleaning of its vivid 13th-to-15th-century frescoes. The track continues southeast to **Asklipío** village, where slightly later frescoes in the church of Kímisis Theotókou are in better condition owing to the dry climate. Together these constitute the finest Byzantine art *in situ* on the island.

From Asklipío you emerge on the southeast coast at **Kiotári** and **Yennádhi,** stretches of open gravel beach in the initial throes of development. Further south, **Plimíri** is sandy and more sheltered, while **Prassoníssi** (Leek Island) at Rhodes' extreme south tip is tethered by a broad, sandy causeway favoured for training by world-class windsurfers. The main island coast road loops back to Monólithos via the villages of **Kattavía** ❾ (which has a church containing remarkable frescoes and ancient sculptures) and **Apolakkiá,** between which stretches utterly wild, surf-pounded beach.

Most inland villages here are moribund, with house owners off in Rhodes town or overseas. They've sold up *en masse* to Germans at **Lahaniá** near

BELOW: ancient Kameiros.

Plimíri, though the wonderful square with its taverna and twin fountains under a plane tree remains traditional. From here head northwest to the fine hilltop village of **Messanagrós**, with its 13th-century chapel hunched amid the larger foundations of a 5th-century basilica. If you're overtaken by darkness and can't face the drive back to town, the kindly keepers at **Skiádhi monastery** ⑩ just west may invite you to use the guest quarters.

Map on page 244

The East Coast

The east coast, sandier and more sheltered than the west, with a warmer sea, was only developed for tourism after the 1970s, though much of it remains unspoiled. **Koskinoú** is famous for its ornate doorways and intricate pebble-mosaic courtyards. Immediately downhill, the spa of **Thérmes Kallithéas** ⑪, undergoing restoration, is a splendid orientalised Art Deco folly of the Italians, complete with domed pavilion and palm trees. Below the spa, a pair of sandy coves flanked by rocky headlands are popular with divers.

Wall-to-wall hotels characterise **Faliráki**, the popular package resort bursting with the young, carefree and single. There are dozens of bland eateries and dance bars behind the long sandy beach, where every kind of watersport, plus para-gliding, is on offer. Immediately south looms **Cape Ladhikó**, with its "Anthony Queen" (*sic*) cove where Quinn starred in *The Guns of Navarone*. Beyond the cape stretches the long pebble-sand beach of **Afándou** ⑫, scarcely developed except for the18-hole golf course just inland. At a junction still further south, a seaward turning leads through the Italians' model-farm scheme of the 1920s at **Kolýmbia** to another resort ranged around a small volcanic cove.

Heading inland, you reach the leafy glades of **Eptá Pighés** (Seven Springs) ⑬,

Skiádhi monastery has a miraculous icon of the Panaghía (Blessed Virgin) which supposedly bled when it was stabbed by a heretic in the 15th century.

BELOW: a full moon over Líndhos.

one of the island's most popular beauty spots. The springs of the name feed a small reservoir dammed by the Italians to irrigate their Kolýmbia colony. Explore a claustrophobic aqueduct-tunnel leading to the pond, or eat at the popular taverna under the trees in the company of screaming peacocks and geese. The Greek answer to fertility drugs, **Tsambíka Monastery** teeters high on the volcanic headland behind Kolýmbia, overlooking a sandy namesake beach to the south. The otherwise undistinguished church is a magnet for childless women who come as barefoot pilgrims to reverence an 11th-century icon at its 8 September festival.

Arhángelos ⓮, 29 km (18 miles) from Rhodes town, is the island's largest village, famous for its *koureloúdhes* (rag rugs), pottery and leather crafts – all goods duly pitched at a large, mostly German, package-tour contingent, here despite the inland position. Good beaches are not far away, however, for example **Agáthi**, reached via the little resort and fishing port of **Haráki**, overlooked by the crumbled Knights' castle of **Feraklós**.

Líndhos

There are regular buses over the 56 km (35 miles) from Rhodes town to **Líndhos** (**Lindos**) ⓯, but it's more relaxing to take a boat trip and enjoy the coastal scenery. Huddled beneath yet another Knights' castle, Líndhos with its tiered, flat-roofed houses appears initially to be the dream Greek village. Medieval captains' mansions – some open for viewing – have ornate gateways and vast pebble-mosaic courtyards. Near the main square, a Byzantine church preserves 18th-century frescoes. The hottest spot on Rhodes, its narrow lanes teem with day-trippers in high season. Donkeys, the Lindian taxi, haul tourists up the steep gradient to the ancient acropolis with its scaffolded Temple of Lindian Athena. It's more accurately a Temple of Tourism, with women selling lace on the way up.

Líndhos in general is a shrine to sun, sea and sex. At night the village throbs to the beat of numerous bars, while by day the sand lining the northerly port below is sardine-can dense. The southern harbour, with a quieter beach, is known as St Paul's Bay, honouring the Apostle who landed here in AD 58. The tiny church dedicated to him celebrates a *panighíri* on 28–29 June.

Ancient Lindos dates back to the Bronze Age, thanks to the only protected harbour on the island aside from Mandhráki. With such barren surroundings, it always lived from the sea. In the 1960s, the light and shade playing on the nearby jagged mountains attracted Italian, German and British painters and drop-outs. Past alumni include the late astrologer Patric Walker and various members of Pink Floyd, but Líndhos' days as a hippie-artist colony are long over, superseded by the era of mass tourism. Supermarkets cater to every foreign whim, and tavernas even do sweets – it's hard to believe you're in Greece.

Around the limestone headland, **Péfki** (**Péfkos**) ⓰ is a good deal less frenetic than Líndhos, originally an annex of the latter but now a package resort in its own right; beaches are small and hidden. At **Lárdhos** 4 km (2½ miles) west, the long, gravelly beach is obvious, and the village elders have not waited for a mooted second civilian airport to appear nearby to begin determined development. ◻

If a childless woman conceives after praying at Tsambíka Monastery, the child is named Tsambíkos or Tsambíka, names unique to Rhodes.

BELOW: a popular beach at Péfki.

Leisurely Líndhos

Líndhos is the last place to visit in Greece. This aphorism was endorsed in the 1960s and 1970s by a score of expatriates who found in this beautiful resort a nirvana where they would write that great novel or paint that ultimate canvas. Most were British, most were in their thirties, most had had a previous career and some had enjoyed limited artistic success – a published novel, articles in a glossy magazine. Then there were young hippies to whom the mere thought of ever holding down a job was anathema. All these expats lived in modest Greek houses and were fortunate in that the corner grocer permitted them to buy "on tick". Finally there were transient expatriates. These included a publisher, an opera star, an art historian, and a couple of architects. They had purchased as holiday homes the magnificent old sea-captains' houses which grace Líndhos.

Ars longa, vita brevis could have been the motto of these drop-outs and, in the privacy of their homes, pot accompanied *oúzo* and the *ménage à trois* was not unknown. Pot was tolerated by the authorities except when Greta, a German student on vacation and not really part of the expat community, was imprisoned for possession. The consensus was that she had been incarcerated because she refused the advances of the police sergeant. Imagine the horror of her parents when they arrived to join their daughter in her Greek idyll and found her in a rural island jail.

So was any work accomplished? Did anyone make a sale?

One day Willard, an enthusiastic snorkler, who years previously had sold a novel but had since collected rejection slips, struck gold. A visiting German television producer was looking for a diving "buddy". After diving, Klaus read Willard's short stories, and knew instantly they would make great television plays. Willard now spends a lot of time in Hollywood.

And then there was David, who appeared waving a cheque for US$5,000 and smiling broadly; and Tiger with rings (made of hand-painted pebbles from the beach) on her fingers and rings on her toes; and... ❏

THE SOUTHERN DODECANESE

Map
on page
254

The islands farthest from the mainland – they didn't even become part of Greece until 1948 – have developed a distinct character, culture and architecture

Kássos

Kássos is the southernmost Dodecanese island, and the poorest. Remote and barren, its plight was accentuated by a comprehensive Ottoman massacre in 1824. Before and since Kassiots took to the seas, distinguishing themselves as pilots, and helping to dig the Suez Canal. In six clustered villages on the north flank, many houses lie abandoned: summer sees a homecoming of expatriated Greek-Americans, especially for the major festivals, 17 July (Aghía Marína) and 15 August (Assumption of the Virgin).

The capital, **Frý ❶** (pronounced "Free"), is a bit shabby but does have a couple of tavernas and an attractively enclosed fishing port, the Boúka, with a narrow entrance, set against a mountain backdrop. **Emboriós** down the coast was the old commercial port, now silted up but still picturesque. The only conventional tourist attraction is **Seláï** stalactite cave beyond **Aghía Marína**, the most attractive inland village.

Except at peak season when a bus and mopeds appear, you face long, shadeless hikes to get anywhere. The only half-decent beach, for instance, is **Helathrós**, nearly four hours' walk from Frý in the southwest, via **Ághios Yeórghios Hadhión**, one of two rural monasteries. The indolent should take up offers of boat excursions to better beaches on the offshore islets of **Makrá** and **Armathiá,** which has a spectacular beach.

Frý has a tiny airstrip with puddle-jumper planes to Rhodes, Kárpathos and Sitía (Crete). Fares are affordable, and a flight may be your only option in heavy seas, when inter-island ferries skip the poor anchorage west of the Boúka.

PRECEDING PAGES: windmills on Kárpathos. **LEFT:** all dressed up for the festival of St John. **BELOW:** a traditional Ólymbos interior.

Kárpathos

Wild, rugged and sparsely populated, Kárpathos is the second largest Dodecanese island, marooned in crystalline sea roughly halfway between Rhodes and Crete. With vast expanses of white-sand beaches, usually underused, and craggy cloud-topped mountains soaring to almost 1,200 metres (4,050 ft), it makes up in natural beauty for what it lacks in attractive villages or infrastructure.

Direct seasonal flights serve Kárpathos from overseas; the alternative involves a domestic flight or ferry from Rhodes. The capital and southerly harbour of **Pigádhia ❷** (also known as **Kárpathos**) has undergone a tourism boom in the last few years; in any case the town only dates from the mid-19th century, and had little beauty to lose before eyesore concrete blocks went up. Many families have returned wealthy from America, and you're as likely to hear "Have a nice day" as "*Kaliméra*".

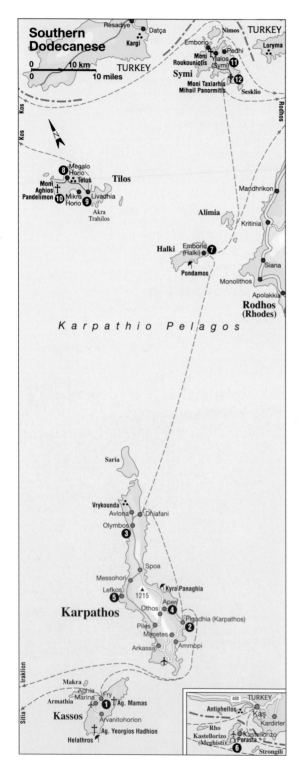

Southern Dodecanese

Karpathos

Kassos

Rodhos (Rhodes)

Karpathio Pelagos

Just north of Pigádhia, massively sandy **Vróndi** beach, with windsurfers and kayaks for rent, sweeps past to the 5th-century basilica of **Aghía Fotiní**. Otherwise you can drive 7 km (4½ miles) south to **Ammopí**, the island's longest established resort, with its three sandy coves, the third for nudists.

Northern Kárpathos is easiest visited via the port of **Dhiafáni**, served both by local caiques from Pigádhia and the occasional main-line ferry. A jetty built in 1996 has made the previous, precarious transfer ashore in small boats history. Dhiafáni is peaceful and congenial except in August, with beaches and coastal walks to them in either direction, but most use it as a stepping-stone to reach **Ólymbos ❸**, the island's most distinctive village, which clings to the mountainside 600 metres (1,860 ft) up.

Remote Ólymbos feels like the capital of a separate island. Older houses consist of one divided room built around a central wooden pole, the "pillar of the house", to which are attached embroideries and usually a wedding portrait of the owners, complete with a *stéfano* or wedding wreath. On a raised wooden platform behind a carved rail are rolled-up bedding, plus chests of dowry linens and festival clothes.

The rest of the room is crammed with plates, lace, crochet and other souvenirs – a kitsch explosion of fairground colours – gathered by seafaring relatives from ports around the world. Even modern villas have their front room decked out in the same way, with the TV draped in garish mats, a shrine for family photos and icons.

Ólymbos long existed in a time warp, but tourism by amateur anthropologists has dragged the place into modern times, and the locals are now well used to visitors. It's best to stay the night, when you'll hear the Dorian-influenced local dialect in the tavernas and see the women clomp off to the terraces below at dawn, in their high leather boots. Older women still wear traditional costumes (intricately embroidered jackets, scarves and pinafores) on a daily basis as well as for festivals, though lately a good deal of the embroidery is imported. Bread and biscuits are baked in communal ovens. The flour was formerly ground by the village's half-dozen 18th-century windmills, two of which were restored as working museum-pieces in the mid-1980s.

Map on page 254

Organised tours serve Ólymbos, complete with bus transfer up from Dhiafáni, but the north is wonderful for walking. Besides the hike between the two, there's the all-day trek via **Avlóna** hamlet to **Vrykoúnda**, where a cave-shrine of St John the Baptist is the focus for a major festival on 29 August.

Exploring further afield can be arduous: paved roads are rough, the many dirt ones appalling, and filling stations few. Mopeds should thus be avoided for long trips, as they'll run out of petrol – and when the *meltémi* wind buffets the west coast you can be blown off the road by gusts. There are buses and pricey taxis to less remote mountain villages like **Menetés** with vine-covered streets; **Apéri ❹**, the elegant medieval capital, said to have the highest per capita income in Greece; **Óthos**, the highest on the island at 700 metres (3,000 ft), where an old Karpathian house serves as a craft museum; and **Voládha** just across a mist-swirled ridge, with a tiny Venetian citadel.

Ólymbos was virtually cut off from the rest of Kárpathos for centuries. The road from the south was only completed in 1979.

Many of Kárpathos' better beaches are most easily reached by excursion boat. Among these, on the east coast, are **Kyrá Panaghiá** (with the most facilities and a lovely pink-domed church), or lonelier, more unspoilt **Aháta** and **Apélla**. **Arkássa** on the western shore is a growing resort, popular with both Greeks and foreigners, between a Mycenaean-Classical acropolis at **Paleókastro** and the working fishing port of **Finíki**. **Lefkós ❺**, further north, presents an outstanding topography of headlands sheltering three horseshoe bays of white sand; there are plenty of places to stay and eat.

BELOW: clouds gather over Ólymbos.

BELOW: the port of Kastellórizo.

Kastellórizo

Kastellórizo's alias, Meghísti, means "Biggest" – biggest, that is, of a local mini-archipelago, for this is actually the smallest inhabited Dodecanese island. It's also the first point in Europe, coming from the east, as signs on the quay proudly announce to wandering yachts, and only a few nautical miles away from Turkey where locals go shopping. Before 1900, Kastellórizo was a thriving town of 14,000, supported by its schooner fleet. The sale of the fleet, World War I bombardment, and an earthquake in 1926 sent the island into terminal decline, despite its role during the 1930s as a sea-plane halt.

The final nail in the coffin came in July 1944, when a fuel depot exploded, levelling more than half the port. The town had already been looted, and few chose to return after the war, when the population dropped to about 200. The US even tried to persuade Greece to cede Kastellórizo to Turkey in 1964 in exchange for limited hegemony in Cyprus. Recovery from this nadir is due to the return of expatriate "Kassies" from Perth and Sydney to build retirement homes, and the island's use as location for the Oscar-winning film *Mediterraneo*, which spurred a wave of tourists.

This limestone island is fringed by sheer cliffs, with no beaches at all. What remains of the red-roofed port town, **Kastellórizo**, is overseen by a half-ruined, red-stone Crusader castle, responsible for the island's Italianate name. The keep houses a small museum (Tue–Sun, 8am–2.30pm) of local finds, relocated here from the quayside mosque, while beyond in the cliff-face is Greece's only Lycian house-type tomb.

Also worth seeing is the remote monastery of **Ághios Yeórghios toú Vounoú** with groin vaulting, pebble flooring and the frescoed subterranean crypt-chapel

of Ághios Harálambos. Boat trips go to the satellite islet of **Rhó**, or to the cathedral-like Blue Grotto of **Perastá** ❻ on the southwest coast which, according to locals, rivals its namesake in Capri. The cave is about 45 metres (140 ft) long and 28 metres (87 ft) high, and the rays of the morning sun create spectacular effects inside. The journey there is a 90-minute round-trip, plus time to swim in the deep, glowing waters.

Kastellórizo lies 70 nautical miles (114 km) from Rhodes, and ferries make the long trip only two or three times a week. The tiny airstrip receives three to five weekly flights from Rhodes, though seats can fill days in advance. Most tourist facilities are basic, ie non-en-suite; the half-dozen tavernas are fairly pricey because most food is imported.

Map
on page
254

Hálki

Ninety minutes by boat from Kámiros Skála on Rhodes, Hálki (also spelt Chálki) is pretty, welcoming and "arrived", despite being barren and harsh, and lacking a fresh water supply. **Emborió** (**Hálki**) ❼, the harbour and only settlement, has numerous waterfront tavernas and abundant accommodation in its restored neo-classical mansions, though most of these are block-booked from April to October by two British tour companies. **Ághios Nikólaos** has the highest bell-tower in the Dodecanese, nearly matched by a free-standing clocktower nearby.

The island's only sandy beach – artificially supplemented – is at **Póndamos** bay, 400 metres (440 yards) west; just overhead, **Horió** village has been deserted since the 1950s but offers spectacular views from its crumbled Knights' fortress. Tarpon Springs Boulevard, built with money from Hálki sponge fishermen who

Hálki was a fertile island until seawater infiltrated its water-table. Now fresh water is imported by tanker.

BELOW: fishing still plays a major role in the Dodecanese economy.

emigrated to Florida, has been extended to the monastery of **Ághios Ioánnis** in the northwest of the island. Without a lift, it's a good two-hour walk from Horió. There are no other good roads, so pebble coves like **Aréta** and **Dhýo Yialí**, on the north shore, or Trahiá under the castle, are reached by boat excursion. Otherwise you can walk to less inspiring **Yialí** or **Kánia**.

The name Hálki comes from the Greek word for copper, which was once mined here.

Floating between Hálki and Rhodes, **Alimiá** (aka **Alimniá**) island has been deserted since World War II, despite having a fresh-water spring and excellent anchorage. The inhabitants aided the Allies under the very noses of the Italian forces manning submarine pens here. When they were detected, the islanders were deported to Rhodes and Hálki as punishment, never to return. With yet another Knights' castle, a pretty church, pebbly beaches, clear waters and ruined houses strafed by bullet holes, the island is now a popular picnic spot for both locals and tourists, and seasonally home to Halkian sheep.

Tílos

Tranquil and unspoiled Tílos has only seen tourism since the late 1980s. It has several thousand goats but only about 350 people (80 in the winter). Though the island is bare on its limestone heights, neighbouring Níssyros deposited rich lava soil in the lowlands, which with ample ground-water allows the Tiliots to farm. Indeed before the 1970s it was the granary of the Dodecanese, with undulating fields of wheat visible far out to sea.

BELOW: most islands have to import fruit and vegetables.

The island's capital, **Megálo Horió 8**, is an inland village, topped by a Venetian castle that incorporates a Classical gateway and stone from the ancient acropolis. It looks south over an orchard-planted plain to red-sand **Éristos** beach, the best on Tílos. The harbour and main resort of **Livádhia 9** has a

long shingle beach, behind which development is accelerating at an alarming rate. There are now half a dozen good tavernas, a score of hotels and even some low-key nightlife. You can walk or moped to most good beaches, so boat trips aren't usually offered. The closest are Lethrá and Thólos, with the Knights' castle of Agriosykiá (one of seven here) en route. Just west of Livádhia is the ghost village of **Mikró Horió**, abandoned in the 1950s. There's another castle here, and a late-hours bar in a restored house.

The trans-island road passes another fort and a cave at **Harkádhi**, in which the fossilised bones of tiny mastodons (extinct elephants) were found in 1971. The bones are kept in a small museum in Megálo Horió.

Map on page 254

At **Ághios Andónios** beach, the surf washes over the petrified remains of three sailors, trapped by an eruption of Níssyros. Road's end is the 15th-century **monastery of Aghíos Pandelímon** ❿, tucked into a spring-fed oasis-ravine. The tower-gate is only opened for the regular Sunday-morning minibus tour from Megálo Horió. The church has a few frescoes and a fine marble floor. The big island knees-up is here, running for three days from 25 July and including the famous "Dance of the Cup". Almost as important is the 23 August festival at **Panaghía Polítissa monastery** near Livádhia, for which special boats are laid on from Rhodes the previous day.

For centuries Sými was the sponge-diving capital of the Aegean, until it was surpassed by Kálymnos (see page 270).

Sými

As you approach Sými on a day-trip boat from Rhodes, flotillas of boats flee the port of **Yialós** ⓫ for remote beaches around the island. The foreign "residents" and overnighters are escaping the daily quota of trippers. Yialós (also called Sými) is a stunning spectacle with its tiers of pastel-coloured houses. But it is

LEFT: island woman. **BELOW:** the ferry from Rhodes approaches Yialós.

Map
on page
254

The Symiots have been renowned for their boat-building since antiquity. In legend they built the Argo in which Jason sailed off to find the Golden Fleece.

BELOW: local transport in Horió.
RIGHT: Yialós, Sými.

a town with two faces. When the tour boats hoot their arrival, it becomes a mini-Rhodes, with mediocre waterside tavernas touting for business, and stalls selling imported spices and sponges, plus other knick-knacks. As soon as the trippers leave in mid-afternoon, peace is restored: there's room to walk on the quay and you'll get stronger drink.

Symiots are famous as boat-builders and you can still see boats taking shape at the Haráni yards. Until it was surpassed by Kálymnos after World War II, Sými was also the sponge-diving capital of the Aegean, a role assured by an Ottoman imperial grant of monopoly in the trade. The Treaty of the Dodecanese, in which Italy formally surrendered the islands to the Allies, was signed in Les Katerinettes restaurant on 8 May 1945.

Built in a protected gulch and thus stiflingly hot in summer, Yialós is beautiful at night when the bay reflects the lights from the houses above. Popular with the yachting fraternity, but still relatively unspoilt because of limited accommodation, the "Hydra of the Dodecanese" has plenty of bars and tavernas scattered about. It's not, however, an island for the unfit, the elderly or the very young, who would have to manage the 357 steps of the **Kalí Stráta**, the broad stair-street climbing to the upper town of **Horió**. Follow arrows to the worthwhile local **museum** (Tue–Sun, 10am–2pm), which highlights Byzantine and medieval Sými. Overhead is the Knights' castle, built on the site of – and using material from – the ancient acropolis.

The only other significant habitation is the valley of **Pédhi** to the east, where flat land and a few wells allow vegetable cultivation. On the south side of the bay here, reached by a marked trail, is the naturally sandy beach of **Ághios Nikólaos**, the only one on Sými.

Beyond Haráni, the coastal track heads north, then west to the bay of Nimborió, where a Byzantine floor mosaic and catacombs can be found up behind an artificial strewn sand beach. The only other notable sacred art outside the museum is at the monastery of **Mihaïl Roukouniótis**, west of Horió, with a peculiar piggy-back church and vivid 18th-century frescoes in the upper one.

Other beaches are pebble; walk across the island, through the remaining juniper forest, to **Ághios Vassílios** in the southwest (no facilities), or take an all-day boat excursion to **Ághios Yeórghios Dhyssálona**, **Nanoú** or **Marathoúnda** (all with tavernas) on the east coast.

The most important monastery is **Taxiárhis Mihaïl Panormítis** ⑫ in the far south. The Archangel Michael is the patron of local sailors, and his feast day (8 November) brings seafaring pilgrims to Panormítis from all over the Aegean. The central church with its myriad oil lamps seems lost amidst a giant pebble-mosaic courtyard; a small museum displays votive offerings from seamen. Things are tranquil once the tour boats have gone – it's usually the first stop coming from Rhodes – and you can rent a cell for whatever you wish to pay. If you're a woman travelling alone, beware: one of the monks is rather lecherous and will insist you sleep inside the compound; its doors are locked at 9.30pm sharp. ❑

THE NORTHERN DODECANESE

Map
on page
264

Closer to Turkey than to Greece, these islands have a discernible eatern influence. As well as the Ottomans, the Italians and the Knights of St John have also left their mark

Astypálea

Bleak, butterfly-shaped Astypálea, with just over 1,000 inhabitants, is geographically nearer to the Cyclades than the Dodecanese. It belongs administratively to the latter group, yet in architecture and culture bears more resemblance to the former. On a clear day both Amorgós and Anáfi appear distinctly on the horizon. In recent years Astypálea's notoriously bad ferry connections have improved, enough to ensure export of the abundant local fish, though still not enough to suit package-tour operators. In high summer the few hotels do fill up, while Athenians have renovated old houses in the capital as summer residences. A domestic airport operates, a single stretch of road has been paved, taverna food has improved, and houses are whitewashed more frequently, but further momentous change is unlikely.

Many visitors stay in the principal (and functional) port of **Péra Yialós** or **Skála**, which dates from the Italian era. A long stair-street connects Skála with the capital, also called **Astypálea ❶**, which incorporates the medieval **Hóra**, the finest such in the Dodecanese outside of Pátmos. A line of derelict windmills trails off to the northwest; at the pinnacle of things sits the tan-walled **kástro**, not for once a legacy of the Knights of St John, but a 13th-century effort of the Venetian Quirini clan. Until World War II several hundred islanders dwelt inside it, but now all is desolation, except for two fine churches: **Evangelístria**, supported by the groin vaulting of the northwest entrance, and **Ághios Yeórghios**.

Just west of the Hóra ridge, **Livádhia ❷** is the island's second resort, between citrus orchards and a sandy but somewhat scruffy beach. Better beaches, like nudist **Tzanáki**, and taverna-equipped **Ághios Konstandínos**, lie further southeast, out on the western "wing". **Kaminákia** and **Vátses** beaches beyond are usually visited on boat excursions.

The "body" of the butterfly is a long isthmus, just 100 metres (110 yards) across at its narrowest point, by Stenó and Mamoúni beaches. **Maltezána** (officially **Análipsi**) to the east has become another resort, more through proximity to the airport than any intrinsic merit. The only habitations on the eastern "wing" are **Éxo Vathý**, favoured by yachts, and **Mésa Vathý**, road's end. A single bus plies between Livádhia and Maltezána, via all points in between; otherwise it's one of three elusive taxis, or a rented moped.

Níssyros

In legend Greek Poseidon, pursuing the Titan Polyvotis, tore a rock from nearby Kós and crushed his adversary beneath it. The rock became Níssyros. The groaning of the Titan is still audible beneath the sur-

LEFT: St John's monastery, Pátmos. **BELOW:** the black volcanic shore of Níssyros.

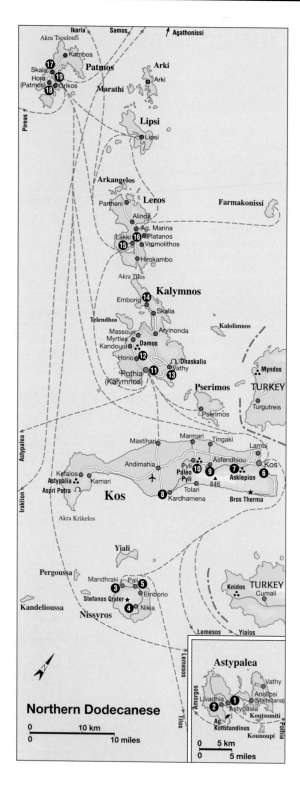

Northern Dodecanese

0 _____ 10 km

0 _____ 10 miles

face of the caldera in Níssyros's most impressive feature, the volcano which forms the heart of the island. Currently dormant, it was last active in 1933, and vulcanism dominates Níssyros, from black pebbles on the shore to a sulphurous spa.

Once you're away from its harbour, **Mandhráki** ❸ proves an attractive capital. Wooden balconies hang cheerfully from tall, white houses ranged around a central communal orchard. Overhead, the Knights' castle shelters the monastery of Panaghía Spilianí, while to the south, the Doric citadel of **Paleókastro** is more impressive.

Mandhráki by night is lively, with most tavernas and *kafenía* found, unusually, inland. There are few hotels, as most folk come just for the day from Kós to tour the volcano. In some establishments, you can order *soumádha*, a non-alcoholic drink made from local almonds. The early-spring almond-blossoming is one of the island's glories, best appreciated by walking some of the remaining trail system.

The main **Stéfanos** crater, 260 metres (810 ft) across, punctuates the nearly lifeless Lakkí plateau, 13 km (8 miles) southeast of Mandhráki. Occasional buses make the trip. With stout shoes, you can visit the caldera floor, braving a rotten-egg stench. Yellow crystals form around hissing steam vents while mud boils out of sight – the voice of Polyvotis.

The Greek power corporation made exploratory geothermal soundings here until 1993, but departed in the face of islander hostility – though not before ruining the best local walking trail.

Two scenic villages perch above Lakkí: **Emborió**, virtually abandoned and bought up for restoration by outsiders, and lively **Nikiá** ❹, with a quirky round *platía* and a few *kafenía*. The Emboriots moved down to the fishing port of **Páli** ❺. The biggest sandy beach is 6 km (3½ miles) around the northeast coast, at **Pahiá Ámmos**. West of Páli, the old spa at **Loutrá** has been well restored with EU funds.

Kós

The second largest Dodecanese in population, Kós is third largest in size after Rhodes and Kárpathos. It follows the lead of Rhodes in most things: a sea-transport hub for a gaggle of surrounding islands; a shared history, give or take a few years; a similar Knights' castle guarding the harbour, plus a skyline of palms and minarets; and likewise an agricultural economy displaced by tourism.

However Kós is much smaller than Rhodes, and much flatter, with only one mountain, Dhíkeos, rising to 846 metres (2,775 ft) in the southeast. The margin of the island is fringed by excellent beaches, most easily accessible by motorbike or even push-bike. Despite the presence of cycle-paths – a Greek first – Kós is by no means unspoilt, and even early or late in the season you'll have plenty of company. Visits in mid-summer, especially without a reservation, are emphatically not recommended. Yet the obvious over-development has compensations: surprisingly good restaurants scattered across the island, ample water-sports opportunities, and a good infrastructure (including cinema summer and winter).

Although the Minoans colonised the site of present-day **Kós town** ❻, during the late Bronze Age and Classical eras, the main island city-state was Astypalaia, on the far southwestern cape of Kéfalos, an ally of Rhodes in the Dorian Hexapolis. Spartan sacking during the Peloponnesian War and a subsequent earthquake (Kós is very susceptible to them) forced a relocation to the northern site, a process completed by the mid-4th century BC. According to Strabo, the new town was a success: "She was not large but inhabited in the best way possible and to the people visiting her by sea pleasant to behold."

Yet another earthquake in 1933 devastated most of Kós Town, except for the Ottoman bazaar of Haluvaziá, but gave Italian archeologists a perfect excuse to

Map on page 264

Kós has been inhabited since Neolithic times. Between 1500 and 1100 BC it had a powerful naval fleet, which took part in the Trojan War.

BELOW: boats take excursions from Kós to Níssyros.

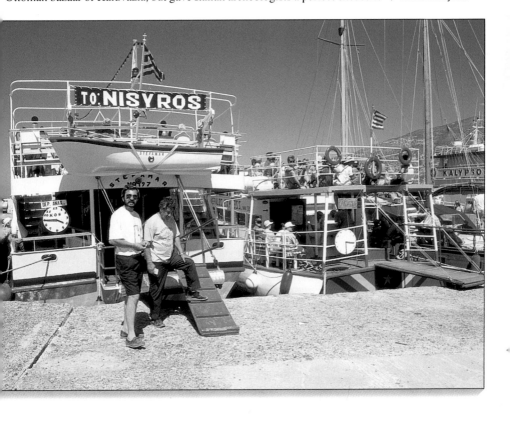

The 18th-century Defterda mosque in Platía Eleftherías is still used by Kós's 50 or so Muslim families, but is not open to the public.

BELOW: the remains of the Asklépion.
RIGHT: in Kós's Archeological Museum.

excavate the ancient city comprehensively. Hence much of the town centre is an archeological park, with the ruins of the Roman *agora*, the eastern excavation, lapping up to the 18th-century Loggia Mosque and the "Plane Tree of Hippocrates", under which the father of medicine is said to have taught. It is not really 2,500 years old, though it probably is one of the oldest trees in Europe, now dependent on a life support system of metal scaffolding.

The western digs offer covered mosaics and the Xystós, the colonnade of an indoor running track. Just south stand an *odeion*, sometimes used for summer performances, and the **Casa Romana** (Tue–Sun, 8.30am–3pm), a restored Roman villa with more mosaics and murals. The Italian-founded **Archeological Museum** (Tue–Sun, 8.30am–3pm) on Platía Eleftherías has a predictable Latin bias in exhibits, though the star statue, purportedly of the great healer Hippocrates, is in fact Hellenistic.

Hippocrates himself (c460–370 BC) was born and practised on Kós, but probably died just before the establishment of the **Asklépion ❼**, the ancient medical school 4 km (2½ miles) southwest of town. The site (Tue-Sun, 8.30am-3pm) impresses more for its position overlooking the straits towards Turkey than for any surviving structures. Their masonry was thoroughly pilfered by the Knights to build their massive **castle** (Tue–Sun, 8.30am–3pm), which unlike the one at at Rhodes was strictly military. It's a double fort, the smaller inner one dating from the mid-15th century, the outer circuit completed in 1514.

Between the Asklepion and Kós Town, pause at **Platáni**, roughly halfway, to dine at one of two excellent Turkish-run tavernas. As on Rhodes, most local Muslims have chosen to emigrate to Turkey since the 1960s. There was a small Jewish community here too, wiped out like the Rhodian one in 1944, leaving

Map on page 264

behind only the marvellous Art Deco **synagogue** by the town agora. The road east of town dead-ends at **Brós Thermá**, enjoyable hot springs which run directly into the sea. West of town, within easy cycling distance, are the package resorts of **Tingáki** and **Marmári** with their long white beaches, and the less frantic **Mastihári**, with a commuter boat to Kálymnos.

All three of these take a back seat, tourism-wise, to **Kardhámena ❽** on the south coast, 25 km (15 miles) from Kós Town but just 7 km (4 miles) from the airport. It's the island's cheap-and-cheerful resort, with little to recommend it aside from suggestively-named cocktails and a long, sandy and jam-packed beach. The only cultural diversion is the Knights' castle near **Andimáhia**, a two-hour walk inland for the energetic.

In the far southwest, facing Níssyros, are more scenic and sheltered beaches, with names like "Banana" and "Magic". At nearby **Ághios Stéfanos**, twin 6th-century basilicas are the best of several early Christian monuments. The Kéfalos headland beyond saw the earliest habitation of Kós: **Asprí Pétra** cave, home to Neolithic man, and Classical **Astypalaia**, the birthplace of Hippocrates, of which only the little theatre remains.

The appealing villages on the wooded northern slopes of Mount Dhíkeos, collectively known as the **Asfendhíou ❾**, have retained their traditional character, with whitewashed houses and attractive Byzantine churches. At Ziá, tavernas seem more numerous than permanent inhabitants, and are especially busy at sunset and after. Asómati's vernacular houses are slowly being bought up and restored by foreigners. The forest that surrounds the villages, the only one on the island, provides welcome relief from the heat in summer.

On the western flank of Mount Dhíkeos, the Byzantines had their island cap-

The Asklépion, Kós's ancient medical school and hospital, has two underground chambers with a statue of Aphrodite, believed to be where venereal diseases were treated.

BELOW: the massive castle built by the Knights at Kós.

Although the sponge-diving industry has declined in Kálymnos (see page 258) there are still workshops in Póthia where you can see sponges being cleaned and trimmed.

BELOW: the silver-domed cathedral of Ághios Hristós on Póthia waterfront.

ital at **Paleó Pylí** (Old Pylí) , today a jumble of ruins – including two 14th-century churches with frescoes – below a castle at the head of a spring-fed canyon. Modern Pylí, 3 km (2 miles) downhill, paradoxically offers something more ancient: the Harmyleio, a subterranean Hellenistic family tomb with 12 niches.

Psérimos

Tiny Psérimos (population circa 60), between Kós and Kálymnos, can be reached from either, though tourist excursions from Kós won't give you a full day here. This is apparently because the massive crowds of day-trippers, who come to flop on the long beach here, exceed the capacity of the few tavernas amidst the 30 or so buildings, so lunch is now taken in Póthia. If you do elect to stay the night, you'll find the islanders more receptive once the excursionists have departed. At sunset, local women wade into the sea, skirts held high, in rarely seen relaxation.

The sea is perfect for children, for several hundred feet away from the shore the water is still only shoulder-deep. If you tire of the main beach – which doubles as the main street – there are others, not as good in the east and north of the islet, or you could visit the monastery of Grafiótissa. After dark, the only sounds will be the wind rustling through calamus thickets, or the tinkle of goat bells.

Kálymnos

First impressions of Kálymnos, north of Kós, are of an arid, mountainous landmass with a decidedly masculine energy in the main port town of Póthia. This is due to the former dominant industry, sponge-diving, only lately supplanted by tourism and commercial fishing. But the former mainstay (*see page 258*) is

amply abundant in home décor of huge sponges and shell-encrusted amphorae, souvenir shops overflowing with smaller sponges, and (in autumn) uproarious celebrations of returned divers in the port's bars and cafés – which single women may choose to avoid or gravitate toward, according to taste.

Póthia ⑪ itself, the third largest town in the Dodecanese with a population of about 11,000, is noisy, colourful and workaday Greek. Its brightly painted houses rise in tiers up the sides of the amphitheatric bay. To the northwest loom two castles: Hryssoherías, the Knights' stronghold, and the originally Byzantine fort of Péra Kástro, above the medieval capital of **Horió** ⑫, which is still the island's second town.

The east coast is harsh and uninhabited except for the green, citrus-planted valley extending inland from the fjord of **Vathý** ⑬, which comes as a surprise amid all this greyness as you round a high curve in the road. Plátanos and Metóhi hamlets used to live from the sweet-smelling mandarin and orange orchards here, though many of these are now for sale. Yachts call at the little port of **Rína**, from where there are boat trips to the nearby cave of **Dhaskalió**, a place of ancient worship, and purportedly of refuge during the Italian era. The limestone strata are riddled with other, visitable stalactite caves. The best are **Kéfala** in the far southwest, and **Skalía** and **Kolonóstilos** in the far north.

Most visitors stay at the beach resorts on the gentler west coast, locally referred to as **Brostá** ("Forward"). Locals and Greek vacationers tend to gravitate towards beaches at **Kandoúni** and **Linária**, though undeveloped **Platýs Yialós** just north is reckoned the island's best. Foreign package tourists patronise **Myrtiés** and **Massoúri**, two adjacent, heavily developed resorts. At Myrtíes, also the port for the idyllic islet of Télendhos, a riot of vegetation

Map on page 264

Póthia has an orphanage where, until recently, Orthodox priests would come to choose a bride before they were ordained. A woman without a dowry was reckoned to have little chance of finding a husband outside the Church.

BELOW: quiet times on Kálymnos.

Sponge Diving

Kálymnos has been a sponge-fishing centre from ancient times, although a combination of fishing restrictions and marine blight have diminished the trade in recent years. Sponges come in various grades: coarser for industry, or finer for cosmetic and artistic use. Although cheap artificial sponges now dominate the market, many people will still pay extra for the more resilient natural sponge.

Sponges were traditionally "cured" in two stages. First the divers trod them underfoot on the caique deck to "milk" them of unwanted organic matter; then they strung them together and dropped them back into the sea for a few more days of cleaning.

Sponge-curing can be observed in Póthia factories (particularly at the Astor Sponge Workshop, open daily 10am-6pm in summer). Older operations have stone tubs of salt water, others bubbling vats of dilute acid which bleach the sponges – a concession to tourist tastes which actually weakens the

fibres. After this optional process, they're rinsed in salt water again and finally laid out to dry in the factory courtyard.

Over the years sponge-fishers developed various methods of gathering their quarry: spearing them in shallow water; dragging a heavy blade and net along the sea-bottom so that everything – stones and seaweed as well as the odd sponge – got pulled up together; and diving.

In the old days, divers used to sink themselves with heavy stones tied to their waists. Holding their breath, they scraped off the rock-fixed sponges spied from the surface. They could usually get two or three before they had to surface for air. Better divers could dive to 40 fathoms before the "machine" was introduced late in the 19th century.

The "machine" is the local term for the first diving apparatus, which consisted of a rubber suit with a bronze helmet connected to a long rubber hose and a hand-powered air-pump. The diver was let out on a long cable and given enough air-hose for his final depth, where he could stay much longer thanks to the constant air supply. Too long and too deep, as it turned out. Compressed air delivered to divers at the greater depths bubbled out of solution in their bloodstream as they rose, invariably too rapidly. The results of nitrogen embolism – known as the "bends" – included deafness, incontinence, paralysis and often death.

By the 1950s the physiological mechanism was understood and the carnage halted, but too late to help hundreds of Kalymnian crewmen. Although the "machine" now seems quaintly antiquated, it was innovative enough for its time to enrich the boat captains and sponge wholesalers.

Ironically, the increased efficiency in sponge-harvesting helped to wind up the industry. The Greek seabed was stripped bare, and Kalymnian boats had to sail increasingly further afield. Over-exploitation of Mediterranean sponge beds was the rule even before a virus devastated them during the 1980s. Today, sponge divers are a rare breed, but two or three caiques still set out from Póthia in late April for six months of sponge diving. ❑

LEFT: the "machine" that revolutionised diving.

– palms, hibiscus, grape arbours – adorns tavernas, rooms and *dhomátia*. You can escape the crowds by heading north towards **Aryinónda** and **Emborió** , the end of the road 19 km (12 miles) from Póthia, but at a price: beaches are rough shingle rather than comfortable round gravel, and the bus service beyond Massoúri is sparse to non-existent. In any case, Kálymnos is just the right size to explore by moped, and boat excursions are also offered.

Map on page 264

Télendhos

Seen from Myrtiés on Kálymnos at dusk, the bulky islet of Télendhos resembles a snail; others claim to see the silhouette of a petrified princess, jilted here by her lover. The caique from Myrtiés runs every 20 minutes in the summer, from dawn until late, and (optimistically) once or twice daily in the winter. Prepare to share the boat with boxes of tomatoes, piles of blankets, and other household goods. The fishermen who are the most frequent passengers are graced with wonderful manners: even if she is three times younger, a lady will not be allowed to stand while they remain seated.

The single waterside hamlet huddles under mammoth **Mount Ráhi** (458 metres/1,420 ft). On the far side of this, a long trek away, is the fortified monastery of Ághios Konstandínos. Less energetic souls content themselves with the ruined Byzantine monastery of **Ághios Vassílios**, at the north edge of the hamlet, or the Byzantine baths at **Ághios Harálambos**. Télendhos is more upmarket than nearby Psérimos, and less set in the day-trip mentality. Tavernas are stylish and friendly, and accommodation designed with intent to lure custom over from the main island. Beaches are limited both in number and size. The best is scenic **Hohlakás**, 10 minutes west, with coin-sized pebbles.

Télendhos was joined to Kálymnos until AD 554, when an earthquake sundered the two. Buildings of a town that sank into the resulting channel are supposedly visible in exceptional circumstances.

BELOW: fishing nets drying in the sun.

Léros

Léros, with its half-dozen deeply indented bays, looks like a jigsaw puzzle piece gone astray. The deepest inlet, that of **Lakkí**  (now the main ferry port), sheltered an important Italian naval base from 1923 onwards, and from here was launched the submarine that torpedoed the Greek battleship *Elli* in Tínos harbour on 15 August 1940.

Today Lakkí town seems bizarre, an Art Deco experiment far too grand for the present token population. The institutional buildings, reminders of colonial subjugation, seem neglected, the landscaped squares and wide boulevards spookily empty. Ferries in all directions tend to arrive after dark, when the prevailing shabbiness is masked by glamorous illumination. The local atmosphere is not cheered by the presence of three hospitals for handicapped children and mentally ill adults, substandard conditions which prompted an uproar when exposed in the late 1980s. More timid travellers thus give Léros a miss, which means that the island is mostly spared the excesses of industrial-strength tourism.

The rest of the island is more inviting, particularly the fishing port of **Pandéli** with its waterfront tavernas, just downhill from the capital of **Plátanos** , draped over a saddle culminating in a well-preserved Knights' castle with its Panaghía tou Kástrou church.

South of both, **Vromólithos** has the best easily accessible, car-free beach on an island not known for good, sandy ones. In most places sharp rock reefs must be crossed. **Ághia Marína**, beyond Plátanos, is the hydrofoil harbour and, like Pandéli, offers good tavernas.

The ancient worship of the goddess Artemis may be responsible for one custom peculiar to Léros: all property is inherited down the female family line.

Álinda, 3 km (2 miles) north around the same bay, is the oldest established resort, with a long beach right next to the road – and a poignant Allied War Graves cemetery containing casualties from the Battle of Léros in November 1943, when the Germans ousted an insufficiently supplied British commando force.

In ancient times Léros was sacred to Artemis, and on a hill next to the airport runway are knee-high remains of the goddess's temple. Artemis' reputed virginity lives on in the place name **Parthéni** (*parthenos* is the Greek for "virgin"), the other side of the airport: an infamous concentration camp during the junta, now a scarcely more cheerful army base. Things perk up at the end of this, with one of the island's better beaches, **Blefoútis**, with a popular taverna.

Other bays tend not to be worth the effort spent getting there. **Goúrna**, in the west, is long, sandy and gently shelving, but also windy, backed by rubble and devoid of facilities. **Xirókambos** in the south refuses to face the facts of a poor beach as it struggles to be a resort; caiques from Myrtiés on Kálymnos call here in season.

Lipsí

The name Lipsí (sometimes spelt Leipsoí) is supposed to derive from Kalypso, the nymph who held Odysseus in thrall for years. The little island (population 450) has been transformed by tourism and a regular ferry service since the 1980s. The single harbour town (also called **Lipsí**) has been spruced up, accom-

BELOW: twilight over Télendhos.

modation has multiplied, bulldozer tracks and paved roads creep across the landscape, and mopeds are now available to explore them.

Map
on page
264

An extraordinarily long esplanade links the ferry quay with the village centre, marked by the three-domed cathedral of Ághios Ioánnis. Behind this is the main square with some cafés and the town hall, whose ecclesiastical museum has some amusing exhibits. As befits a dependency of Pátmos, the older houses have their windows outlined in bright colours which change by the year, just as in Skála. Beaches are scattered across the island. The best and sandiest are the town beach of **Liendoú**, **Platýs Yialós** in the northwest, with a seasonal taverna, and **Katsadhiá**, a double cove in the south, facing Léros, with two tavernas.

Lipsí appears green, but farming is dependent on well water; there is only one spring in the west of the island. Though tractors and pumps are audible by day, nights are given over to the sea's lapping, the crowing of errant roosters, or a snatch of music from the seasonal dance bar.

Three remoter islets north of Lipsí are far less developed and can be more easily reached from Pátmos. The permanent population of **Arkí** is just 39, and falling. There's no real village, beach, fresh water, or ferry dock. Electricity is solar, and two ferries each call once a week. Likewise two tavernas keep rooms for guests. **Maráthi**, across a channel, gets some day-trips from Pátmos for the sake of its sandy beach. It is inhabited only in summer, when there are a couple of places to stay. **Agathoníssi**, off towards Sámos, is more of a going concern with its three hamlets and population of about 160. Connections are better too, with hydrofoils dovetailing well with the small ferries. Most tourists stay at the little port of **Ághios Yeórghios**, with a convenient beach. More secluded beaches lie around the headland at Spiliás, or in the far east of the island at Thóli.

BELOW: café society in Lipsí.

The monastery of St John was built as a fortress to protect its treasures from pirates (there are even slits for pouring boiling oil over attackers). The massive walls were restored after an earthquake in 1956.

BELOW: a courtyard in St John's Monastery, Pátmos.

Pátmos

Pátmos has been indelibly linked to the Bible's Book of Revelations (Apocalypse) ever since tradition placed its authorship here, in AD 95, by John the Evangelist. The volcanic landscape, with its strange rock formations and sweeping views, seems suitably apocalyptic. In 1088 the monk Khristodoulos Latrenos founded a monastery here in honour of St John the Theologian (as the Evangelist is known in Greek), which soon became a focus of scholarship and pilgrimage. A Byzantine imperial charter gave the monks tax exemption and the right to engage in sea-trade, concessions respected by the island's later Venetian and Ottoman rulers.

Although Pátmos is no longer ruled by the monks, their presence tempers the rowdier elements found in most holiday resorts. There is no nudist beach on the island, nightlife is genteel and those who elect to stay (as opposed to those who arrive by hydrofoil from Kós or Sámos) appreciate the unique, even spiritual, atmosphere that Patmos exudes once the day-trippers have departed.

Skála ⓘ is the port and largest village, best appreciated late at night when crickets serenade and yacht-masts are illuminated against a dark sky. By day Skála loses charm, but all island commerce, whether shops, banks or travel agencies, is here. Buses leave regularly from the quay for the hilltop **Hóra** ⓘ, but a 40-minute cobbled path short-cutting the road is preferable.

Hóra's core, protected by a massive, pirate-proof fortress and visible from a great distance, is the **monastery of St John the Theologian** (daily 8am–2pm; also Mon, Tue, Thur, Sun 4–6pm). A photogenic maze of interlinked courtyards, stairways, chapels and passageways, it occupies the site of an ancient Artemis temple. The Treasury houses the most impressive monastic collec-

ion in Greece outside Mount Áthos. Priceless icons and jewellery are on display, though the prize exhibit is the edict of Emperor Alexios Komnenos granting the island to Khristodhoulos. The library, which is closed to all but ecclesiastical scholars, is rather diminished from its heyday but still contains 4,000 books and manuscripts.

Away from the tourist thoroughfares, Hóra is pregnantly silent, its thick-walled mansions with their pebble courtyards and arcades the preserve of wealthy foreigners who snapped them up in the 1960s. Short-term rooms are thus hard to come by, but there are a few good tavernas and, from Platía Lótzia on the north, one of the finest views in the Aegean, taking in at least half a dozen islands on all but the haziest of days.

Just over halfway up the path from Skála to Hóra stands the small **monastery of the Apocalypse** (same hours as main monastery), built around the grotto where John had his Revelation. A silver band on the wall marks where John laid his head to sleep. In the ceiling is a great cleft in the rock through which the divine Voice spoke.

The rest of the island is inevitably something of an anticlimax, but the beaches of Pátmos are surprisingly good. Buses connect with the beach resort of **Gríkos** ⑲, whose population in winter falls to a dozen people, and to the fertile village of **Kámbos**, whose beach is popular with Greek families. The biggest sandy beach is **Psilí Ámmos** in the far south, accessible by boat trip or a half-hour walk from road's end. Beaches north of Skála include (in order) **Melóï**, with a good taverna and an outdoor cinema; long **Agriolivádhi**; isolated **Livádhi Yeranoú**, with an islet to swim to; and finally **Lámbi**, with irresistible, multicoloured volcanic pebbles. ❏

BELOW: a young monk at St John's Monastery.

CRETE

Greece's southernmost island – and the largest – is characterised by soaring mountains, a proudly independent people, and unique remains of the first great European civilisation

Map on pages 288–9

Crete (Kríti), claimed by many Greeks to be the most authentic of the islands, is by far the largest. It stretches 256 km (160 miles) east to west and is between 11 and 56 km (7 to 35 miles) wide. A massive mountainous backbone dominates, with peaks stretching skywards to over 2,400 metres (8,060 ft). In the north the mountains slope more gently, producing fertile plains, while in the south they plunge precipitously into the sea. Megalónissos ("Great Island") is what Cretans call their home and "great" refers to far more than size.

Great can certainly be applied to the Minoan civilisation, the first in Europe and one with which Crete is inexorably entwined. Visitors by the thousand pour into the ruins of Knossós, Festós, Mália and Káto Zákros, before heading towards one of the scores of excellent beaches. With two major airports, Crete cannot be classified as undiscovered, but through its size and scale it manages to contain the crowds and to please visitors with widely divergent tastes. While a car is essential for discovering the best of the island, car hire is, unfortunately, comparatively expensive.

Most of Crete's 500,000 people live in the north. The mountains to the south, honeycombed with caves, nurture a proud and ruggedly independent people whose fierce mustachioed menfolk still sometimes dress in jodhpurs, black leather knee-boots and black crochet headscarves. Unlike islands more integrated with the mainland, Crete has its own songs, characterised by the *mantinádes*, and its own dances such as the spectacular *pentozáli*. These are almost invariably accompanied by the *lýra*, a ubiquitous Cretan instrument.

For more than half the year snow lies on the highest peaks, which provide a dramatic backdrop to verdant spring meadows ablaze with flowers. This, as botanists and ornithologists know well, is *the* time to visit. The former arrive to view more than 130 plant species that are unique to the island, while the latter are thrilled by more than 250 types of birds heading north. These migrants briefly join such rare residents as Bonelli's eagle and Eleonora's falcon. And it is in spring that the island is redolent with sage, savory, thyme and oregano. Dittany however is the endemic Cretan herb – did you know that bathing in an infusion of dittany increases sexual desire?

Crete, much more than other Greek islands, is a place both for sightseeing and for being on the beach. Minoan ruins are the major magnets: as well as the archeological sites, the Archeological Museum in the capital, **Iráklion ❶**, houses a unique collection of artefacts from Europe's oldest civilisation. But there are also Greek, Roman and Venetian remains for

PRECEDING PAGES: evening in Iráklion; sunset on the mountains of Crete. **LEFT:** the harbour at Haniá. **BELOW:** a religious festival.

which many tourist authorities would give their eye teeth, and literally hundreds of Byzantine churches, many with rare and precious frescoes. These paintings often have a distinct Cretan style recognisable by elongated figures and attention to detail. (Many churches will be locked: enquire at the nearest café for the key.) Dozens of monasteries have fallen into disuse, but others still function and have rich treasures and histories.

Homer's "island of 100 towns" can also be called an island of 100 beaches. Some are simply a place where a boat can be beached, but many are superb stretches of sand. On some, nudity, though not officially sanctioned, is tolerated. The season is long, stretching from Easter until late autumn.

Minoan glory

Most of the Minoan ruins visited at such renowned sites as Knossós, Festós, Mália and Káto Zákros date from the neo-palatial era (1700–1380 BC). Great unfortified palaces, brilliantly decorated, were built and beautiful pottery and magnificent jewellery, used for both religious purposes and personal adornment, were produced.

The first palaces, which were built during the proto-palatial period (2000–1700 BC) and of which scant remains exist today, are generally though to have been destroyed by an earthquake. Debate still rages as to what brought the neo-palatial era to an end. By the post-palatial period (1300–1100 BC) the Minoan leadership in the eastern Mediterranean was waning, and by the Early Iron Age (1100–650 BC) Crete was under the sway of mainland Greece. Surviving Minoans – Eteo-Cretans – retired to the mountains and continued to maintain their old traditions.

BELOW: large pots (*pithi*) are still made as in Minoan times.

Iráklion (Iráklio, Heráklion)

The capital of Crete since 1971, Iráklion has a population of 125,000 and is the fifth largest in Greece. It vaunts the highest per capita income of any Greek city, but this does not show in the civic infrastructure. Look not for extensive elegance or great public works. Much of Iráklion resembles a building site because of the tendency of the inhabitants to spend money on starting buildings without sufficient capital for completion.

Most tourists head for the Minoan ruins of Knossós, but this should be combined with a visit to the outstanding **Archeological Museum ⒶA** (daily, 8am–7pm, except Mon mornings) in order fully to comprehend the site and its contents. The tourist office is almost next door, and both are moments from the cafés and restaurants of **Platía Eleftherías** (Freedom Square) **ⒷB**, popular with both locals and visitors.

Iráklion's other major attractions, other than the Minoan, are from the Venetian era, testifying that this was Crete's most prosperous period in historical times. Head seawards to the old harbour and visit the Venetian **Arsenali ⒸC** (covered boat-building yards) and the restored **Koúles fortress ⒹD** (Mon–Sat, 8am–6pm; Sun 10am–3pm) whose three high-reliefs of the Lion of St Mark announce its provenance. Observe Mount Yioúhtas, ever present in the background, resembling a recumbent figure said to be that of Zeus. The fortress is illuminated after dark – a fine spectacle from the quayside cafés.

A few minutes to the west of the old harbour on S. Venizélou Street is the **Historical Museum ⒺE** with collections from early Christian times onwards (Mon–Sat, 9am–2pm).

Head towards the city centre and the upmarket cafés of **Platía Venizélou**

> **Map on page 284**

The Archeological Museum in Iráklion is best visited in the afternoon, when it is quieter. You can take a break in the garden café – but remember to retain your museum ticket for re-admission.

BELOW: the Venetian fort overlooking Iráklion harbour.

Iráklion's Morosíni Fountain, built by the Venetians in the 1620s, originally had a giant statue of Poseidon on top (matching the sea gods around the basin below the lions) but he went missing during the Turkish occupation.

(Venizélou Square, also known as Lion or Fountain Square) which takes its popular names from the stylish 17th-century **Morosíni Fountain ❻** and guardian marble lions. Overlooking the square is the Venetian **Loggia ❻** (city hall) flanked by the churches of **Ághios Márkos ❶** and, in its own little square, **Ághios Títos ❶**. All three of these buildings have been heavily restored. Since 1966, when it was returned from St Mark's Basilica in Venice, the skull of St Titus, St Paul's apostle to Crete and the island's first bishop, has been housed in Ághios Títos.

Walk south through the "market street", redolent with tantalising smells, jammed with people and resonant with decibels, but now very touristy (the true city markets now take place in Iráklion's suburban streets) and then west to the cathedral of **Ághios Minás ❶**. More interesting than the cathedral is the **Icon Museum** (Mon–Sat, 9am–1pm), housed in the small church of **Aghía Ekateríni ❶**, which contains some exquisite icons, six of them the work of 16th-century master, Mihaíl Damaskinós.

Challenging but rewarding is a circumambulation of the 15th-century city walls which, in their day, were the most formidable in the Mediterranean. The walls stretch for nearly 4 km (2½ miles) and in parts are 29 metres (95 ft) thick. En route, pause a moment at the tomb of the great Irákliot author and iconoclast Níkos Kazantzákis to enjoy the views and perhaps to consider the brief inscription on fear, hope and freedom.

The best beaches near Iráklion are at **Ammoudára**, just west of town, and at **Karterós**, **Toumbroúk** and **Amnissós** to the east. The latter, which was the port for **Knossós**, has the best sands and ambience, and spectacular views of incoming planes at the airport.

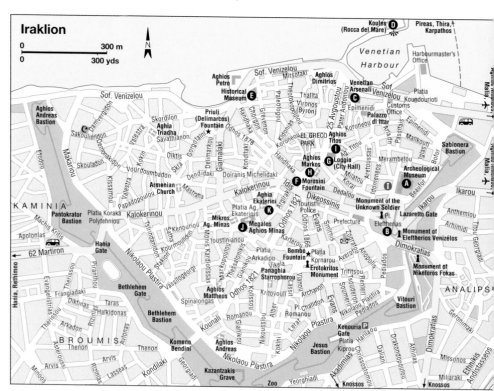

To Knossós and beyond

Several short excursions from Iráklion will delight the lover of Minoan sites, providing opportunities to view the attractive countryside and to savour village life. The most famous site, of course, is the palace of **Knossós ❷**, a mere 5 km (3 miles) southwest of the city centre, and easily reached on a No. 2 bus from Iráklion. (*For a full exploration of the remains at Knossós, see pages 302–3.*) In and around the village of **Arhánes ❸**,12 km (8 miles) south of Knossós, are three churches with interesting frescoes and icons, and three Minoan sites. **Turkoghitoniá** has a Minoan palace; **Fourní** possesses the outstanding cemetery in the prehistoric Aegean; and the remains of a Minoan temple have been unearthed at **Anemóspilia**.

A steep climb from Arhánes (allow 1 hour) leads to the summit of **Mount Yioúhtas** (811 metres/2,660 ft), from where you can admire the panorama while griffon vultures soar overhead. At the top are a Minoan peak sanctuary, a 14th-century chapel and caves in which Zeus is said to be buried. This would seem to prove the truth of the aphorism that "all Cretans are liars" because, in the opinion of most Greeks, Zeus is immortal.

Týlissos ❹, 13 km (8 miles) southwest of Iráklion, possesses three well-preserved small palaces or large villas (daily 8.30am–3pm) and is one of the few present-day villages to retain its original prehellenic name. Twenty kilometres (13 miles) further west on the same road, the elongated village of **Anóghia**, where wool is spun and where many homes have looms, is a weaving and embroidery centre. Many Anoghians wear native dress with the picture-book men looking like rebels in search of a cause. This is no stage setting: Anóghia has a long tradition of resistance and revolt. The village was razed in 1944 and

Maps:
City 284
Area 288

Human remains found at Anemóspilia suggest that when the temple was destroyed by an earthquake (around 1700 BC) a priest was in the act of ritually sacrificing a youth.

BELOW: a market street in Iráklion.

Zorba's Legacy

Seldom has a fictional character so engulfed its creator as did Zorba the Greek swallow Níkos Kazantzákis (1883–1957), the most renowned Greek writer of the modern era. Although Kazantzákis's output was large and varied, it is to the rugged, warm and happy-go-lucky Zorba that he owed his reputation.

At least, that was so until another of his books was also made into a film, *The Last Temptation of Christ*. When this book was first published, the Orthodox Church sought to prosecute him. When the film was screened in 1988, many church leaders the world over sought to have it banned. In Athens, priests marched on the cinemas where the movie was playing and screens were slashed.

When Kazantzákis was born in 1883, Crete had not yet become a part of the Greek nation but was still embroiled in attempts to free itself from the Turkish yoke, a struggle which drove the Kazantzákis family to move

to the island of Náxos soon after Níkos was born. But it is here on the "Great Island" that he is buried: once a Cretan, always a Cretan – indeed, no self-respecting Cretan refers to himself as a Greek.

Yet, because of his non-conformist views and writings, Kazantzákis was denied burial in a Christian cemetery with the full rites of the Orthodox church. He was buried in the Martinengo bastion of the Iráklion walls and his tomb carries this inscription: "I hope for nothing. I fear nothing. I am free." A statue in Eleftherías (Freedom) Square in Iráklion honours him more than does his grave on the town's battlements.

His admirers will make for the Kazantzákis Museum in the village of Mirtiá (24 km/ 15 miles) due south of Iráklion (when Kazantzákis was born here, it was called Varvári). Well arranged displays illustrate his personal, literary and political life both in Greece and abroad, with one room entirely devoted to Zorba. And in the Historical and Ethnographic museum in Iráklion, a complete room has been set aside to represent a study of Kazantzákis.

Those who favour fiction rather than fact have much to see in Crete. Ierápetra was the home of Madame Hortense, the French courtesan who featured in *Zorba*. Visitors may be shown where her still body was washed and where, even before the body was cold, the old harpies rushed in and stripped her apartment of all her possessions. And, in Ierápetra, Spýros Hrisofákes, a sprightly 65-year-old with a waxed moustache, still remembers the French courtesan who was the model for Kazantzákis's Madame Hortense and whose favours he, although a mere child, so desired.

Much of *Zorba* was filmed in Pláka and, high above it, Kókkino Horió, which lie on the coast midway between Réthymnon and Haniá. Here habitués of the local tavernas may not recall the name of Kazantzákis but remember well that of Anthony Quinn. Then, in the northwest corner of the Akrotíri Peninsula, there is Stavrós with its pleasant beach, shallow waters and towering cliffs – known to the locals as "Zorba's Mountain" – where the film's climax was shot. ❏

LEFT: Spýros Hrisofákes with a photograph of the courtesan who inspired Kazantzákis.

its men, many of whom still wear traditional Cretan dress, are among the fiercest and bravest in Crete.

From Anóghia the road climbs to the magnificent **Nída plateau** from where it is a 20-minute uphill stroll to the **Idean Cave** which was the nursery, if not the birthplace, of Zeus. Here the god was hidden and guarded by the Kourétes, who clashed their weapons to drown the sound of his cries, while the nymph Amalthée fed him goats' milk. Climbers might wish to push on to the summit of **Mount Ida (Psilorítis)** ❺, at 2,456 metres (8,060 ft) the highest point on Crete. A guide can be hired: allow up to 8 hours for the round trip.

East from Iráklion

Return to Iráklion and continue eastwards along the expressway for 24 km (15 miles), but then forget the "express". You have reached the Cretan Riviera, a stretch reminiscent of Blackpool or Coney Island with the resorts of **Hersónissos** ❻, **Stalídha** (Stális) and **Mália** ❼. Search not for elegance: bars and pizzerias abound. Ethnic it ain't. However the beaches are among the best although most of the sand is occupied by tourists. Hersónissos has scanty Greek and Roman remains while, close to the beach near Mália is a renowned Minoan site. Stalída has to settle for native palm trees.

The **Palace** at Mália (Tue–Sun, 8.30am–3pm), traditionally associated with King Sarpedon, brother of Minos, is contemporary with that at Knossós. The ruins are not as extensive as those at Knossós or Festós but, even without reconstruction, are more readily understood. The remarkable number of store rooms and workrooms suggests a country villa more than a palace. Recent excavations have unearthed the Hrysólakkos (Golden Pit) from the proto-

Map on pages 288–9

Black crochet headscarves (along with baggy jodhpurs and high boots) are the traditional dress still worn in many parts of Crete.

BELOW: woven goods in Anóghia.

There are thousands of cloth-sailed wind pumps across the Lasíthi Plain, but only a few are still used to pump up water for irrigation.

palatial period (1900–1700 BC). This name is derived from the numerous gold artefacts found in this enormous necropolis.

From either Mália or Hersónissos, twisting mountain roads lead up to the **Lasíthi Plain** ❽, around 840 metres (2,750 ft) above sea level and 57 km (36 miles) from Iráklion. This fertile and impeccably cultivated land supports a cornucopia of potatoes and grain crops, apples and pears. The visitor can well believe that Crete was the granary of Rome and may recall Pliny's statement that whatever is produced in Crete is incomparably better than that produced in other parts. However, rare is the day when you will see the unfurled sails of the 10,000 wind-pumps that irrigate the rich alluvial soil.

Proceed counter-clockwise around the plateau. **Psyhró** is the starting point for the descent to the giant **Díktian Cave**, supposedly the birthplace of Zeus. Guides here can be irritating but how, without one, will you be able to distinguish from all the other stalactites and stalagmites those nipples upon which Zeus suckled? Before leaving the plain, try to visit **Tzermiádho** and its **Trapéza Cave** which is the mythical home of Kronos and Rhea, the parents of Zeus.

Eight km (5 miles) after leaving Mália, the main coastal road passes the chapel of **Ághios Yeórghios Selenáris**. Public transport stops here to allow passengers to give thanks for a journey completed and to pray for a safe continuation. If you had travelled in the days of the old road, you would have been eager to do just this. Such shrines are not uncommon at the midpoint of dangerous roads.

Safely on to **Ághios Nikólaos** ❾, 69 km (43 miles) from Iráklion, invariably abbreviated by tourists to "Ag Nik" and once the St-Tropez of Crete. This

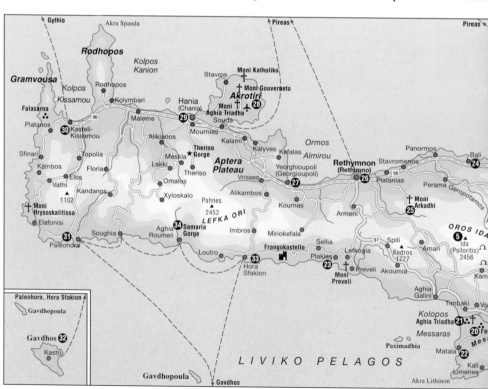

picture postcard paradise, overlooked by the eastern mountains, is magnificently situated on the Gulf of Mirabello. Here, and at neighbouring **Eloúnda ❿** (10 km/6 miles away), are some of the island's best and most expensive hotels. Unfortunately Ag Nik does lack a decent beach, having built a football pitch over its best one, although there are some passable sands a couple of miles to the east. Restaurants and hotels, discos and cafés cluster Ag Nik's Mandhráki harbour and the small, so-called, bottomless lake. The latter is connected to the harbour by a canal. Hedonists have been known to occasionally tear themselves away from their sybaritic lifestyles to visit the town's archeological museum (Tue–Sun, 8.30am–3pm) and folk museum.

The nearby island of **Spinalónga** with its ruined Venetian fortress is readily reached from Ághios Nikólaos by boat. (In 1589 the Venetians made the peninsula of Spinalónga an island by cutting a canal.) Aristotle Onassis considered building a casino here, but fortunately did not.

Clinging to the hillside 11 km (7 miles) from Ag Nik is **Kritsá ⓫** "the largest village in Crete", where lovely frescoes adorn the church of **Ághios Yeórghios**. Immediately below Kritsá is the church of **Panaghía Kerá** which is Crete's greatest Byzantine treasure. The entire interior is a picture-book bible consisting of 12th- to 15th-century frescoes. Indicative of changing times, until a few years ago Panaghía Kerá was a functioning church: it is now a museum and charges admission.

A couple of miles beyond and above Kritsá are the ruins of **Lató**. The pleasure here lies not so much in the fairly extensive remains of a Greco-Roman city but the superb views. From the northern acropolis, look across plains covered with an infinity of olive and almond trees to the coast and to Ághios

Map on pages 288–9

Lake Voulisméni at Ághios Nikólaos was said to be bottomless, and the home of spirits. Unromantic modern surveyors have found that it is about 70 metres (230 ft) deep and fed by an underground river.

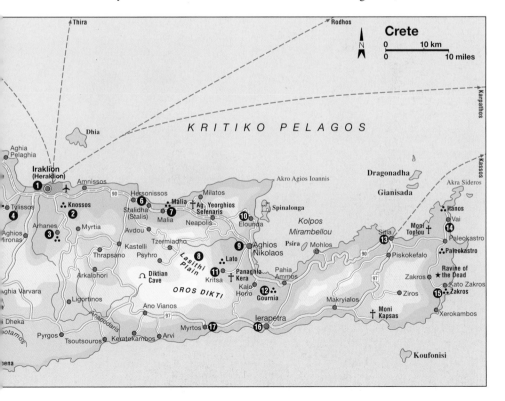

The 16th-century Venetian fortress on Spinalónga, near Ághios Nikólaos, was used as a leper colony until 1957 – the last in Europe.

BELOW: roasting a lamb for Easter.

Nikólaos (once the port for Lató) and beyond, to the Gulf of Mirambello and the Sitía mountains. To sit here and absorb the view with the background music provided by the bells of unseen sheep is to feel completely chaste.

Leave Ághios Nikólaos and head eastwards for Sitía. After 19km (12 miles), **Gourniá** , the poor man's Pompeii, is reached (Tue–Sun, 8.30am–3pm). Spread over a ridge, overlooking the sea, are remains, not of another palace, but of streets and houses of a Minoan town. Especially in spring, when the site is covered with a riot of flowers and their perfume fills the air, even those bored with old stones will be delighted to be there.

A few miles further and a poorly surfaced side road drops to the unspoiled fishing village of **Móhlos**. The tiny island opposite, which can be readily reached by strong swimmers, bears the same name as the village and has scanty Minoan ruins. Some way beyond is the larger island of **Psíra** where a Minoan town and port are being excavated. (Both islands can, on occasions, be reached by boat from Ághios Nikólaos.)

Sitía ⓭, 70 km (44 miles) from Ag Nik, is a somewhat laid-back town which, to the delight of visitors and the chagrin of locals, has not yet hit the big time. Here are the almost obligatory Venetian fort, archeological museum (Tue–Sun, 8.30am–3pm), and a disappointing beach. There is also a folklore museum.

Toploú Monastery, its tall 16th-century Italianate bell-tower beckoning like the minaret of a mosque, stands in splendid isolation in the middle of nowhere beyond Sitía. The monastery derived its name from a renowned artillery piece (*top* is Turkish for cannon) which formerly protected it. The monks also had other methods of protecting themselves: observe the hole above the monastery gate through which they poured hot oil over their assailants.

After a further 9 km (6 miles) is **Váï** ⑭, renowned for its myriad palm trees and the large, sandy beach that suggests far-away tropics. Don't believe it. The palm trees are native, not the species associated with desert islands, and the beach is usually crowded. For a more relaxed time, better make for the quiet, palm-free **Ítanos**, a couple of miles farther north.

Southwards from Váï is **Paléokastro**, which hit the headlines because of outstanding finds at the largest Minoan town yet to be uncovered. Beaches about a mile away, especially at the southern end of the bay, are well worth visiting. Further on is **Ano Zákros**, the starting point to **Káto Zákros** ⑮, the fourth great Minoan site (Tue–Sun, 8am–2pm). Hikers will prefer to make their way from Upper to Lower Zákros by walking through the spectacular **Ravine of the Dead**, where caves were used for Minoan burials.

The ruins at Káto Zákros, 43 km (27 miles) from Sitía, are from the neopalatial era, but there are intrusions from the proto-palatial era. They are often waterlogged because Crete is tipping over longitudinally, with its eastern end sinking below and its western end rising above the water table. The main dig has its customary central courtyard and royal, religious and domestic buildings and workshops radiating outwards. Close by are the remains of a Minoan town and of a sheltered Minoan harbour ideally situated for trade with the Levant and Egypt. As at many Minoan sites, the setting is everything.

Unusually, the dig at Káto Zákros is privately funded. In the 1960s Dr Nikólas Pláton, director of the Archeological Service, was asked by the Pomerances, a New York business couple, if any Minoan sites had still to be excavated. Yes, he told them. So what, they asked, was the problem? Money, was the reply. With that, the Pomerances underwrote the dig with no strings attached.

> Map on pages 288–9

The plantation of palm trees at Váï, which has existed since Classical times, may be unique in Europe. The trees are now fenced in to protect them.

LEFT: taking it easy on Váï's palm-fringed beach.

Back at Gourniá, a flat road crosses the island's isthmus to **Ierápetra**  (35 km/22 miles from Ag Nik), the largest town on the south coast. Over the past decade Ierápetra has enjoyed a boom, not only because of tourism but also because of market gardening and the uncovering of archeological sites. The town, scarcely atmospheric, has a promenade at the rear of a not-so-good beach, the inevitable archeological museum and a small Venetian fort.

Fifteen km (9 miles) to the west lies the pretty village resort of **Mýrtos**, which takes advantage of mild weather to remain open through the winter. Eastwards 24 km (15 miles) from Ierápetra, is the new and inchoate summer resort, and reasonable beach, of **Makryghiálos**. From here a side road leads to the 14th-century **Kapsás Monastery** built snugly into the cliffs at the entrance to a gorge. Monks will show you, encased in a silver casket, the skull of Gerondoyánnis, a 19th-century faith healer, who is a kind of cult figure. Káto Zákros is practically round the corner but cannot be reached without returning to Makrýialos and then taking the twisting mountain roads to Sitía.

South from Iráklion

Head south from Iráklion, over a lower point in the island's spine, and you reach the very centre of the island, at **Aghía Varvára**. Straight on brings you to a breath-taking view of the Plain of Mesará. Rich soil and a benign climate make this a cornucopia where the wild flowers are said to be taller and larger than anywhere else in Crete.

At the edge of the plain, 40 km (25 miles) from Iráklion is the almost sacred village of **Aghíi Dhéka** (Holy Ten) with its heavily restored medieval church into which are incorporated fragments from the nearby site of Górtyn. Aghíi

BELOW: Zarós in the Plain of Mesará.

Dhéka is renowned because in AD 250, during the persecution of the Christians, 10 men were executed who are not only among the most revered of Cretan saints but also glorified as the first in a long line of Cretans willing to sacrifice themselves to oppose the tyrannical occupiers of their beloved island.

After another 1 km, you reach **Górtyn (Górtys)** ⓲. This was the capital of the Romans who came to Crete in the 1st century BC to settle feuds but who stayed to conquer. Outstanding and upstanding are the Roman *odeion* and a triple-naved basilica. The latter is by far the best preserved early church in Crete and was built to house the tomb of St Titus, Crete's first bishop, who died in AD 105. (daily, 8.30am–3pm). However, the most renowned artefacts are some stone blocks incorporated into the *odeion*. About 2,500 years ago more than 17,000 characters were incised on these to produce the Code of Górtyn which consists of rules governing the behaviour of the people.

Those in search of more classical ruins, of health and good swimming might wish to head south to **Léndas** ⓳ (72 km/45 miles from Iráklion) over a mountainous road that provides magnificent vistas. Nearby ancient **Lebéna** was the port for Górtyn and its therapeutic springs made it a renowned healing sanctuary with an **Asklipíon** (temple to Asklipiós, the god of healing). Traces of this sanctuary, with mosaic floors and large baths, can be seen. In an attempt to equal if not emulate the ancients, nude bathing is popular at Léndas's best beach, beyond the headland at the western end of the village.

Festós (Phaestos) ⓴, Crete's second great Minoan site, occupies a magnificent location 16 km (10 miles) west of Górtyn (daily, 8am–7pm). Most of the remains are from the neo-palatial period, although part of the floor plan of the proto-palatial palace is discernable. State-rooms, religious quarters,

Map
on pages
288–9

The text of the Code of Górtyn is written in "ox-plough" fashion, reading left to right along one line, then right to left along the next.

BELOW: shepherds milking in the mountains.

The remains of two palaces can be seen at Festós: the first was built around 1900 BC and destroyed by an earthquake 200 years later; the other was seriously damaged around 1450 BC, possibly by a tidal wave.

BELOW: Mátala's sandstone caves.

workshops, store-rooms and functional plumbing can all be identified. An outstanding sight is the Grand Stairway. At Festós those purists who bristle at Knossós's reconstruction can let their imaginations run riot unhindered.

Nearby, again on a glorious site with views of the Libyan Sea, are the attractive Minoan ruins of **Aghía Triádha** ㉑ (daily, 8.30am–3pm) whose exact function – palace or villa – still causes speculation.

Next, to **Mátala** ㉒, 70 km (44 miles) from Iráklion. The resort first gained renown when the sandstone caves in the cliffs around the small, excellent sandy beach became home of the world's hippies and Joni Mitchell wrote a song about it. Today the small village can be busy, yet not frenetic. The scenic 30-minute walk south to Red Beach is highly recommended, though Kómmos beach to the north is much larger and has a recently excavated Minoan site.

The larger south coast resort of **Aghía Galíni** also lies on the Gulf of Mesará, though a little further west, 70 km (44 miles) from Iráklion. If Mátala proved too boisterous, then Aghía Galíni will be far more so. The harbour, with a short wide quay and a tiny main street jammed with tavernas and bars, is enclosed within a crescent of steep hills covered with modest hotels. Nightlife goes on into the wee small hours. Not for the faint-hearted.

Into western Crete, and **Plakiás** ㉓ is reached, with its five large beaches and spectacular mountain backdrop, 112 km (70 miles) from Iráklion. An almost mandatory pilgrimage from here is to the **Monastery of Préveli** (13 km/8 miles), passing en route the evocative ruins of the **Monastery of Ághios Ioánnis**. Préveli has a superb position, an interesting museum whose highlights include a piece of the True Cross, and a courtyard fountain with the inscription "Wash your sins, not just your face". Below the monastery is a beach from

where Allied troops in World War II escaped to waiting submarines after being sheltered by the monks. The provincial town of **Réthymnon** is 35 km (22 miles) to the north.

West from Iráklion

Back in Iráklion, an oleander-lined expressway runs west towards Réthymnon. Some however, might prefer more leisurely travel on the picturesque but winding old road. Alternatively, leave the new road 25 km (16 miles) from the capital to arrive in **Fódhele (Phódele)**, a small village rich in orange trees and locally made embroidery. A restored house here is said to be the birthplace in 1545 of Domínikos Theotokópoulos, better known as El Greco. Fódhele's fame may be fleeting, for the latest word is that El Greco was probably born in Iráklion. Back on the expressway, turn seawards after a further 18 km (11 miles) to reach the idyllic resort of **Balí ㉔** which is clustered around three small bays at the foot of a hill.

At **Stavroménos** or **Plataniás**, just before Réthymnon, turn southeast for the beautifully situated **Arkádhi Monastery ㉕** (80 km/50 miles from Iráklion), Crete's most sacred shrine. If the elaborate 16th-century western façade of the double-naved church seems familiar, it is because it is pictured on the 100-drachma note. In 1886, the monastery, sheltering hundreds of women and children, was attacked by the Turks. Rather than surrender, the abbot ordered that gunpowder stored in the now roofless room in the northwest corner of the courtyard be ignited, thus killing both enemy and refugees. This act of defiance brought the plight of the Cretans to the public eye and gained for them the sympathy and assistance of much of Europe.

When Arkádhi Monastery exploded, one infant was blown into a tree and survived. She grew up to become a nun.

BELOW: Arkádhi Monastery.

Map on pages 288–9

A Cretan Custom

Travellers who take the road in western Crete from Kastélli to Ano Paleókastro are in for an unusual, yet typical Cretan surprise. The road climbs and twists past olive groves and, after 8 km (5 miles), terminates at Ano Paleókastro. From here the ruins of Polyrínia can be reached only by walking through the gardens of villagers.

The barking of an especially ferocious fenced-in dog serves not only to terrify the tourist but also to alert Mr Pirounákis to the approaching stranger. Mr Pirounákis welcomes you with *Elláte! Kathíste*! (Come! Sit down!). The greeting is timely for you are sure to be panting, completely unnerved and uncertain as to which is the route to the ruins.

Within the house all is bare and whitewashed. Mr Pirounákis immediately pours for you a glass of *tsikouthiá*, Cretan fire-water, but he abstains on account of a heart condition. Sweetmeats follow and then comes the interrogation. And, be sure, whether you are from England or America, Singapore or Switzerland, Mr Pirounákis is sure to have hosted previous visitors from there. In evidence, he produces his three large guest books and hundreds of picture postcards sent by those he has entertained. Simple arithmetic reveals that Mr Pirounákis plays host to about 500 tourists annually and dispenses many litres of the lethal *tsikouthiá*.

Mrs Pirounákis soon appears and refills your glass. It is difficult to depart and continue onto Polyrínia, for the Pirounákis pair believe it is a matter of pride and honour to offer comfort to strangers. Cretans pay more than lip service to Xenios Zeus, the patron god of hospitability.

Farewells are finally permitted and you can continue your sightseeing. A stiff climb of a few more minutes and you reach the scattered, inchoate ruins of Polyrínia. But it is not for the mute stones but rather for the superb views of the Gulf of Kissamos and, above all, for Cretan hospitality in the shape of Mr and Mrs Pirounákis that the traveller visits Ano Paleókastro and Polyrínia. ❏

Réthymnon (Réthimno) ㉖, 77 km (48 miles) from Iráklion, which prides itself on being Crete's intellectual capital, still possesses an intact old town with a small, picturesque Venetian harbour. Its major attraction is a quayside choc-a-bloc with colourful but expensive fish restaurants guarded by an elegant lighthouse. West of the harbour is the immense ruined **Fortétsa**, said to be the largest Venetian castle, and from where excellent views may be enjoyed (daily, 9am–4pm). Réthymnon's other attractions – the **Rimóndi Fountain**, the **Archeological Museum** (Tue–Sun, 8.30am–3pm) and the **Neradzés Mosque** – all lie between the harbour and the fortress. If it's open, a climb to the top of the mosque minaret is rewarding.

Venetian houses with unexpected architectural delights can be found in the narrow streets linking these sights, while oriental delights in the shape of minarets and overhanging wooden oriels give Réthymnon a Turkish-style raffishness. Besotted shoppers, especially those in search of leather and textiles, will find their nirvana in narrow, crowded Arkadhíou Street. Sun-worshippers will make for Réthymnon's wide beach. There are decent sands, backed by a palm-shaded promenade which starts immediately east of the harbour and stretches for several miles past the new part of town.

Réthymnon and Haniá to the west are joined by an expressway and an old road. Leave the highway after 23 km (14 miles) and enter **Yeorghioúpoli (Georgioúpoli)** ㉗ at the mouth of the River Armyrós. This delightful princely hideaway has a good long beach and a eucalyptus-shaded square.

Áptera, a flat plateau above Kalýves, provides not only excellent panoramas of the enormous **Gulf of Soúda** and the **Akrotíri peninsula** ㉘, but also insights into Crete's history. Visit the recently restored monastery of **Ághios Ioánnis Theológos**, the ruined Turkish fort, and the Greco-Roman remains. The name Áptera ("wingless ones") is derived from the Sirens.

Haniá (Chaniá, Khaniá) ㉙, 59 km (37 miles) from Réthymnon, is Crete's second city and its capital until 1971. It is a larger version of Réthymnon and claims to be one of the oldest continuously inhabited cities in the world. Its jewel is the boat-free outer Venetian harbour. The quayside is wide and backed by characterful, colourful old buildings whose reflections shimmer in the water. The ambience is of the Levant and this is the place for the *vólta,* the evening stroll.

The restored 17th-century **Mosque of Hassán Pasha**, the oldest mosque in Crete, stands at one end of the quay and is now the tourist office, while the restored **Firkás Sea Fortress**, which houses the naval museum (Tue–Sun, 10am–2pm), occupies the other end. Here in December 1913 the king of Greece officially raised the national flag for the first time on Crete. The Old Town, where artisans, especially leather workers, still occupy workshops, can be entered from this point by way of Angélou and Theo-tokopoúlou Streets. Both have splendid examples of domestic Venetian architecture. More leather is for sale on narrow, crowded Skrídlof Street.

The **Archeological Museum** (Tue–Sun, 8.30am–3pm) occupies the church of the Franciscan Friary, one of the best preserved and largest of a score of

Map on pages 288–9

The appearance of the town [Haniá] was striking, as its irregular wooden buildings rose up the hill sides from the sea, interspersed with palm trees, mosques and minarets. There was no mistaking we were in Turkey.

– HENRY FANSHAW TOZER, 1890

BELOW: Réthymnon harbour.

The lighthouse at Hánia, designed like a minaret, dates from the period 1830–40, when Crete was handed over to Egypt in reward for helping the Turks crush the rebellious Greeks.

BELOW: Hánia harbour in the early morning light.

still-standing Venetian churches. The Church of **Ághios Nikólaos**, after various architectural and religious conversions, displays both a minaret and a campanile. Another example of ecumenicalism is the small, drab Orthodox Cathedral, built by a grateful Turkish Muslim whose son's life had been saved by the intervention of the Virgin Mary.

In the New Town, visit the lofty glass-roofed cruciform **market**, and the less exciting **historical museum** (Mon–Fri, 9am–1pm; free) and archives with a collection of objects from the estate of Elefthérios Venizélos, father of the modern Greek nation.

Those with a sense of history will visit **Mourniés** and **Thériso**, villages south of Haniá. The house in which Venizélos was born, now a museum, is in Mourniés. From here, a delightful journey through the Thériso Gorge brings the visitor to the village of that name. Much revered by the Cretans is the house of Venizélos's mother which served as a revolutionary headquarters and is now a national shrine.

Akrotíri, a limestone peninsula stretching northeastwards from Haniá, is full of interest. First visit the hill of **Profítis Ilías**, where revolutionary Cretans gathered in 1897 to demand union with Greece. Here are the simple graves of Venizélos and his son Sofoklís.

Other graves, 1,527 of them, are found at the nearby immaculately maintained **Commonwealth Cemetery** where British and Commonwealth troops killed during the 1941 Battle of Crete are buried. Equal honour is given to three times that number of Germans who are buried in the well-tended cemetery at **Máleme**, 16 km (10 miles) west of Haniá. And on the western outskirts of Haniá stands a massive memorial topped by a diving eagle honouring Germans

killed while attempting to oppress the Cretans: an unusual example of tolerance.

Farther out on the Akrotíri, 16 km (10 miles) from Haniá is the important **monastery of Aghía Triádha**. A further 4 km (2½ miles) and reached by a deteriorating road, is the **Gouvernéto Monastery**, a century older. Both have many treasures and shaded courtyards where visitors can chat with monks. From Gouvernéto a rough 40-minute downhill scramble leads to the abandoned, enchanting and possibly enchanted **Katholikó Monastery**, concealed in a ravine populated only by goats. Dating from about 1200, this is, if not the oldest, certainly one of the first monastic settlements on Crete.

St John the Hermit is thought to have lived and died in a cave near the Katholikó Monastery.

West from Haniá

The road west from Haniá hugs the coast, passing several busy small resorts that merge imperceptibly with each other, before arriving at the **Kolymbári** crossroads. Proceed westwards through low hills. Emerge through a cleft to memorable views of the plain of Kastéli and the Bay of Kíssamos enclosed within the peninsulas of Rodhopós and Gramvoúsa. These are sometimes compared to a bull's horns, but more resemble rabbit's ears on the map. The road makes a tortuous descent to the plain and to pleasant but rather characterless **Kastéli-Kíssámou (Kastélli) ㉚** with its wide, broad beach, Roman ruins and a seldom open museum (42 km/26 miles from Haniá).

Turn left at **Plátanos** and a twisting road, reminiscent of a corniche, leads after 44 km (28 miles) from Kastéli, to **Váthi** and several splendidly frescoed Byzantine churches. From Váthi a poor road through a ravine leads in 10 dusty kilometres (6 miles) to the **Hrysoskalítissa Convent**. The name means "Golden Stairway" and refers to one of the 90 steps descending from the terrace being

BELOW: shadows in the afternoon.

Map
on pages
288–9

*The Samariá Gorge
is the home of the
rare and elusive
Cretan wild goat, the
agrími or krí-krí.*

BELOW: the "Iron
Gates", Samariá
Gorge. **RIGHT:** a
warm welcome at a
Cretan *kafenéon*.

made of solid gold. Failure to recognise that step is considered proof that you
have sinned. From Hrysoskalítissa a barely negotiable road terminates at the
broad sands of **Elafonísi**, bordering a shallow lagoon – possibly the best spot in
the whole island for beach lovers.

Around the corner to the southwest lies **Paleóhora** ❸ (76 km/48 miles from
Haniá), a self-contained resort that has a ruined castle and both sand and shingle
beaches, the latter for windy days. Occasional boats leave for **Gávdhos** ❸
island, Europe's southernmost point.

Hóra Sfakíon (Sfakiá) ❸, 75km (47 miles) by road from Haniá, is the home
of the Sfakians, who epitomise the independent and unmanageable Cretans. A
small, cliff-hanging, picturesque port with a brave past. Sadly, its sole *raison
d'être* today – but don't tell this to the Sfakians – is to transfer exhausted tourists
returning by ferry from their Samariá Gorge excursion.

Samariá Gorge

The most exciting and spectacular adventure which Crete offers the average
visitor is a walk through the **Gorge of Samariá** ❸, at 18 km (11 miles) one of
the longest in Europe. The walk starts by descending a steep stairway at
Xylóskalo, 1200 m (3,936 ft) above the sea, at the southern end of the vast
Omalós plain, itself some 45 km (28 miles) tortuous drive from Haniá.

Within a couple of kilometres' walking, the path is 600 metres (2,000 ft)
lower, then after a further 8 km (5 miles), the abandoned village of Samariá
and its church come into view. Stop and admire the church's lovely 14th-century
frescoes: an opportunity to regain your breath without loss of face.

The going now gets tough and involves criss-crossing the river-bed. Be
warned: flash floods can occur and wardens' warnings
should be observed. The gorge narrows and the walls
soar straight upwards for 300 to 600 metres (1,000–
2,000 ft). Soon after passing the church of Aféndis
Hristós, the **Sidheróportes** (Iron Gates) are reached
and the gorge, scarcely penetrated by sunlight here, is
little more than 3.5 metres (11 ft) wide. However,
only a giant can, as sometimes claimed, stretch out
and touch each side of the gorge.

If, overcome by exuberance, you are tempted to
burst into song – don't. The park is under the strict
aegis of the Haniá Forest Service which specifically
forbids singing, among other activities. Even the most
innocent of botanists will be delighted by the gorge,
and ornithologists have been known to spot bearded
vultures overhead.

And so to **Aghía Rouméli** and the church of the
Panaghía. However, all is not over: this is old semi-
abandoned Aghía Rouméli and the goal is new Aghía
Rouméli on the coast. This means a further 3 km
(2 miles) of hot and anticlimactic walking before
celebrating with that longed-for swim or cold drink.
Refreshed, the only practical exit from the gorge,
other than retracing the same route is by boat
eastwards to Hóra Sfakíon or westwards to Paleóhora.
There are no roads. The gorge is open from about the
beginning of May until the end of October (entrance
fee). Allow four to six hours for the walk. ❑

CENTRE OF EUROPE'S FIRST CIVILISATION

Until a century ago, the Minoan civilisation was little more than a myth. Now its capital is one of the largest and best restored sites in all Greece

Knossós is a place of questions, many of them unanswered. Some visitors to the site find the concrete reconstructions and repainted frescoes (often from very small existing fragments) aid comprehension. But for many, used to other, more recent, ruins that are clearly defensive or overtly religious, the site is mysterious. Can we hope to look back at fragments of a culture from 3,500 years ago and understand its imperatives and subtleties?

In legend, Knossos was the labyrinth of King Minos, where he imprisoned the minotaur, the human-bovine child of his wife Pasiphae. In reality, the role of the Minoan palace was probably not in the modern sense of a palace, but perhaps as an administrative and economic centre, unified by spiritual leaders.

Among the 1,300 rooms of the main palace were both the sacred and the commercial: lustral baths for holy ceremonies; store rooms for agricultural produce; workshops for metallurgy and stone-cutting. Nearby are the Royal Villa and the Little Palace.

Try to visit early or late in the day, to avoid the worst of the crowds, and to avoid being swept along by the flow. Look for the subtle architectural delights – light wells to illuminate the larger rooms; hydraulic controls providing water for drinking, bathing and flushing away sewage; drains with parabolic curves at the bends to prevent overflow.

Combine that with a midday visit to the archeological museum on the site – to take full advantage of the air-conditioning inside.

△ **OVERVIEW**
The scale of the site is most apparent from the air – nearly 2 hectares (4 acres) of palaces ruled a population of perhaps 100,000.

▽ **EMPTY VESSELS**
Huge earthenware jars, *píthi*, were used to store grain, olive-oil, wine or water. Similar jars are still made in a few Cretan villages today.

△ **CHAIR OF STATE**
The throne room, possibly a court or council room, has a gypsum throne flanked by benches, and frescoes of griffins. These may have symbolised the heavenly, earthly and underworldly aspects of the rulers.

CONTROVERSIAL EXCAVATIONS

△ THE PLAY'S THE THING
The theatre was used for plays and processions. An engineered road, one of the oldest in Europe, leads from here to the Little Palace.

▽ ALL AT SEA
The fresco in the Queen's apartments (which included an *en suite* bathroom) features dolphins, fishes and sea urchins.

◁ BULL AND GATE
A (replica) fresco depicting the capture of a wild bull decorates the ramparts of the north entrance, leading to the road to Knossos' harbour at Amnissos.

▽ DILEMMA OF HORNS
The famous double horns now sitting on the south façade were once regarded as sacred symbols, though perhaps this is an overworking of the bull motif of the site.

◁ COLOUR CODING
The South Propylon (pillared gateway) has near life-size frescoes of processionary youths, including the famous slender-waisted cup-bearer. In Minoan art, male figures were coloured red, female white.

In 1878 a local merchant, Mínos Kalokairinós, uncovered a fragment of the remains at Knossos, but the Turkish owners of the land prevented further excavation and even the wealthy German Heinrich Schliemann couldn't afford their asking price when he attempted to buy the site.

However, once Crete gained autonomy from the Turks at the turn of the century, the way was open for the English archeologist Arthur Evans (later knighted) to purchase the area and begin excavating. He soon realised that this was a major discovery. He worked at Knossós over a period of 35 years, though by 1903 most of the site had been uncovered.

Evans' methods of using concrete to reconstruct the long-gone timber columns, and to support excavated sections of wall have received much criticism. While these preserved some of the structure *in situ*, it also involved much interpretative conjecture on the part of Evans (pictured above with a 1600 BC steatite bull's head from the Little Palace).

Excavation continues to this day, under subtler management.

INSIGHT GUIDES
TRAVEL TIPS

Insight Guides portray destinations in depth, providing the complete picture and the top photography

Insight Pocket Guides focus on the best choices for places to see and things to do and include large fold-out maps

Insight Compact Guides' portability makes them the perfect books to carry with you for on-the-spot reference

Three types of guide for all types of travel

INSIGHT GUIDES Different people need different kinds of information. Some want *background information* to help them prepare for the trip. Others seek *personal recommendations* from someone who knows the destination well. And others look for *compactly presented data* for on-the-spot reference. With three carefully designed series, Insight Guides offer readers the perfect choice. Insight Guides will turn your visit into an experience.

The world's largest collection of visual travel guides

CONTENTS

Getting Acquainted

The Place

Area Some 25,000 sq. km (10,000 sq. miles) of the Aegean and the Ionian seas are covered by islands.
Situation Greece is one of the southernmost European countries, ensuring a high sunshine rate throughout much of the year.
Population The most populated island is Crete, with just over 500,000 inhabitants, followed by Corfu (97,000), Lésvos (89,000), and Rhodes (88,000). The least populated islands covered in this book are the "Back Islands" of the Cyclades: tiny Donoússa, Iráklia, Shinoússa and Koufonísi have only 100–200 inhabitants each.
Language Greek.
Religion Greek Orthodox.
Time Zones Greek time is 2 hours ahead of Greenwich Mean Time. So when it is noon in Greece it is 10am in London, 5am in New York, and 8pm in Sydney. Like the rest of the European Union, the clock is advanced 1 hour from the end of March to the end of September to give extended daylight hours.
Currency Drachma.
Weights and Measures Metric.
Electricity 220 AC; round two-pin plugs.
International Dialling +30 (country code for Greece), followed by the relevant area code (omitting the 0).

Climate

If you visit Greece in the summer months bring lightweight, casual clothing. If you visit during the winter months, bring the same kind of clothes you would wear during spring in the northern part of the United States or northern Europe: that is, be ready for rainy, windy days and temperatures ranging between 40° and 60°F (3° and 16°C).

On the whole, islands are ill-equipped for visitors during the winter months. Heating can be basic or non-existent, boats infrequent, food tinned on the smaller islands and amenities scarce. The tourist season is officially "over" in late October, although it extends well into November on Rhodes and Crete, but ends mid-September in northern Greece. Should you find yourself on the pertinent islands during this period, you will be treated to a curious spectacle: an emerging ghost town. Cafés and shops close down daily, sometimes locking their doors directly after you have left, and remaining closed until the following April or even May.

In general, the north coast of each island is subject to more summertime gales and cooler temperatures than the protected south coast; be sure to check on a map exactly where a holiday resort is before making a final booking. Many travellers underestimate the differences in climate between individual island chains. The green, cool Ionian islands, for instance, are prone to rainy spells from mid-September through to the end of March. By contrast, the southern coasts of Crete and Rhodes can offer swimming for the hardy as late as mid-December. If planning to visit any island between mid-September through to the end of April, a good rule to follow is this: the further south the island geographically, the better the sunshine rate.

Government and Economy

Greece is a republic with a president, elected by parliament, who holds ceremonial executive power. The parliament has a single chamber made up of 300 elected members and led by the prime minister.

King Constantine went into exile in December 1967, following the April seizure of power by the infamous colonels' junta, and the monarchy was abolished after a referendum held after the collapse of the dictatorship in 1974. Since then two main parties, New Democracy (conservative) and PASOK (socialist), have taken turns at governing; PASOK has been in power since 1993, with the next elections not required by law until 2000.

Strikes and demonstrations are a way of life in Greece. Think yourself lucky should there not be one in Athens as you're passing through.

The late 1980s and early 1990s saw a huge rise in the cost of living throughout the country; a shock for anyone who remembers the islands as a "cheap and cheerful" holiday destination. Although the islands are no longer the place for bargain-basement breaks, the drachma tends to steadily devalue against other currencies at a rate slightly faster than the current domestic inflation of about 4 percent, so Greece remains good value for travellers.

Spelling and Place Names

This book has employed a transliteration system which attempts to guarantee proper pronunciation by foreigners as much as it represents, letter for letter, the Greek alphabet in Roman characters. If you find a place name that is unfamiliar, check on more than one map or ask at a local ticket office if the destination has another name or spelling.

Some examples include:
● **Sýntagma Square** in Athens is also known as **Sindagma, Platía Syntágmatos** or (in English) **Constitution Square**.
● The island of **Lésvos** is known as **Lesbos, Mytilene,** or **Mytilíni**.
● **Corfu** can be called by its Greek name **Kérkyra**
● **Itháki** can be known by its English name **Ithaca**.

Planning the Trip

Visas & Passports

Citizens of EU nations have unlimited visitation rights in Greece; your passport will not be stamped upon entry or exit. With a valid passport, citizens of the United States, Canada, Australia and New Zealand can enter Greece and stay in the country for up to 3 months. No visa is necessary. To stay longer than 3 months, you must obtain a permit from the **Aliens' Bureau** in Athens (173 Alexandras Avenue, tel: 642 1616 or 770 5711).

No visa is required for citizens of the following non-EU countries:
For a stay of 3 months: United States, Australia, New Zealand, Canada, Andorra, Argentina, Bahamas, Barbados, Brazil, Cyprus, Gambia, Granada, Iceland, Israel, Japan, Liechtenstein, Malta, Mexico, Monaco, Morocco, Norway, South Korea, Switzerland.
For a stay of 2 months: Republic of South Africa, Venezuela, Chile, Colombia, Dominican Republic, El Salvador, Haiti, Honduras, Guatemala, Ecuador, Kenya, Mozambique, Nicaragua, Panama, Paraguay, Peru, Uruguay, Zambia.
For a stay of 1 month: Tunisia and Hong Kong.

Citizens of other countries should contact the nearest Greek embassy or consulate with regard to visa requirements.

Currency

The Greek national currency is the *dhráhma*, rendered drachma in English, which comes in coins of 1, 2, 5, 10, 20, 50 and 100dr, plus notes of 50, 100, 500, 1,000, 5,000 and 10,000dr. Especially

Customs

It is prohibited to import narcotics, medicine (except limited quantities prescribed by a licensed physician for your own use), explosives and weapons. For other specific restrictions regarding the importation and exportation of such things as animals, plants, shotguns, pleasure craft and antiquities, contact the nearest Greek embassy, consulate or tourist organisation. Exporting antiquities without a permit is a serious offence.

Duty Free

The current allowances for goods bought duty-free (ie at a duty-free shop or on a plane or boat) when travelling between EU countries are:
● 200 cigarettes or 100 cigarillos or 50 cigars or 250g tobacco;
● 2 litres table wine; ● 1 litre spirits or 2 litres fortified wine, sparkling wine or other liqueurs;
● 60 ml perfume; 250 ml cologne.
NB At the time of writing, duty-free shopping for EU citizens within the

since the devaluation of March 1998, nobody bothers much with amounts of 10dr or under, and such coins – as well as the 50dr note – are approaching extinction.

Exchange Rates

Rates of exchange go up or down daily. To find out the current rate of exchange, check illuminated displays in bank windows, or the newspapers; you can read the tables even in Greek.

Credit Cards

The plusher hotels, shops and restaurants of Athens and larger islands all recognise the major international credit cards, but many tavernas will not. Stickers in the front windows advise on which cards are acceptable, but be sure to check before ordering or buying that the arrangement is still valid.

EU could be phased out by 1999. Check with your local customs and excise office before travelling.
US citizens and other non-EU citizens may import duty free:
● 200 cigarettes or 50 cigars or 250g tobacco; ● 1 litre spirits or 4 litres wine; ● 250 ml cologne or 50 ml perfume.

Duty Paid

For EU citizens: Provided goods obtained in an ordinary shop in an EU country are for your personal use there are, in principle, no restrictions. EU law sets out recommended guide levels, however, and if you bring more than the amounts in the guide levels you must be able to show that the goods are for personal use. Guide levels are:
● 800 cigarettes; 400 cigarillos; 200 cigars; 1 kg smoking tobacco;
● 10 litres spirits; 20 litres fortified wine; 90 litres (of which not more than 60 litres sparkling) wine; 110 litres beer.

However, you will find that most brands of card are accepted by the numerous cash dispensers, found even on fairly small islands like Léros, Náxos or Skópelos, upon entry of your PIN number – for example, the National Bank of Greece takes Mastercards; the Commercial Bank serves Visa; and the Alpha Credit Bank accommodates Visa and American Express cardholders. You will find that this is the most convenient and least expensive way of getting funds, and many of the machines operate around the clock.

Travellers' Cheques and Eurocheques

These can be cashed at any bank (except certain branches of the Agrotiki Trapeza/Agricultural Bank) and – at a poor rate and/or for high commissions – at travel agencies and many hotels. Much the best place for these transactions, especially on small islands without a bank, is the post office; queues are short and commissions tend to be less than elsewhere. You'll need to order both sorts of cheques from a high-street bank and, in the case of Eurocheques, a matching security card to prevent cheques from being used fraudulently.

Cash

Every island, no matter how remote, will have some form of banking system – often just the post office, as noted above. Some islands set up banking facilities in tourist shops and ote (telephone offices); offices and hours are irregular, never over weekends except perhaps Saturday morning. Cash is often the only form of guaranteed legal tender on these far-flung islands. If you plan to island-hop or follow on any itinerant whims, carry quantities of both drachmas and crisp bills of your native currency. Islanders are honest and your cash will almost certainly be safe, but be careful.

Animal Quarantine

Dogs and cats require health and rabies inoculation certificates issued by a vet in the country of origin before being allowed to enter Greece. The certificate must be issued not more than 12 months in advance in the case of dogs and 6 months in the case of cats (and not less than 6 days prior to arrival). Parrots and other birds must have a health certificate stating they are free from psittacosis.

Health

Residents of EU countries are eligible to receive free emergency medical care. In Britain, it is necessary to obtain form E111 from the post office (resident aliens must apply directly to DSS) before leaving home. It's strongly recommended to take out medical insurance as well.

Read the small print thoroughly before you travel. Be sure your policy covers the cost of an air taxi as, in an emergency, this is the quickest way off the smaller islands to the nearest hospital. If you plan to hire a car, a motorcycle or a moped, ensure that your policy covers all motoring accidents. The number of accidents, especially on mopeds, mounts annually.

DRINKING WATER

Carrying a large plastic bottle of mineral water is as common a sight on Greek islands as carrying a baguette around Paris, but it is rather deplorable, as sunlight releases toxic PVC into the water, and the spent bottles contribute enormously to Greece's litter problem. Buy a sturdy, porcelain-lined canteen and fill it from the cool-water supply of bars and restaurants you've patronised; nobody will begrudge you this. Although unfiltered tap water is generally safe to drink if not brackish, having a private water supply is much handier, as village-centre springs are rare and the sun is fierce. If you do want bottled water, it can be bought almost anywhere that sells food, even in beach cafés and tavernas.

INSECTS & PESTS

Snakes and scorpions can be found in rocky areas. They tend not to attack unless disturbed, but you should always dress in long trousers and socks when hill walking. Jellyfish (*tsoúkhtres*) are less common these days but can still occasionally be seen (and should be avoided) near the shores of some beaches. Sea urchins embed their spines painfully in you if stepped on in the water; a local Greek remedy is to douse the wound with olive oil and then gently massage the foot until the spines pop out. This rarely works unless you're willing to perform minor surgery with pen-knife and sewing needle, so wear plastic shoes when walking in shallow water.

The most common pest is the mosquito, which loves virgin white

skin. Avoid perfumes and deodorants (it attracts them even more) and invest instead in either of two items. The first is a pyrethrin coil, which when lit and placed by the window, acts as an effective means of combat by smothering the mosquito (and you) in foul-smelling smoke. Even the smaller islands sell these coils in chemists or grocers. The second method is a plug-in electric pad, which vapourizes smokeless rectangular tablets. Practically odourless, it's worth seeking out in chemists, supermarkets or hardware shops.

DRUGS

All prescribed drugs you take with you should be packed in their original bottles, carefully labelled and marked. Failure to do so could result in an arrest for the possession of dangerous drugs – codeine compounds in particular are banned, labelled or not. Greek authorities take the unauthorised use of drugs very seriously indeed; this is not the country in which to carry cannabis, no matter how small the quantity. Err on the side of caution at all times.

Sunburn

Each year hundreds of tourists are badly burnt by ignoring an obvious rule: do your tanning slowly.
● For the first few days wear a sunhat and a sun block.
● Observe, like sensible Greeks, the afternoon siesta when the sun is at its hottest, and stay on the beach for just a couple of hours in the mornings and the early evenings. Gradually work up to staying out longer.
● Remember to re-apply suntan lotion whenever you come out of the sea.
● It's possible to get burned while swimming or sightseeing too. Wearing a T-shirt over your swimsuit for the first couple of days or, when touring the island, dressing in long sleeves, avoids senseless burning.

What To Wear

On the whole, island life is casual. It's possible to get by without offending anyone by dressing simply, in a cotton dress and sandals (if a woman) or long trousers and a T-shirt (if a man). Bathing costumes can be slipped on underneath. Disco clothes or wash-and-wear cottons are sold on most larger islands, though of variable quality.

Like any other country, Greece has a set of codes, both stated and implicit, which defines the socially acceptable range of attire. The Greeks will not expect you as a tourist to dress as they do. However, in certain places and regions you will encounter requirements or conventions concerning dress which do reflect on you as a visitor.

To enter a church, men must wear long trousers and women, sleeved dresses. Makeshift wraps will occasionally be provided at the church entrance if you do not have them. Not complying with this code will be taken as insulting irreverence on your part. It's also important to conform to the socially acceptable dress code of the region you are visiting. On Mýkonos, for example, male and female tourists alike will shock no one by wearing shorts, a swimsuit or going bare-chested, even in many public places. But this same dress will be severely alienating if worn in a mountain village in Crete. The best approach is to observe what people around you are wearing and to dress accordingly.

FOOTWEAR

Sandals are appropriate day or night. Plastic flip-flops are invaluable for walking in shallow water containing rocks, rubbish or sea urchins, as well as for walking on the red-hot volcanic beaches of Santoríni and Híos. Such footwear can usually be bought on the islands. Sturdier walking shoes are required for mountain-climbing or uphill strolls as path surfaces can be ankle-turningly rough, and snakes are common in the hills.

Greek National Tourist Offices

● **Australia & New Zealand** 51–57 Pitt Street, Sydney, N.S.W. 2000, tel: (02) 9241 1663.
● **Canada** 1233 rue de la Montagne, Montreal, Quebec H3G 1Z2, tel: 514 871 1535; 1300 Bay Street, Toronto, Ontario M5R 3K8, tel: 416 968 2220.
● **Japan** 11 Mori Building, 2-6-4 Toranomon, Minato-Ku, Tokyo 5, tel: 503 5001.
● **United Kingdom** 4 Conduit Street, London W1R 0DJ, tel: 0171 734 5997.
● **United States** Olympic Tower, 645 Fifth Avenue, New York, N.Y. 10022, tel: 212 421 5777; 611 West 6th Street, Los Angeles, CA 92668, tel: 213 626 6696; 168 North Michigan Avenue, Chicago, IL. 60601, tel: 312 782 1084; National Bank of Greece Building, 31 State Street, Boston, Mass. 02109, tel: 617 227 7366.

What To Bring

These items should appear on every dedicated island-hopper's checklist, but again, most can be bought in Athens or the larger island cities: compact binoculars; can-opener, corkscrew, sharp knife, plastic fork and spoon (a good Swiss Army knife includes most of these domestic items); plastic drinking cup; torch (very important for steep island paths late at night); vacuum flask; face cloth (unavailable in Greece); bath towel (expensive in Greece); beach towel (silly novelty ones available everywhere); travel pack of soap powder (Greek detergent boxes do not reclose); sticking plasters; antiseptic cream; universal sink plug; portable clothes line and pegs; insect repellent; aspirin; indigestion tablets; earplugs; alarm clock and/or a watch. These last two items are for catching ferries, caiques and island buses; no two island clocks tell the same time and ferries wait for no one.

Baggage

The old saying, which applies to travellers everywhere, applies especially to those travelling on Greek islands: pack your suitcase, then unpack it and leave half the contents behind. Nothing ruins a holiday more than having to heave a heavy backpack or hold-all around unsuitable terrain, ie hills and ferry decks. Not many hotels have minibus services to/from the harbour or airport. If you plan to find accommodation when you arrive, you'll have to carry your suitcase while you look around or store it somewhere – a few of the more popular islands offer temporary luggage storage facilities near the harbour. If your luggage is still too heavy for prolonged island-hopping, consider investing in a suitcase- or backpack-compatible trolley

A handy tip: packing a smaller, collapsible holdall or day-pack inside a larger one can be useful. The smaller one can be brought out for the beach or for short trips to other islands, while the larger one and its contents stay safely stored in the hotel.

Left Luggage

There is a left-luggage facility immediately opposite the Athens West Airport Terminal, but none at the East Terminal. Most hotels in Greece, however, will be willing to store locked suitcases for up to a week if you want to take any short excursions. This is usually a free service, provided you've stayed a night or two, but the hotel accepts no responsibility in the highly unlikely event of theft. Commercial left luggage offices operate in many harbour towns on the islands. For a small charge, space can be hired by the hour, by the day, by the week, or longer. Although contents will probably be safe, take any valuables with you.

Getting There

BY AIR

Quite a few of the more popular islands have international airports. These include Crete (Iráklion and Hania), Rhodes, Corfu, Kefalloniá, Kós, Skiáthos, Mýkonos, Lésvos, Sámos and Zákynthos, and new charter destinations open each season. Many people, however, fly to Athens first; then take a ferry or a domestic aeroplane to the islands.

Greece has good air connections and is serviced by numerous international airlines. There are ways of flying at a much lower cost than the standard airline ticket (eg apex, stand-by, last-minute seats, "bucket shops"), and you may want to look into the different options before buying a ticket. By far the cheapest is by buying a seat on a charter flight, which can cost as little as £100 return from London. These often arrive in the middle of the night (or depart at dawn).

Athens Airports

Athens has three air terminals. The **East Air Terminal** is for international scheduled flights; a separate **charter terminal** has been created at the old American airbase; while the **West Air Terminal** is for all Olympic Airways flights and flights to the islands. Taxis or buses connect the three. During the peak summer season you can't walk through the special charter terminal without tripping over sleeping bodies and rucksacks, stranded by cancelled or delayed flights. It's all part of the fun.

Reservations

The dual perils of Greek civil aviation strikes and package tour operators' double-booking practices means nothing should be left to chance. Confirm travel arrangements and hotel accommodation with your tour operator or travel agent 3 days before leaving for Greece. When returning home, call the airline or the appropriate authority before

setting off for Athens to catch a flight home; on the islands, your local rep is supposed to confirm your return charter flight, but it's best not to assume this. Inexpensive charter flights are often subject to several hours' delay, so be sure to slip a bottle of water, a good novel or a pack of cards into your hand luggage. For information on transfer to the islands' domestic airlines, or of how to reach Athens or Piraeus from the airports, see *Getting Around*, page 315.

BY SEA

By far the majority of visitors entering Greece by sea do so from the west, from Italy. You can catch a boat to Greece from Venice, Ancona, Trieste and Bari, but the most regular service is from Brindisi. Daily ferry lines (less frequent in the low season) connect Brindisi with the three main western Greek ports: Corfu, Igoumenítsa and Pátra. Corfu is a 9-hour trip; Igoumenítsa 11 hours; and Pátra 16 to 18 hours, depending on whether you take a direct boat or one that makes stops in Corfu and Igoumenítsa. The "Superfast" ferries between Ancona and Pátra, introduced in 1997, offer an efficient 22-hour crossing, and daytime hydrofoils operate sporadically between Igoumenítsa and Brindisi.

Igoumenítsa is the ideal port of call for those setting off to see central-western Greece. Pátra is best if you want to head directly into Athens or into the Peloponnese. Regular buses and trains connect Pátra and Athens (4 hours by bus, 5 hours by train). If you plan to take your car with you on the boat, you should definitely make reservations well in advance. Otherwise, arriving a few hours before departure time should suffice, except during peak season when booking in advance for seats and berths is essential.

Eastward, boats run weekly between Haifa, Limassol, Rhodes and/or Crete, and Piraeus, not to mention the numerous crossing points between the East Aegean Islands and the Turkish coast.

BY LAND

From Europe: It's some 3,000 km (1,900 miles) from London to Athens, and it has always been a rather impractical travel option if you're just trying to get to Greece for a brief holiday. Ongoing troubles in former Yugoslavia now mean even longer detours. Check with your local Greek tourist office or motoring organisation for the latest information before leaving.

There are one or two reputable bus lines that connect Athens and Thessaloníki with many European cities (eg, 3½ days from London).

Various trains you can take from northwest Europe will take about as long as the bus, cost considerably more, but fares include the Italy–Greece ferry crossing, and you may arrive feeling more intact.

From Asia via Turkey: If you are travelling overland to Greece from Asia you will pass through Istanbul and cross into Greece at the Evros River. The recommended method is by car or bus. The road is good and the journey from Istanbul to Thessaloníki takes approximately 15 hours; several companies serve the route.

The train follows the old Orient Express route, with better scenery than the road, but unless you're a great rail fan, journey times are off-putting: 17 hours by the timetables, up to 19 hours in practice.

Coming Home

Leave plenty of time to reach Athens for your flight home, especially if you are on a remote island. Any situation involving more than one Greek vehicle (plane, boat, taxi) is courting disaster.

If the distance is far, or merely complicated, break the journey into stages to prevent calamities along the way. Leaving Hálki or S´ymi, for instance, it would be wise to arrive on Rhodes the day before your flight departs; 2 days before if flying back from Athens via Rhodes.

Practical Tips

Tourist Information

ATHENS

The 24-hour tourist police number in Athens is 171; their walk-in premises are in Koukáki in Athens at Veïkoú 98, just south of the intersection with Anastasíou Zínni.

The Athens headquarters of the Greek National Tourist Organisation (GNTO or EOT – Ellinikós Organismos Tourismoú) is located at 2 Amerikís Street, tel: 322 3111. Visiting hours are from Mon–Fri 12–2.30pm.

There is also an information desk at the East Air Terminal which is open during the day and displays ferry sailings even when closed, as well as another in Piraeus at Zéa Marina, tel: 413 5716.

THE ISLANDS
At least one-third of all the islands operate semi-official municipal tourist information centres from June until September. These are prominently sited near the centre of the main harbour town and often located in picturesque buildings, ie a windmill on Páros, a clocktower on Sými, an Art Deco pile on Pátmos. They serve the usual function of all tourist information centres, and some can even help with accommodation.

These information centres are not to be confused with the numerous ticket and tourist agencies at every port and promenade. The latter are run by private individuals, usually to promote excursions and activities of their own. Although they may be helpful and provide details when asked, information from tourist agencies is not comprehensive. Occasionally, this will be the only

Tour Guides

A tour of the island Kálymnos is fondly remembered by one traveller as the highlight of her trip to Greece. The guide, an ebullient former seaman, arrived at her hotel in a battered '68 Chevy, and kept up a steady stream of repartee and island facts in a Greek/Australian accent.

A tour guide is a good idea for anyone who wants to study an island in detail, who has no transport, or who enjoys the idea of spending several hours in close

office on an island where anyone speaks English.

Most islands also devote a special section of the police force to deal solely with visitors and their requirements. Tourist Police can also help with accommodation. For a list of conventional police telephone numbers on the islands, see *Security & Crime*, page 313.

The larger islands have nationally coordinated GNTO tourist information centres. Although opening times vary with the island and the season, a weekday visit in the morning between 9am and 1pm is sure to find the following open:
● **Corfu**: Rizospáston Vouleftón, Kérkyra, tel: (0661) 37 520/37 640.
● **Kefalloniá**: Customs Dock, Argostóli, tel: (0671) 22 248.
● **Sýros**: 10 Dhodhekaníssou, Ermoúpoli, tel: (0281) 86 725/ 82 375.
● **Kós**: Information Office, Vassiléos Gheorghíou 3, tel: (0242) 28 724/24 460.
● **Rhodes**: Arhiepiskópou Makaríou & Papágou streets, Rhodes Town, tel: (0241) 23 655/23 255; City of Rhodes Information Booth, tel: (0241) 35 945; Líndhos Information Office, tel: (0244) 31 428.
● **Sámos**: 4, 25-Martíou, Vathý, tel: (0273) 28 582.
● **Haniá**: 40 Kriári Street, tel: (0821) 92 943/92 624.
● **Iráklion**: 1 Xanthoudídhou Street, tel: (081) 228 203/228 225.

proximity with a local. Whether all the "facts" are actually true remains anyone's guess, but an entertaining companion can be worth the price. Guides generally hire themselves out by the half day, full day or even week; ask the tourist police or ask around at various ticket agencies. There are no set fees and few regulations governing the tour guide business, so negotiate everything in advance, including petrol and lunch.

Réthymnon: S. Venizélou, beachfront, tel: (0831) 29 148.
Ághios Nikólaos: Marina waterfront, tel: (0841) 82 384.

Embassies

All embassies in Athens are open from Monday to Friday, usually from 8am until 2pm.
● **Australia**: 37 D. Soutsou Street, tel: 644 7303.
● **Canada**: 4 I. Genadiou Street, tel: 723 9511-9.
● **Ireland**: 7 Vas. Constantinou SE, tel: 723 2771.
● **New Zealand**: 24 Xenias Street, tel: 771 0112.
● **United Kingdom**: 1 Ploutarchou Street, tel: 723 6211.
● **United States**: 91 Vas. Sofias Avenue, tel: 721 2951.

Postal Services

Signs denoting post offices are usually bright yellow, as are post boxes (though red ones are for express mail). Post boxes are often tiny, wall-mounted affairs which look as if they are rarely opened and can be hard to find; often they are on the outside walls of tavernas or shops obscured by flowers. Island post offices can be large and efficient (on Rhodes, there are separate mail slots to separate European destinations), or cramped and chaotic. If on a remote island, mail your postcards on the return journey on a larger island; they will arrive home quicker. Opening hours of post offices vary, but can most often be visited Mon–Fri 7.30am–2pm. The post office in Sýntagma Square, Athens, is open usually from Mon–Sat 7am–8.30pm; and on Sun 9am–1pm.

Stamps can be bought at post offices and most kiosks (*períptera*), although a commission of 10–15 percent is added by the kiosk. If sending the attractive, large-format postcards, additional, letter-rate postage may be required, so it's best to have them weighed first. If you want to send a parcel from Greece, remember not to wrap it until a post office clerk has inspected it, unless it's going to another EU or EFTA country, in which case you can present it sealed. Some post offices stock various sizes of cardboard boxes for sale in which you can pack your material, as well as twine, but bring your own tape and scissors. Letters can be sent Post Restante to any post office. Take your passport when you go to pick up mail.

Telecommunications

The easiest way to make telephone calls is to purchase a telephone card from a kiosk and use a phone booth. Cards come in three sizes: 100 units, 500 units and 1,000 units, with the largest ones representing the best value. Otherwise, you may find a telephone at a kiosk, for which you will pay around 25 or 30dr for a local call, depending on whether the phone is digital (*psifiakó*) or not.

You can also make long-distance calls from any one of the many kiosks which have metered phones. However, a call from a kiosk will cost considerably more than from a cardphone, or from the new-style coin-op counter phones which take 10, 20 and 50dr pieces, often found in hotel lobbies and restaurants. Calls from hotel rooms typically have a 100 percent surcharge on top of the standard OTE rates, though this can be worth it for the quiet and privacy.

Post offices also offer fax transmission services; a growing number of cybercafés are also springing up in the larger towns.

With the proliferation of card-phones and mobile phones, OTE branch offices have largely withdrawn their attended phone booths where you paid upon completion of a call. In the very largest cities, the central OTE may be open 7.30am–10pm or 11pm, occasionally around the clock, to sell cards for its inside booths; elsewhere you'll be lucky to find OTE open past 7pm, and occasionally they close as early as 3pm.

Dialling Codes

The dialling code from Greece to the UK is 0044. From Greece to the US or Canada it is 001. From the UK to Greece the code is 0030; for Athens, 00301.

Media

PRINT

Kiosks on the major islands receive most British newspapers the day after publication, up to two days later at weekends. The *International Herald Tribune* can usually be bought on the day of publication. Rhodes, Crete, Corfu and Kós produce local "What's On" guides (several languages for each publication) which can be found in kiosks or tourist information centres.

English-language newspapers can be purchased around Sýntagma Square in Athens from kiosks; again, the British press and a smattering of American papers are well represented.

Local quality sources of news in English are limited since the demise of several weekly and monthly magazines. The daily (except Monday), four-colour *Athens News* is interesting and informative, with both international and local news, particularly good for the Balkans, with complete TV and cinema progammes as well. *Odyssey* is a glossy, bi-monthly

magazine created by and for the wealthy Greek diaspora, somewhat more interesting than the usual airline in-flight mag.

RADIO & TV STATIONS

ER 1 and ER 2 are the two Greek State radio channels. ER 1 is divided into three different "programmes". First (728 KHz) and Second (1385 KHz) both have a lot of Greek popular music and news, some foreign pop and occasional jazz and blues. Third Programme (665 KHz) plays a lot of classical music. ER 2 (98 KHz) is much like the first two programmes. News can be heard in English, French, German and Arabic on the First Programme at 7.40am every day of the week; in English twice a day on ER 2 at 2pm and 9pm. The BBC World Service offers news on the hour plus other interesting programmes and features.

Additionally, a plethora of private stations broadcast locally from just about every island or provincial town, no matter how tiny.

There are two state-owned and operated television channels (ET1 and ET2) and at least six private television channels (Antenna, New, Mega, Seven-X, Skaï, Star). Often they transmit movies and programmes which, conveniently for the English-speaking viewer, are not dubbed, but rather carry Greek subtitles. Most fancier hotels now broadcast satellite TV.

BOOKSHOPS

Most popular islands have at least one bookshop located near the harbour with books in English. Don't expect grand literature, however; the stock-in-trade tends to be dire thrillers, international bestsellers, and bodice-rippers. Many island kiosks (as in Athens) sell second-hand paperbacks throughout the summer, probably rescued from beaches and hotels. These can be found in a heap on the pavement and are usually even more down-market in quality than the bookshop books, though you may often be surprised.

Athens has numerous bookshops

which sell quality books in English. Distributors often import from the United States, so you may find some books which are unavailable in Britain.

Pharmacies

In Greece there are certain pharmacies that are open outside normal shop hours and work on a rotating basis. If you need a pharmacy after hours or on weekends, you can find out which ones are open either by looking at the card posted in any pharmacy's window (which gives details on late-night pharmacies), or by consulting a local newspaper.

In Athens, the doctor's roster can be obtained by dialling 105; the 24-hour pharmacy roster can be obtained by dialling 107. In the largest resorts – eg Rhodes or Crete – there will be at least one pharmacy open 24 hours.

Hospitals

In case of a medical emergency, summon an ambulance by dialling 166. If for some reason this fails, call the local Tourist Police. They should speak English and will be able to tell you which hospitals have emergency facilities.

To find your way around the Greek health system, particularly in emergencies, try to find a competent speaker of both Greek and English who can inform you of what is going on.

If this isn't possible and you feel you need help, call your embassy. US citizens can call the "emergency" telephone number 721 2951 in Athens

Security and Crime

Crime is rare on the islands, and the petty theft which does occur might well be carried out by other tourists, rather than locals. If you have left something in an Athens taxi or bus, call 523 0111. Should trouble arise, each island has a

Emergencies

If you need emergency assistance, dial the following:
● **Ambulance:** 166
● **Police:** 100
● **Tourist police:** 171 (Athens)
● **ELPA** (the Greek automobile association): 104

police number,listed below, which can be rung in emergencies. Special officers known as "tourist police", whose duties are concerned solely with visitors, are also assigned to some islands and can even help with accommodation, and they usually speak English

The Ionian Islands
Corfu, tel: (0661) 39 503/30 265
Paxí, tel: (0662) 31 222
Lefkáda, tel: (0645) 92 696
Kefalloniá, tel: (0671) 22 200
Zákynthos, tel: (0695) 22 550

The Saronic Gulf Islands
Aegina, tel: (0297) 23 333
Hydra, tel: (0298) 52 205
Póros, tel: (0298) 22 256
Salamína, tel: (01) 465 1100
Spétses, tel: (0298) 73 100

The Cyclades
Amorgós, tel: (0285) 71 210
Anáfi, tel: (0286) 61 216
Andíparos, tel: (0284) 61 202
Ándhros, tel: (0282) 22 300
Folégandros, tel: (0286) 41 249
Íos, tel: (0286) 91 222
Kéa, tel: (0287) 51 205
Kímolos, tel: (0287) 51 205
Kíthnos, tel: (0281) 31 201
Mýkonos, tel: (0289) 23 990
Mílos, tel: (0287) 21 378
Náxos, tel: (0285) 22 100
Páros, tel: (0284) 23 333
Santoríni, tel: (0286) 22 649
Sérifos, tel: (0281) 51 300
Sífnos, tel: (0284) 31 210
Síkinos, tel: (0286) 51 222
Sýros, tel: (0281) 22 620
Tínos, tel: (0283) 22 255

The Sporades
Alónissos, tel: (0424) 65 205
Skiáthos, tel: (0427) 21 111
Skópelos, tel: (0424) 22 235
Skýros, tel: (0222) 91 274

The NE Aegean Islands
Híos, tel: (0271) 23 211
Ikaría, tel: (0275) 22 222
Lésvos, tel: (0251) 22 776
Límnos, tel: (0254) 22 200
Psará, tel: (0272) 61 222
Sámos, tel: (0273) 27 980
Samothráki, tel: (0551) 41 203
Thássos, tel: (0593) 22 500

The Dodecanese
Astypálea, tel: (0242) 61 207
Hálki, tel: (0246) 71 213
Kálymnos, tel: (0243) 22 100
Kárpathos, tel: (0245) 22 218
Kássos, tel: (0245) 41 222
Kastellórizo, tel: (0241) 26 068
Kós, tel: (0242) 22 222
Léros, tel: (0247) 22 221
Níssyros, tel: (0242) 31 201
Pátmos, tel: (0247) 31 303
Rhodes, tel: (0241) 27 423
Sými, tel: (0241) 71 238
Tílos, tel: (0241) 53 222

Crete
Ághios Nikólaos, tel: (0841) 26 900
Haniá, tel: (0821) 73 333
Iráklion, tel: (081) 283190
Réthymnon, tel: (0831) 28 156
Sitía, tel: (0843) 22 266 (ordinary police, not tourist police)

Athens/Piraeus
Tourist Police, tel: 171 (24 hours)
4 Leoharous Street, tel: 323 0263
58 Sokratous Street, tel: 522 6067
37 Iroon Politehniou Street, tel: 412 0325
East Air Terminal, tel: 969 9523
West Air Terminal, tel: 981 4093

Electricity

The standard electric current throughout Greece is 220 AC. This means that non-switchable appliances (most shavers and hair dryers) from North America require transformers, which are difficult to get in Greece. Greek outlets and plugs are the standard round, two-pin European continental type, different from both UK and North American types; plug adaptors for American appliances are easy to find, three-to-two-pin adaptors for UK appliances much less so, and best purchased before departure.

Business Hours

The schedule for business and shop hours is a complicated affair, varying according to the type of business and the day of the week. The main thing to remember is this: if you're after something important, go shopping for it between 10am and 1pm, Monday to Friday, the only hours when everything is almost guaranteed to be open. Many shops take a long lunch break, then most will open again in the late afternoon, but you can never be sure... Since 1994, Athens has experimented with "straight" hours during the winter to bring the country more in line with the EU, but it appears to be discretionary rather than obligatory, with some stores observing it, others adhering to traditional schedules. Whether this will catch on and spread to the islands is anyone's guess.

WINTER OPENING HOURS – ATHENS

Non-food shops: Open Mon–Wed 9am–5pm; Tues, Thur–Fri 10am–7pm; Sat 8.30am–3.30pm. **Food shops**: Mon 9am–2.30pm; Tues–Fri 9am–6.30pm; Sat 9am–3.30pm.

SUMMER OPENING HOURS – ATHENS

Most businesses: Mon, Wed, Sat 8am–2.30pm; Tues, Thur, Fri 9am–1.30pm, then reopen 5–8.30pm.

The shops in Athens' Pláka district remain open until 10pm or longer to take advantage of anyone who wants to browse. Tourist shops (selling clothes, sandals, suntan oil) and kiosks will almost always be open until midnight on popular islands like Corfu, Rhodes, Páros, Mýkonos and Kós.

Butchers and fishmongers are not allowed to open on summer evenings (though a few wink at the law), and pharmacies (except for those on rota duty, see page 313) never open Saturday mornings.

Rush Hours

One reason for turning to "straight" opening hours is to combat Athens' horrendous rush hours. Traffic jams and pollution have reached such high levels in Athens that a law was introduced: on even days of the month only cars with even-numbered licence plates are allowed into the city centre; on odd days, only those cars with odd-numbered licence plates. Taxis are also subject to this law – an "M" on top means "odd-numbered"; a "Z" means even – but foreign-registered vehicles are exempt.

BANKING

All banks are open to the public from Mon–Thur 8am–2pm; Fri 8am–1.30pm. In heavily touristed areas, like central Athens and the popular islands, however, you may find at least one bank open on some summer evenings and/or weekends for currency exchange. This will always be in or around the main harbour area. On the smallest, rarely visited islands, expect only minimum (or no) banking facilities so travel with emergency cash.

Around Sýntagma Square in Athens, at the time of going to press, these banks offered extended hours: **General Bank of Greece**, 1 Ermoú Street, tel: 324 6451, and the **National Bank of Greece**, 2 Karaghéorghi Servías Street, tel: 323 6481.

There are several banks in the East and the West Air Terminals in Athens, all with extended opening hours. There are also cash dispensers which accept Visa, Mastercard, Plus and Cirrus.

● **East Air Terminal**
Agricultural Bank of Greece, tel: 962 2791. Open daily 24 hours.
Commercial Bank of Greece, tel: 961 3611. Open daily 8am–8pm.
General Bank of Greece, tel: 961 3700. Open daily 7am–9.30pm.
National Bank of Greece, tel: 961 2728. Open daily 7am–11pm.
● **West Air Terminal**
Agricultural Bank of Greece, tel: 984 1282. Open daily 8am–8.30pm.
Commercial Bank of Greece, tel: 981 1093. Open daily 8am–7pm.
Ionian Bank of Greece, tel: 982 1031. Open Mon–Fri 8am–2pm.
National Bank of Greece, tel: 982 4699. Open daily 7am–11pm.

In the busier resorts and around Sýntagma Square in Athens you will find exchange booths, which will change notes for you. Check commission rates, and for smaller amounts of cash, look for booths charging a percentage commission rather than a flat rate. Some travel agents may also change notes or cash Eurocheques and travellers' cheques.

Public Holidays

● 1 January	New Year's Day/ *Ághios Vassílios*	
● 6 January	Epiphany/ *Theofánia*	
● February/ March (48 days before Easter)	"Clean" (Shrove) Monday	
● 25 March	Feast of the Annunciation/ *Evangelísmos & Independence Day*	
● variable	Good Friday	
● variable	Greek Orthodox Easter	
● 50 days after Easter	Pentecost Monday/*Aghíou Pnévmatos*	
● 1 May	Labour Day	
● 15 August	Assumption of the Holy Virgin	
● 28 October	*Ohi* Day (anniversary of defiance of Mussolini)	
● 25 December	Christmas Day	
● 26 December	*Sýnaxis tis Theotókou* (Gathering of the Virgin)	

Siesta

Siesta is strictly observed on many islands, when, between the hours of 3pm and 6pm, the driving of motorbikes and scooters through residential neighbourhoods is often prohibited. This provides a wonderful respite in even the noisiest of tourist towns, and is the ideal time to take a nap or extend a leisurely lunch into the afternoon. Most shops will close, perhaps to reopen again in the evening.

Although the sun is fierce during these hours, anyone with a strong constitution and protective clothing will be rewarded if they choose this time to visit otherwise-busy archeological sites (a few of which stay open after 3pm): crowds will have diminished considerably.

Nude Bathing

Nude bathing needs discretion. It is legal on very few Greek beaches, though socially acceptable on many. The main rule-of-thumb is this: if it is a secluded beach and/or a beach that has become a commonly accepted locale for nude bathing, you probably won't be bothered by, nor offend, anyone. Avoid stripping off on beaches near towns or principal harbours.

If the island you are visiting has only recently joined the mainstream ferry route, also strip with discretion. Shortly after Íos, now one of the most hedonistic islands, joined the Mýkonos/Náxos boat route, two young visitors were thrown into jail for a week, then taken to a Sýros court in handcuffs, merely for removing their bathing trunks in public – so be warned.

Getting Around

From The Airport

TO ATHENS

Between central Athens and the three airport terminals at Hellenikon there are various connecting services.

● **By taxi:** A taxi ride from the West Terminal to Athens (Sýntagma/Omónia) should cost approximately 2,100dr and will take 25–40 minutes depending on traffic. From the East Airport, it should cost slightly more and will take slightly longer. There's a fee of 50dr per bag as well, plus supplements for leaving the airport, and bonuses at Christmas or Easter week.

● **By bus:** The bus service is much cheaper and works well if you're not in a rush. Take bus 091 leaving approximately every 20 minutes (200dr), or every hour from midnight–5am (400dr) for Sýntagma and Omónia squares.

TO PIRAEUS

● **By taxi:** From the East and West Terminals to Piraeus the taxi fare costs about 2,000dr. From the centre of Athens to Piraeus, expect to pay around the same amount.

● **By bus:** Between Piraeus and the East-West Terminals, bus number 019 runs about hourly from 5am–10.20pm to Aktí Tzelépi and then on to the main harbour in Piraeus for 200dr. Green bus number 40 runs to Piraeus from a stop on Filellínou, but the route is circuitous and slow – count on nearly an hour at peak traffic times.

● **By metro:** It is easiest to get from Athens to Piraeus in about 25 minutes by catching one of the clean and safe metro trains. The stations nearest the centre of Athens are Viktória, Omónia, Monastiráki, and Thissío. The fare is cheap (100dr) and the metro is open from 5.15am until around midnight.

Domestic Flights

Travelling on one of the domestic planes operated by Olympic Airways to an island is an alternative to the ferry. The air fare, by European standards, is reasonable and the time saved is huge: it can take up to 6 hours to sail from Piraeus to Mýkonos, but only 50 minutes to fly. The flights are fun – the planes are too tiny (sometimes only 16 seats) to treat the journey as anything but a bus ride in the sky. Carry your own luggage aboard (maximum 5–10 kg, otherwise you'll have to check it), store it where possible, then grab a window seat for a magnificent view of low-lying hills, sparkling seas, and evocative islets crowned by chapels.

Upon arrival, a taxi will transfer you to the principal harbour town; most airport buses (Kós and Límnos are exceptions) have been withdrawn.

There are drawbacks to inland air travel, however. Demand can be greater than the number of seats, and having a ticket doesn't guard against being unceremoniously bumped when you arrive at the West Terminal. (During the summer, Athenians with island homes "block book" seats, often more than 2 months ahead. Tourists rate as a low priority when it comes to check-in.) The domestic terminal itself is chaotic and confusing; check-in desks seem to appear or disappear at whim, and for once it's a good idea to treat minimum prior check-in times (45 minutes) with respect. Less frequented islands can, at the height of the season, be difficult to reach as planes are pulled from their routes to make up a shortfall elsewhere.

Having said that, if you approach domestic air travel as a treat rather than as a necessity and actually do achieve lift-off, the experience is worthwhile. Early morning flights have the most advantages. Not only do you gain extra time to book on the next flight if you get bumped, but watching the sun rise over the Aegean, or arriving on Mýkonos in time to watch the revellers go to bed and the old ladies sweep the streets clean, is an island adventure on its own.

Pick up a current timetable and reserve seats at any **Olympic Airways** office. The Athens headquarters is at 96 Syngrou Avenue, tel: 929 2111. The most central office is at 15 Filellínon Street, Sýntagma Square, tel: 926 7444. Major credit cards accepted.

Air Greece is a smaller airline that is gaining popularity among Greeks for internal flights. They fly from Athens to Thessaloníki, Rhodes, Iráklion and Hánia in Crete, and also Iráklion–Thessaloníki. The Air Greece head office is at Daidalou 36, Iráklion, Crete, tel: (081) 330 533/330 074. There is also an Athens office, tel: 325 5011/324 4457/960 0646.

Water Transport

FERRIES

In 1997 the GNTO finally had a stab at producing a comprehensive, impartial advance ferry timetable, a fat booklet entitled *Greek Travel Routes*. Whether they will be able to continue with this is uncertain, but it was a long overdue effort; the only alternative is the privately published *Greek Travel Pages*,

pricey at over 6,000dr and unreliable because if you don't pay to advertise with them, they may or may not list you in their editorial content. It can be purchased in Athens at major bookstores, or from the GTP headquarters at the corner of Psylla and Filellínon streets.

The mimeograped/cyclostyled ferry schedules, published weekly and free, are given out at tourist information points in Athens and on the islands. Most offices hang a schedule in a conspicuous place, so even though the desk itself might be closed the information is still obtainable.

Once there was no need to buy a seat in advance unless you wanted a berth or first-class seat. You could imply arrive at Piraeus a couple of hours before departure and cruise the various ticket agencies.

But in response to high-season scandals in 1996 – in which captains were fined for loading boats to double their safe passenger capacity – advance purchase of computerised tickets is now, in theory, required for all classes of ferry travel. In practice, in the past, top-drawer lines like Minoan or ANEK instituted this system of their own accord, and you always had to book passage in advance for cars, cabins or travel at peak times. Now, however, it appears that the days of strolling up to the gangplank and buying from a chap at a booth under a sunshade will soon be well and truly over, if they aren't already.

Agencies handle different boats

which are often sailing to the same destinations at the same times. Many agents will claim "their" boat is the quickest, most powerful, sometimes the only way to get to an island that day. It pays to shop around – you may find an "express" sailing to your destination as opposed to a "milk run" which stops at four islands en route. Cynical travellers will add at least 1 hour to the time any Greek claims it takes to sail to a specific destination.

Although the situation is improving, catching a ferry on one island to sail to a distant island can be a frustrating experience. Ferries may arrive 2, 3, even 5 hours late, but to leave the port is to risk missing the boat entirely. Just occasionally, the boat can arrive early, and there is no guarantee it will wait until the scheduled departure time to leave. The only way to guarantee accurate, up-to-the-minute information on the erratic ways of ferries is to contact the Port Authority (Limenarhío), which can (and does) monitor the movements of individual boats. Port Authority offices are usually located on the far end of the waterfront of each island's principal harbour, away from the cafés and boutiques. It would help to ask a Greek-speaking person to do the enquiring, as English is not widespread.

Port Authority telephone numbers are as follows:

The Ionian Islands
Corfu, tel: (0661) 39 918
Itháki, tel: (0674) 32 909
Kefalloniá, tel: (0671) 22 224
Lefkádha, tel: (0645) 22 322
Paxí, tel: (0662) 31 259
Zákynthos, tel: (0695) 22 417

The Saronic Gulf Islands
Aegina, tel: (0297) 22 328
Hydra, tel: (0298) 52 279
Póros, tel: (0298) 22 274
Salamína, tel: (01) 465 3252
Spétses, tel: (0298) 72 245

The Cyclades
Ándhros, tel: (0282) 22 250
Íos, tel: (0286) 91 264

Ferry Survival Tips

● Once aboard, position yourself on the top deck for sun-bathing after the boat has left the harbour and turned around; otherwise, you may find yourself in the shade.
● Food bought beforehand is a better idea than eating overpriced grease in one of the snack bars, although overnight sailings always offer full-menu lunch and supper in a self-service *trapezaría* or (for

the lucky few) waiter service in an amiably old-fashioned first-class salon. Food tends to be indifferent or worse, with the major lines to Crete and the Dodecanese being honourable exceptions.
● Bring plenty to read.
● Prepare for a mild dose of sea-sickness on any journey longer than 3 or 4 hours; the Aegean can be rough.

Kéa, tel: (0287) 31 344
Kýthnos, tel: (0281) 31 290
Mílos, tel: (0287) 41 607
Mýkonos, tel: (0289) 22 218
Náxos, tel: (0285) 22 300
Páros, tel: (0284) 21 240
Santoríni, tel: (0286) 22 239
Sérifos, tel: (0281) 51 470
Sífnos, tel: (0284) 31 617
Sýros, tel: (0281) 22 690
Tínos, tel: (0283) 22 348

The Sporades
Alónissos, tel: (0424) 65 595
Skiáthos, tel: (0427) 22 017
Skópelos, tel: (0424) 22 180
Skýros, tel: (0222) 91 475

The NE Aegean Islands
Foúrni, tel: (0275) 51 207
Híos, tel: (0271) 23 097
Ikaría (Ághios Kírykos), tel: (0275) 22 207
Ikaría (Évdhilos), tel: (0275) 31 007
Lésvos (Mytilíni), tel: (0251) 28 647
Lésvos (Sígri), tel: (0253) 54 433
Límnos, tel: (0254) 22 225
Psará, tel: (0272) 61252
Sámos (Vathý), tel: (0273) 27 318
Sámos (Karlóvassi), tel: (0273) 32 343
Sámos (Pythagório), tel: (0273) 61 225
Samothráki, tel: (0551) 41 305
Thássos, tel: (0593) 22 106

The Dodecanese Islands
Astypálea, tel: (0242) 61 208
Hálki, tel: (0241) 45 220
Kálymnos, tel: (0243) 29 304
Kárpathos (Pigádhia), tel: (0245) 22 227
Kássos, tel: (0245) 41 288
Kastellórizo, tel: (0241) 49 270
Kós, tel: (0242) 28 507
Léros, tel: (0247) 22 224
Níssyros, tel: (0242) 31 222
Pátmos, tel: (0247) 31 231
Rhodes, tel: (0241) 27 690
Sými, tel: (0241) 71 205
Tílos, tel: (0241) 44 350

Crete
Ághios Nikólaos, tel: (0840) 22 312
Haniá, tel: (0821) 98 888
Iráklion, tel: (081) 244 956
Kastélli, tel: (0822) 22 024
Réthymnon, tel: (0831) 22 276
Sitía, tel: (0843) 22 310

Cruises

Apparently one in six of all visitors to Greece embarks on an Aegean cruise. Cruises can range from 1-day trips to the Saronic Gulf islands, to 21-day packages on a "floating hotel" departing from Piraeus taking in Gibraltar and Morocco. Many people elect for the 7-day excursion, which offers an opportunity to see a couple of islands in the Cyclades, a few Dodecanese islands, and a stop-over in Turkey for good measure. Accommodation, prices and standards vary widely and it might be an idea to shop around for a good price.

Ticket agencies in Athens are the places to visit, with cruise opportunities prominently displayed in windows. (Although, if you have ever been at Mýkonos harbour when the ships arrive and watched the frantic

● Piraeus Port Authority, tel: 451 1311 or 452 7107 (Zéa Marina).
● For more information on island hopping by ferry, see *Island hopping* on page 75, and *Coping with Piraeus* on page 115.

HYDROFOILS
Hydrofoils ("Flying Dolphins") are twice as quick and twice as expensive as ferries. A service between Piraeus and the Saronic Gulf islands continues throughout the year. Seasonally (from around May to October), hydrofoils connect islands in the Sporades with Vólos and Thessaloníki; Kavála with Thássos; from a variable Attic port to certain of the Cyclades; and all the smaller Dodecanese between Sámos and Rhodes, inclusive.

There are also limited, high-summer services linking Alexandhroúpoli with Samothráki and sometimes Límnos or Thássos.

Modern hydrofoils show videos and have bar facilities. However, as hydrofoils need a calm sea to travel, they are highly prone to cancellation because of bad weather.

preparations of shop managers adjusting their prices upwards, it may change your mind about a cruise entirely.)

The most comprehensive company is Royal Olympic Cruises, formed by the merger of Epirotiki and Sun Lines. It is accustomed to dealing with foreigners, and offers four-day, seven-day and 14-day cruises. Details can be found from any travel agent or by contacting Royal Olympic's headquarters at Aktí Miaoúli 18538, Piraeus, tel: 429 1000.

London-based **Swan Hellenic Cruises** offer all-inclusive holidays on large luxury liners, with guest speakers instructing passengers on anything from archeology to marine biology. Swan Hellenic are at 77 New Oxford Street, London WC1A 1PP, tel: 0171 800 2200.

"EXCURSION" BOATS
If a tourist island boasts a major attraction, it has scores of package trips to view it/visit it/swim off it. Ticket agencies promote excursions aggressively, so you can pick and choose at your leisure. Unless you enjoy the company of gregarious strangers, the site is of premier importance, or if time is limited, it's often nicer to make your own way to attractions as local transport is usually available, too.

Lots of "excursion" boats offering daytrips to neighbouring islands leave and depart at more convenient times than regular ferries. The other difference? Excursion boats are twice as expensive, since they are effectively travel-agent charter craft.

Public Transport

BUSES
Island buses can be converted school buses or modern coaches, or even pick-up trucks with seats installed in the payload space to transport tourists. Some drivers

ricochet through mountain roads at death-defying speeds; accidents, however, appear to be rare. Just stow your luggage carefully to be on the safe side.

Almost without exception, a bus of some description will meet arriving ferries (even if a boat is delayed) to transport passengers up the hill to the island's *hóra*, or capital. Bus stops are usually in main squares or by the waterfront in harbours and vehicles may or may not run to schedule. A conductor dispenses tickets on the bus itself; often the fare required and the ticket will not show the same price, with the lower old price over-stamped. This isn't a con, but merely a practice – island companies use pre-printed tickets until the supply is gone, which may take several years.

TAXIS

Taxis in Greece, especially in Athens, merit a guidebook to themselves. It may well be that your taxi "experience" will figure among the most prominent memories of your holiday. Perhaps the Greek taxi experience is best divided into three stages for analytical purposes.

First: getting a taxi. It's almost impossible at certain times of the day, and probably worst before the early afternoon meal. When you hail a taxi, try to get in before stating your destination. The drivers are very picky and often won't let you in unless you're going in their direction. If you see an empty taxi, run for it, be aggressive – otherwise you'll find that some quick Athenian has beaten you to it.

Second: the ride. Make sure the taxi meter is on when you start out, and not on "2" – that's the double fare, which is only permitted from midnight to 5am, or outside designated city limits. Once inside, you may find yourself with company. Don't be alarmed. It is traditional practice for drivers to pick up two, three, even four individual riders, provided they're going roughly in the same direction. In these cases, make a note of the meter count

when you get in. In fact, because taxis are so cheap, they can end up functioning as mini-bus services. Packed in with a Greek mother with her shopping bags, a chic businessman and a university student, you may find yourself in the middle (literally) of some rather interesting conversations.

Third: paying up. If you've travelled with other passengers, make sure you aren't paying for the part of the trip that happened before you got in. You should pay the difference in meter reading between embarking and alighting, plus the 200dr minimum. Otherwise, the meter will tell you the straight price, which may be adjusted according to the tariff regulations that should be on a laminated placard clipped to the dashboard. There are extra charges for each piece of luggage in the boot, for leaving (but not entering) an airport or seaport, plus bonuses around Christmas and Easter.

Some drivers will quote you the correct price, but many others will try to rip you off, especially if it seems you're a novice. If the fare you're charged is clearly above the correct price, don't hesitate to argue your way, in whichever language, back down to a normal price.

Obviously these rules apply more to Athens than to the islands, although it's still necessary to be pretty aggressive on Crete and Rhodes. On the smaller islands, expect to share your taxi, not only with the aforementioned group of passengers, but also an animal or two.

In recent years various radio taxi services have started up in Athens and most other larger towns. They can pick you up within a short time of your call to a central booking number.

CARS

Car hire is somewhat expensive in Greece (though fuel costs the same as in the UK), and taking your car to the islands is not generally recommended. Only on Crete, Rhodes, Lésvos, Híos, Évvia, Kefalloniá and Corfu, will you benefit greatly from having a car at your disposal; otherwise it's more fun to rely on island buses and taxis. There are desks manned by the major car hire firms at island airports and in the ticket agencies on the waterfront. Shop around for the best price.

The Automobile and Touring Club of Greece (ELPA) provides foreign motorists with assistance and information. Offices in Crete can be found in Haniá at Leofouros Soudas 163, tel: (0821) 96 611/97 177, and in Iráklion at Papandhréou 46–50, tel: (081) 289440/288180. In Athens, ELPA offices are located at 2–4 Messoghíon Avenue, tel: 779 1615, and at 6 Amerikís & Panepistimíou streets, tel: 363 8632.

Driving a car in Athens is unpleasant and confusing. Greek tempers are short and road signs or adequate warning of mandatory turning lanes practically non-existent. Cars are, however, fun for daytrips out of the city.

Car Hire Companies

Major international chains such as Avis, Hertz, InterRent/Europcar and Budget all have rental desks at both the East and West air terminals. Otherwise, head for Syngroú Avenue in central Athens, where most of the smaller, less expensive international and Greek chain franchise-holders cluster.

A few tried-and-true examples:

● **Speedo Rent A Car**, 8 Syngroú Avenue, tel: 922 6102
● **Thrifty Rent A Car**, 24 Syngroú Avenue, tel: 922 1211
● **European**, 36–38 Syngroú Avenue, tel: 924 6777
● **Reliable**, 3 Syngroú Avenue, tel: 924 9000
● **Just**, 43 Syngroú Avenue, tel: 923 9104

MOTORCYCLES, BICYCLES AND SCOOTERS

On most Greek islands you will find agencies that rent small motorcycles, various types of scooters, 50cc and under, and even mountain bikes. On the smaller islands these are certainly the way to go. For a good price (weekly rates are quite reasonable), they give you the freedom to travel where you will and also to delight in the smell of a place, impossible on buses or in cars. For any bike of over 50cc displacement, helmets and a motorcycle driving licence are both theoretically required, and occasionally these rules are enforced.

Before you set off, make sure the bike of whichever sort works by taking it for a test spin down the street (be on the look-out for lethal "staircase" alleys). Brakes in particular are badly set, lights may need new fuses or bulbs, and spark-plugs get fouled – ask for a spare and the small wrench to change it. Otherwise you may get stuck with a lemon or, worse, be held responsible for its malfunctioning when you return it. Reputable agencies now often give you a phone number for breakdown pick-up service.

Above all, don't take any unnecessary chances, eg by riding two on a bike designed for one. Many a holiday in Greece has been ruined by a serious moped accident. Wear protective clothing and check that your holiday insurance covers any problems.

Where to Stay

Hotels

The Greek National Tourist Organisation (GNTO) governs the construction and classification of all hotels. The classification awarded is determined by the size of the rooms, size of public areas including lobby and restaurant (if any), decor and furnishings and services provided by the hotel.

All hotel accommodation is divided into classes: luxury class, then classes A–E. The price in each category is fixed, ie, an A-class hotel will always cost more than a B-class hotel, even with seasonal variations in price. The categories are not an indication of quality but of space and facilities available. A C-class hotel, for instance, may not have conference rooms but its accommodation may be just as comfortable as an A- or B-class hotel. Anyone who rates charm above lobby space, or yoghurt and honey above an all-inclusive breakfast, will probably be just as happy in a lower-class hotel as in one of the luxury versions; almost all accommodation from C-class upwards can be guaranteed to have a high standard of cleanliness.

GNTO offices around the world can help with accommodation. See page 309 for names and addresses of international GNTO offices. All GNTO offices offer free pamphlets on each island chain, giving information on hotels in the A–C classes.

There is normally a 10 percent surcharge for a stay that is less than 3 nights and a larger increase if you want an extra (third) bed in the room. VAT, and any municipal tax, are also not included.

ATHENS

Divani-Palace Acropolis
19–25 Parthenonos,
11742 Athens
tel: 922 2945
Luxurious hotel with swimming pool, restaurant, bar, a few blocks down from the Acropolis, often has tour groups. $$$

Grande Bretagne
Sýntagma Square,
10563 Athens
tel: 323 0251
The grand old lady of Athenian hotels, the venue for innumerable political, cultural and society events. Very expensive. The GB Corner is wonderfully comfortable for meals. $$$

Park
10 Leoforos Alexandras,
10682 Athens
tel: 883 2712
Across the street from the Pedion tou Areos park and conveniently near the National Archeological Museum. $$$

St George Lycabettus
2 Kleomenous Street,
10673 Athens
tel: 729 0711
On the slopes of Lycabettus in the comfortable neighbourhood of Kolonaki, with a fine view down over Athens towards the Acropolis. Small swimming pool on the roof. $$$

Amalia
10 Amalias Avenue,
10557 Athens
tel: 323 7301
A thoroughly comfortable place to stay on Sýntagma Square. $$$

Electra Palace
18 Nikodhímou Street,
10557 Athens
tel: 324 1401
In Pláka, with a pleasant roof bar

and swimming pool, providing a sharply angled view up to the Acropolis. $$$

Christina
15 Petemeza Street and Kalirois Avenue, 11743 Athens
tel: 921 5353
Comfortable hotel on the edge of the neighbourhood of Koukáki. $$

Pláka
7 Kapnikareas,
10556 Athens
tel: 322 2096
The bright white lobby is impressive, as is the roof garden's view towards the Acropolis. In Pláka, near the Roman agora. $$

Achilleas
21 Lekka Street,
10562 Athens
tel: 323 3197
Despite the entrance off the street, this is good value. Completely renovated in 1995. Near both Pláka and Sýntagma Square. $$

Acropolis View
10 Webster Street,
11742 Athens
tel: 921 7303
Fine, small hotel on a quiet side street near the Herodes Atticus theatre, with some rooms and a rooftop bar looking on the Acropolis. In the upper area of Koukáki. $$

Athenian Inn
22 Háritos Street,
10675 Athens
tel: 723 8097
Quiet location, three blocks from fashionable Kolonaki Square. Lawrence Durrell wrote in the guest book, "At last, the ideal Athens hotel, good and modest in scale but perfect in service and goodwill." This is still the case. $$

Attalos
29 Athinás Street
10554 Athens
tel: 321 2801
Two blocks from Monasteraki Square, friendly and attentive staff, good value. Athinas Street is busy during the day, but quiet at night. Rooms are plain but clean. The roof garden has fine views of the city and the Acropolis. Free luggage storage. $$

Austria
7 Mousson,
11742 Athens
tel: 923 5151
Owned by an Austrian-Greek family, this hotel is near the Acropolis on a quiet street, with front rooms overlooking a park. The view of the Acropolis is marvellous. In the upper area of Koukáki. $$

Museum
16 Bouboulina and Tositsa,
10682 Athens
tel: 360 5611
Conveniently located, one block from the National Archaelogical Museum. $$

Nefeli
16 Yperidhou Street,
10558 Athens
tel: 322 8044
Small, clean, well-run hotel in a quiet area of Pláka. $$

Pella Inn
Ermou and 1 Kareskaki,
10554 Athens
tel: 322 8044
Family-run hotel between Monasteraki Square and the Thission tram station. By no means posh, but clean and friendly. The upper floors facing Ermou Street have a wonderful view of the ancient Greek agora and the Acropolis. $

Tempi
29 Aiolou, 10551 Athens
tel: 321 2229
Three blocks north of Monasteraki Square. Because it is a pedestrian street, Aiolou is quiet at night. The rooms are clean and the staff friendly. Free luggage storage, laundry room. $

Hostel Aphrodite
12 Einardhou Street
10440 Athens
tel: 881 0589
e-mail: hostel-aphrodite @ath.forthnet.gr.
Clean, unpretentious, friendly this small hotel is a good deal. Slightly off the beaten track but conveniently near the tram station in Victoria Square. Pleasant basement bar and an excellent deal on the inter-island boat pass. Free luggage storage. $

Marble House
35 A. Zinni
11741 Athens
tel: 923 4058
Inexpensive, clean, friendly atmosphere. Two blocks from Syngroú Avenue and the Olympic Airlines office. Not air conditioned, but with powerful ceiling fans. Koukáki area. $

Student Inn
16 Kydhathinéon,
10588 Athens
A good deal for inexpensive accommodation in Pláka. $

THE IONIAN ISLANDS
Corfu

There are more than 200 hotels on Corfu, from the luxurious Corfu Palace down. Choose according to where you want to be and what is available. In Corfu Town, avoid hotels in Kanóni , because they are in the airport flight path. Visit the GNTO at the corner of Rizospastón Vouleftón and Iakóvou Políla, tel: (0661) 37 520/37 639/40, for information about hotels and less formal accommodation.

Cavalieri Hotel
Corfu Town
tel: (0661) 39 336
Pleasant, well run hotel, with attractive roof garden. $$$

Corfu Palace Hotel
Corfu Town
tel: (0661) 39 485
Plush, expensive. $$$

Louis Grand Hotel
Glyfada
tel: (0661) 94 140
Large hotel on the beach with all the trimmings. $$$

Arkadion
Corfu Town
tel: (0661) 37 670
Centrally located, right by the Listón, facing the esplanade. No frills. $$

Astron
Corfu Town
tel: (0661) 39 505
Medium-sized hotel in the old harbour, near the law courts, overlooking the sea. TV. $$

Bella Venezia
Corfu Town
tel: (0661) 46 500
Near Platía Dimarhíou, behind the

Cavaliéri Hotel. Rooms have TV, air conditioning, small refrigerator. $$

Ermónes Beach Hotel
Ermónes
tel: (0661) 94 241
This large hotel/bungalows on a hillside, provides a cable car to take guests down to the beach. $$

Glyfada Beach Hotel
Glyfada
tel: (0661) 94 258
Medium-sized hotel on the beach, no frills. $$

Paxí

Paxos Beach
Gáïos
tel: (0662) 32 211
Attractive bungalows, above beach, 2 km (1¼ miles) from town. $$

Lefkádha

Ammoudia
Nydhrí
tel: (0645) 92 771
Pleasant, small hotel on the edge of Nydhrí, 45 metres (50 yds) from the sea. Bar, snack bar, pool. $$

Price Categories

Our price categories are based on the cost of a double room for one night in the high season:

$$$ Expensive: above 24,000dr
$$ Moderate: 12–24,000dr
$ Inexpensive: under 12,000dr

Apollon
Vasilikí
tel: (0645) 31 122
Small, family-run hotel in the village, 270 metres (300 yds) from the harbour. Rooms have small refrigerators. $$

Léfkas Hotel
Lefkádha Town
tel: (0645) 23 916
The larger and more pretentious of the two hotels facing the sea as you enter town, with large arches on the facade. Rooms have TV and air conditioning. Restaurant, bar. $$

Nirikos Hotel
Lefkádha Town
tel: (0645) 24 132
Next to the Léfkas, it's smaller and

less expensive. Rooms have TV and ceiling fans. Restaurant, bar. $$

Vasilikí Bay
Vasilikí
tel: (0645) 31 077
Pretty similar to Apollon. In the village 55 metres (60 yds) from the harbour. $$

Itháki

Tourist agencies, Della, tel: (0674) 32 104, and Polyctor, tel: (0674) 33 130, can arrange rooms on Itháki.

Captain's Apartments
Kióni
tel: (0674) 31 481
Family-run rented apartments, each with kitchen and TV. Overlooking over the sea. $$$

Hotel Kióni
Kióni
tel: (0674) 31 362
New, simple, good. $$

Mentor
Vathý
tel: (0674) 32 433
Basic, clean, sometimes noisy. $$

Nostos Hotel
Fríkes
tel: (0674) 31 644
Attractive, family-run hotel, 180 metres (200 yds) from the sea. $$

Odysseas
Vathý
tel: (0674) 32 381
Smaller and less expensive than the Mentor. $$

Kefalloniá

The GNTO, tel: (0671) 22 248, in the harbour across from the police station, can help you find the full range of accommodation available on the island.

Filoxenia
Fiskárdho
tel: (0674) 41 319
A 19th-century house beautifully refurbished as a small hotel. In the village, 9 metres (10 yds) from the water. $$$

White Rocks
Platý Yialó
tel: (0671) 23 167
The best of the resort area, set in among the trees and 45 metres (50 yds) from the water. Hotel and bungalows. $$$

Lara
Lourdháta
tel: (0671) 31 157
Wonderful, quiet family-run hotel shaded by tall olive trees, 250 metres (280 yds) from the beach. Rooms have small refrigerators; some have ceiling fans. $$

Mouikis Hotel
Argostóli
tel: (0671) 23 032
In town, some 50 yds from the harbour, has wonderful view over the water. Well kept rooms, with TV and air conditioning. $$

Mouikis Village
Argostóli
tel: (0671) 41 562
Wonderful, small apartments 6 km from Argostoli, with pool, tennis, children's playground. Moderately expensive, although a good bargain for the larger apartments. $$

Panormos
Fiskárdho
tel: (0674) 41 203
Six rooms above restaurant, right on the water. $$

Zákynthos

Caravel Zante
Plános
tel: (0695) 45 261
6 km (3½ miles northwest of Zákynthos town. Beautifully set on a small cove, right by the water. $$$

Plágos Beach
Tragáki
tel: (0695) 45 997
Arguably the most beautiful hotel on the island, surrounded by gardens and on the water. Large swimming pool. $$

Hotel Diana
46 D. Roma, Zákynthos Town
tel: (0695) 28 547
In town on a quiet pedestrian sreet. Rooms have air conditioning, TV balcony with view of the sea. $$

Hotel Bitzaro
Kapodistriou & 2 Mitropoleos, Zákynthos Town
tel: (0695) 23 644
Near the town beach, ivy-covered, quiet. Rooms have TV, ceiling fans. $$

SARONIC GULF ISLANDS
Salamína
Gabriel
Eándio
tel: (01) 466 2275
Not posh but the best hotel on the island, in a pleasant village right by the water. $$

Aegina
Areti
Aegina town
tel: (0297) 23 593
Across from the ferryboat landing, no frills. Also has rooms to let. $$
Danae
Aegina town
tel: (0297) 22 424
Family-run, friendly hotel 650 metres (700 yds) from harbour on a bluff overlooking the sea. Restaurant, bar, pool. $$
Apollo
Aghia Marina
tel: (0297) 32 271
Large cement block accommodation with all the trimmings, restaurant, bar, swimming pool, tennis, right on the sea. $$
Argo
Aghia Marina
tel: (0297) 32 266
Near the Apollo and similar to it, but smaller and less expensive. $$

Póros
Epta Adelfia (Seven Brothers)
Platía Iroön, Póros town
tel: (0298) 23 412
Small family-run hotel on the main square, near the harbour. Some rooms have air conditioning. $$
Latsi
Póros town
tel: (0298) 22 392
150 metres from the harbour, just before the naval school. Restaurant, bar. $$
Pavlou
Neórion, Póros
tel: (0298) 22 734
2 km (1 mile) from town, 15 metres from the water. Refurbished in 1998. Restaurant, bar, swimming pool, 2 tennis courts. $$

Hydra
Miranda
Hydra town
tel (0298) 52 230
Renovated traditional island mansion on top of a hill in the west of the town. Rooms have air conditioning and a small veranda. Best rooms are those facing the harbour. Breakfast served in the garden. $$

Price Categories

Our price categories are based on the cost of a double room for one night in the high season:

$$$ Expensive: above 24,000dr
$$ Moderate: 12–24,000dr
$ Inexpensive: under 12,000dr

Orloff
Hydra town
tel (0298) 52 564
Renovated old island mansion now offering the most attractive accommodation on the island. Rooms have air conditioning, TV, small refridgerator. Generous buffet breakfast in the garden. $$
Angelika
Hydra town
tel (0298) 53 202
Another renovated mansion, 250 metres from the harbour, not as posh as the Orloff but very pleasant. Rooms have air conditioning and TV. Breakfast served in the courtyard. $$
Leto
Hydra town
tel (0298) 52 280
200 metres from the harbour, up the road by the clock tower. Air conditioning. $$

Spétses
Spétses Hotel
Spétses town
tel: (0298) 72 602
In Kounoupítsa, 800 metres (½ mile) from the Dápia. Rooms have air conditioning and TV. Restaurant, bar and a second bar on the hotel's pleasant private beach. $$$
Léka Palace
Spétses town
tel: (0298) 72 311
Once the Xenia, then the Kastelli, now with a new name and new management, just renovated and upgraded. Beyond Kounoupítsa, northwest from the Dápia, 5 minutes walk to the beach. Large rooms with TV, mini fridge, air conditioning. Bar and restaurant overlooking the sea. Large swimming pool, tennis courts, extensive gardens. $$
Soleil
Spétses town
tel: (0298) 72 488
Small hotel on the water near the Dápia, between the fish market and the town beach. Rooms have TV and small fridge. Scrupulously clean. $$
Villa Martha
Aghía Marína
tel: (0298) 72 147
Out of town, southeast of the Old Harbour, 250 metres from the sea, set among trees and flowers. Rooms overlook either the sea or the wooded mountain. Ceiling fans. Cafeteria/bar. $$

THE CYCLADES
Ándhros
Paradissos
Ándhros town
tel: (0282) 22 187
An elegant Neo-Classical mansion near the centre of town, 700 metres (760 yds) from the beach. Airy rooms with superb views from the balconies. $$$
Andros Holiday Hotel
Gávrio
tel: (0282) 71 209
Right on the beach just outside town. Attractive rooms, pool, tennis courts, sauna, gym. $$
Hryssí Aktí
Batsí
tel: (0282) 41 236
Deservedly popular for its location, in the centre of town, across from the beach. $$

Kéa
Ioulis
Kéa town
tel: (0288) 22 177
Delightfully quiet spot in the *kástro*, with views from the terrace. $$

Kéa Beach
Koundoóros Bay
tel: (0288) 31 230
Luxury bungalow complex built in traditional Cycladic style, with all facilities from a nightclub to watersports. 5 km (3 miles) south of Písses. $$

Tínos
Tinion
Hóra
tel: (0283) 22 261
Charming old-world hotel with tiled floors, lace curtains and a large balcony. $$

Aeolos Bay Hotel
Ághios Fókas
tel: (0283) 23 339
Smart, comfortable hotel a short walk out of town, overlooking the beach. Pool, pleasant gardens, breakfast on the terrace. $$

Kýthnos
Kythnos
Mérihas Bay
tel: (0281) 32 247
Basic but friendly hotel situated right on the waterfront. Rooms at the front have balconies overlooking the sea. $$

Sýros
Omiros
Ermoúpoli
tel: (0281) 24 910
A 150-year-old neoclassical mansion recently restored to a high standard. Rooms furnished in traditional style, with views of the lively harbour. $$$

Dolphin Bay Hotel
Galissás
tel: (0281) 42 924
The largest and most modern hotel on the island, with all facilities, large swimming pool and beautiful views over the bay. $$$

Europe Hotel
Ermoúpoli
tel: (0281) 28 771
An early 19th-century hospital converted into a pleasant hotel with large rooms round a cloister-like pebbled courtyard. $$

Mýkonos
Princess of Mýkonos
Ághios Stéfanos beach
tel: (0289) 23 806
A five-star hotel popular with stars such as Jane Fonda. 2 km (1 mile) from Hóra and just 30 metres above the beach, with all the luxury facilities. Air conditioned rooms (some with kitchenettes), satellite TV, Italian restaurant, swimming pool and gym. $$$

Cavo Tagoo
Hóra
tel: (0289) 23 692
Jet-set luxurious, set on a hillside 500 metres north of Hóra. Prize-winning Cycladic architecture, beautiful furnishings, impeccable service, friendly atmosphere and views over the Aegean. $$$

Despotiko Hotel
Hóra
tel: (0289) 22 009
A converted 18th-century mansion named after a 19th-century bishop, an ancestor of the family that runs the hotel today. Bar, swimming pool. $$$

Hotel Elena
Hóra
tel: (0289) 23 457
Located in the heart of town, yet quiet and impeccably clean, with great views of the harbour. Rooms have air conditioning and TV. Good buffet breakfast. Watch the sunset from the veranda bar. $$

Apollonia Bay Hotel
Ághios Ioánnis
tel: (0289) 27 890
Traditionally Cycladic cluster of small villa-studios located on its own bay about 3½ km (2¼ miles) from Hóra. Gracious, friendly service, incomparable views. Rooms have air conditioning, TV, hairdryers. Large swimming pool, bar. $$

Sérifos
Areti
Livádi
tel: (0281) 51 479
Family-run hotel (and cake-shop) near the ferry landing, built on a hill with superb views. Peaceful terraced garden overlooking the sea. $$

Sífnos
Platýs Yialós Hotel
Platýs Yialós
tel: (0284) 31 324
Large, Cycladic-style hotel at far end of beach. Well furnished and decorated with wood-carvings and wall paintings. Rooms have air-conditioning and fridge. $$$

Artemón Hotel
Artemón
tel: (0284) 31 303
Simple, beautiful, family hotel with rooms that overlook fields rolling towards the sea. $$

Apollonia
Apollonía
tel: (0284) 31 490
Charming small hotel (only 9 rooms) with traditional island architecture and friendly service. $

Moní Hrysopighí
Apókofto
tel: (0284) 31 255
This 17th-century monastery, situated on an islet reached by footbridge, rents out simple cells in summer. Book well in advance. $

Andíparos
Hryssí Aktí
near Kástro
tel: (0284) 61 220
Elegant hotel with good rooms right on the beach on the island's east coast. $$

Mandalena
Kástro
tel: (0284) 61 206
Clean but simple rooms on the waterfront, with good views of the harbour and across to Páros. $

Páros
Astir of Paros
Náousa
tel: (0284) 51 976
One of Greece's finest deluxe hotels, right on the beach. Spacious rooms with all the facilities, balconies and bathrooms lined with Parian marble. Large pool, three-hole (sic) golf course, horseback riding, art gallery. $$$

Golden Beach
Hrysí Aktí
tel: (0284) 41 366
Modern low-rise hotel on the beautiful east coast. Good rooms

with balconies overlooking the Golden Beach. Excellent service. Very popular with windsurfers. $$
Dina
Parikía
tel: (0284) 21 325
Small friendly hotel in the heart of the old town. Spotlessly clean rooms set around a lovely flowered courtyard. Only 8 rooms, so book early. $

Náxos
Chateau Zevgoli
Hóra
tel: (0285) 22 993
Quiet, plush and exclusive, high up in the old town. A mansion with only 10 rooms (book early). One has a four-poster bed, most have great views. $$$
Grotta
Hóra
tel: (0285) 22 215
Modern Cycladic-style hotel beautifully situated on a headland with good views over the sea and the *kástro*. $$
Anixi
Hóra
tel: (0285) 22 112
Modest, very Greek, family-run pension overlooking the sea and the Grotta quarter. Communal bathroom, garden. $

Mílos
Venus Village
Adamás
tel: (0287) 22 030
Fairly new, large hotel and bungalow complex on the beach. Efficient service, great location. $$$
Popi's Windmill
Trypití
tel: (0287) 22 286
A unique establishment: a luxuriously converted windmill with all the amenities of an elegant hotel, plus beautiful views towards Adamás port. $$$
Kapetan Tassos
Apollónia
tel: (0287) 41 287
Modern apartments in traditional blue-and-white island architecture, with good sea views. $$

Panorama
Klíma
tel: (0287) 21 623
Small seafront hotel, family-run with friendly service. The owner sometimes takes guests fishing. $

Folégandhros
Anemomylos
Hóra
tel: (0286) 41 309
A fully-equipped apartment complex built in traditional Cycladic style around a courtyard. Stunning views from the balconies overhanging the cliff edge. $$$
Fani-Venis
Hóra
tel: (0286) 41 237
Comfortable hotel in a Neo-Classical mansion with rooms overlooking the sea. $$
Kástro
Hóra
tel: (0286) 41 230
A 500-year-old traditional house that is actually part of the ancient Kástro walls. Quaint rooms have pebble mosaic floors, barrel ceilings and spectacular views down sheer cliffs to the sea. $

Síkinos
Porto Síkinos
Aloprónia
tel: (0286) 51 220
The best accommodation on the island: a complex of 18 Cycladic-style buildings right on the beach. Bar and restaurant. $$$
Kamares
Aloprónia
tel: (0286) 51 234
Traditional-style, affordable hotel with average but comfortable rooms. $$
Flora
Aloprónia
tel: (0286) 51 214
Another Cycladic-style development, this time simple chalet rooms built around courtyards on the hillside above the port. Great sea views. $

Íos
Íos Palace
Mylopótas
tel: (0286) 91 269
Modern hotel designed and

decorated in the traditional style. Near the beach, with very comfortable rooms, marble-lined bathrooms and balconies overlooking the sea. $$$
Philippou
Hóra
tel: (0286) 91 290
Small, comfotable hotel in the centre of Íos's nightlife. Great location if you plan to party all night. Otherwise, bring earplugs or choose somewhere out of town. $$
Acropolis
Mylopótas
tel: (0286) 91 303
Clean, simple rooms with balconies overlooking the beach below. $

Amórgos
Aegiali
Órmos Aigiális
tel: (0285) 73 393
Smart modern hotel complex with good facilities, including a taverna and large swimming pool. Lovely views over the bay from the veranda. $$$
Minoa
Katápola
tel: (0285) 71 480
Pleasant rooms in traditional-style hotel on the harbour square. Can be noisy. $

Santoríni
Atlantis
Firá
tel: (0286) 22 232
Elegant hotel built in the 1950s and recently renovated. Spacious rooms, most with balconies with magnificent views of the town and the volcano. $$$
Fanari
Ía
tel: (0286) 71 008
Traditional *skaftá* cave houses converted into luxury holiday accommodation. Swimming pool, breakfast terrace, bar, and 240 steps down to Ammoudiá Bay below. $$$
Ermis
Kamári
tel: (0286) 31 664
Family-run hotel set in beautiful gardens not far from the town centre and the black beach. $$

Esperides
Kamári
tel: (0286) 31 185
Small, friendly new hotel which
includes the ruins of a Byzantine
town in its pistachio grove. $

THE SPORADES
Skiáthos
Atrium Hotel
Plataniás
tel: (0427) 49 345
Casual elegance, with traditional
architecture, resembles monastery.
Chic, beautiful, expensive. $$$
Boúrtzi Hotel
Skiáthos Town
tel: (0427) 21 304. $$
Troúlos Bay
Koukounariés
tel: (0427) 49 390
Attractive, comfortable, on the
beach. $$
Póthos Hotel
Skiáthos town
tel: (0427) 22 694
Both clean, simple and good value
for money. $

Skópelos
Adrina Beach
Pánormos
tel: (0424) 23 373/5
Casual elegance, with private
beach. No single rooms. $$$
Skópelos Village
Skópelos town
tel: (0424) 22 517
Spacious maisonettes on the far
side of the harbour, with pool and
playground. $$$
Kyr Sótos Hotel
Skópelos town
tel: (0424) 22 549
Remodelled family house set on the
waterfront, inexpensive, casual and
tiny rooms. $

Alónissos
Liadromia
Patitíri
tel: (0424) 65 521
Private traditional house on
peninsula overlooking the sea.
Carefully refurbished, garden. $$
Nerídes
Patitíri
tel: (0424) 65 643

Studio apartments (no single
rooms), swimming pool. $$
Paradise Hotel
Patitíri
tel: (0424) 65 160
Family-run hotel above the harbour.
Has pool and is close to the rocks
for sea bathing. $$

Skýros
Skýros Travel, tel: (0222) 91 123,
can advise you where to stay.
Skýros Palace
Magaziá
tel: (0222) 91 994
About 1 km (½ mile) from the
Mólos and about 45m (50 yds) from
the beach, a new hotel in traditional
island style.Seawater pool,
restaurant, superior rooms. $$$

Price Categories

Our price categories are based
on the cost of a double room for
one night in the high season:

$$$ Expensive: above 24,000dr
$$ Moderate: 12–24,000dr
$ Inexpensive: under 12,000dr

Linariá Bay
Linariá
tel: (0222) 96 274/5
Small hotel on the promontory
above the pier. Rooms have fridges
and air conditioning. $$
King Likomides
Linariá
tel: (0222) 96 249
Slightly less expensive than the
Linariá Bay, this is a small hotel by
the pier where the ferries dock.
Rooms have small fridges. $$
Xenia
Magaziá
tel: (0222) 91 209
One of the cement boxes that
usually disfigure the landscape, but
this "modern" hotel directly behind
the beach is now part of the
scenery. The location is wonderful,
the rooms comfortable. $$

Évvia
Agápi
Loutrá Edhipsoú
tel: (0226) 23 883/4

Medium-sized hotel, 100 yds from
the sea and separated by a park
from the GNTO-run thermal baths. All
rooms have TV, small refrigerator,
air conditioning. $$
Aígli
Loutrá Edhipsoú
tel: (0226) 22 215
Across the road from the sea, this
circa 1930 hotel in the centre of
town is now faded but it is a well
maintained, historical building. The
hot baths, for which many people
visit, are inside the hotel. $$
Karystion
Kárystos
tel: (0224) 22 191/291
Small hotel, 360 metres (400 yds)
from the port, right on the water.
10 percent discount for bookings
made through the Internet on
http://agn.hol.gr./hotels/karystio.htm.
$$
Plaza
Límni
tel: (0227) 31 235
Centrally situated, very small 19th-
century hotel with arches right on
the water. $$
Akti Aetos
Kárystos
tel: (0224) 23 447
Small, two-storey white hotel and
bungalows. Restaurant, bar, with
view down to beach about 60
metres (70 yds) away. $
Límni
Límni
tel: (0227) 31 316
Medium-sized hotel towards the
far end of the village, 10 metres
from the sea. Fine rooms with
balconies. $

THE NE AEGEAN ISLANDS
Samothráki
Kaviros
Thermá
tel: (0551) 98 277
Pricey, 1980s-built hotel under the
plane trees at this spa resort; well
landscaped and traffic-free. $$$
Xenia
Paleópoli (Sanctuary of the Great
Gods)
tel: (0551) 41 166
This old stone-clad, one-storey
outfit, originally built to accommodate
archeologists, is much in demand –

no wonder, poised as it is on a knoll between sea and ruins. $$

Thássos
Alkyon
Liménas
tel: (0593) 22 148
Spacious rooms, with harbour or garden view, plus gregarious Anglo-Greek management and afternoon tea, make this a firm favourite with English-speaking travellers. $$
Mirioni
Liménas
tel: (0593) 23 256
Very well priced and comfortable spot with a large breakfast salon; also with a cheaper annexe. $
Thassos Inn
Panayía village
tel: (0593) 61 612
Quiet except for the sound of water in runnels all around, this modern building in traditional style has most rooms facing the sea. $

Price Categories

Our price categories are based on the cost of a double room for one night in the high season:

$$$ Expensive: above 24,000dr
$$ Moderate: 12–24,000dr
$ Inexpensive: under 12,000dr

Límnos
Akti Myrina
Mýrina
tel: (0254) 22 310
Elegant, very expensive bungalows with private beach and all activities to hand; try not to get booked into the ugly new annexe. $$$
Villa Afrodite
Platý beach
tel: (0254) 23 141
Run by returned South African Greeks, this comfortable small hotel has a poolside restaurant and sumptuous buffet breakfasts. $$
Ifestos
Mýrina
tel: (0254) 24 960
Attractive, quietly located behind Romeïkós Yialós town beach. $

Lésvos
Clara
Pétra
tel: (0253) 41 532
The designer-furnished rooms of this bungalow complex look north to Pétra and Mólyvos. Short walk to a beach. $$$
Olive Press
Mólyvos
tel: (0253) 71 205
Converted from an old olive mill, this stone-clad hotel offers a mix of rooms and self-catering studios. $$$
Vatera Beach
Vaterá
tel: (0252) 61 212
Rambling, well-run hotel, just opposite the best beach on the island. $$
Villa 1900
Mytilíni
tel: (0251) 23 448
Rooms in a restored neoclassical mansion with period furnishings and ceiling murals. $$

Híos
Kyma
Híos Town
tel: (0271) 44 500
A converted neoclassical mansion with a modern extension; family management, good breakfasts in a salon with a painted ceiling. $$
Perivoli
Kámbos
tel: (0271) 31 513
A tasteful renovation project utilizing an old mansion. $$
Volissos Houses
Volissós
tel: (0274) 21 128
Stunning old-house restoration project, British-built and managed; currently five self-contained, self-catering units. $$

Sámos
Galaxy
Vathý
tel: (0273) 22665
Garden surroundings, a fair-sized pool, ordinary rooms; takes packages but there are often vacancies. $$
Olympia Beach
Kokkári
tel: (0273) 92420
Small hotel facing the west beach, not blocked out by tours. $$
Galini Hotel
Pythagório
tel: (0273) 61 167
Modern, small, quiet hotel near the top of town, welcomes (unusually here) walk-in clientele. $
Vathi
Áno Vathý
tel: (0273) 28 124
Slight remoteness is offset by the honest and welcoming management; a favourite of independent travellers. $

Ikaría
Messakhti Village
Armenistís
tel: (0275) 71 331
Imposing common areas and large private terraces compensate for rather plain rooms at this self-catering complex; the large pool is a necessity, as the sea here can be dangerously rough. $$

THE DODECANESE
Rhodes
Grand Hotel Astir Palace
Rhodes town
tel: (0241) 26 284
Deluxe hotel with nightclub, casino, tennis courts and reputedly the largest swimming pool in Greece. On Aktí Miaoúli, separated from the beach by the promenade. $$$
Steps of Lindos
Vlyhá Bay
tel: (0244) 42 262
Luxury 320-bed hotel set into a hillside with magnificent views of Lindos. Variety of watersports. $$$
Lydian's Village
Yennádi
tel: (0244) 44 161
A hotel complex (97 rooms) build like a Cycladic village on the sea between Lárdhos and Yennádi. $$$
S. Nikolis
Rhodes town
tel: (0241) 34 561
Rambling restoration project in the heart of the Old Town with hotel plus self-catering studios; rooftop breakfast terrace. $$

Sabina
Theologos Beach
tel: (0244) 41 613
Pleasant 70-room hotel with pool
and tennis court. Friendly
atmosphere with some non-smoking
rooms (unusual in Greece). 7 km
(4 miles) from the Valley of the
Butterflies. $$

Cava d'Oro
Rhodes town
tel: (0241) 36 980
The inner courtyard adjoins the old
town wall.All 13 rooms have shower
and toilet. $$

Andreas Hotel
Rhodes town
tel: (0241) 34 156
Imaginative old-house restoration,
perennially popular, reasonably
priced; wood-trimmed rooms have
wash-basins only. $

Nymphi
Sálakos
tel: (0246) 22 206
A converted Italian-era mansion,
makes a fine woodland base near
the centre of the island. Only 4
rooms. $

Kássos

Anessis $
Frý
tel: (0245) 41 234 and
Anaghenessis $
Frý
tel: (0245) 41 495
Exceedingly modest though they
are, these two hotels represent
nearly half the beds available in Frý,
the port town. Comfortable rooms,
some with sea views.

Kárpathos

Possirama Bay
Pigádhia
tel: (0245) 22 916
A 5-minute wak from the town
centre, quiet, apartments with fully-
equipped kitchens and balconies
overlooking the beach. $$$

Aphrodite
Ólymbos
tel: (0245) 51 454
The only en-suite rooms here, plus
views south to the ocean. $$

Blue Bay Hotel
Pigádhia
tel: (0245) 22 479

Monasteries

Monasteries and convents can
occasionally provide refuge for
the adventurous and solitary
traveller. Enquiries must be
conducted on the spot, or
through a specific island's
Tourist Police (see page 313).
Remember that you must dress
and behave according to their
rules; no shorts and skirts for
women. The doors may be closed
as early as sunset and some
kind of donation may be
expected.

Comfortable and just a few steps
back from Vróndi beach. $$

Kastellórizo

Megisti
Kastellórizo
tel: (0241) 49 272
Overpriced but the only really
luxurious place, at the north end of
the waterfront, with its own
swimming lido. $$

Mavrothalassitis Pension
Kastellórizo
tel: (0241) 49 202
In the centre of town, one of the
very few here with en-suite
plumbing. In a lovely restored
mansion, where Australian-Greek
family also runs a restaurant. $

Hálki

The Captain's House
Emborió
tel: (0241) 57 201
English-and-Greek-run, this is a
delightful outfit in an old mansion,
recently converted to en-suite. $

Hotel Halki
Emborió
tel: (0241) 45 208
In a fomer sponge-processing plant.
28 rooms, restaurant and bar. $

Tílos

Livadia
Livádhia
tel: (0241) 44 266
Upgraded in 1994, this hotel
is good value, especially the
upper floor "suites"; also offers
self-catering studios nearby. $

Eirini
Livádhia
tel: (0241) 44 293
Long the top hotel on the island,
now being challenged by others, but
still wins on points for its beautiful
grounds and common areas. $

Sými

Alyki
Sými Town
tel: (0241) 71 665
Genuinely olde worlde – this used to
be the opera house – next to the
clock tower on the quay. $$$

Horio
Sými Town
tel: (0241) 71 800
Mock-traditional architecture, and
great views, at the top of the
stair-street up from the port
(minibus transfer available). $$

Astypálea

Studios Electra
Livádhia
tel: (0243) 61 270
Castle-view studios, just inland at
the island's main beach resort. $

Vangelis
Skála port
tel: (0243) 61 281
Newish (1994) studio units above a
respected restaurant, on the less
congested side of the bay. $

Níssyros

Porfyris Hotel
Mandhráki
tel: (0242) 31 376
Comfortable, with gardens, a good
swimming pool and views over the
kámbos of communal orchards. $$

Pension Nissyros
Mandhráki
tel: (0242) 31 052
More modest, close to the sea. $

Kós

Hippocrates Palace Hotel
Kos town
tel: (0242) 24 401
Trading on the ancient tradition of
the Asklepeion, this new complex
includes an "Olympic Health
Centre" and a medical spa. $$$

Hotel Afendoulis
Kos town
tel: (0242) 25 321

Small family-run hotel offering large en-suite rooms and full breakfasts. Lovely garden full of jasmine. $$

Pension Alexis
Kós Town
tel: (0242) 28 798
This pension, run by the same friendly family in a quiet back street in the town centre, is a backpacker's home-from-home. $

Kálymnos

Villa Themelina
Póthia
tel: (0243) 22 682
In a 19th-century mansion with a pool and a gardens, this is the town's top choice; unfortunately package companies seem to be aware of this. $$

Greek House Pension
Póthia
tel: (0243) 23 752
En suite, eccentrically furnished rooms and almost manically friendly proprietress. $

Télendhos

Most accommodation here is in tavernas – surprisingly numerous for such a small, one-hamlet islet.

Hotel Port Potha
tel: (0243) 47 321
An exception to the above rule, this is the debut of relative luxury. $$

Uncle George's
tel: (0243) 47 502
Simple but clean rooms above an excellent taverna, this is more typical for Télendhos. $

Léros

Hotel Yianna
Álinda
tel: (0247) 23 153
Modern hotel overlooking the Allied World War II cemetery and Álinda's narrow but clean beach. $$

Pension Fanari
Pandhéli
tel: (0247) 23 152
Secluded setting, with views across to the castle, make this a winner. $

Lipsí

Aphrodite Hotel
Lipsí
tel: (0247) 41 000
A 1997-built, attractive studio

bungalow complex, just inland from the town beach of Liendhoú. $$

Apartments Galini
Lipsí
tel: (0247) 41 212
By the ferry jetty; well-appointed rooms with balconies. $

Pátmos

Hotel Australis
Skála
tel: (0247) 31 576
Peaceful family-run pension in gardens near Mérihas. Plain, en-suite rooms but big breakfasts and very kind management ensure a loyal following. $$

Artemis
Gríkos
tel: (0247) 34 016
Modern but traditional-style complex with simply furnished rooms, sea views, pleasant gardens and an athletic centre. $$

CRETE

Ághios Nikólaos

Minos Beach
tel: (0841) 22 345
Exclusive resort hotel: whitewashed bungalows in landscaped gardens, with private beach. $$$

Haniá

Creta Paradise
tel: (0821) 61 315
New beach resort development on the beach outside town. Large rooms, all sports facilities, friendly service. $$$

Teresa
tel: (0821) 92 798
Renovated Venetian house, rooms decorated with local crafts and antiques. Views of the harbour from the terrace and some rooms. $$

Hersónisos

Creta Maris
tel: (0897) 22 115
Luxury seafront hotel, with individual bungalows, outdoor theatre and cinema. $$$

Iráklion

Atlantis
tel: (081) 229 103
Large modern hotel in quiet side

street with panoramic views over the port and city. $$$

Galaxy
tel: (081) 238 812
Attractive modern hotel set around a central court and swimming pool. Sauna and summer café. $$$

Dedalos
tel: (081) 244 736
Conveniently located, recently refurbished, decorated with paintings by local artists. $$

Mirabello
tel: (081) 285 052
Clean, simple family hotel in an old building near El Greco Park. $

Mátala

Orion
tel: (0892) 42 129
Modest but smart hotel in wonderfully secluded spot just outside Mátala. Large swiming pool and several fine beaches nearby. $

Réthymnon

Grecotel Creta Palace
tel: (0831) 55 181
Large resort hotel on its own beach at Misiría, 4 km (2 miles) east of Réthymnon. Extensive facilities, including fitness club. $$$

Fortetsa
tel: (0831) 55 551
On a quiet back street a minute's walk from the seafront. Good facilities, courtyard, pool. $$

Zanya
tel: (0831) 28 169
Spacious rooms in an old Turkish house. Friendly atmosphere, communal bathroom. $

Private Rooms

On the islands, the most widespread type of inexpensive accommodation is renting private rooms (dhomátia). These are rented out by local residents at prices controlled by the tourist police. In general, when looking for any kind of accommodation, the tourist police can be of considerable help. If you arrive without any accommodation and none seems to be available, enquire at their office. If you'd like to make a reservation or arrangement in advance call them and they'll often be able to help. For a list of police telephone numbers on individual islands, see *Security & Crime* on page 313.

Except at the height of summer, when rooms are scarce, *dhomátia* can be secured just by stepping off the ferry. Housewives meet any and all ferries until late into the evening. "Room? Room?" they will ask, and a deal is often struck there on the spot. The price is normally for the room itself, rather than per bed; a single, therefore, usually costs little less than a double, unless business is slack or you commit to stay a while. Within 10 minutes of the ferry departing both the women and the rooms have disappeared. As most accommodation on the islands is clean and perfectly acceptable, upon arrival it might be an idea to take the first room offered for 2 nights (cheaper than 1 night) and shop around in the meantime. Men with rooms to offer, or when a car journey is involved, often bring their children along, a gesture which makes women travelling alone feel more secure

Pensions

A pension tends to be a casual, family-run establishment, falling somewhere between a private room and a hotel. As the accommodation has been purpose-built, many rooms have balconies and, whenever possible, a sea view. They are divided into classes A–C, but rates tend to be less expensive than hotels. First-class pensions are listed in the GNTO hotel guide and can be pre-booked directly. Lists of pensions in lower categories can only be obtained on the spot through the Tourist Police (see page 313).

Villas & Apartments

Self-catering is increasingly popular in Greece, especially for those holidaying with young children. Villas and apartments are clean, and comfortably, if sparsely, furnished. Like hotels and pensions, they are graded according to fixed-price categories. Expect to pay slightly less for a first-class apartment as for a luxury hotel room.

Rental Agencies

● **Alexander Travel**
4 Stadiou Street, Athens
tel: 322 7668
Apartments throughout Greece, especially Skiáthos and Corfu.
● **Ameridian Ltd**
Room 63
3 Filellínon Street, Athens
tel: 323 2608
Houses throughout Greece.
● **Corfu Sun Club**
tel: (0661) 33 855
Self-catering on Corfu.
● **Polytravel**
25 August Street
Iráklion, Crete
tel: (081) 282476
All types of accommodation throughout Crete.
● **Skópelos Tours**
tel: (0424) 22 721
Self-catering on Skópelos.
● **Ikos Travel**
tel: (0424) 65 320
Self-catering on Alónnisos.

Camping

A certain portion of tourists who come to Greece decide to "rough it", although this type of holiday is now being discouraged by the GNTO. Those who want to camp at organised campsites with facilities will find scores of them all over the islands, some run by the Greek Touring Club, and others – including recently sold-off GNTO ones – privately.

The most beautiful campsites, however, are usually the ones you find on your own. While in most places it is officially illegal just to lay out your sleeping bag or pitch a tent, if you're discreet you'll probably not be bothered. That means asking permission if you seem to be on private property, avoiding "unofficial" campsites set up in popular tourist areas, and always leaving the place looking better than when you came.

The GNTO issues a useful booklet, *Camping in Greece*, listing all the officially recognised sites, with codes for facilities on offer.

Youth Hostels

Theoretically, you need a member's card to stay in a Greek youth hostel, though in practice you can often just pay an extra fee, and must defer to cardholders for space. An international membership card can be obtained before you travel by applying to your national Youth Hostel Association, or once in Greece to the Greek Youth Hostels Association at 4 Dragatsaniou Street, 10559 Athens, tel: 323 4107.

Youth hostels can be found in the following locations:

ATHENS
● 75 Damareos Street, Pangráti, tel: 75 19 530.
● YWCA Youth Hostel, 11 Amerikis Street, tel: 36 26 180.

CRETE
● **Iráklion** Youth Hostel
5 Výronos Street
tel: (081) 28 6281
● **Mália** Youth Hostel
just east of village
tel: (0897) 31 555
● *Mýrthios* Youth Hostel
tel: (0832) 31 202
● **Plakiás** Youth Hostel
tel: (0832) 31 306
● **Réthymnon** Youth Hostel
41 Tombázi Street
tel: (0831) 22 848

THE CYCLADES
Santoríni
There are three in **Firá town:**
● International Youth Hostel
tel: (0286) 22 387
● Kamares Youth Hostel
Erythroú Stavroú
tel: (0286) 24 472
● Kondohóri Youth Hostel
Ághios Elefthérios
tel: (0286) 22 722.

Where to Eat

What To Eat

Eating out in Greece is above all a social affair. Whether it be with your family or your *paréa*, that sacred circle of friends, a meal out is an occasion to celebrate. This may have something to do with the fact that eating out in Greece continues to be affordable and popular, not something restricted to those with credit cards.

And the predominance of the *tavérna*, that bastion of Greek cuisine, reflects this popularity. There is also considerable regional variety in Greek cuisine and you should keep an eye out for those specialities of the house which you haven't seen before. Another thing you'll quickly learn in Greece is how strikingly different the same dish can be when it is prepared well or prepared badly. It is therefore worth shopping around for your *tavérna* (especially in heavily visited areas), asking the locals what they suggest, walking into the kitchen to look at the food (a customary practice), instead of being stuck with a tourist trap which spoils your appetite for *moussaká* for the rest of the trip.

Island cuisine can be more than just *moussakás*, and holds a few surprises. Seafood can be difficult to find, even impossible on some remote islands, and is quite expensive by local standards. The Aegean has been over-fished, and often the proceeds of a successful day are sent straight to Athens or the large island hotels. To enjoy the meal of a lifetime you must stay on one island for some time, and strike up a friendship with a fisherman. The rewards will be worth it: the best of a daily catch often goes straight into the fisherman's family pot.

Here are few notes about Greek eating habits. The main meal is eaten at midday, between 2pm and 3.30pm and is usually followed by a siesta break lasting until 5.30pm or 6pm. The evening meal can either be another full meal, or an assortment of *mezédhes*. This is usually eaten between 9pm and 11pm. Breakfast in Greece is rather meagre, usually consisting of bread, butter, jam and coffee.

Some *tavérnes* may not have menus, some have menus without prices. It is also a good idea to ask how much things cost before you eat. For a list of items you may see on the menu, see the Language section on page 340.

Restaurants

ATHENS

Bajazzo
Ploutarchou and Dinokratous, Kolonáki, tel: 729 1420
Unusual food combining nouvelle cuisine and traditional Greek dishes; expensive by Greek standards but cheap by world-wide standards for innovative, high-quality food. Closed Sunday.
Gerofínikas, 10 Pindarou, tel: 362 2719
Cosmopolitan Greek cuisine with Constantinople specialities included. Fresh fish, lamb with artichokes and tempting desserts. Pricey but recommended.
Kostoyiannis, 37 Zaimi (Pedion Areos), Exárhia, tel: 821 2496
Large selection of appetisers. Main dishes include rabbit stifado and quail. Spiced quince with whipped cream and walnut cake for dessert.
Themistokles, 31 Vas. Georgiou, Pangráti, tel: 721 9553. Fine taverna fare on the first floor of an old Athenian dwelling.

THE IONIAN ISLANDS
Corfu
Tripa restaurant in village of Kinopiástes in the hills, just south of Corfu Town. Fixed, moderately high price but an endless supply of very good food.
Yanni's, near church of Saints Iason and Sosipater, at Anemómilos, just south of the town.

All Types of Greek Restaurants

Restaurants in Greece come in many guises:

● **Tavérnes** These casual eating establishments have more or less the same style and set-up throughout Greece, and the menu is similar. Which is to say no frills, no packaging which tries to convince the consumer that this *tavérna* is different from the others, special, distinct. The place, and your being there, is somehow taken for granted: you eat the good food at Yannis's or Yeorghios's, you enjoy yourself, and you don't end up paying an arm and a leg for it.

● The **estiatório**, is the restaurant as we usually think of it, which ranges from the tradesmen's lunch-hour hangout, with ready-cooked (*maghireftó*) food and bulk wine, up to pricey linen-tablecloth places with bow-tied staff.

● The **psistariá** is a barbecue-style restaurant specialising in lamb, pork or chicken on a spit.

● The **psarotavérna** specialises in fish; while the **ovelistírio** (*yíros* stall) and **souvlatzídhiko** purvey *yíros* and *souvláki* respectively, sometimes to a sit-down trade, garnished with salads.

● **Kultoúra** restaurants, more popular of late among students and urban intellegentsia, offer nouvelle Greek cuisine based on updated traditional recipes.

● **Ouzeri** (called *tsipourádhika* in the North), where the local tipple serves as accompaniment to *mezédhes* or small plates of specialty dishes.

Lefkádha

Reganto, Lefkádha Town. Off the main square. Colourful atmosphere, good food, inexpensive.
Breath of Zorba, Nikiána.Tables right up to the water, moderately expensive.
Nick the Greek's, Nydhrí. Standard, good Greek taverna on the harbour.

Itháki

Gregory's, Vathý. Just outside of town, in a romantic setting under the trees. Good food, both meat and fish.

Kefalloniá

Kaliva, Argostóli. Pleasant garden to match the food.
Saoulis, Sámi. Waterfront taverna serving fish, regular Greek dishes and specialities (eg octopus pie).

Zákynthos

Arekia taverna, Zákynthos Town. Wonderful, with singing.
Oraia Ellas, Zákynthos Town Village Inn, near Strata Marina hotel. Good, expensive French food.

SARONIC GULF ISLANDS

Aegina

Vostitsano, in Aegina Town. Plus any of the numerous fish tavernas in Pérdhika.

Póros

Dolphin, in town near post office. Good seafood taverna.

Hydra

Three Brothers taverna, in town, up from the harbour.
Kseri Elia, in town, up from the harbour.

Spétses

Siouras, in Paleó Limáni, in the old harbour. Taverna over the water, popular, noisy, expensive.
Il Padrino Bar and Pizzeria, on the water, in the old harbour.
Patralis, near the Spétses Hotel. Usually good, often excellent fish.

THE CYCLADES

Santorini

Nikolaos, Firá. Fine old taverna, very popular locally.
Selene, Firá. Elegant garden restaurant overlooking Caldera.
Camille Stefani, Kamári, on beach.

Síkinos

Ostria, affiliated with Kamares Hotel, see *Hotels*, page 326.

Náxos

Elli, Hóra. Good Greek restaurant with a fine view of the temple.
Castro, Hóra, Kástro.

Páros

Porphyra, Parikiá. Seafood.
Tamarisko, Parikiá.
Tsitanis, Pródhromos. Local favourite for Greek food.
Kargas, Náoussa harbour. Old *ouzeri*, picturesque, seafood on charcoal.

Andíparos

Galini Hotel, Hóra. Good taverna in hotel (see *Hotels*, page 323).
Pepinos, Ághios Yórgos. Fresh fish.

Mýkonos

Katrin, Hóra. Excellent, but expensive, French restaurant.
Antonini, by taxi square on quay. Good Greek food since 1955.
Sesame Kitchen, Hóra, next to Maritime Museum. Inventive international food.
Osteria del Pesce da Lu, near Kalafáti. One of Greece's best authentic Italian restaurants, excellent food.

Sýros

Eleana, Ermoúpoli. First-rate Greek cuisine.
Lilis, Ermoúpoli, Áno Sýros. Greek taverna.

Tínos

Ksinari, Hóra, on main shopping street. Greek food with a Lebanese accent.
Tsambia, in Kiónia, near Tínos Beach Hotel. Typical Greek taverna food.

Ándhros

Yiannouli's, on beach between Gávrio and and Batsí. Popular place for lunch, home cooking.
Stamatis, in Batsí, up the stairs at far end of town.

Mílos

Trapatsellis, in Adhámas.
To Diporto, in Pláka.

Sífnos

Manganas, in Artemónas, near bus stop. Simple, good Greek food.
Liotrivi, in Artemónas. First-rate Greek food in beautiful garden.

THE SPORADES

Skiáthos

Agnantia, near road to Evangelístria. Offers refined Greek cuisine, elegance and views, expensive.
Asprolithos taverna in town, and **Asprolithos taverna** in Megali Ammos, just outside town. Both have great variety, fresh food, excellent cuisine.
Chez Julien, in town. French restaurant, seafood.
Messogeia, near Trión Ierarhón Square. Greek home cooking, inexpensive.

Skópelos

Spyros taverna in town on waterfront. Inexpensive, popular.
Perivóli, in town. Refined Greek cooking. Needs reservation, moderate price.
Térpsis, near Stáfylos Beach. Good for grilled chicken.

Alónissos

Astrofengiá, at entrance to Hóra. Old family house, innovative cuisine.
Paraport, at base of castle in Hóra. Stunning view, grill.
To Kamaki, just up from port. *Ouzerí*.

Skýros

Kristina's, Horió, downtown branching away from the post office. Up market, with very good food, expensive.
Margetis, Horió, on main street. Good Greek food, inexpensive.

Anna's at the windmill on the beach. Wonderful lobster.

THE NE AEGEAN ISLANDS

Samothráki

Orizontas, Kamariótissa. Quick-served *maghireftá* and good bulk wine make this by far the best of several tavernas in the port.
To Kastro, Kentrikí Platía, Hóra. Excellent, unpretentious *ouzerí*.

Thássos

O Glaros, south end of the beach, Alykí hamlet. Least expensive and most authentic of several tavernas here; local fresh fish.
O Platanos, under the tree, Sotíros village. Summer-only taverna; elaborate dishes when trade justifies it, simple grills otherwise, and powerful homemade *tsípouro* if you ask.
Iy Pighi, Kentrikí Platía, Liménas. Old warhorse dishing out dependable *maghireftá* next to the spring of the name; best at supper.

Límnos

Platanos, Mýrina Town. Traditional purveyor of *maghireftá* in the bazaar, beneath two plane trees.
Iliovasilemata, Ághios Ioánnis beach. Excellent seafood.
Zimbabwe, Platý village. Secluded but popular grill-*ouzerí*.

Lésvos

The Captain's Table, old port, Mólyvos. Greek and Australian-run fish restaurant with grills and good vegetarian *mezédhes*, too.
Ya Mas, Skála Eressoú, waterfront. Canadian-Greek-run breakfast and after-hours bar with pancakes, whole-grain bread and decadent chocolate desserts.
Dhouladhelli, south entrance to Aghiássos village. Inexpensive taverna with local specialties.
Iy Eftalou, just before the thermal baths, Eftaloú. Reliable favourite, much liked by locals.

Híos

O Dholomas, Karfás. Frankly tacky decor, but this is an excellent *ouzerí*; open May–Sept.
Ouzeri Theodhosiou, Neoríon quay,

Híos Town. Oldest and still one of the best *ouzerí* in town
O Tsambos, Katarráktis. Fish tavernas are often a rip-off; this place near the anchorage isn't.
Stelios's (Tou Koupelou), waterfront, Langádha. Last remaining – and happily one of the best – of the seafood tavernas that once graced the quay here.

Sámos

Nissi, Aghía Paraskeví bay. Grilled seafood, and abundant *dhískos* (tray) of *mezédhes*; seafront terrace.
Iy Haravghi, Kérveli beach. Beach *tavérna* with a full bar, good *mezédhes* and *maghireftá*.
Remataki, town beach, Pythagório. This is one of the few places locals will be seen at.
Blue Chairs, Vourliótes. Four tavernas compete hotly in the photogenic central square here; this one has an edge.
To Kyma, Ághios Konstandínos. Full-service taverna at the east end of the quay with good bulk wine.

Ikaría

Paskhalia, Armenistís. Wonderful breakfasts, and reasonable fish, washed down by good bulk wine at supper.
Delfini, Armenistís. More traditional, less polished, even more popular than its neighbour, Paskhalia.

Foúrni

Rementzo (Nikos'). Best of the three full-service waterfront tavernas; here you'll almost definitely find *astakós*, Aegean lobster, and the succulent *skatharí* or black bream.

THE DODECANESE

Rhodes

Le Bistrot, Omírou 22–24, old town. A genuine French-run bistro; pricey and a bit nouvelle, but good.
O Meraklis, Aristotélous 32. The last surviving *patsatzídhiko* (*patsás* kitchen) in town attracts a rather lurid clientele from 3–7am only; just the thing if you've stumbled off the overnight ferry from Kastellórizo.
Alatopipero, Mihaïl Petrídhi 76, new town near Rodhíni park. Nouvelle-Greek *ouzerí* with recherché dishes. Supper only; closed Mon.
O Yiannis, in Koskinoú village, 5 km (3 miles) south of Rhodes town. Very reasonable *mezédhes* and bulk wine.
Tommy's, Haráki. Best of the waterfront fish tavernas, run by a professional fisherman.
Epta Pighes, Eptá Pighés. This streamside *exohikó kéndro* has been going since 1948, and because of its Rhodian clientele is far better than its location would have you believe.

Kárpathos

Kali Kardhia, Pigádhia shore road. The spot for fish, though they do other things, too.
To Limanaki, Vróndi beach. Quite good, with nice touches like homemade rice pudding. Lunch only.
Parthenonas, centre, Ólymbos village. The place to go for local titbits like *makaroúnes* (homemade pasta with onions and cheese)

Hálki

Mavri Thalassa, Emborió

waterfront. None of the half-dozen tavernas here is bad, but this has the edge for its carefully prepared *mezédhes* and crab salad.

Kastellórizo
Ouzeri Megisteas, behind the arcaded market building in Kastellórizo town. Best value for money, with a good line in goat chops (generally better than lamb in Greece).
Little Paris, waterfront. Longest-running and most reliable of several fish tavernas, most of which cater to not-very-discriminating yachties.

Tílos
Blue Sky, above the ferry dock, Livádhia. The more reasonable of two spots for grilled fish.
Stelios, east end of Livádhia bay. Newish (1997) entrant on the scene, about the best for *maghireftá*.
Kali Kardhia, Megálo Horió. Much the best food in the western half of the island and fine views over the kámbos to Éristos beach.

Sými
Yeorghios's, Horió. An island institution, decades old and still very good; nouvelle Greek cuisine in non-nouvelle big portions.
O Meraklis, rear of Yialós bazaar. Well-executed dishes, if a bit pricey (especially the baby native shrimp).
Tholos, past the Haráni shipyards. *Ouzerí* with excellent views.

Níssyros
Taverna Nissyros, inland lane of Mandhráki. The oldest and one of the most popular outfits here.
Taverna Irini, Platía Ilikioméni, Mandhráki. Big portions of fish and meat, unlike many other *mezédhes*-orientated spots in town.
Aphroditi, Páli fishing port. Good for *maghireftá*, homemade desserts and bulk Cretan wine.

Kós
Ambavris, Ambávris hamlet, 800m (900 yds) south of Kós Town. Outdoor courtyard seating means summer operation only; go for the *pikilía* or house medley.
Gin's Palace, Platáni. Turkish

management dishes out tasty Anatolian-style *mezédhes* and grills.
Psistaria Apostolis, Marmári access road. Fresh fish and own-produced meat, an amazing wine list and reasonable prices.
Olympiada, Ziá village. Perhaps the only one of a dozen tavernas here without a sunset view, so the food – lots of stews with *pligoúri* (bulgur wheat) on the side – has to be good.
Iy Pighi, Pylí village. Inexpensive, basic taverna serving nourishing food, best for lunch while touring.
Limionas, Limiónas fishing anchorage, near Kéfalos. Where you go for fresh fish on Kós; limited menu otherwise. Open most of the year.

Kálymnos
Barba Petros/Adherfi Martha, east quay, Póthia. Excellent seafood, if rather plainly served.
Xefteris, inland. Good traditional *maghireftá* dishes, though not as cheap as they might be – they're famous.
Iliovasilema, Myrtiés. Run by the local butcher, so good grills; never mind the tacky decor.

Astypálea
Iy Monaxia/Viki's, inland from ferry jetty, Skála. Most reliable purveyor of *maghireftá* on the island; open much of the year.

Léros
Ouzeri Kapetan Mihalis, little alley in Aghía Marína. Basic but authentic and cheap place (no sea view), where you can sample local salt-marinated (*pastós*) seafood. Open for lunch.
Mezedhopolio Kapaniri, Aghía Marína seafront. Plenty of fried vegetable first courses, then meat or seafood. Best for supper.
To Stéki, next to Allied war cemetery, Álinda. Good grills and *mezédhes*, open all year for a local clientele.
Iy Thea Artemi, Blefoútis beach. Better-than-average beach taverna.

Lipsí
Barbarosa. Good for vegetable-based *maghireftá*; great view from the terrace.
Delfini, by the police station.

Eclectic menu, including fish and vegetables, popular with British.
Fish Restaurant, on the quay. Opens only when the owner has freshly caught something.

Pátmos
O Grigoris, Skála waterfront. Seating is noisy – at the corner with the road up to Hóra – but the food is carefully prepared and abundant.
Vangelis, main square, Hóra. Long-running classic *maghireftá* spot. Check out the amazing juke-box, if it's still there.
Melloi/Stefanos', Melói beach. A superb taverna; well-executed *maghireftá*, plenty for vegetarians.
Lambi, Lámbi beach. Besides Stefanos', the most reliable of Pátmos' various beach eateries.

CRETE
Haniá
Dino's. Seafood. Expensive.
Karnaghio, in old harbour. Moderate.
Tholos. Cretan food. Moderate.

Réthymnon
Agrimia, Cretan food. Moderate.
Famagusta, Cypriot and Cretan food. Moderate.

Iraklión
Ippokambos. Best *meze* in town. Moderate.
Kyriakos. Reliable. Moderate.

Drinking Notes
GREEK WINES
Greek wines have yet to obtain the status of their French counterparts, though young oenologists trained abroad are definitely having a go at it, and there are an increasing number of quality micro-wineries on the mainland. Additionally, many islands produce excellent vintages which they can't or won't export, so they remain unknown. Miles Lambert-Gócs' *The Wines of Greece* (Faber & Faber) is recommended as a guide to the better bottles, though coverage ceases in 1993. All this wonderfulness, however, costs as much as anywhere else; cheaper

but palatable mainland labels include **Carras** (Macedonia), **Boutari** (Macedonia), **Cambas** (Attica), and **Tsantali** (Macedonia). Examples include:

● **Boutari Nemea** the best mid-range red. Full bodied, not too much tannin. Other, premium versions of Nemea – merely a region in the north-central Peloponnese– exist; the pricier, the smoother, as a rule.

● **Boutari Lacs des Roches** their upper mid-range white, considered superior to Rotonda.

● **Katoghi** a wonderfully smooth red from Métsovo.

● **Hatzimihali**, red and white the first, and still one of the best of the central Greece micro-wineries; what fancy tavernas tend to have as a premium wine, and can be found even in rather provincial bottle-shops.

● **Athanasiadhi**, red and white remarks as for Hatzimihali.

● **Gheorghiadi** the best bottled retsina, from Thessaloníki, far superior to the usually preferred Kourtaki or Malamatina. Retsina, wine flavoured with pine resin, is an acquired taste but in hot weather is an ideal "solvent" for greasy, heavy food.

ISLAND WINES

Many islands bottle (or barrel) wines which are sold only locally. Although barreled (*me to kiló, híma*) wines tend to be rough and ready, they're very cheap and certainly authentic. You may have to ask around for the following:

The Ionian Islands

Kefaloniá: **Robola**, a delicate expensive white.

Corfu: **Theotoki** is the local wine (red or white); the speciality of the island is a very sweet orange liqueur called **Kumquat**.

Andípaxi: The local grapes are much appreciated; ask for wine from the barrel.

Zákynthos: Try the wines made from grapes grown in Zákynthos's lush green vineyards – **Comouto** rosé or the white **Verdea**.

Island Brew

Níssyros in the Dodecanese islands produces a non-alcoholic drink called *soumádha*, similar to Italian orgeat, made from almonds; you dilute the syrup 3:1 with water for a refreshing drink.

The Cyclades

Náxos: **Ariadne** wine is delicious; also white, red or rosé **Prombonas**. Try also the lemon-based local liqueur **Kitron**.

Páros: Of the two major locals, **Kavarnis** is more expensive (and better) than **Lagari**. All in red, white and rosé.

Santoríni: Two white wines worth trying are **Visanto** (sweet) and **Nichteri** (dry).

Sérifos: A full-bodied retsina called **Marko**. Try it from the barrel.

The Sporades

Skópelos: Plums are the speciality here, and their dried-up cousins, prunes. Locally produced plum wine is delicious; that produced from prunes is disgusting.

The Dodecanese

Rhodes: A visit to one of the numerous off-licences in Rhodes Town will find a whole range of locally-produced drinks; wines from Rhodes are consumed all over the Dodecanese. CAIR, the co-operative originally founded by the Italians, has the ubiquitous white **Ilios** (named after the sun god) and red **Chevalier du Rhodes**, but the private, Émbonas-based winery Emery is more esteemed for its **Mythiko** and **Villaré** red and white labels. CAIR Brut "champagne" is exported to many islands and can also be found in Athens.

The NE Aegean islands

Sámos: Sámos is one of the few islands to export wine, not only to the mainland but also abroad; the French in particular like the sweet dessert wines. A number of premium white bottles in particular

are produced, but surprisingly the *oúzo* is reckoned better: try the Ghiokarinis brand.

Híos: Particularly around Mestá, a heavy, sherry-like but very palatable wine is made from raisins. *Oúzo* is made here too – try the **Tetteris** brand.

Lésvos: Quite a few local *oúzos* emanate from the distilling centre of Plomári; **Varvaghiannis** is the most celebrated, and expensive, but many consider it too sweet. EPOM is the principal co-operative, marketing among others the **"Mini"** brand, with its rampantly sexist label, a staple of *ouzerí* across the country.

Límnos: Like most volcanic islands, Límnos produces excellent whites, fewer reds; almost anything is worth trying, and easily available from Mýrina bottle shops.

Thássos: Not wine, not *oúzo*, but *tsípouro* – often flavoured with exotic spices or pear extract rather than the anise of *oúzo* – is the tipple here. Homemade firewater gets lethally strong; anything over 50 percent alcohol must be barrelled, not bottled, lest it explode.

Crete

White wines include **Regalo** (dry) and **Vilana** (medium dry). Peza and Minos bottle a number of reds and whites of varying quality. Red wines include **Castello**, **Mantiko** and **Saint Antonio**. There are also local variations on brandy and raki.

Culture

Sound and Light Spectacles

Throughout the summer, Athens, Corfu and Rhodes offer "sound and light" shows projected onto the frontages of their ancient ruins. These performances are perfect for children, and the lights are exciting to watch from the comfort of a nearby terrace. The words, however, are dire. Try attending a show in a language other than your own.

● **Athens**: 9pm (English); 10pm (German – Tuesday and Friday only); 10.15pm (French – except for Tuesday and Friday). Tickets available at the Pnyx before the show. For information, tel: 332 1459.

● **Corfu**: 9.30pm (English – except Saturday and Sunday); 9pm (French – Sunday); 9pm (Greek – Saturday). Ticket price includes Greek folk dances. Reduced rates for students. Tel: (0661) 30 520.

● **Rhodes**: The spectacle at the Palace of the Knights is performed several times each evening in English, French, German and Greek. For information, tel: (0241) 23 255.

Greek Folk Dances

Athens, Corfu and Rhodes have regular performances of Greek folk dancing during the summer months.

● In **Athens**, the renowned Dora Stratou Group perform at the Filopappou Theatre most nights at 10.25pm. On Wednesday and Sunday there is an extra performance at 8.15pm; for information, tel: 324 4395.

● Performances are held each evening at 9pm on **Corfu** at the Old Venetian Castle. The ticket price includes the Sound and Light spectacle. Information from (0661) 39 730.

● On **Rhodes**, the Nelly Dhimoglou Group holds sway at the Old Town Theatre, off Platía Ariónos, most evenings at 9.15pm. Call (0241) 27 524 for details.

Religious Festivals

The Greek Orthodox Church still exerts enormous influence on contemporary life, both in Athens and on the islands. Sunday is the official day of rest, and even in mid-season on some tourist-laden islands, shops and activities will be suspended on the Holy Day. Excursion boats to other islands might well be running to schedule, but often what no one bothers to point out is that nothing on the destination island will be open when you arrive; check beforehand to avoid disappointment.

The most important holiday in Greece is Easter, celebrated by the Greek Orthodox calendar usually a week or two to either side of Catholic Easter. Traditional foods include *tsouréki*, plaited bread with red eggs inside, and *magherítsa*, tripe and lettuce soup. It is advisable to find out before booking a spring holiday exactly when Easter might be, as services, shops and even aeroplane flights experience disruptions during the week before and after Easter.

On 15 August, the Assumption of the Virgin Mary, many islands hold a *paniyiri* (celebration) to mark the reception of the Panaghía (as she is in Greek) into heaven. Greeks make pilgrimages from all over the country to **Tínos** in the Cyclades where the icon of the Panaghía Evangelístria is said to work miracles. Pilgrims flock to **Pátmos**, too, where St John is said to have written the book of Revelations.

The most colourful festival of the

Name Days

Nearly every day is a cause for celebration for someone in Greece. Instead of marking birthdays, Greeks have *yiortés*, name days, which celebrate Orthodox baptismal names. When the day commemorates a popular name-saint like John or Helen, practically the whole nation has a party. You'll hear locals say: *"Yiortázo simera"* (I'm celebrating today). To which you may reply: *"Hrónia pollá"* (Many years, ie happy returns).

Virgin, however, takes place on 15 August in the hillside town of Ólymbos on the island of **Kárpathos**, where the women wear brilliant traditional dress and the *paniyíria* can last for days.

Other important celebrations include Ághios Spyrídhon in **Corfu**, when the relics of the patron saint are paraded around the streets (12 December, Palm Sunday, Easter Saturday and 11 August); the *Theofánia* (Epiphany) on 6 January with a big ceremony in **Piraeus**, and on **Crete** where the seas are blessed and boys dive for the cross thrown into the waves; the feast of St George on 23 April, where especially on **Kós** and **Límnos** the patron saint of Greece is remembered in festivities, and the important rural festivals of Aghía Marina (17 July), coinciding with the first grape crop; Aghía Paraskeví (26 July) and John the Baptist (29 August).

Worthwhile festivals, with their origins in religion but now largely secular, are the Pentecost Saturday bull-sacrifice and horse-racing festival at Aghía Paraskeví on **Lésvos**; Metamórfosis tou Sotíros (6 August), when it is the custom to have fights with eggs, flour and yoghurt; and Ághios Dhimítrios on 26 October, when the first wine is ready to drink.

Seasonal Festivals

● **May–September** Folk dancing by the Dora Stratou Group at the Filopáppou Theatre, **Athens**, and Nelly Dhimoglou Group in **Rhodes Old Town**.
● **June** Jazz & Blues Festival, Lykavittós Theatre, **Athens**
● **Mid-June–September Pátras** International Festival: ancient drama, classical music and contemporary theatre up in the medieval castle grounds, and odeion.
● **June–September Athens** Festival. Ancient drama, opera, music and ballet at the Herod Atticus Odeon, among other venues.
● **Late June–late September Sými** Festival. Concerts and musical events; newish but apparently set for success.
● **July–August Epídhavros** Festival. Performances of ancient drama in the open-air Epidaurus amphitheatre on the Peloponnese.
● **Late July** Music Festival on the island of **Itháki**.
● **Early August Iráklion, Crete**, concerts; theatre; opera etc.
● **August Lefkádha** Festival of Music, Folklore and Theatre; participation by overseas groups.
● **August** Ippokratia Festival, **Kós**; art exhibits, concerts, films plus a cermony at the Asklepion.
● **August** Kavála Festival; includes ancient drama performed at **Philippi**.
● **Late August** Wine Festival in Rodhíni Park, south of **Rhodes** town.
● **July–August** "Epirot Summer" at **Ioánnina**; includes ancient drama performances at nearby **Dodona** amphitheatre.
● **August–September Santoríni** Music Festival
● **August–October Rhodes** Festival
● **August–September Réthymnon** Renaissance Fair. Various cultural activities at the Venetian Fort.
● **October Thessaloníki** Dhimitria Festival. Theatre, music, ballet, followed by self-contained film-festival.

Information and tickets for the Athens Festival events in particular can be obtained from the GNTO (EOT) Festival Office, 2 Spýrou Milíou Arcade, (entrance from 4 Stadou Street), tel: 322 1459 or 322 3222, ext. 240.

Outdoor Movies

One of the delights of an island evening is to sit under a starry sky and enjoy an outdoor movie. Many of Greece's outdoor cinemas, like an American drive-in without the cars, do not attempt to compete with mainstream movie houses, screening instead kung fu flicks, Hollywood war movies and B-movies you've never heard of. However, on larger islands like **Lésvos, Crete** or **Rhodes**, you will often get – if not exactly first-run fare – quality stuff from four to eight months back, or old classics. Films are usually in English with Greek subtitles, but the background noise (Greeks talk through screenings) often makes the dialogue incomprehensible. Take snacks (though nuts and drinks are sold), a warm jacket and wear lots of mosquito repellent.

Nightlife

Most island nightlife consists of strolling from taverna to *zaharisplastíon* to a café on the promenade. Having said that, discos or musical bars abound on any island with a sizeable influx of tourists. The best are out of town and out of doors; dancing under the stars is an unforgettable Greek experience. Canny managers of discos located some distance from the port hire a nightly minibus which transports revellers to the premises. Discos on small islands are the most fun when, around midnight, traditional island music is played and older folks join young foreigners on the dance floor.

For a more sophisticated evening out, both Rhodes and Corfu have casinos.

Shopping

What To Buy

Most Greek tourist tat is instantly forgettable; it also takes up room on ferries and aeroplanes. Much better to concentrate on small local items like sponges from **Kálymnos**, leather bags from **Rhodes**, hand-made pottery from **Sífnos**, woollen shoulder bags from **Crete**, and extremely attractive silver jewellery from a number of islands. Much of this jewellery is made by local craftsmen, and styles range from the traditional to the fashionable.

Other good buys include baskets, copper pots and other copperware, honey, olive oil, and the ubiquitous *loukoúmia* (Turkish Delight), made on **Sýros** but exported to other islands, too. **The Dodecanese** are particularly rich in fur-coat shops and are also a source of inexpensive booze, both local and imported.

Hydra, Mýkonos and **Páros** have some of the most fashionable boutiques to be found in Greece. Much of their stock outclasses Athens but not, unfortunately, London, Paris or New York.

Bargaining is expected in markets and stalls. In these places, even if an item has a price tag, try offering a lower price. Even better, show interest and then walk away. (You can always return if the ploy doesn't work. It usually does.) Bargaining is unacceptable in department stores, chain stores and most boutiques.

Department stores implement a complicated service system not recommended for anyone in a hurry. If you happen to go to a large stationers to purchase a notebook, a pencil, some envelopes and perhaps a birthday card, you could find yourself standing in six different queues: one for each department (where an assistant writes a receipt for each item), one to pay the cashier the total amount, and one for delivery of the goods. If you're lucky, all four items will have arrived from their various departments (only a few steps from each other) at the delivery desk to be wrapped or placed into a bag with four separate receipts taped on top.

PERÍPTERA (KIOSKS)

Life in Greece would be unmanageable without a neighbourhood *períptero*: always open days, nights, holidays and Sundays. Although they may appear limited by their diminutive structures, kiosks are really multi-purpose powerhouses. Besides filling the function of newsagent and tobacconist, these businesses, many family-run, also double as mini-amusement parks with kiddie rides, sporting goods stores, ironmongers, locksmiths, and for many customers with problems, the proprietor may dispense psychiatric or medical advice. Here, too, is a quick place to buy tourist requisites: shampoo, nail clippers, postcards.

There are over 3,000 kiosks in Athens alone. It is not unusual for a *períptero* to work shifts of 12 hours in conditions that vary from furnace-like in summer to chill and damp in winter. The kiosks started as gifts from the government to wounded veterans of the Balkan Wars and the First World War. Many people remark on the similarity between the architecture of kiosks and that of military guardposts such as those used by the honour guard in front of Parliament on Sýntagma Square.

Sport

Golf

Greece has a few golf courses dotted around the country. In **Athens**, the course is at Glyfádha, tel: 894 6875. **Rhodes**' golf course is at Afándou, tel: (0241) 51 255). **Corfu**'s Ermónes Bay golf club, tel: (0661) 94 220 is particularly nice. Lessons and rental equipment available at all courses.

Yachting

The GNTO publishes an excellent booklet called *Sailing the Greek Seas*. Included is information on weather, coastal radio telephone stations, entry and exit regulations. The pamphlet is particularly detailed on marinas, bunkering ports and supply stations. There are four marinas within striking distance of Athens. Information on services or facilities may be obtained by calling:
● Vouliagméni Marina, tel: 896 0012.
● Zéa Marina, tel: 451 3944.
● Álimos Marina, tel: 982 8642.
● Flísvos Marina, tel: 982 8537.

If you prefer to charter a yacht, the GNTO can provide lists of yacht brokers and consultants. All charter agreements have to be made in the manner and on the official form prescribed by the Greek government. The following organisations can also offer help and advice:
● **Greek Yacht Brokers & Consultants Association**
PO Box 30393, 10033 Athens
tel: 985 0122
● **Hellenic Yachting Federation**
Possidonos 55, Piraeus
tel: 930 4825

● **Hellenic Professional and Bareboat Yacht Owners Association**
Office A8, Zéa Marina, 18536 Piraeus, tel: 452 6335.
● **Thalassa Charter and Yacht Brokers**
Grypári 72, Kallithéa, Athens, tel: 956 6866.
● **Sunsail**
Port House, Port Solent, Portsmouth PO6 4TH, UK, tel: 01705 210345.

Anyone planning to sail independently around the islands is advised to become familiar with the list of Port Authorities (see *Getting Around*, page 316). The Port Authority Harbour Police are the only people who can provide up-to-the-minute information on conditions concerning a specific island. Fuelling facilities and other provisions are available at: Adhámas (Mílos); Aegina; Ághios Nikólaos (Kéa); Ághios Nikólaos (Crete); Argostóli (Kefalloniá); Corfu Port; Ermoúpoli (Sýros); Hánia. (Crete); Híos Town; Hydra; Kálymnos; Kamáres (Sífnos); Kapsáli (Kýthira); Kastellórizo; Kástro (Ándhros); Katápola (Amorgós); Kós Town; Lakkí (Léros); Lefkádha Town; Linariá (Skýros); Mýrina (Límnos); Mytilíni (Lésvos); Mýkonos; Náxos; Parikía (Páros); Pigádhia (Kárpathos); Póros; Pythagório (Sámos); Mandhráki (Rhodes); Skála (Pátmos); Skiáthos; Skópelos; Spétses; Tínos; Vathý (Itháki); Zákynthos.

Sport in the Resort

Many of the larger hotels have tennis courts and facilities for water-skiing. Major beaches can provide windsurf boards, pedaloes, kayaks, snorkelling and windsurfing equipment: there's even scope for parascending in many popular island resorts.

Language

About the Greek Language

The language of Greece is Modern Greek. Modern Greek is the outcome of developments that have taken place in the Greek language since the Classical period (5th–4th centuries BC). Modern Greek is still very close to Ancient Greek: it uses the same alphabet and much of the same vocabulary, and it retains much of the same complex grammar.

This guide to Greek phrases cannot deal with the complexities of the grammar, but aims to provide the simplest (if not the most elegant) way of saying some basic things. It's worth investing in a good phrase-book, and possibly a pocket dictionary.

All Greeks learn English at school, and many speak it very well. There are also plenty of Greeks who have lived abroad (in America, Australia, Germany or elsewhere) and have picked up an excellent command of English there. More importantly, Greeks aren't used to foreigners knowing any Greek at all, and even a couple of words from you in their native language are likely to provoke admiration and encouragement.

Pronunciation Tips

The words and phrases in this language section are transcribed into the Roman alphabet; the only items given in Greek characters are a few words and phrases commonly used in notices. Most of the sounds of Greek aren't difficult for English speakers to pronounce. There are only five vowel sounds: *a* is pronounced as in northern English "bath"; *e* is as in "red"; *i* as in "bid"; *o* is like the vowel sound in standard English "more"; and *u* is as in "pull". The letter *y* here is always pronounced as in "yes", not as in "why" or in "silly". The letter *s* in this guide is always pronounced "s", never "z". The sound represented here as *th* is always pronounced as in "thin", not "that"; the first sound in "that" is represented by *dh*. The only difficult sounds are *h*, which is pronounced like the "ch" in Scottish "loch", and *gh*, which has no equivalent in English, but you can try producing it by pronouncing the "ch" in "loch" and humming at the same time! If that doesn't work, just pronounce it as a rough "g".

Even some of the most common Greek words tend to be quite long: four or five syllables are quite

Our Transliteration System

In Greece, all town and village names on road signs, as well as most street names, are written in both the Greek and the Roman alphabets. There's no single, universally accepted system of transliteration into Roman, and in any case the Greek authorities are gradually replacing old signs with new ones that use a slightly different system. This means you will have to get used to seeing different spellings of the same place on maps and signs and in this book. For instance, the word "saint" (masculine) in place names may be spelled "Agios", "Ághios", "Ayos" or "Ayios".

Below is the transliteration scheme we have used in this book: beside each Greek letter or pair of letters is the Roman letter(s) we have used. (Note that sometimes this will vary according to which letter follows it, or whether the letter occurs at the beginning or in the middle of a word.) Next to that is a rough approximation of the sound in an English word.

A α	a	father	N ν	n	no	EI ει (ei)	i	ski
B β	v	vote	Ξ ξ	x	taxi	EY ευ (eu)	ef	heffer
Γ γ	g	got	O o	o	long		or ev	ever
	or gh	throaty version	Π π	p	pen	OI οι (oi)	i	ski
		of get	P ρ	r	room	OY ου (ou)	ou	tourist
	or y	yet	Σ σ/ς	s	set			
Δ δ	dh	then	T τ	t	tea	ΓΓ γγ (gg)	ng	long
E ε	e	egg	Y υ	y	ski	ΓK γκ (gk)	ng	long
Z ζ	z	zoo	Φ φ	f	fish	ΓΞ γξ (gx)	nx	anxious
H η	i	ski	X χ	h	loch	ΜΠ μπ (mp)	b	beg
Θ θ	th	thin	Ψ ψ	ps	maps		or mb	limber
I ι	i	ski	Ω ω	o	cord	NT ντ (nt)	d	dog
K κ	k	kiss					nd	under
Λ λ	l	long	AI αι (ai)	e	hay	TZ τζ (tz)	dz	adze
M μ	m	man	AY αυ (au)	af	daft			
				or av	lava			

Greek words is of the utmost importance, and Greeks will often fail to understand you if you don't stress the right syllable; in this guide, stress is marked by an accent (á): compare *póli* "town" (pronounced something like "Polly") and *polí* "much", "many" or "very" (pronounced "poll-ee")

Greek word order is flexible, so you may often hear phrases in a different order from the one in which they are given here.

Like the French, the Greeks use the plural of the second person when addressing someone politely. We have used the polite (formal) form throughout this language section, except where an expression is specified as "informal".

Communication

Yes	*ne*
No	*óhi*
Thank you	*efharistó*
You're welcome	*parakaló*
Please	*parakaló*
Okay/All right	*endáxi*
Excuse me (to get attention, or I'm sorry)	*me sing-horíte*
Excuse me (to ask someone to get out of the way)	*sighnómi*
Can I ask you something? (normal way of beginning a request for information)	*na sas rotíso káti?*
Could you help me?	*boríte na me voithísete?*
Certainly	*vevéos* or *efharístos*
Can I help you?	*boró na sas voithíso?*
Can you show me...	*boríte na mou dhíxete...*
I want...	*thélo...*
I need...	*hriázome*
Wait a minute!	*periménete!*
I'm lost	*éhasa to dhrómo*
I don't know	*dhen xéro*
I don't understand	*dhen katálava*
Do you speak English/Greek?	*xérete angliká/eliniká?*

Please speak more slowly	*parakalo miláte sighá-sigha*
Could you say that again, please?	*parakaló hanapéste to*
Slowly/quietly	*sighá-sigha*
Here	*edhó*
There	*ekí*
Up/above	*páno*
Down/below	*káto*
Now	*tóra*
Early	*norís*
Late	*arghá*
What?	*ti?*
When?	*póte?*
Why?	*yatí?*
Where?	*pu?*
Where is the toilet?	*pu íne i twaléta?*

Greetings

Good morning	*kaliméra*
Good evening	*kalispéra*
Good night	*kaliníhta*
Hello/Goodbye	*yásas* (informal *yásu*)
Mr/Mrs/Miss	*kírios/kiría dhespinís*
Pleased to meet you (formal)	*héro polí*
What is your name?	*pos léyeste?/ pos íne t'onomá sas?*
(informal	*pos se léne?*)
I am English/American	*íme ánglos/ amerikanós*
(feminine	*anglídha/ amerikanídha)*
Irish/Scottish	*irlandhós/ skotsézos*
(feminine	*irlandhéza/ skotséza*)
Canadian/Australian	*kanadhós/ afstralós*
(feminine	*kanadhéza/ afstraléza*)
I'm here on holiday	*káno dhiakopés edhó*
Is this your first trip to Greece/ Athens?	*próti forá érheste stin Eládha/Athína?*
Do you like it here?	*sas arési edhó?*
How are you?	*ti kánete?*
(informal	*ti kánis?*)
Fine, thanks, and you?	*kalá, esís?*
(informal	*esí*)

Cheers/Your health! (when drinking)	*yámas!*
Do you like...?	*sas arési...?*
Very much	*pára polí*
It's lovely/ beautiful	*íne polí oréa*
Never mind/ It doesn't matter	*dhembirázi*

Telephone Calls

The telephone	*to tiléfono*
Phone-card	*tilekárta*
May I use the phone please?	*boró na tilefoníso parakaló?*
Hello (on the phone)	*embrós*
My name is...	*léghome...*
Could I speak to...	*boró na milíso me...*
Wait a moment	*periménete mya stighmí*
He/she isn't here	*dhen íne edhó*
When will he/ she be back?	*póte tha íne ekí?*
Should he/she call you back?	*na sas pári?*
I'll try again later	*tha xanapáro arghótera*
I didn't hear what you said	*dhen ákusa*

In the Hotel

The hotel	*to xenodhohío*
Do you have any vacant rooms?	*éhete dhomátia?*
I've booked a room	*ého kratísi éna dhomátio*
I'd like...	*tha íthela...*
a single/double room (with double bed)	*éna monó/dhipló dhomátio*
a twin-bed/ three-bed room/	*éna dhíklino/ tríklino*
a room with a bath/shower	*éna dhomátio me bányo/dus*
How long will you stay?	*póso tha mínete?*
One night	*éna vrádhi*
Two nights	*dhío vrádhya*
How much is it?	*póso káni?*
Is breakfast included?	*mazí me to proinó?*
It's expensive	*íne akrivó*
Is it quiet?	*íne ísiho?*

Is there a balcony?	éhi balkóni?
Do you have a room with a sea-view?	éhete dhomátio me théa pros ti thálasa?
Is the room heated/air-conditioned?	to dhomátio éhi thérmansi/air condition?
Can I see the room please?	boró na dho to dhomátio parakaló?
What floor is it on?	se pyo órofo íne?
On the first floor	stom bróto órofo
Is there a lift?	éhi asansér?
The room is too hot/cold/small	to dhomátio íne polí zestó/krío/mikró
It's noisy	éhi polí fasaría
Could you show me another room please?	boríte na mu dhíxete álo dhomátio parakaló?
I'll take it	tha to páro
Sign here please	mya ipoghrafí parakaló
What time is breakfast?	ti óra servírete to proinó?
Please give me a call at...	parakaló xipníste me stis...
Come in!	embrós!
Can I have the bill please?	mu kánete to logharyazmó parakaló?
Can you call me a taxi, please?	tha kalésete éna taxí parakaló?
dining room	trapezaría
key	klidhí
towel	petséta
sheet	sendóni
pillow	maxilári
soap	sapúni
hot water	zestó neró
toilet paper	hartí twalétas

At a Bar, Café or Patisserie

bar/café/patisserie	bar/kefenío (or kafetéria)/zaharoplastío
I'd like...	tha íthela...
a coffee	éna kafé
Greek (Turkish) coffee	elinikó kafé
filter coffee	ghalikó kafé/kafé fíltro

instant coffee	neskafé
capuccino	kaputsíno
white (with milk)	me ghála
black (without milk)	horís ghála
with sugar	me záhari
without sugar	horís záhari (or skéto)
a cup of tea	éna tsái
a lemon tea	éna tsái me lemóni
(bottled/canned) orange/lemon juice	mia portokaládha/lemonádha
fresh orange juice	éna himó portokáli
a glass/bottle of water	éna potíri/bukáli neró
with ice	me págho
a whisky/ouzo/brandy/	éna whisky/oúzo/cognac
a beer (draught)	mya bíra (apó varéli)
an ice-cream	éna paghotó
a pastry	mya pásta
Anything else?	típot'álo?
kinds of sweet oriental pastries	baklavá/kataífi

In a Restaurant

restaurant	estiatório/tavérna
Have you got a table for...	éhete trapézi ya...
How many are you?	pósa átoma íste?
There are (four) of us	ímaste (téseris)
Could we change tables?	borúme n' aláxume trapézi?
I'm a vegetarian	íme hortofághos
Can we see the menu?	borúme na dhúme ton katálogho?
What have you got to eat?	ti éhete na fáme?
Come and see what we've got	eláte na dhíte ti éhume
We would like to order	thélume na parangílume
What will you have?	ti tha párete?
What would you like to drink?	ti tha pyíte?
Have you got wine by the carafe?	éhete krasí híma?
a litre/half-litre	éna kiló/misókilo

of white/red wine	áspro/kókino krasí
Would you like anything else?	thélete típot' álo?
No, thank you	óhi efharistó
glass	potíri
knife/fork/spoon	mahéri/pirúni/kutáli
plate/napkin	pyáto/petséta
The bill please	to logharyazmó parakaló

Food

MEZÉDHES

taramosaláta	smoked fish-roe salad
dzadzíki	yoghurt with garlic
melidzánes	sliced aubergines (eggplant) or
tighanités/kolokithákia	courgettes fried in batter
tighanitá	
lukánika	sausages
tiropitákya	cheese pies
andzúyes	anchovies
elyés	olives
dolmádhes	vine-leaves stuffed with rice
saghanáki	fried cheese
fáva	pease pudding

MEAT DISHES

kréas	meat
arní	lamb
hirinó	pork
kotópulo	chicken
mos-hári	veal, beef
kunéli	rabbit
psitó	roast or grilled
sto fúrno	roast
sta kárvuna	grilled
sti súvla	on the spit
suvláki	spit-roast
kokinistó	stewed in tomato sauce
krasáto	stewed in wine sauce
tighanitó	fried
kapnistó	smoked
brizóla	(pork or veal) chop
paidhákya	lamb chops
sikóti	liver
biftéki	hamburger (without bap)
keftédhes	meat-balls (fried or grilled)
sutzukákya/yuvarlákya	meatballs (stewed)

kimá	minced meat	domátes	tomatoes	méli	honey
makarónya	spaghetti with	fakés	brown lentils	záhari	sugar
me kimá	minced meat	fasólya	stewed white		
piláfi me kimá	rice with minced		beans		

FRUIT (TA FRÚTA)

	meat	fasolákya	green beans	apple	mílo
makarónya	spaghetti with	(fréska)	stewed in	apricots	veríkoka
me sáltsa	tomato sauce		tomato sauce	bananas	banánes
	(may contain	hórta	various kinds of	cherries	kerásya
	meat gravy)		boiled greens	figs	síka
piláfi me sáltsa	rice with tomato	karóta	carrots	grapes	stafílya
	sauce (may	kolokithákya	courgettes	lemon	lemóni
	contain meat	kunupídhi	cauliflower	melon	pepóni
	gravy)	kukyá	broad beans	orange	portokáli
musaká	minced meat	láhano	cabbage	peach	rodhákino
	and aubergine	marúli	lettuce	pear	ahládhi
	topped with	melidzánes	aubergine/	strawberries	fráules
	béchamel		eggplant	watermelon	karpúzi
	sauce	pandzárya	beetroot		
pastítsyo	minced meat	patátes	potatoes		

Visiting a Site

	and macaroni	(tighanités/	(chips/		
	topped with	sto fúrno)	roast)	Is it possible	
	béchamel sauce	piperyés	peppers	to see the	borúme na
yíros me píta	doner kebab	radhíkya	dandelion leaves	church/	dhúme tin
	(slices of grilled	revíthya	chickpeas	archeological	eklisía/ta
	minced meat	rapanákya	radishes	site?	arhéa?
	served in pitta	spanáki	spinach	Where can I	
	bread)	spanakópita	spinach pie	find the	pu boró na vro
domátes/	stuffed	tyrópita	cheese pie	custodian/key?	to fílaka/klidhí?
	tomatoes/	vlíta	boiled greens	We've come a	írthame apo polí
piperyés	peppers	yíghandes	stewed butter	long way to see	makriá na to
yemistés	(stuffed with		beans	it. It's a pity	dhúme. kríma
(me rízi/kimá)	rice/minced	saláta	salad	it's closed	pu ína klistó
	meat)	domatosaláta	tomato salad	(this can be	
		angurodomáta	tomato and	tried if entry	

SEAFOOD

			cucumber salad	seems a problem!)	
frésko/	fresh/	horyátiki	"Greek salad"		
katepsighméno	frozen		(tomato,		
psári	fish		cucumber,		

Sightseeing

ghlósa	sole		onions, olives		
xifías	swordfish		and feta cheese)	art gallery	pinakothíki
kolyós	mackerel			beach	plaz
barbúnya	red mullet			bridge	yéfira

BASIC FOODS

sardhéles	sardines			castle	kástro/frúrio
marídhes	whitebait	psomí	bread	cathedral	mitrópoli
mídhya	mussels	aláti	salt	church	eklisía
bakalyáros	dried salted cod	pipéri	pepper	excavations	anaskafés
strídhya	oysters	ládhi	(olive) oil	forest	dhásos
kidhónya	clams	xídhi	vinegar	fresco	ayoghrafía
kalamarákya	squid	mustárdha	mustard	garden	kípos
supyés	cuttlefish	kremídhya	onions	icon	ikóna
htapódhi	octopus	skórdho	garlic	lake	límni
gharídhes	prawns	vútiro	butter	library	vivliothíki
kávuras	crab	tirí	cheese	market	aghorá
astakós	lobster	féta	feta (sheeps-	minaret	minaré
			milk cheese)	monastery/	

VEGETABLES AND VEGETARIAN FOOD

		avghá (tighanitá)	(fried) eggs	convent	monastíri
		omeléta	omelette	monument	mnimío
angináres	artichokes	marmeládha	jam, marmalade	mosque	dzamí
arakás	peas	rízi	rice	mountain	vunó
		yaúrti	yoghurt	museum	musío

old town	*palyá póli*	grey	*grízo*
park	*párko*	pink	*roz*
river	*potamós*	red	*kókino*
ruins	*erípia/arhéa*	silver	*aryiró*
sea	*thálasa*	white	*áspro*
temple	*naós*	yellow	*kítrino*
information	*pliroforíes*	It's lovely	*íne polí oréo*
open/closed	*anihtó/klistó*	No thank you,	*óhi efharistó,*
		I don't like it	*dhe m'arési*

At the Shops

shop	*maghazí/*	I'll take it	*tha to páro*
	katástima	I don't want it	*dhen to thélo*
What time do	*ti óra*	This is faulty.	*aftó éhi éna*
you open/close?	*aníyete/klínete?*	Can I have a	*elátoma. boró*
Are you being		replacement?	*na to aláxo?*
served?	*exiperitíste?*	Can I have a	*boró na páro*
Whose turn		refund?	*píso ta leftá?*
is it?	*pyos éhi sirá?*	Anything else?	*típot' álo?*
What would	*oríste/ti*	Pay at the	*plirónete sto*
you like?	*thélete?*	cash desk	*tamío*
I'm just looking	*aplós kitázo*	a kilo	*éna kiló*
How much		half a kilo	*misókilo*
does it cost?	*póso éhi?*	a quarter	*éna tétarto*
Do you take	*pérnete*	(of a kilo)	
credit cards?	*pistotikés*	two kilos	*dhío kilá*
	kártes?	100 grams	*ekató*
I'd like...	*tha íthela...*		*ghramárya*
this one	*aftó*	200 grams	*dhyakósa*
that one	*ekíno*		*ghramárya*
one of these	*éna tétyo*	300 grams	*trakósa*
Have you got...?	*éhete...?*		*ghramárya*
Yes, of course	*málista/ne*	more	*perisótero*
	vévea/vevéos	less	*lighótero*
(Unfortunately)	*(dhistihós)*	a little	*lígho*
we haven't got	*dhen éhume*	very little	*polí lígho*
(any)		with/without	*me/horís*
size (for		That's enough	*ftáni*
clothes & shoes)	*número*	That's all	*tipot'álo*
Can I try it on?	*boró na to*		
	dhokimáso?		

TYPES OF SHOP

What size do	*ti número*	bakery	*fúrnos*
you take?	*pérnete?*	bank	*trápeza*
It's too		barber's	*kurío*
expensive	*íne polí akrivó*	bookshop	*vivliopolío*
cheap	*ftinó*	butcher's	*hasápiko/*
Don't you have	*dhen éhete*		*kreopolío*
anything	*típota pyo*	chemist's	*farmakío*
cheaper?	*ftinó?*	department	*megálo*
Please write it	*to ghráfete*	store	*katástima*
down for me	*parakaló?*	dry cleaner's	*steghnotírio*
It's too small/	*íne polí mikró/*	fishmonger's	*ihthiopolío/*
big	*meghálo*		*psarádhiko*
colour	*hróma*	florist	*anthopolío*
black	*mávro*	greengrocer's	*manáviko*
blue	*ble*	grocer's	*bakáliko*
brown	*kafé*	hairdresser's	*komotírio*
gold	*hrisó*	(women's)	
green	*prásino*	kiosk (for	
		newspapers	
		and a variety	

of other goods)	*períptero*		
laundry	*plindírio*		
liquor store	*káva*		
market	*aghorá*		
photographer's	*fotoghrafío*		
(eg for film			
processing)			
post office	*tahidhromío*		
stationer's	*hartopolío*		
supermarket	*supermárket*		
tobacconist	*kapnopolío*		
travel agency	*taxidhiotikó*		
	ghrafío/		
	praktorío		

Times and Dates

(in the) morning/	*to proí/*		
afternoon/	*to apóyevma/*		
evening	*to vrádhi*		
the middle of			
the day	*to mesiméri*		
(at) night	*(ti) níhta*		
yesterday	*htes*		
today	*símera*		
tomorrow	*ávrio*		
the day before			
yesterday	*proxtés*		
the day after			
tomorrow	*methávrio*		
now	*tóra*		
early	*norís*		
late	*arghá*		
a minute	*éna leptó*		
five/ten	*pénde/dhéka*		
minutes	*leptá*		
an hour	*mya óra*		
half an hour	*misí óra*		
a quarter of			
an hour	*éna tétarto*		
at one/	*sti mia/*		
two (o'clock)	*stis dhío (i óra)*		
a day	*mya méra*		
a week	*mya vdhomádha*		
(on) Monday	*(ti) dheftéra*		
(on) Tuesday	*(tin) tríti*		
(on) Wednesday	*(tin) tetárti*		
(on) Thursday	*(tin) pémti*		
(on) Friday	*(tin) paraskeví*		
(on) Saturday	*(to) sávato*		
(on) Sunday	*(tin) kiryakí*		
on the first	*tin próti (tu*		
(of the month)	*minós)*		
on the second/	*stis dhío/*		
third	*tris*		

Transport

airport	*aerodhrómio*
aeroplane	*aeropláno*
boarding card	*kárta epivívasis*
boat	*plío/karávi*
bus	*leoforío*
bus station	*stathmós leoforíon*
bus stop	*stási*
coach	*púlman*
ferry	*feribót*
first/second class	*próti/défteri thési*
flight	*ptísi*
hydrofoil	*iptámeno*
motorway	*ethnikí odhós*
No smoking	*apaghorévete to kápnisma*
port	*limáni*
return ticket	*isitírio me epistrofí*
single ticket	*aplo isitírio*
station	*stathmós*
taxi	*taxí*
train	*tréno*
WC	*twaléta*

TRAVELLING BY PUBLIC TRANSPORT

Can you help me please?	*boríte na me voithísete parakaló*
Where can I buy tickets?	*pu na kópso isitírio?*
At the counter	*sto tamío*
Does it stop at...	*káni stási sto...*
You need to change at...	*tha prépi n'aláxete sto...*
When is the next train/bus/ferry to...	*póte févyi to tréno/leoforío/feribót ya...*
How long does the journey take?	*pósi óra káni to taxídhi?*
What time will we arrive?	*ti óra tha ftásume?*
How much is the fare?	*póso íne to isitírio*
Next stop please	*stási parakaló*
Can you tell me where to get off?	*tha mu píte pu na katévo?*
Should I get off here?	*edhó na katévo?*
Excuse me, I want to get off	*signómi na katévo*
delay	*kathistérisi*

AT THE AIRPORT

Where are the offices of BA/Olympic?	*pu íne ta ghrafía tis British/olimbiakís?*
I'd like to book a seat to Thessaloniki	*tha íthela na kratíso mya thési ya thesaloníki*
When is the next flight to...	*póte tha íne i epómeni ptísi ya...*
Are there any seats available?	*párhun i thésis?*
How many suitcases have you got?	*póses valítses éhete?*
Can I take this with me?	*boró na to páro aftó mazí mu?*
My suitcase has got lost	*háthike i valítsa mu*
My suitcase has been damaged	*i valítsa mu épathe zimyá*
The flight has been delayed	*i ptísi éhi kathistérisi*
The flight has been cancelled	*i ptísi mateóthike*
I can put you on the waiting list	*boró na sa válo sti lísta anamonís*

DIRECTIONS

right/left	*dexiá/aristerá*
Take the first/second right	*párte ton próto/déftero dhrómo dexiá*
Turn right/left	*strípste dexiá/aristerá*
Go straight on	*tha páte ísya/efthía*
after the traffic lights	*metá ta fanárya*
Is it near/far away?	*ína kondá/makriá?*
How far is it?	*póso makriá íne?*
It's five minutes' walk	*íne pénde leptá me ta pódhya*
It's ten minutes by car	*íne dhéka leptá me to aftokínito*
100 metres	*ekató métra*
opposite/next to	*apénandi/dhípla*
up/down	*páno/káto*
junction	*dhiastávrosi*
house/building/apartment block	*spíti/ktírio/polikatikía*
Where is/are...	*pu íne...*
Where can I find a bank/petrol station/	*pu boró na vro mya trápeza/éna venzinádhiko/*

bus stop/hotel?	*mya stási/éna xenodohío?*
How do I get there?	*pos na páo ekí?*
Can you show me where I am on the map?	*boríte na mu díxete sto hárti pu íme?*
Am I on the right road for...	*ya... kalá páo?*
No, you're on the wrong road	*óhi, pírate láthos dhrómo*

ON THE ROAD

Where can I rent a car?	*pu boró na nikyáso aftokínito?*
What is it insured for?	*ti asfália éhi?*
Can another driver drive it?	*borí na to odhiyísi álos odhighós?*
By what time must I return it?	*méhri ti óra prépi na to epistrépso?*
driving licence	*dhíploma*
licence plate	*pinakídha*
petrol	*venzíni*
petrol station	*venzinádhiko*
oil	*ládhi*
How much should I put in?	*pósi na válo?*
Fill it up please	*óso pérni*
lead-free	*amólivdhi*
My car won't start	*to aftokínito dhen pérni bros*
My car has broken down	*hálase to aftokinitó mu*
I've had an accident	*íha éna atíhima*
How long will it take to repair?	*pósi óra thélete na to ftyáxete?*
Can you check...	*boríte na elénxete...*
There's something wrong with...	*káti éhi... (plural káti éhun...)*
• accelerator	*to gázi*
• the brakes	*ta fréna*
• the clutch	*to ambrayáz*
• the engine	*i mihaní*
• the exhaust	*i exátmisi*
• the fanbelt	*i zóni*
• the gearbox	*i tahítites*
• the headlights	*ta fanárya*
• the radiator	*to psiyío*
• the spark plugs	*ta buzí*
• the tyre(s)	*to lástiho (ta lástiha)*
• the windscreen	*to parbríz*

Emergencies

Help!	voíthia!
Stop!	stamatíste!
I've had an accident	íha éna atíhima
Watch out!	proséxte!
Call a doctor	fonáxte éna yatró
Call an ambulance	fonáxte éna asthenofóro
Call the police	fonáxte tin astinomía
Call the fire brigade	fonáhte tus pirozvéstes
Where's the telephone?	pu íne to tiléfono?
Where's the nearest hospital?	pu íne to pyo kondinó nosokomío?
I would like to report a theft	éyine mya klopí
Thank you very much for your help	efharistó polí pu me voithísate

Health

Is there a chemist's nearby?	ipárhi éna farmakío edhó kondá?
Which chemist is open all night?	pyo farmakío dianikterévi?
I don't feel well	dhen esthánome kalá
I'm ill	íme árostos (feminine árosti)
He/she's ill	íne árostos/ árosti
Where does it hurt?	pu ponái?
It hurts here	ponái edhó
I suffer from...	pás-ho apo...
I have a headache/ sore throat/ stomach ache	éxo ponokéfalo/ ponólemo/ kilyópono
Have you got something for travel sickness?	éhete típota ya ti naftía?
It's nothing serious	dhen íne sovaró
Do I need a prescription?	hriázete sindayí?
It bit me (of an animal)	me dhángose
It bit me (of an insect)	me tsímbise
It stung me	me kéntrise

bee	mélisa
wasp	sfíka
mosquito	kunúpi
sticking plaster	lefkoplástis
tissues	hartomándila
toothpaste	odhondókrema
diarrhoea pills	hápya ya ti diária

Numbers

1	éna/mya
2	dhío
3	tris/tría
4	tésera
5	pénde
6	éxi
7	eptá
8	ohtó
9	enéa
10	dhéka
11	éndeka
12	dhódheka
13	dhekatrís/
14	dhekatéseris/
15	dhekapénde
16	dhekaéxi
17	dhekaeptá
18	dhekaohtó
19	dhekaenéa
20	íkosi
30	triánda
40	saránda
50	penínda
60	exínda
70	evdhomínda
80	oghdhónda
90	enenínda
100	ekató
200	dhyakósa
300	trakósa
400	tetrakósa
500	pendakósa
1,000	hílyes/hílya
2,000	dhyo hilyádhes
a million	éna ekatomírio

Notices

ΤΟΥΑΛΕΤΕΣ	toilets
ΑΝΔΡΩΝ	gentlemen
ΓΥΝΑΙΚΩΝ	ladies
ΑΝΟΙΚΤΟ	open
ΚΛΕΙΣΤΟ	closed
ΕΙΣΟΔΟΣ	entrance
ΕΞΟΔΟΣ	exit
ΑΠΑΓΟΡΕΥΤΑΙ	forbidden/no entry
ΕΙΣΙΤΗΡΙΑ	tickets

ΑΠΑΓΟΡΕΥΤΑΙ ΤΟ ΚΑΠΝΙΣΜΑ	no smoking
ΠΛΗΡΟΦΟΡΙΕΣ	information
ΠΡΟΣΟΧΗ	caution
ΚΙΝΔΥΝΟΣ	danger
ΑΡΓΑ	slow
ΔΗΜΟΣΙΑ ΕΡΓΑ	road works
ΠΑΡΚΙΝ/ ΧΩΡΟΣ ΣΤΑΘΜΕΥΣΕΩΣ	car park
ΑΠΑΓΟΡΕΥΤΑΙ Η ΣΤΑΘΜΕΥΣΗ	no parking
ΤΑΞΙ	taxi
ΤΡΑΠΕΖΑ	bank
ΤΗΛΕΦΩΝΟ	telephone
ΤΗΛΕΚΑΡΤΕΣ	phone cards
ΕΚΤΟΣ ΛΕΙΤΟΥΡΓΙΑΣ	out of order

Further Reading

Ancient History & Culture

Burkert, Walter **Greek Religion** (Basil Blackwell). Translation of the German-language classic study of belief in ancient Greece.

Burn, A.R. **The Penguin History of Greece**. (Penguin, various reprints). Good, single-volume introduction to ancient Greece.

Dodds, E.R. **The Greeks and the Irrational**. (University. of California Press, various reprints). Modern Greeks like you to think that their seers put reason on a pedestal; this explores the prevalence of the Other and the unconscious in ancient Greece.

Finley, M.I. **The World of Odysseus**. (Penguin, various reprints). Mycenean myths as borne out by archeological facts.

Fox, Robin Lane **Alexander the Great** (Penguin). Psychobiography wedded to a conventional history.

Grimal, Pierre, ed **Dictionary of Classical Mythology** (Penguin). Considered to be tops among a handful of available alphabetical gazetteers.

Hornblower, Simon **The Greek World, 479–323 BC** (Routledge). Covers the eventful period from the end of the Persian Wars to Alexander's demise.

Byzantine History & Culture

Michael Psellus. **Fourteen Byzantine Rulers**. (Penguin, various reprints). That many changes of rule in a single century (10th–11th), as told by a near-contemporary historian.

Norwich, John Julius, **Byzantium** (three volumes): **The Early Centuries, The Apogee & The Decline** (Viking-Penguin, 1988-1995). The most readable and masterful popular history, by the noted Byzantinologst.

Runciman, Steven. **Byzantine Style and Civilization**. (Penguin, UK only). Art, culture and monuments.

Runciman, Steven. **The Fall of Constantinople, 1453** (Cambridge-Canto). Definitive study of an event which continues to exercise modern Greek minds.

Ware, Bishop Kallistos (Timothy) **The Orthodox Church** (Penguin, various reprints). Good introduction to what's essentially the established religion of modern Greece.

Anthropology & Culture

Campbell, John. **Honor, family and patronage: A study of institutions and moral values in a Greek mountain community**. (Oxford University Press). Classic study of Sarakatsáni in the Píndhos, with much wider application to Greece in general, which however got the author banned from the area by touchy officialdom.

Du Boulay, Juliet. **Portrait of a Greek Mountain Village** (Oxford/ Clarendon Press). Ambeli, a mountain village in Évvia, as it was in the mid-1960s.

Holst, Gail. **Road to Rembetika: Songs of Love, Sorrow and Hashish** (Denise Harvey, Athens). The most user-friendly introduction to the enduringly popular musical form; with translated lyrics of standards, and updated discographies.

Cuisine

Davidson, Alan **Mediterranean Seafood** (Penguin). Recently re-issued 1972 classic that's still the standard reference, and guaranteed to end every argument as to just what that fish is on your taverna plate. With recipes.

Harris, Andy. **A Taste of the Aegean**. Photographs by Terry Harris. (Pavilion Books). Two Greek-resident brothers take you on a gastronomic tour, with recipes.

Stavroulakis, Nicholas. **Cookbook of the Jews of Greece**: Athens: Lycabettus Press/Phildelphia, Kadmos Press). Followable recipes interspersed with their relation to the Jewish liturgical year, and a potted history of the Greek Jewish community.

Modern History and Politics

Clogg, Richard. **A Concise History of Greece** Cambridge UP). Clear and lively account of Greece from Byzantine times to 1991, with helpful maps. The best single-volume summary.

Fourtouni, Eleni. **Greek Women in Resistance**. New Haven: Thelphini Press). Accounts and journals of women interned post-civil-war on Tríkeri and Makrónissos – as much, one suspects, for being uppity in a patriarchal society as for being communists or fellow travellers.

Mazower, Marc. **Inside Hitler's Greece: The Experience of Occupation 1941–1944** (Yale UP). Shows, among other things, how the complete demoralisation of the country and imcompetence of establishment politicians fueled the rise of ELAS – and guaranteed civil war. Harrowing photos as well.

Ward, Michael **Greek Assignments, SOE 1943-UNSCOB1948** (Lycabettus Press, Athens). Another parachuted-in guerrilla who walked from Píndhos to Pílion and survived to marry a Greek and serve as British consul in Thessaloníki.

Ancient Greek Literature & History

Aeschylus. **The Oresteia**. (Viking-Penguin). The trilogy of tragedies from 5th-century BC Athens.

Aesop. **Fables of Aesop** (Penguin). Moral tales, complete with talking animals, by the native of Lésvos and resident of ancient Sámos.

Aristophanes. **Lysistrata/The Acharnians/The Clouds**. (Penguin). Three plays from the greatest ancient comedian.

Herodotus. **The Histories** (Penguin). Fifth-century BC chronicle of the Persian Wars, and the peoples of Anatolia caught up in the conflict.

Homer, tr. Richard Lattimore. His verse translations of **The Iliad** (University of Chicago) and **The**

Odyssey (Harper Collins) remain unsurpassed. The first relates the semi-mythical Bronze Age campaign against Troy; the latter follows the hero Odysseus on his convoluted journey home to Ithaca from the war. Plato. **The Republic** and **The Symposium** (Penguin). The standard undergraduate philosophy texts, perhaps even more meaningful if read on the spot.
Thucydides **History of The Peloponnesian Wars** (Penguin). Bleak, month-by-month account of the conflict by a relegated Athenian general, a pioneer of the genre; lots of islands were deeply involved. Xenophon **The History of My Times** (Penguin). Thucydides ceases coverage in 411 BC; this continues events up to 362 BC

Modern Literature by Greeks

Cavafy, C.P. **Collected Poems**, trans. by Edmund Keeley and Philip Sherrard (Princeton UP) or **The Complete Poems of Cavafy**, tr. by Rae Dalven (Harcourt Brace Jovanovich) Considered the two best versions available in English.
Elytis, Odysseus. **The Axion Esti**. (Anvil/University of Pittsburgh) , **Selected Poems** (Anvil/Penguin) and **The Sovereign Sun** (Bloodaxe/Temple UP). Pretty much the complete works of the Nobel laureate, in translation.
Leontis, Artemis, ed **Greece: a Traveler's Literary Companion** (Whereabouts Press, San Francisco). Regions of the country as portrayed in fiction or essays by modern Greek writers; an excellent corrective to the condescending Grand Tourist accounts.
Myrivilis, Stratis. **Life in the Tomb**, tr Peter Bien (Quarter/New England UP). Harrowing account of the Macedonian front during World War I; first part of a loose trilogy comprising **The Mermaid Madonna** and **The Schoolmistress with the Golden Eyes**, the last two set on the author's home island of Lésvos.
Papandreou, Nick **Father Dancing** (Penguin). Thinly disguised, page-turning *roman-a-clef* by the late

prime minister's younger son.
Papadiamantis, Alexandros. **The Murderess**. Trans. by Peter Levi (London: Writers and Readers). Landmark demotically written novel, set on Skiáthos at the turn of the century. An old woman concludes that little girls are better off dead than grown up into drudgery.
Seferis, George. **Collected Poems 1924–1955/Complete Poems**. Trans. by Edmund Keeley. (Princeton University Press). The former, out of print, has Greek-English texts on facing pages and is preferable to the Complete Poems of Greece's other Nobel literary laureate.
Sotiriou, Dido **Farewell Anatolia** (Kedros, Athens). A best-selling classic since its appearance in 1962, tracing the end of the millennial presence of Greeks in Asia Minor from 1914 to 1922.
Tsirkas, Stratis. **Drifting Cities**. Trans. by Kay Cicellis. (Athens: Kedros). Wartime leftist intrigue in Alexandria, Cairo and Jerusalem.

Foreign Writers on Greece

De Bernieres, Louis **Captain Corelli's Mandolin** (Secker & Warburg/Minerva). Heart-rending tragicomedy set on occupied Kefalloniá during World War II which has acquired cult status and seemingly permanent best-seller-list tenancy since 1994.
Durrell, Lawrence. **Prospero's Cell** and **Reflections on a Marine Venus** (Faber and Faber/Penguin). Corfu in the 1930s, and Rhodes in 1945–47, now looking rather old-fashioned, alcohol-fogged and patronising of the "natives", but still entertaining.
Fowles, John. **The Magus**. (Vintage/Dell). Blockbuster, inspired by author's spell teaching on Spétses during the 1950s, of post-adolescent manipulation.
Miller, Henry. **The Colossus of Maroussi**. (Minerva/New Directions). Miller takes to Corfu, the Argolid, Athens and Crete of 1939 with the enthusiasm of a first-timer in Greece who's found his element.
Pettifer, James **The Greeks: the Land and People since the War**

(Penguin). Useful, if hastily written and edited, general introduction to politics, family life, food, tourism and other contemporary topics.
Spencer, Terence **Fair Greece, Sad Relic** (Denise Harvey, Athens). Literary and Grand Tour philhellenism, from the fall of Constantinople to the War of Independence.
Storace, Patricia **Dinner with Persephone** (Granta/Panthon). New York poet resident a year in Athens takes the pulse of modern Greece. Very funny, very spot-on.

Regional & Archeological Guides

Burn, A.R. and Mary **The Living Past of Greece** (The Herbert Press). Worth toting into the field for the sake of lively text and clear plans; covers most major sites from Minoan to medieval.
Stavroulakis, Nicholas, and Timothy J. DeVinney **Jewish Sites and Synagogues in Greece** (Talos Press, Athens). Alphabetical gazetteer to the communities and suriviving Jewish monumentsr.

Botany

Baumann, Helmut **Greek wildflowers and Plant Lore in Ancient Greece** (Herbert Press). As the title says; lots of interesting ethnobotanical trivia.
Polunin, Oleg and Anthony Huxley **Flowers of the Mediterranean** (Hogarth Press). Has lots of colour plates to aid in identification.

Other Insight Guides

Other **Insight Guides** highlight destinations in this region. and titles include **Greece, Athens** and **Crete** as well as **Cyprus** and the **Turkish Coast**. Apa Publications has two other series of guide books: **Insight Pocket Guides**, which give detailed tours and daytrips, and **Compact Guides**, which are mini encyclopedias. There are **Pocket Guides** to the **Aegean Islands, Athens, Rhodes** and **Crete** and **Compact Guides to Greece, Crete** and **Rhodes**.

ART & PHOTO CREDITS

B. & E. Anderson 91R
Heather Angel 88
Ashmolean Museum 22
David Beatty 40/41, 42/43, 54/55, 104, 127, 171, 175, 180, 220, 225, 231, 236, 247, 250/251, 252, 253, 255, 258, 252R, 269, 270, 272, 273, 274, 275, 281
Benaki Museum 23, 26, 27, 28, 29, 30, 32,33, 34, 35, 36, 37
Marcus Brooke 71, 72, 79, 115, 153, 199, 224, 246, 239L, 239R, 259L, 282, 283, 286, 296
J. Allan Cash Ltd 45, 74
Lance Chilton 300T
Bruce Coleman 90L, 90R, 91L
Pierre Couteau 6/7, 8/9, 12/13, 16/17, 14, 18, 44, 50, 60, 68/69, 84/85, 86/87, 94, 100/101, 108, 116/117, 140/141, 154/155, 156/157, 160, 165, 166, 194/195, 212, 228, 298, 304
Marc Dubin 46, 136, 138, 151, 164, 167, 168, 176, 179, 181, 167, 202, 210/211, 214, 217, 293, 295
Faltaïts Museum 203, 204
Guglielmo Galvin 61, 149T, 239, 240, 240T, 241, 242T, 243, 245T, 245L, 245R, 248, 248T, 259R, 259T, 260, 261
Glyn Genin 52/53, 78, 185, 280, 284, 285, 287, 287T, 288, 289, 290T, 291, 292, 293T, 294T, 298T, 300, 301
Blaine Harrington 169, 201
Terry Harris/Just Greece 47, 58, 77, 80, 95, 120, 161, 165T, 170, 171T, 178T, 183, 215, 256T
Markos G. Hionos 51, 57, 63, 75, 97, 102/103, 122, 123, 133, 135, 150, 158, 198, 205, 238, 290, 299

Ideal Photo 114T
Michael Jenner 148, 265, 266L, 266T
Ann Jousiffe 109, 147, 221, 223, 232/233, 257L, 257R
Michele Macrakis 16, 17, 48, 59, 82, 83, 125, 134, 187, 208/209
Emil Moriannidis 1, 152, 219
Susan Muhlauser 226, 227
Museum of Cycladic Art 24
National Tourist Organisation of Greece 19, 263
Rhoda Nottridge 1124
Richard T. Nowitz 113, 114
Steve Outram 118/119, 139
A. Pappas/Ideal Photo 172T, 178, 224T
Anita Peltonen 144, 218, 210
M. Pharmaki/Ideal Photo 256
Planet Earth Pictures 137
Princeton University Library 20/21
Brian Rogers/Biofotos 89
Spectrum Colour Library 186
Tony Stone Worldwide 98/99
Karen Van Dyke 38, 48
C.Vergas/Ideal Photo 70, 132, 172, 173, 174, 202T, 297
Bill Wassman 2–3, 4–5, 10/11, 56, 73, 76, 111, 169T, 177, 189, 192/193, 234/235, 242, 262, 267, 268, 271, 294
Amanda Eliza Weil 49
Marcus Wilson Smith 25, 33
Phil Wood/Apa Publications 15, 62, 81, 110, 112, 113T, 125T, 126, 126T, 128, 129, 131, 131T, 133T, 134T, 142/143, 146, 149, 175T, 184, 185T, 188, 188T, 196, 197, 223T, 226T, 230T, 230

Maps Polyglott Kartographie
© 1998 Apa Publications GmbH & Co.
Verlag KG (Singapore branch)

Picture Spreads

Pages 64/65
Top row, left to right: Terry Harris, C. Vergas/Ideal Photo, Terry Harris, Steve Outram. Centre row: both by C. Vergas/Ideal Photo. Bottom row, left to right: Terry Harris, C. Vergas/Ideal Photo, Terry Harris, Steve Outram.
Pages 92/93
Top row, left to right: Terry Harris, Steve Outram, Terry Harris, B. & E. Anderson. Centre: Steve Outram. Bottom row: G. Sfikas/Ideal Photo, G. Sfikas/Ideal Photo, Terry Harris, Terry Harris.
Pages 190/191
Top row, left to right: Terry Harris, C. Vergas/Ideal Photo, C. Vergas/Ideal Photo, Terry Harris. Centre row, left to right: Terry Harris, Terry Harris, C. Vergas/Ideal Photo. Bottom row, left to right: Steve Outram, Natasha/Ideal Photo, Terry Harris.
Pages 302/303
Top row, left to right: Steve Outram, C. Vergas/Ideal Photo, Steve Outram, AKG Berlin. Dolphin fresco: Glyn Genin. Centre, left to right: Steve Outram, D. Ball/Ideal Photo. Bottom row: all by Steve Outram.

Cartographic Editor **Zoë Goodwin**
Production **Stuart A. Everitt**
Design Consultants
Carlotta Junger, Graham Mitchener
Picture Research **Hilary Genin**

Index

The Insight Approach

The book you are holding is part of the world's largest range of guidebooks. Its purpose is to help you have the most valuable travel experience possible, and we try to achieve this by providing not only information about countries, regions and cities but also genuine insight into their history, culture, institutions and people.

Since the first Insight Guide – to Bali – was published in 1970, the series has been dedicated to the proposition that, with insight into a country's people and culture, visitors can both enhance their own experience and be accepted more easily by their hosts. Now, in a world where ethnic hostilities and nationalist conflicts are all too common, such attempts to increase understanding between peoples are more important than ever.

Insight Guides:
Essentials for understanding

Because a nation's past holds the key to its present, each Insight Guide kicks off with lively history chapters. These are followed by magazine-style essays on culture and daily life. This essential background information gives readers the necessary context for using the main Places section, with its comprehensive run-down on things worth seeing and doing.

Finally, a listings section contains all the information you'll need on travel, hotels, restaurants and opening times.

As far as possible, we rely on local writers and specialists to ensure that information is authoritative. The pictures, for which Insight Guides have become so celebrated, are just as important. Our photojournalistic approach aims not only to illustrate a destination but also to communicate visually and directly to readers life as it is lived by the locals. The series has grown to almost 200 titles.

Compact Guides:
The "great little guides"

As invaluable as such background information is, it isn't always fun to carry an Insight Guide through a crowded souk or up a church tower. Could we, readers asked, distil the key reference material into a slim volume for on-the-spot use?

Our response was to design Compact Guides as an entirely new series, with original text carefully cross-referenced to detailed maps and more than 200 photographs. In essence, they're miniature encyclopedias, concise and comprehensive, displaying reliable and up-to-date information in an accessible way. There are almost 100 titles.

Pocket Guides:
A local host in book form

However wide-ranging the information in a book, human beings still value the personal touch. Our editors are often asked the same questions. Where do *you* go to eat? What do *you* think is the best beach? What would *you* recommend if I have only three days? We invited our local correspondents to act as "substitute hosts" by revealing their preferred walks and trips, listing the restaurants they go to and structuring a visit into a series of timed itineraries.

The result: our Pocket Guides, complete with full-size fold-out maps. These 100-plus titles help readers plan a trip precisely, particularly if their time is short.

Exploring with Insight:
A valuable travel experience

In conjunction with co-publishers all over the world, we print in up to 10 languages, from German to Chinese, from Danish to Russian. But our aim remains simple: to enhance your travel experience by combining our expertise in guidebook publishing with the on-the-spot knowledge of our correspondents.

66 I was first drawn to the Insight Guides by the excellent "Nepal" volume. I can think of no book which so effectively captures the essence of a country. Out of these pages leaped the Nepal I know – the captivating charm of a people and their culture. I've since discovered and enjoyed the entire Insight Guide series. Each volume deals with a country in the same sensitive depth, which is nowhere more evident than in the superb photography. **99**

Sir Edmund Hillary

The World of Insight Guides

400 books in three complementary series cover every major destination in every continent.